comics
ONE

Translators
Alex Mizuno
Dominic Mah

Editor
Akira Watanabe

Production Artists
Will Chen
Yu-Kai Chieh
Gary Lin

US Cover Design
Yuki Chung

Lettering Fonts
Comicraft
www.comicbookfonts.com

President
Robin Kuo

Publisher
ComicsOne, Corporation.
47257 Fremont Blvd
Fremont, CA 94538
www.ComicsOne.com

First Edition: August 2001
ISBN 1-58899-079-6

KAZAN

4

GAKU★MIYAO

CONTENTS

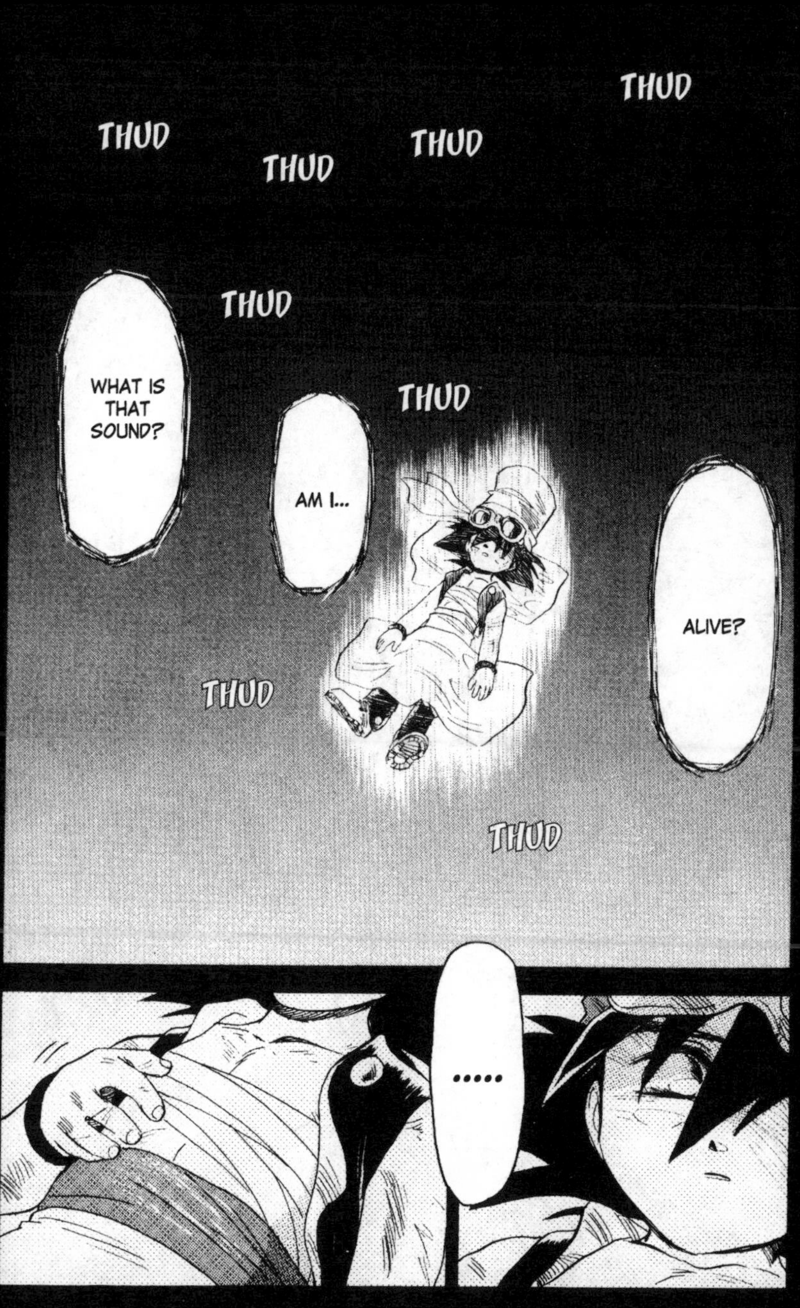
THUD
THUD
THUD
THUD
THUD
WHAT IS THAT SOUND?
AM I...
THUD
ALIVE?
THUD
THUD
.....

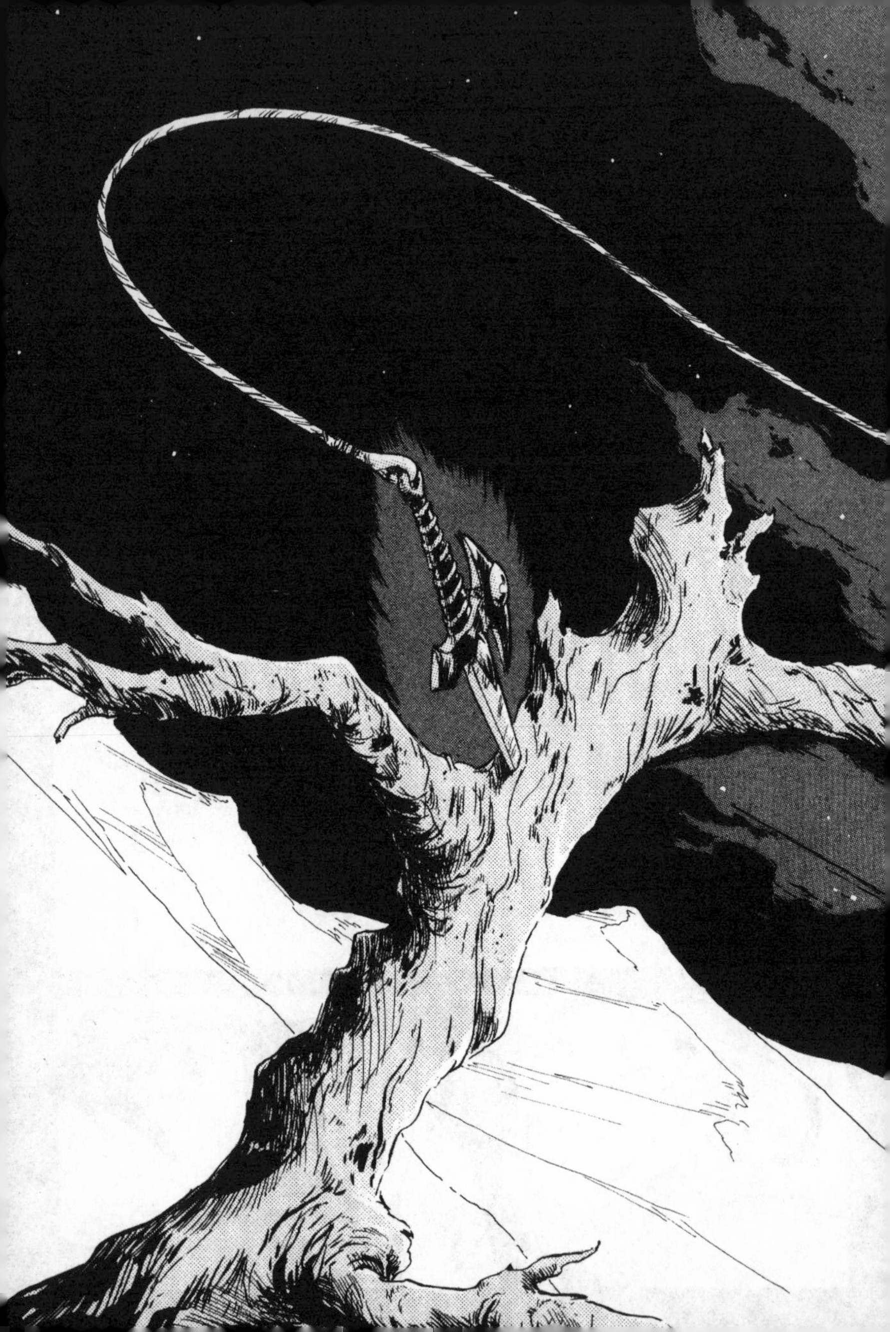

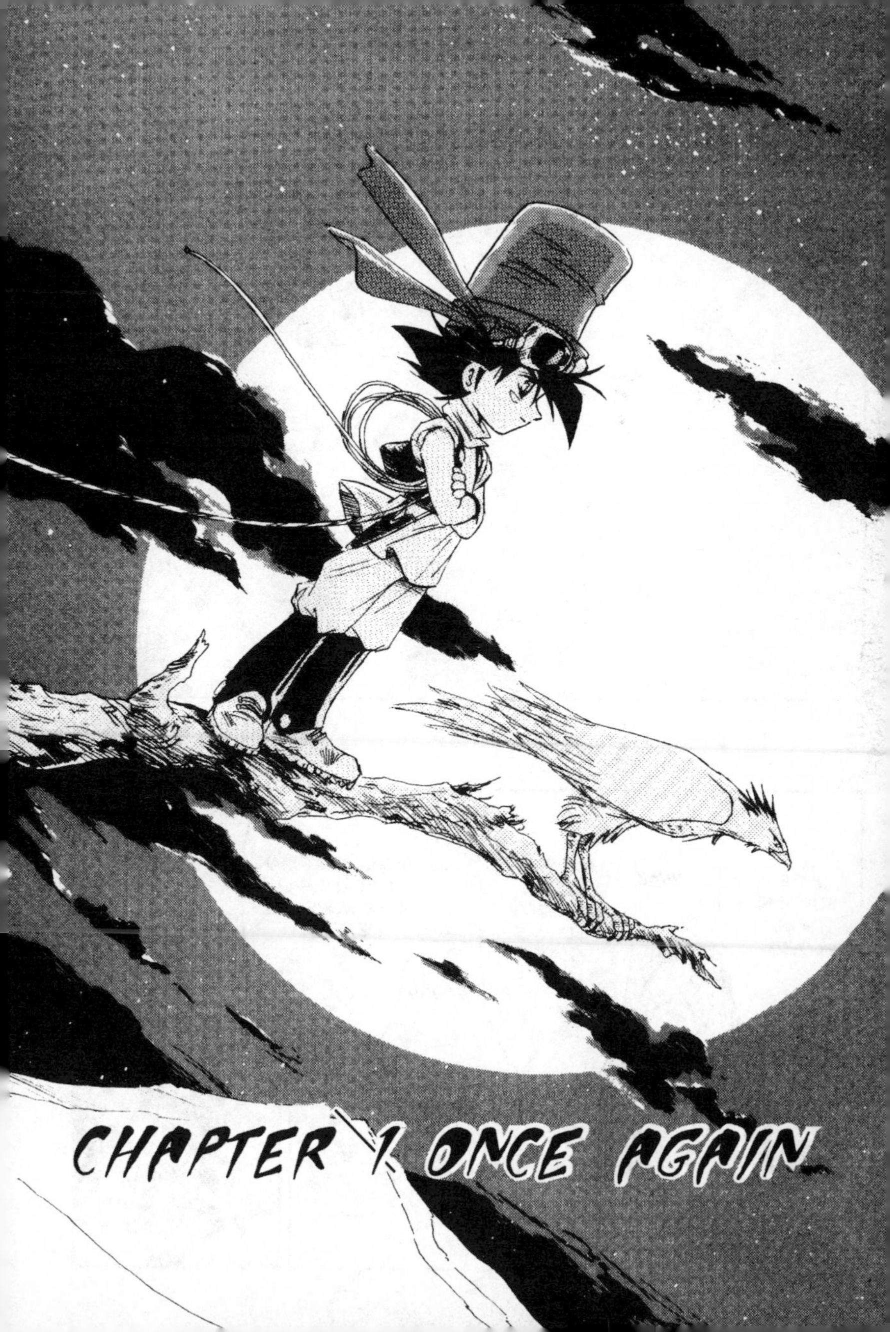
CHAPTER 1 ONCE AGAIN

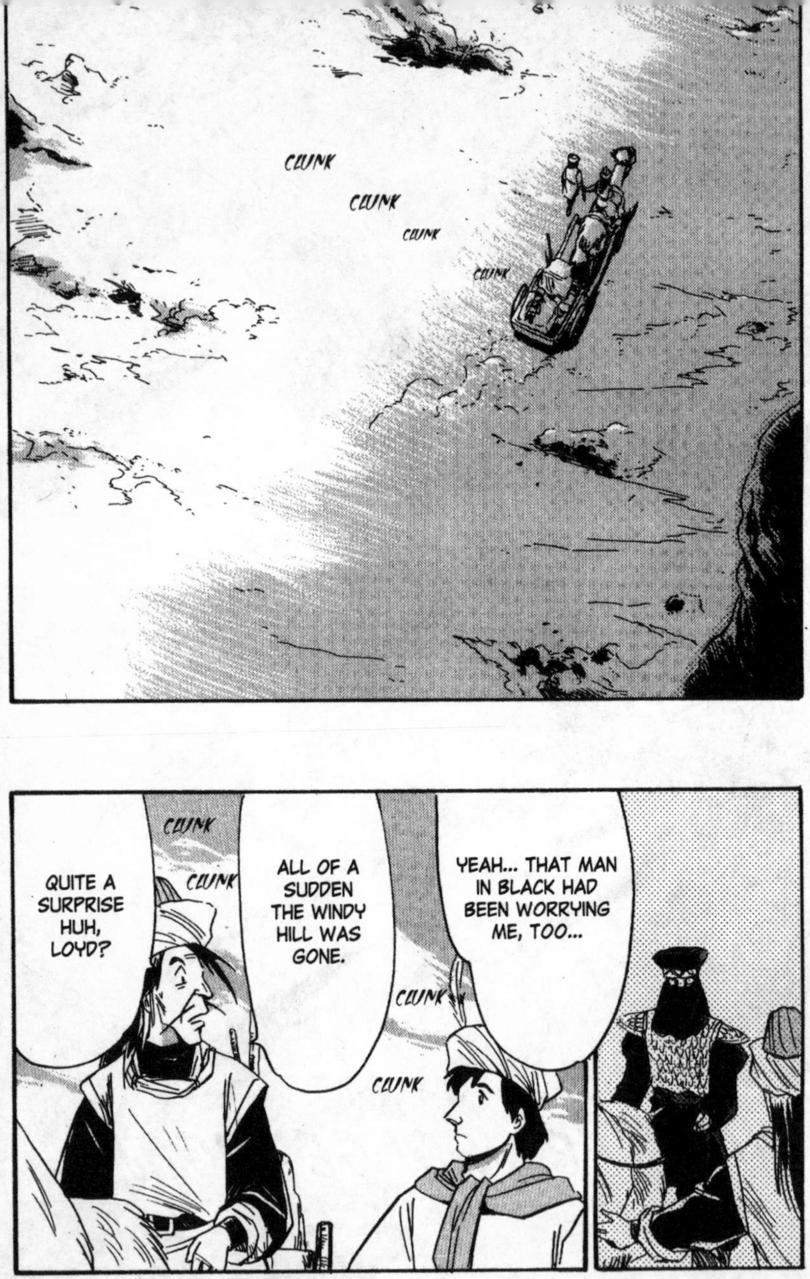
CLUNK
CLUNK
CLUNK
CLUNK
CLUNK
CLUNK
QUITE A SURPRISE HUH, LOYD?
ALL OF A SUDDEN THE WINDY HILL WAS GONE.
CLUNK
CLUNK
YEAH... THAT MAN IN BLACK HAD BEEN WORRYING ME, TOO...

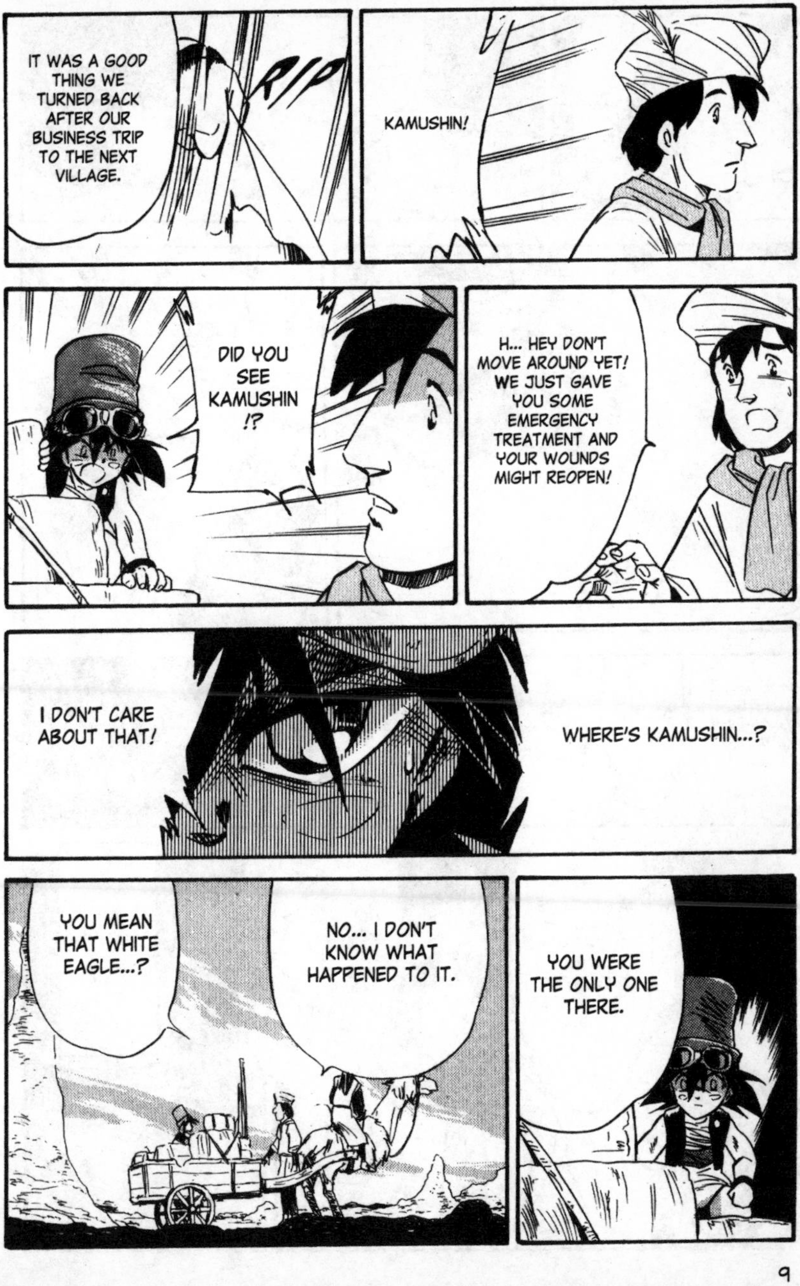
IT WAS A GOOD THING WE TURNED BACK AFTER OUR BUSINESS TRIP TO THE NEXT VILLAGE.
RIP
KAMUSHIN!
DID YOU SEE KAMUSHIN !?
H... HEY DON'T MOVE AROUND YET! WE JUST GAVE YOU SOME EMERGENCY TREATMENT AND YOUR WOUNDS MIGHT REOPEN!
I DON'T CARE ABOUT THAT!
WHERE'S KAMUSHIN...?
YOU MEAN THAT WHITE EAGLE...?
NO... I DON'T KNOW WHAT HAPPENED TO IT.
YOU WERE THE ONLY ONE THERE.

CRACKLE   CRACKLE

HERE, IT'S READY.

HAVE SOME.

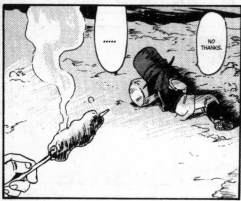

.....

NO THANKS.

SHEEESH.

WHAT A DEPRESSING LITTLE BRAT!

AHHH, GEEZ. HE'S MAKING MY FOOD TASTE BAD.

STOP IT DAD.

THE TWO THINGS I DON'T LIKE ARE SCORPIONS AND DEPRESSING BRATS.

LOYD YOU MUST BE BLIND.

A BRAT LIKE THIS CAN'T BE THE MAN WHO DREAMT OF THE WHITE EAGLE.

QUIT IT. THIS KID HAS BEEN HURT BECAUSE HE WAS SEPARATED FROM HIS FAMILY.

WHATEVER ...

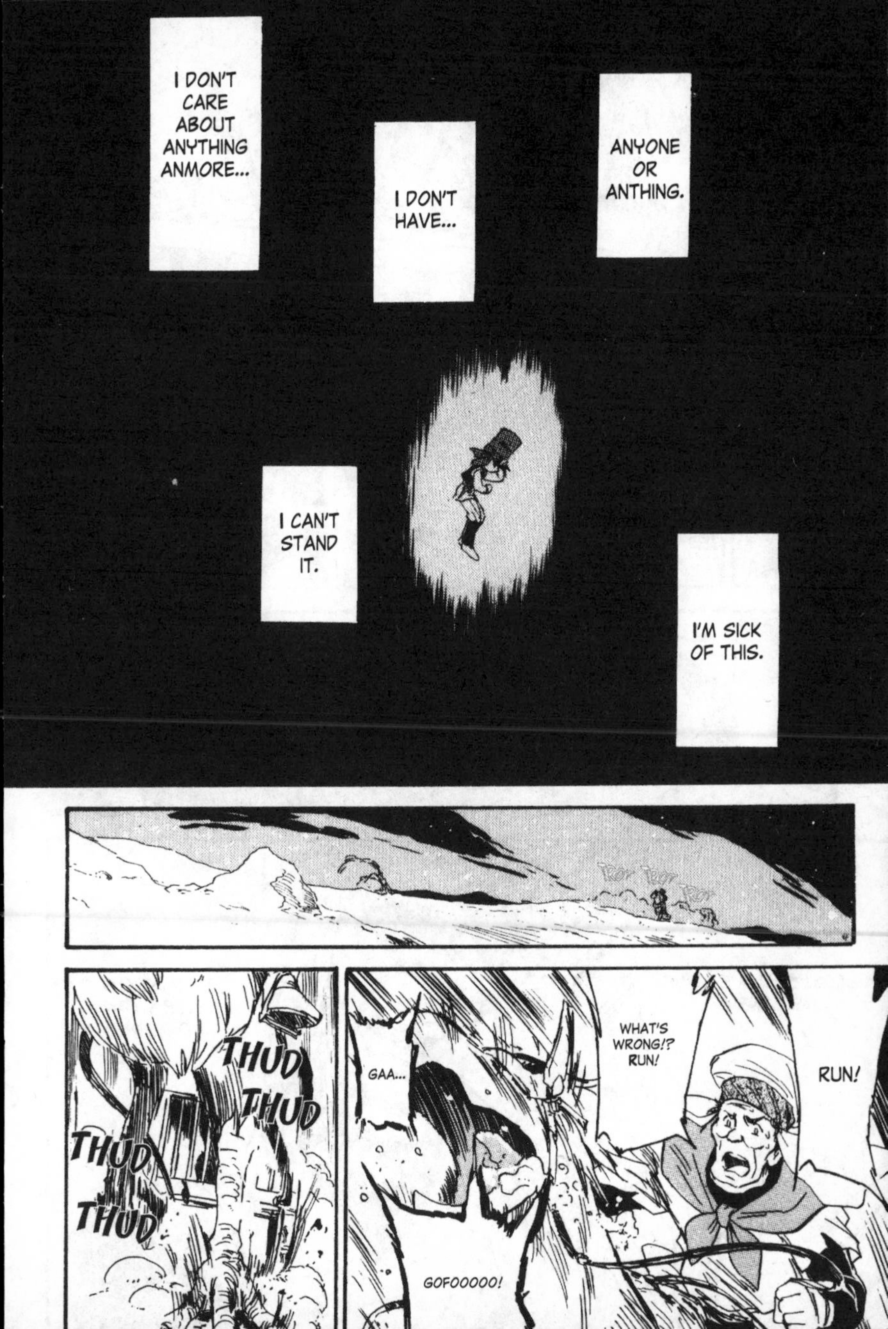
I DON'T CARE ABOUT ANYTHING ANMORE...
I DON'T HAVE...
ANYONE OR ANTHING.
I CAN'T STAND IT.
I'M SICK OF THIS.
THUD
THUD
THUD
THUD
GAA...
WHAT'S WRONG!? RUN!
RUN!
GOFOOOOO!

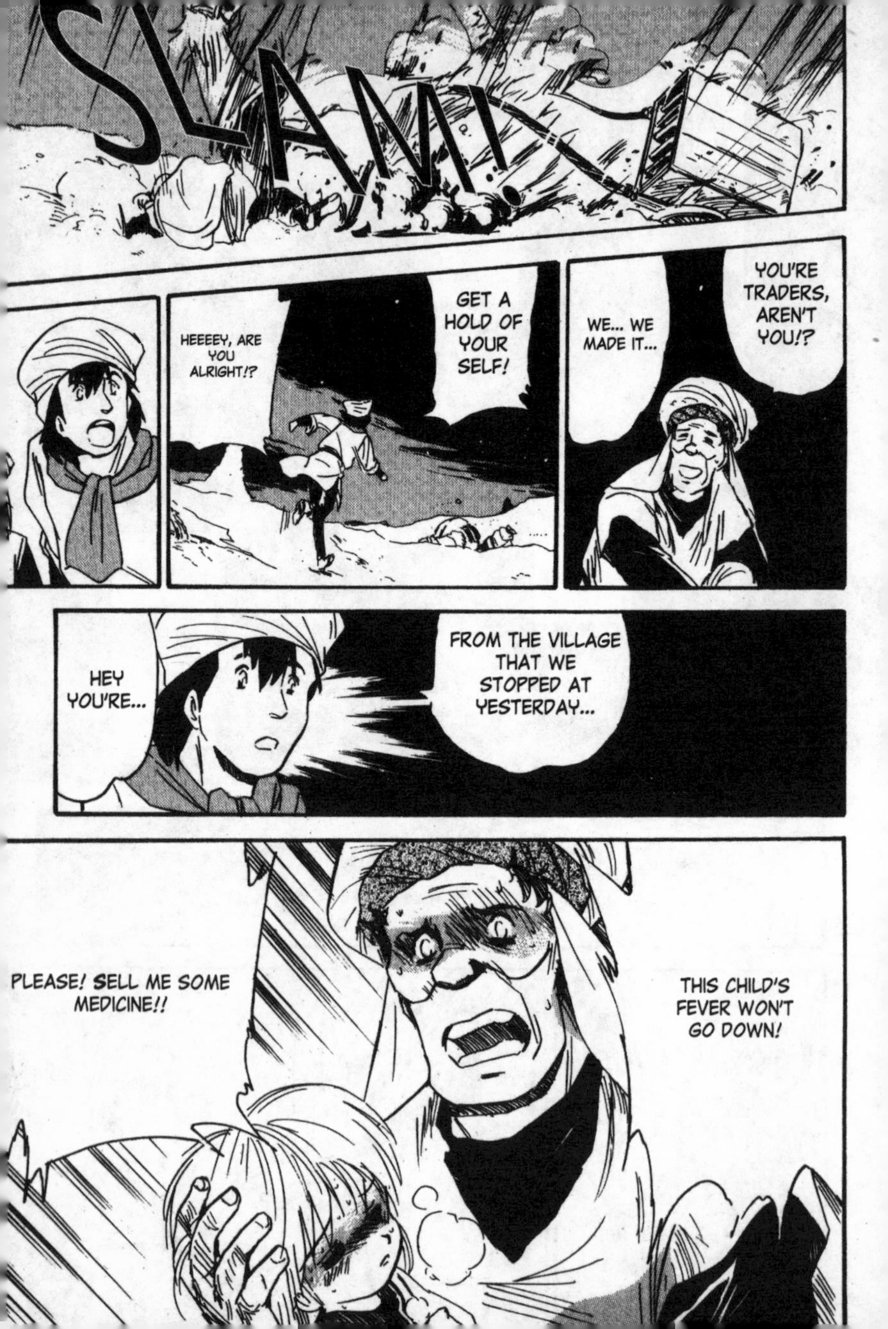
SLAM!
HEEEEY, ARE YOU ALRIGHT!?
GET A HOLD OF YOUR SELF!
WE... WE MADE IT...
YOU'RE TRADERS, AREN'T YOU!?
HEY YOU'RE...
FROM THE VILLAGE THAT WE STOPPED AT YESTERDAY...
PLEASE! SELL ME SOME MEDICINE!!
THIS CHILD'S FEVER WON'T GO DOWN!

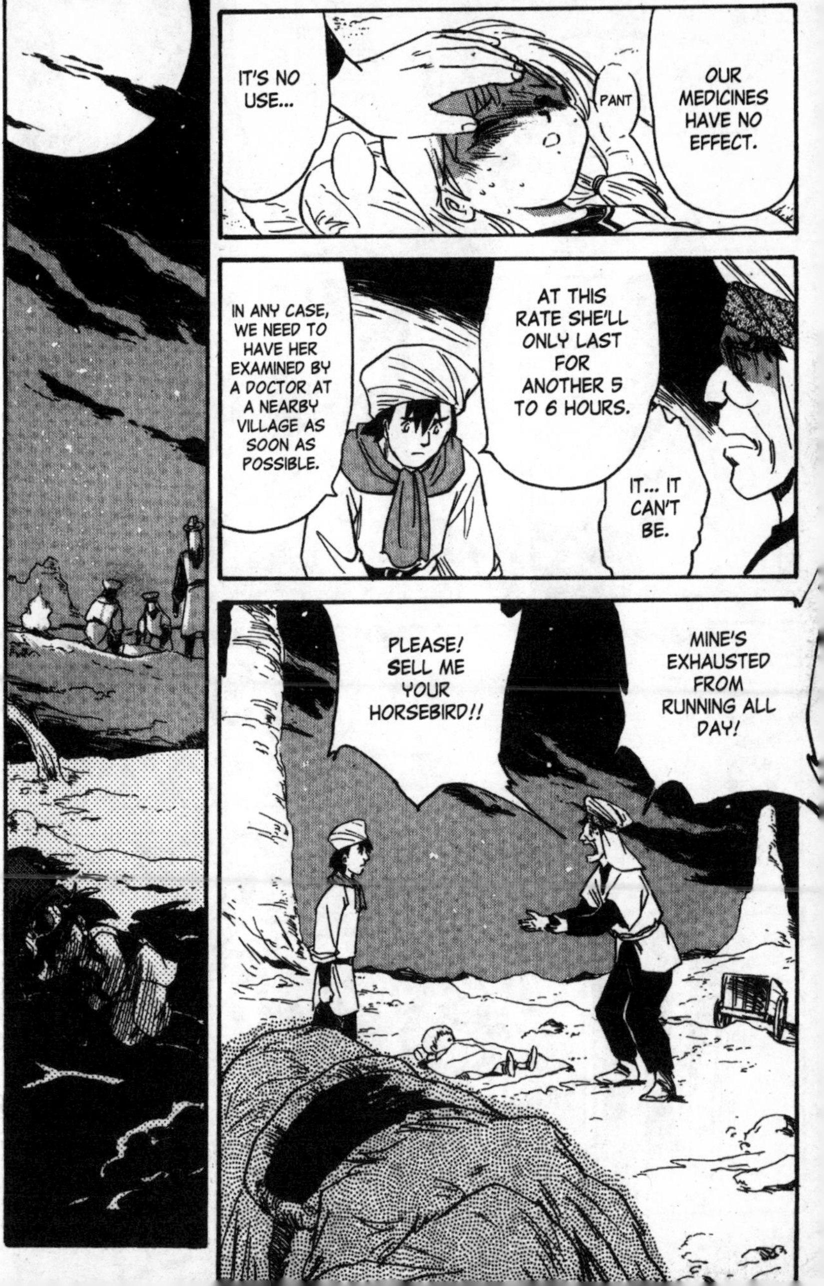
OUR MEDICINES HAVE NO EFFECT.
PANT
IT'S NO USE...
AT THIS RATE SHE'LL ONLY LAST FOR ANOTHER 5 TO 6 HOURS.
IT... IT CAN'T BE.
IN ANY CASE, WE NEED TO HAVE HER EXAMINED BY A DOCTOR AT A NEARBY VILLAGE AS SOON AS POSSIBLE.
MINE'S EXHAUSTED FROM RUNNING ALL DAY!
PLEASE! SELL ME YOUR HORSEBIRD!!

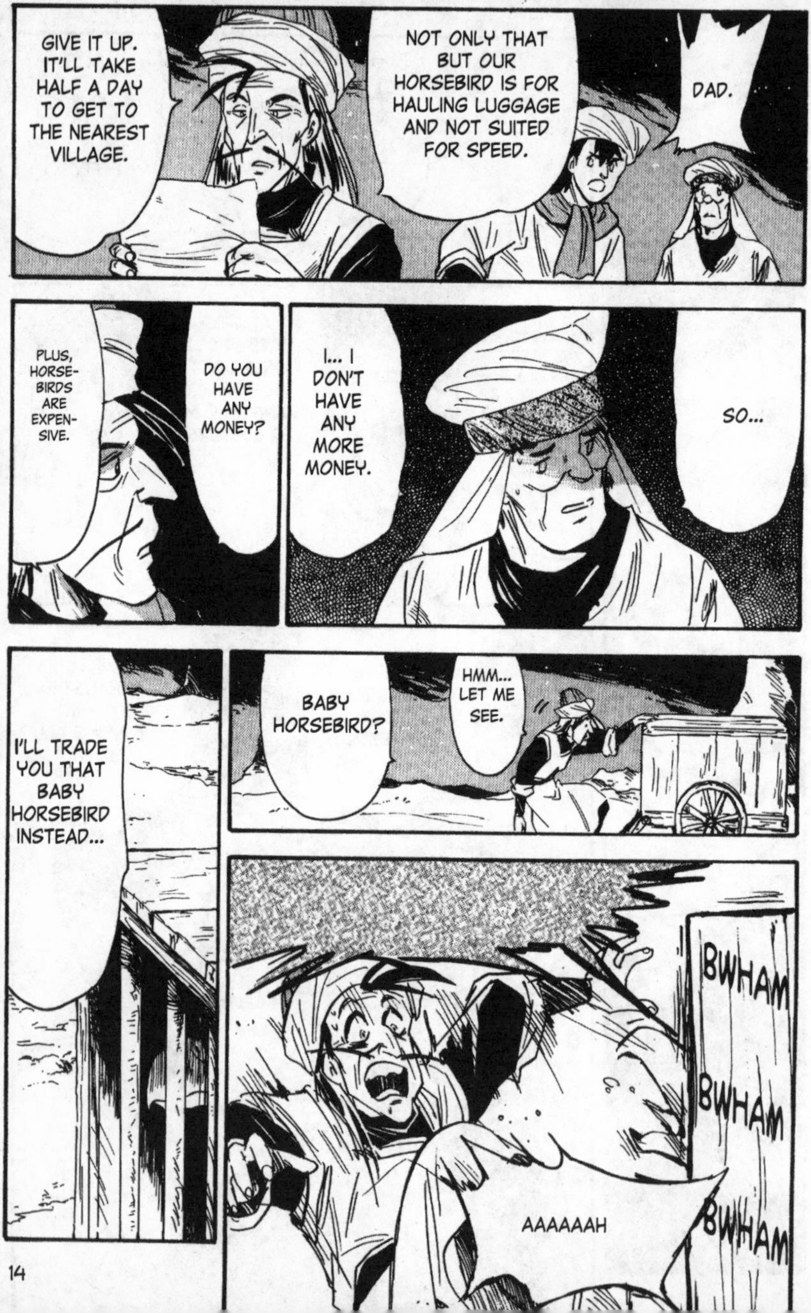

GIVE IT UP. IT'LL TAKE HALF A DAY TO GET TO THE NEAREST VILLAGE.
NOT ONLY THAT BUT OUR HORSEBIRD IS FOR HAULING LUGGAGE AND NOT SUITED FOR SPEED.
DAD.
PLUS, HORSE-BIRDS ARE EXPEN-SIVE.
DO YOU HAVE ANY MONEY?
I... I DON'T HAVE ANY MORE MONEY.
SO...
I'LL TRADE YOU THAT BABY HORSEBIRD INSTEAD...
BABY HORSEBIRD?
HMM... LET ME SEE.
BWHAM
BWHAM
BWHAM
AAAAAAH

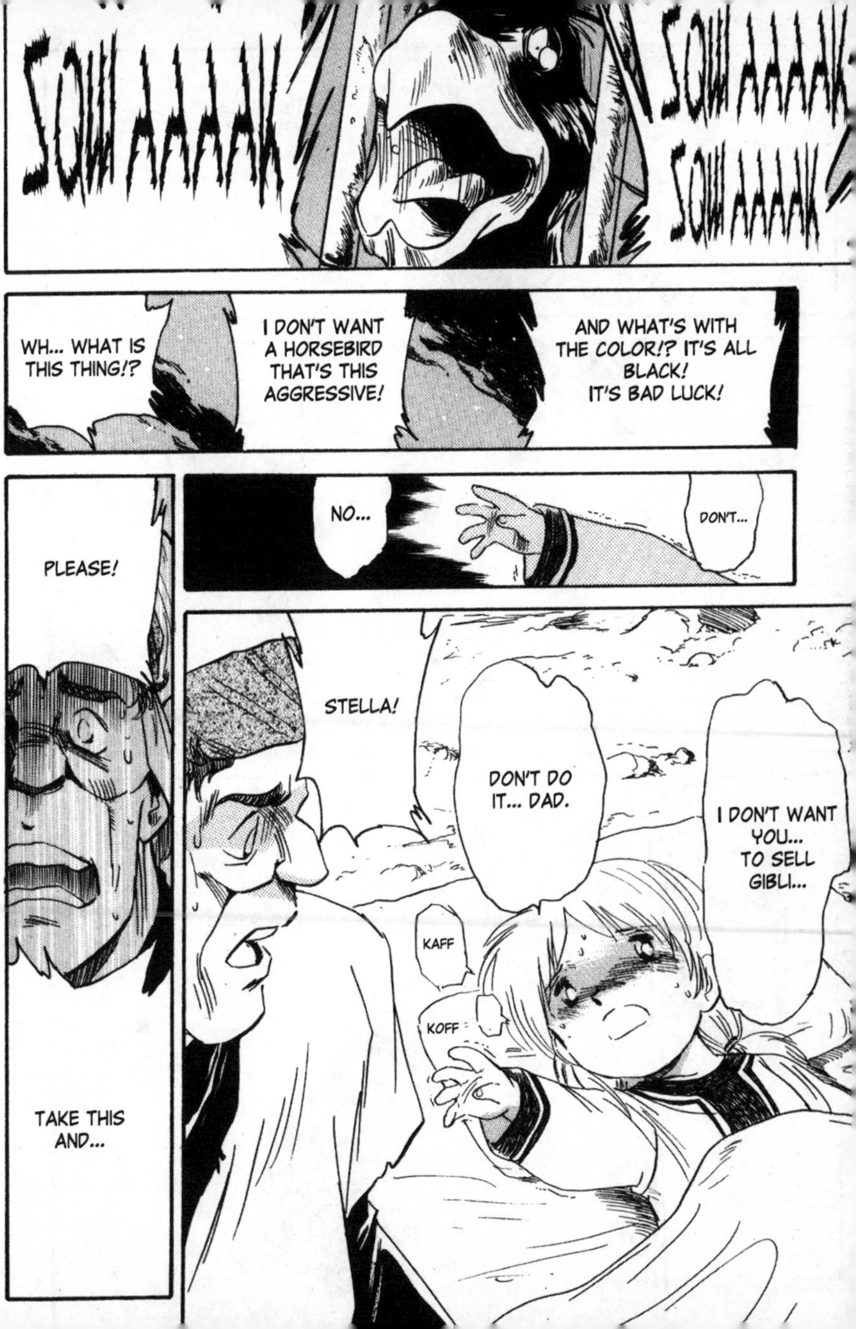
SQW AAAAK
SQW AAAAK
SQW AAAAK
WH... WHAT IS THIS THING!?
I DON'T WANT A HORSEBIRD THAT'S THIS AGGRESSIVE!
AND WHAT'S WITH THE COLOR!? IT'S ALL BLACK! IT'S BAD LUCK!
PLEASE!
NO...
DON'T...
TAKE THIS AND...
STELLA!
DON'T DO IT... DAD.
I DON'T WANT YOU... TO SELL GIBLI...
KAFF
KOFF

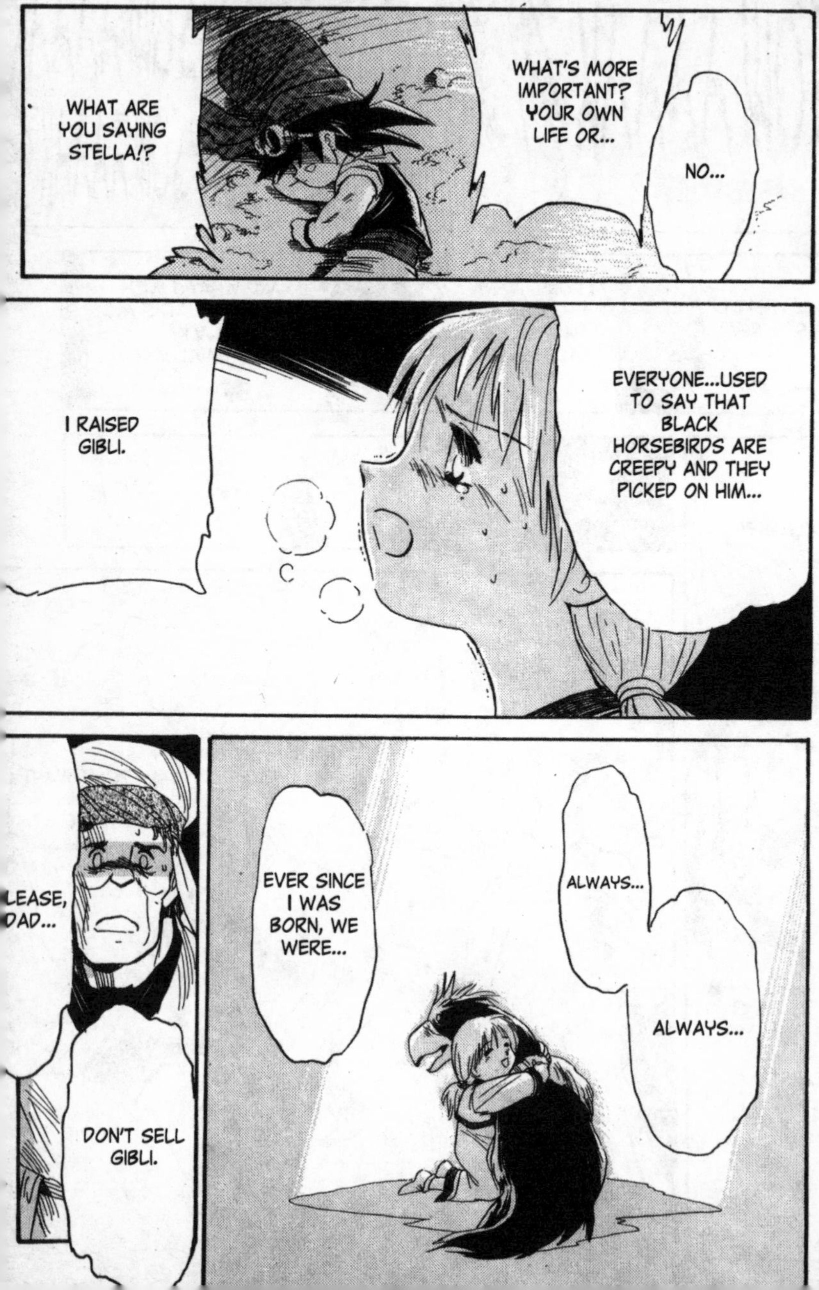
WHAT'S MORE IMPORTANT? YOUR OWN LIFE OR...
NO...
WHAT ARE YOU SAYING STELLA!?
EVERYONE...USED TO SAY THAT BLACK HORSEBIRDS ARE CREEPY AND THEY PICKED ON HIM...
I RAISED GIBLI.
ALWAYS...
ALWAYS...
EVER SINCE I WAS BORN, WE WERE...
LEASE, DAD...
DON'T SELL GIBLI.

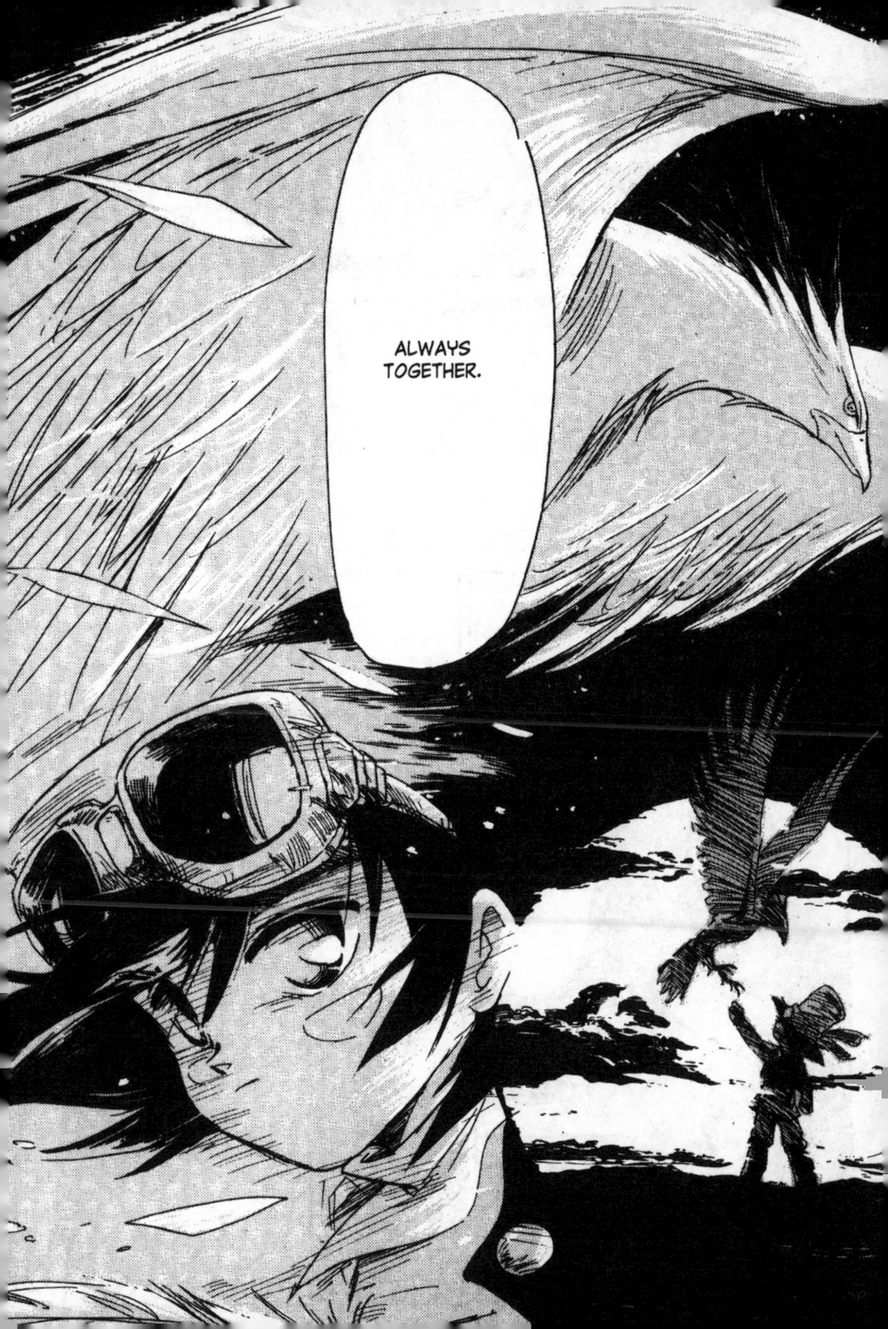
ALWAYS
TOGETHER.

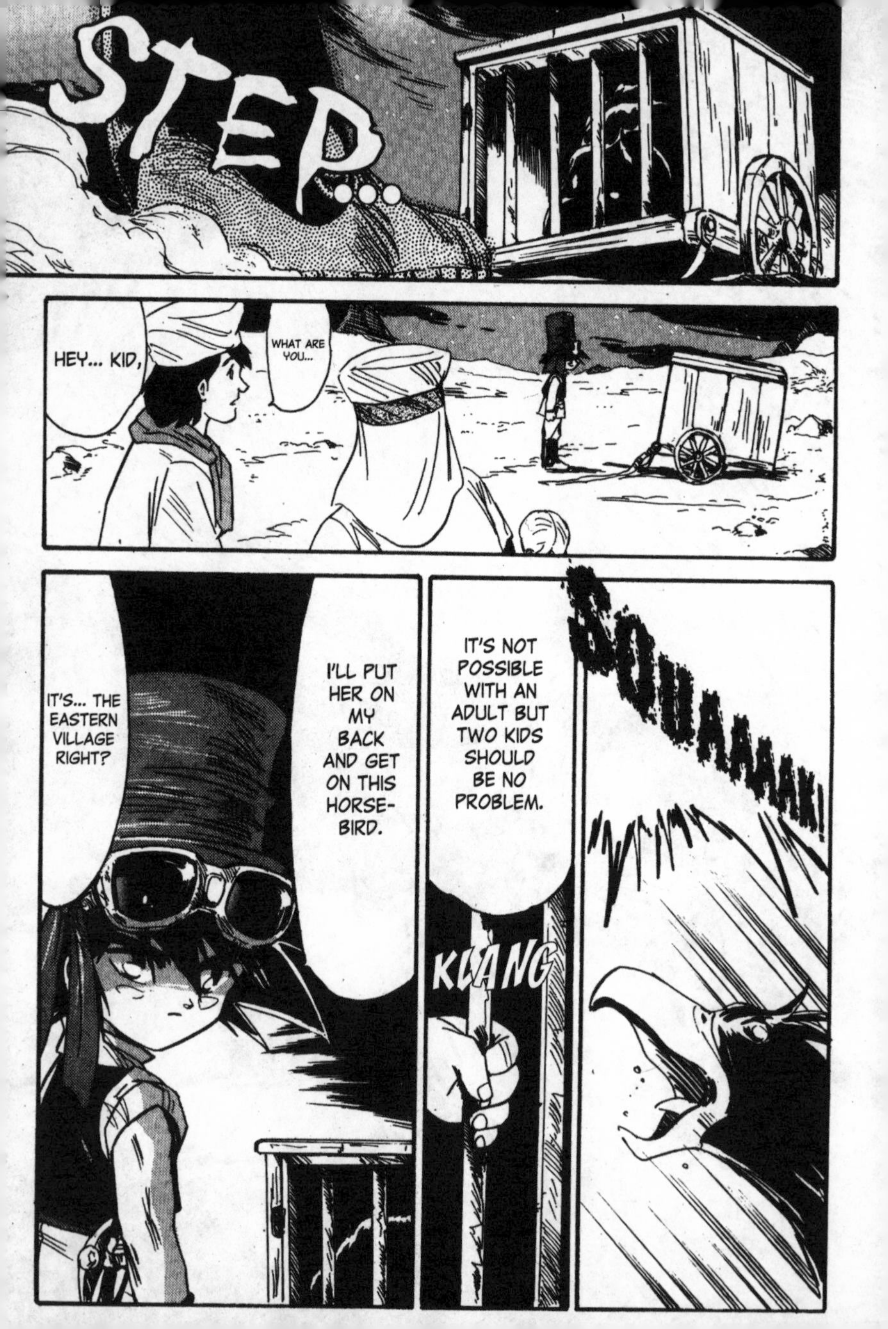
STEP...
HEY... KID,
WHAT ARE YOU...
IT'S... THE EASTERN VILLAGE RIGHT?
I'LL PUT HER ON MY BACK AND GET ON THIS HORSE-BIRD.
IT'S NOT POSSIBLE WITH AN ADULT BUT TWO KIDS SHOULD BE NO PROBLEM.
KLANG
SQUAAAAK!

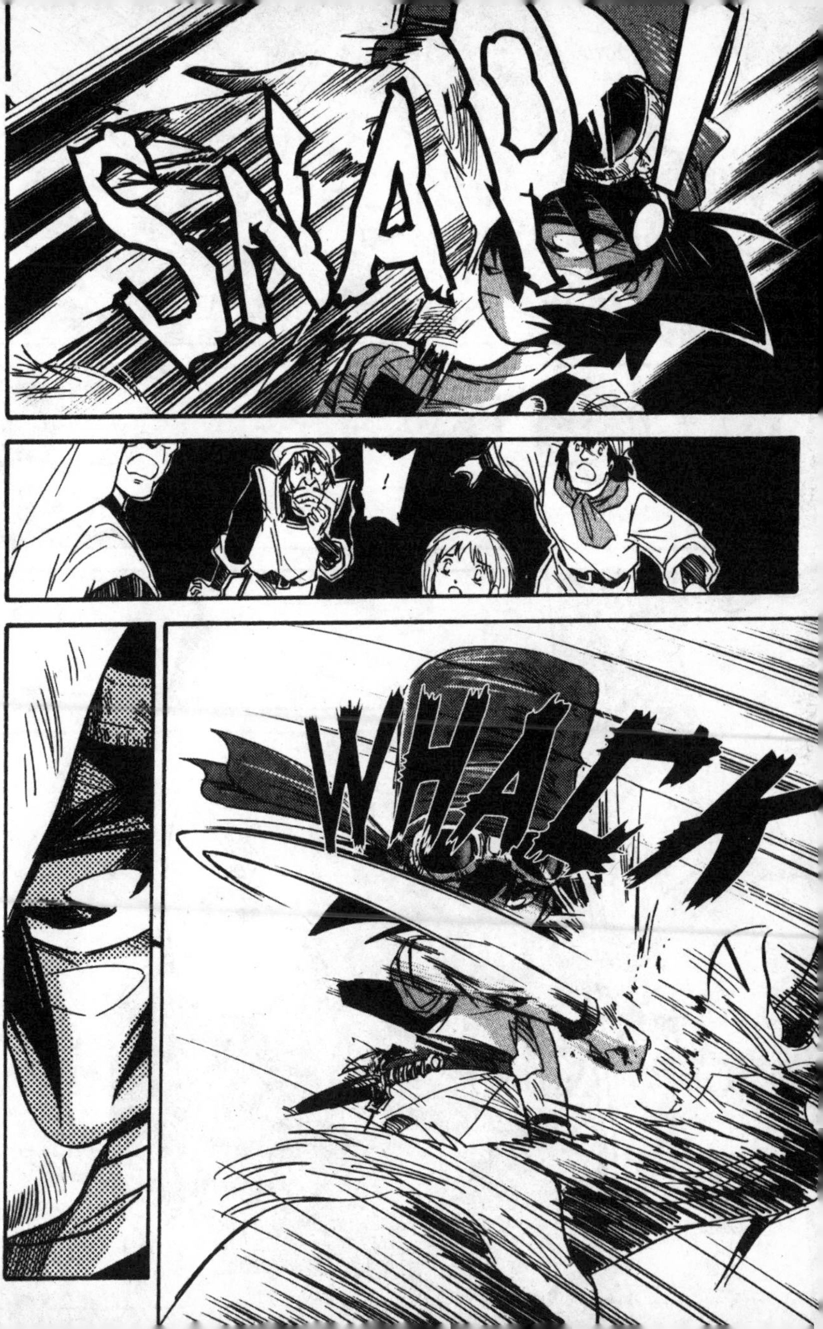
SNAP!
!
WHACK

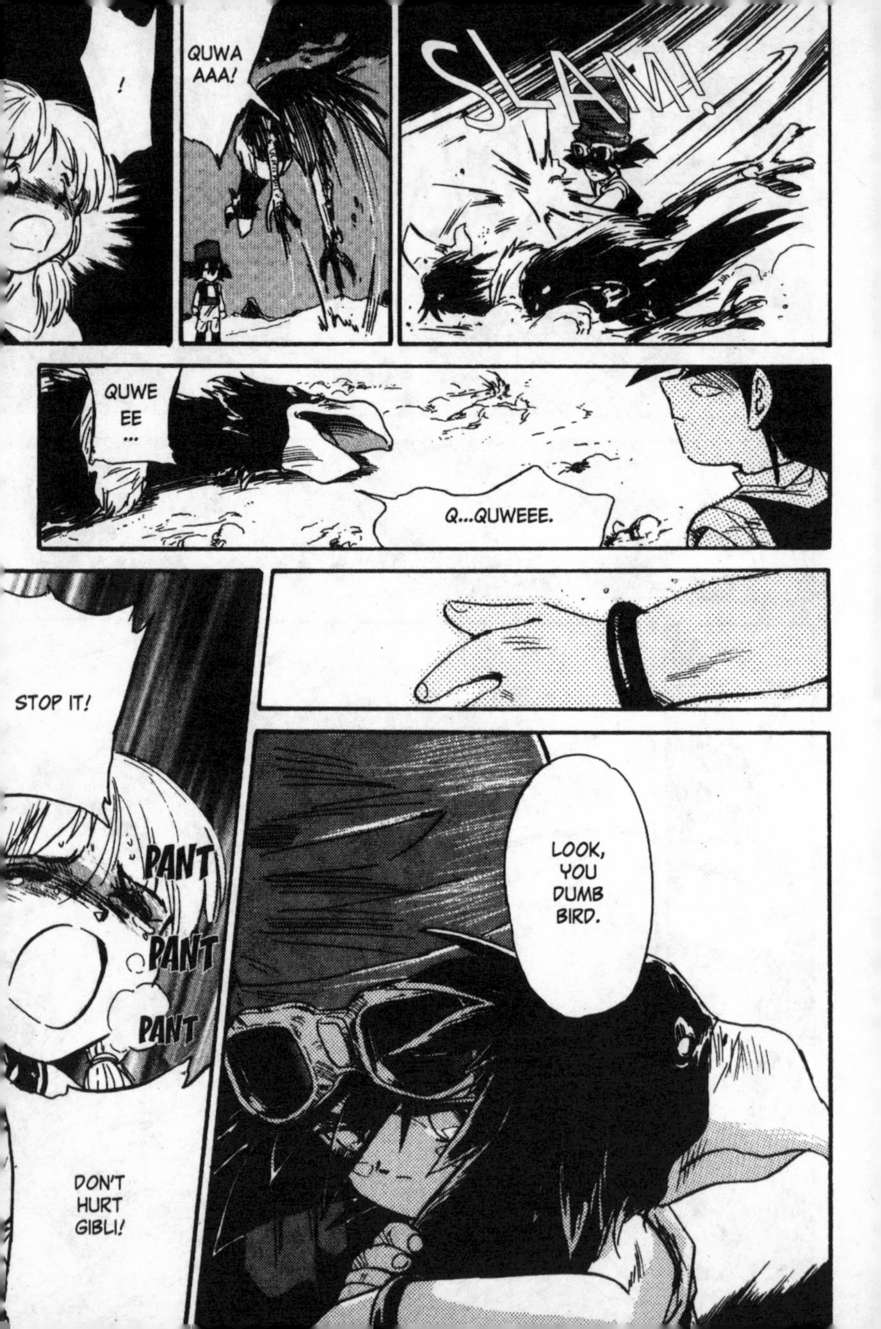
!
QUWA AAA!
SLAM!
QUWE EE ...
Q...QUWEEE.
STOP IT!
PANT
PANT
PANT
DON'T HURT GIBLI!
LOOK, YOU DUMB BIRD.

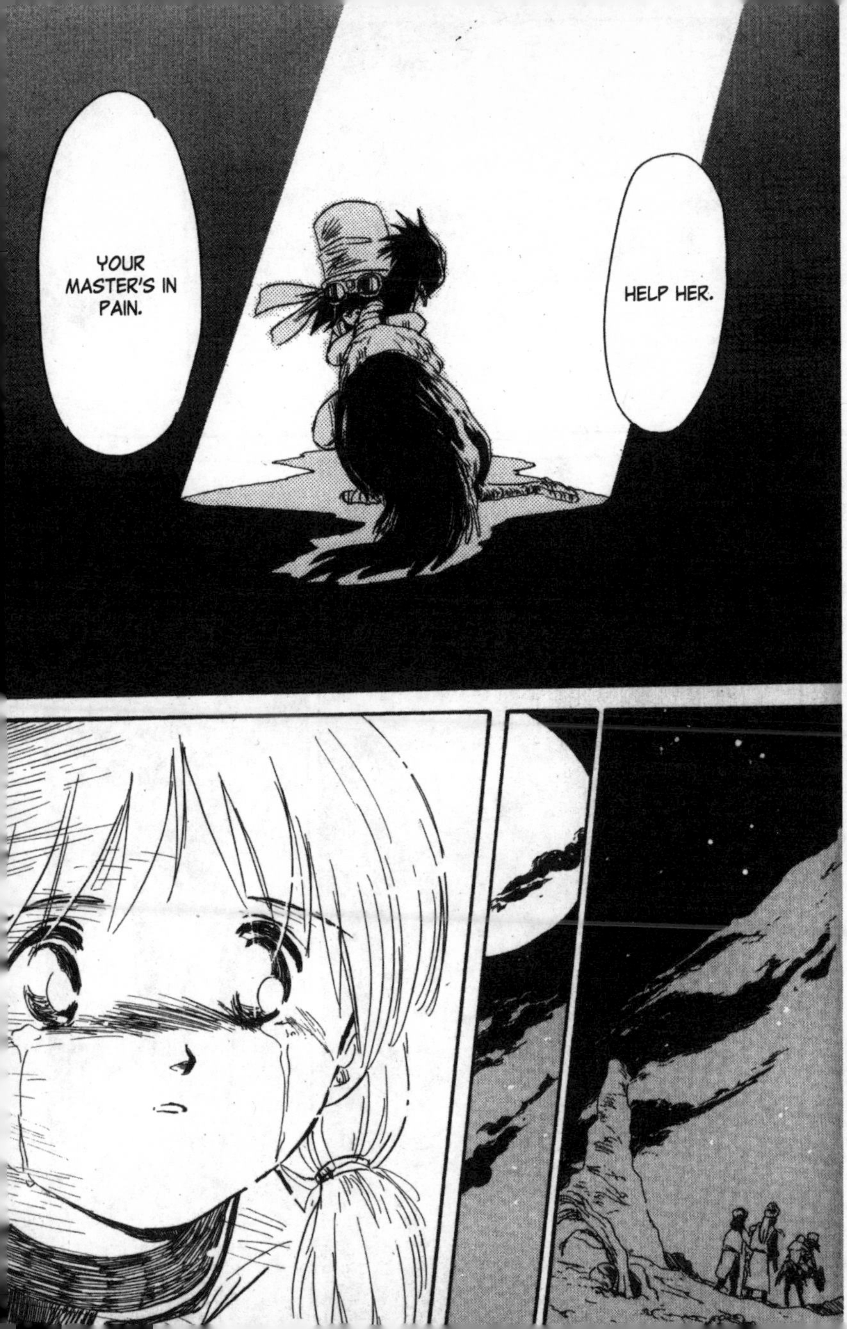
HELP HER.
YOUR MASTER'S IN PAIN.

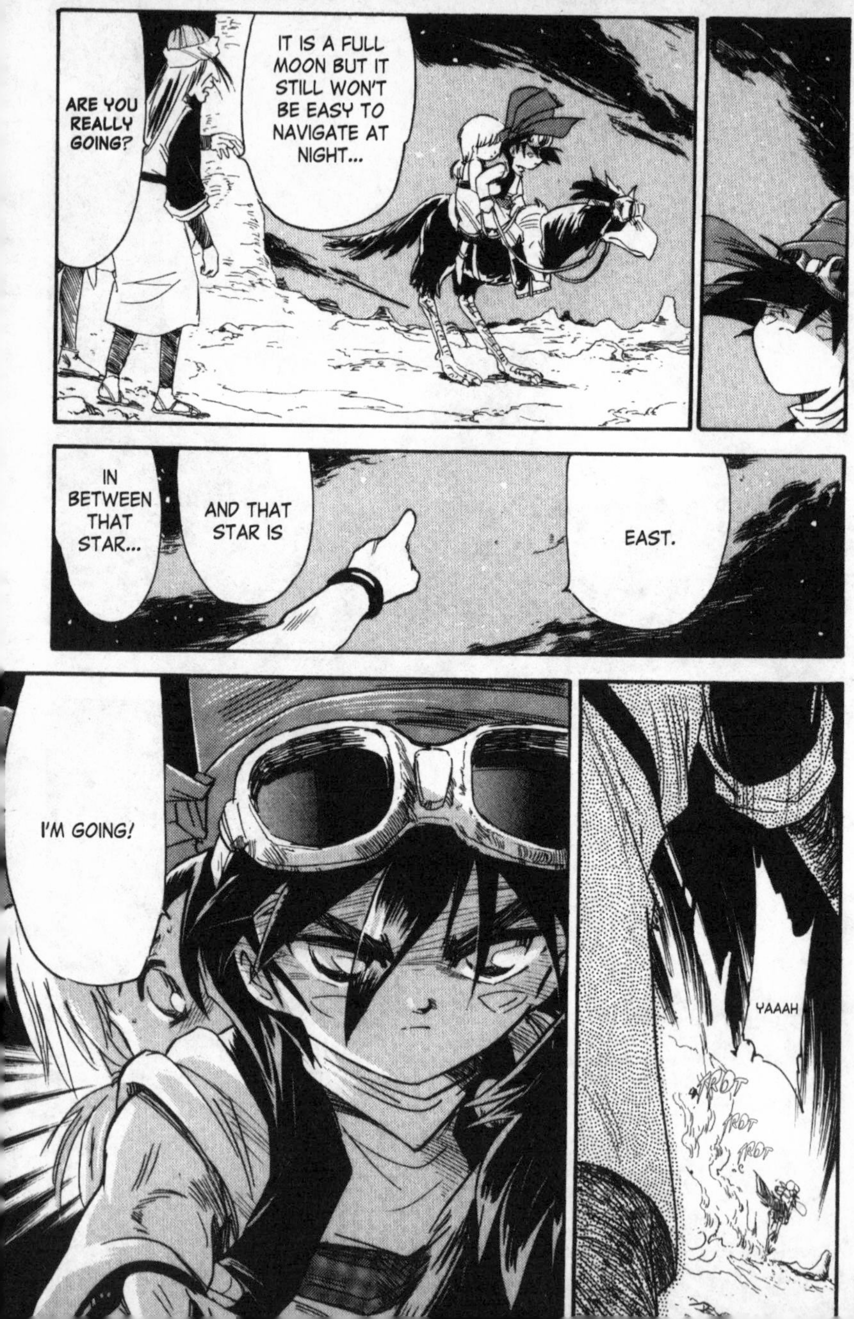

IT IS A FULL MOON BUT IT STILL WON'T BE EASY TO NAVIGATE AT NIGHT...
ARE YOU REALLY GOING?
IN BETWEEN THAT STAR...
AND THAT STAR IS
EAST.
I'M GOING!
YAAAH

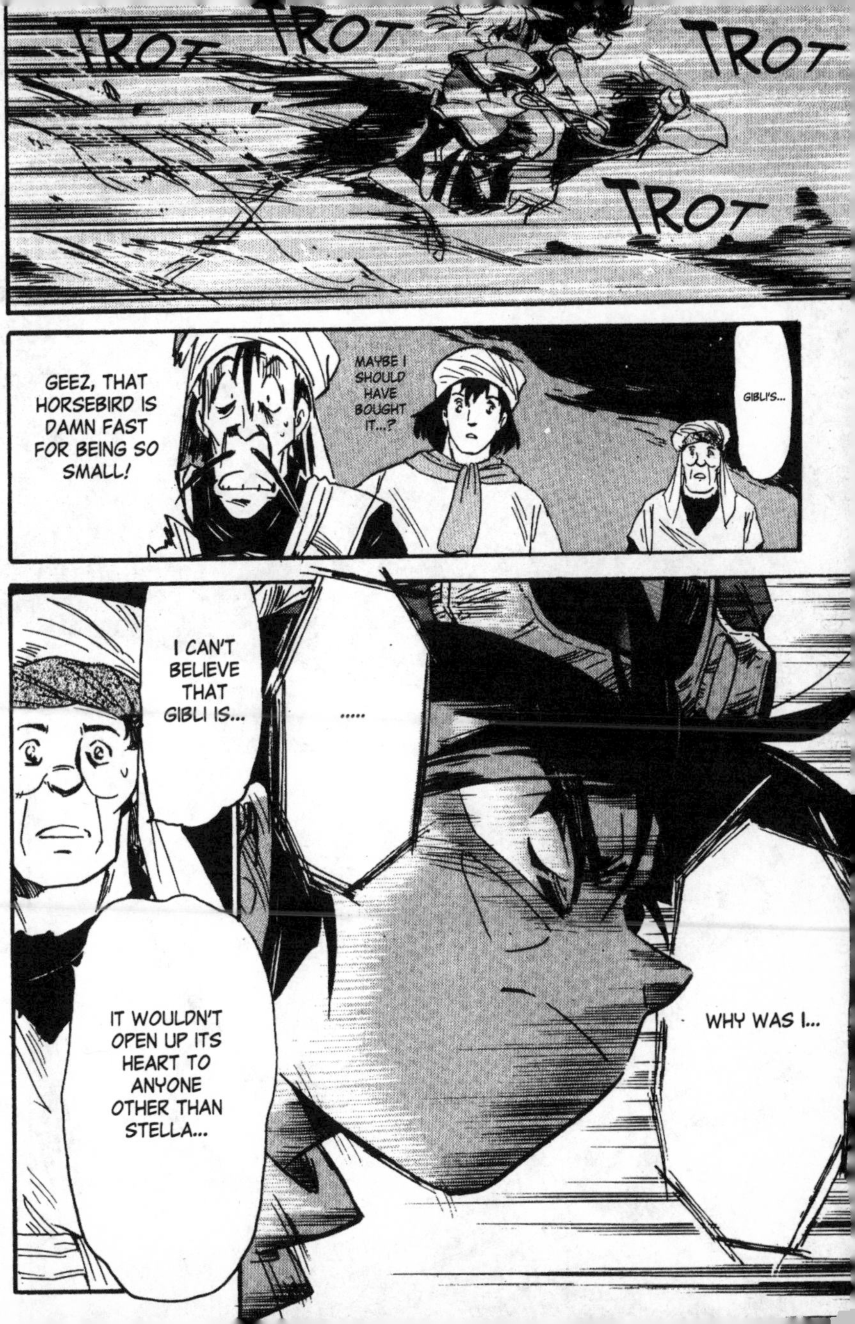

TROT TROT TROT
TROT
GEEZ, THAT HORSEBIRD IS DAMN FAST FOR BEING SO SMALL!
MAYBE I SHOULD HAVE BOUGHT IT...?
GIBLI'S...
I CAN'T BELIEVE THAT GIBLI IS...
.....
IT WOULDN'T OPEN UP ITS HEART TO ANYONE OTHER THAN STELLA...
WHY WAS I...

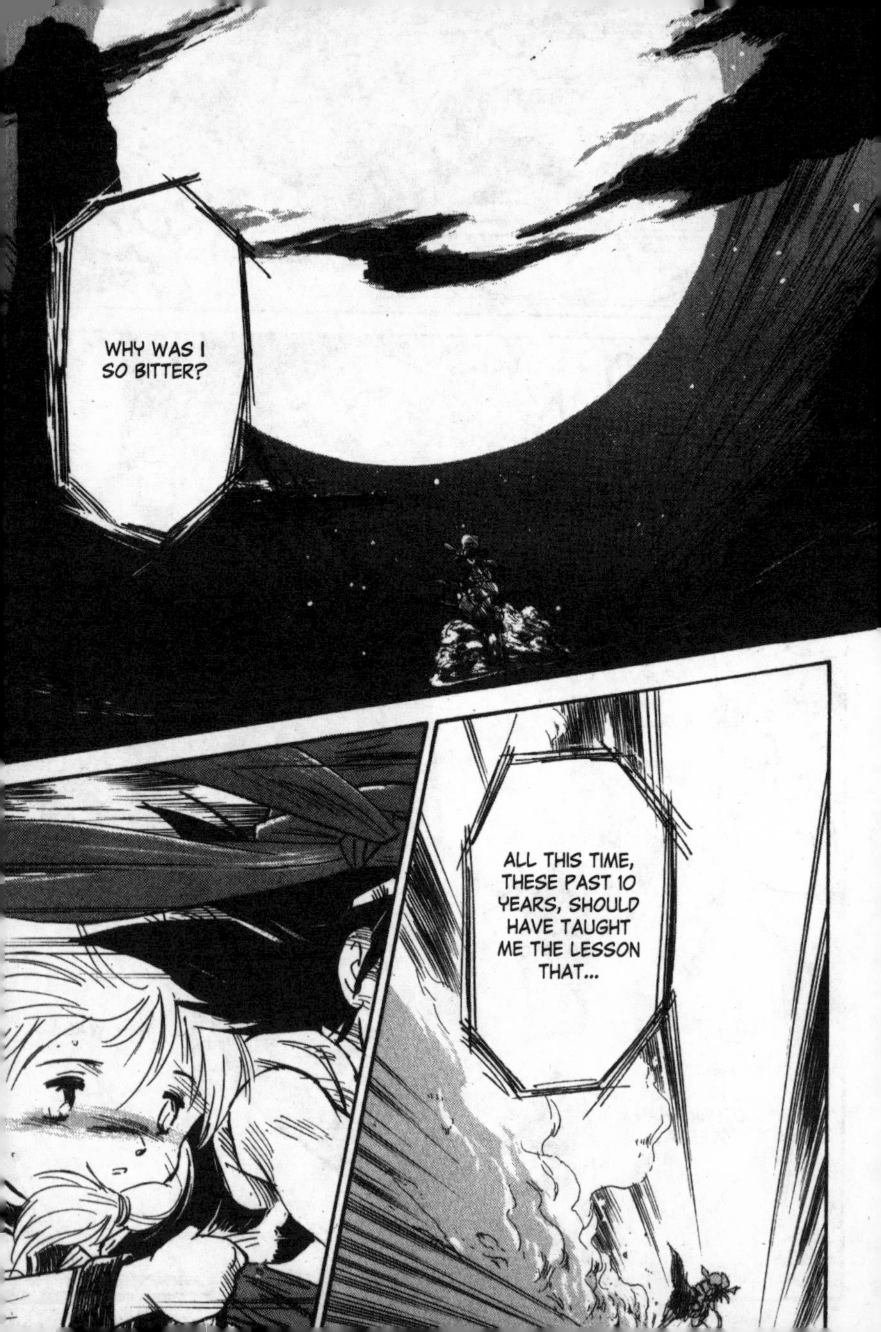
WHY WAS I SO BITTER?
ALL THIS TIME, THESE PAST 10 YEARS, SHOULD HAVE TAUGHT ME THE LESSON THAT...

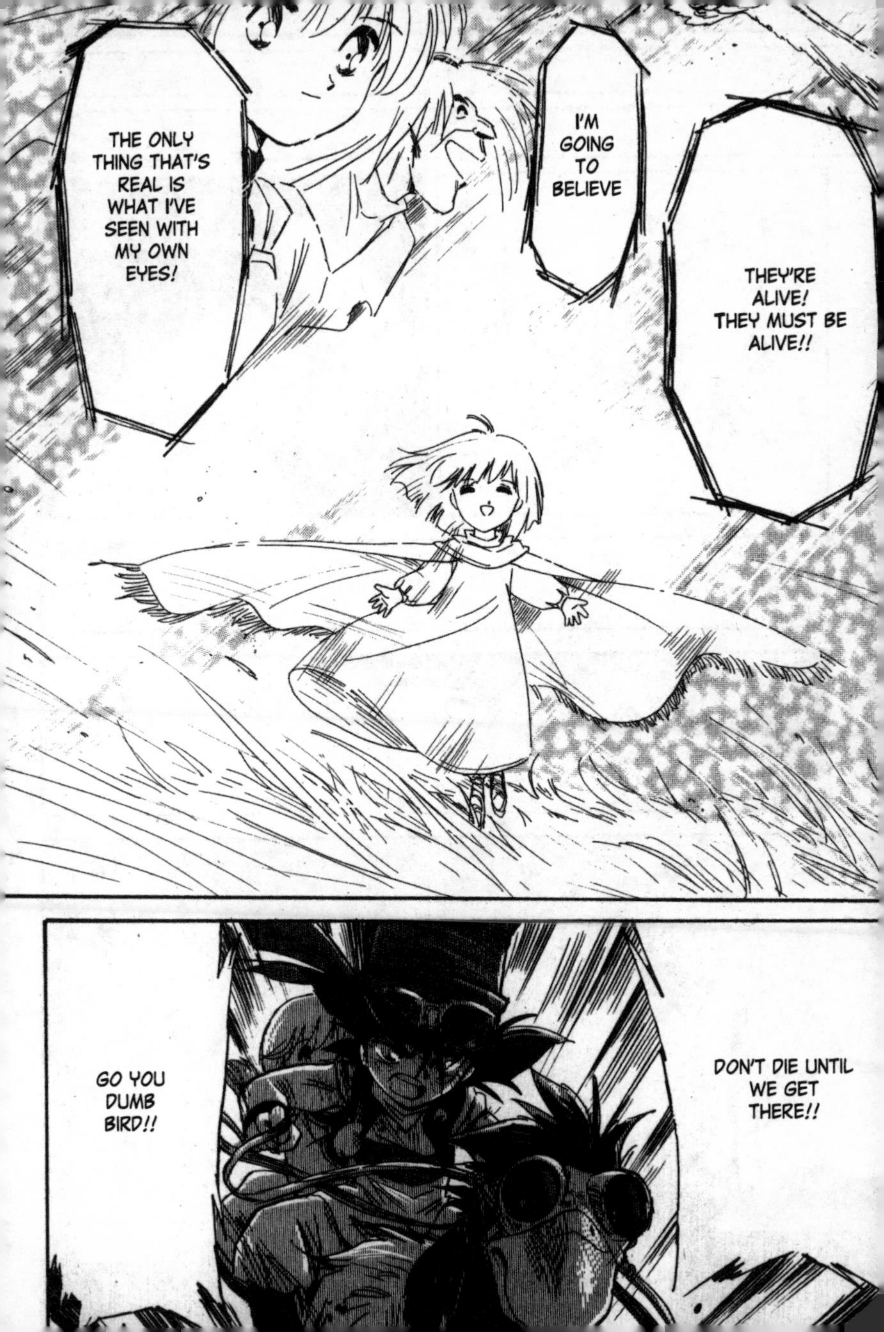

I'M GOING TO BELIEVE
THEY'RE ALIVE! THEY MUST BE ALIVE!!
THE ONLY THING THAT'S REAL IS WHAT I'VE SEEN WITH MY OWN EYES!
DON'T DIE UNTIL WE GET THERE!!
GO YOU DUMB BIRD!!

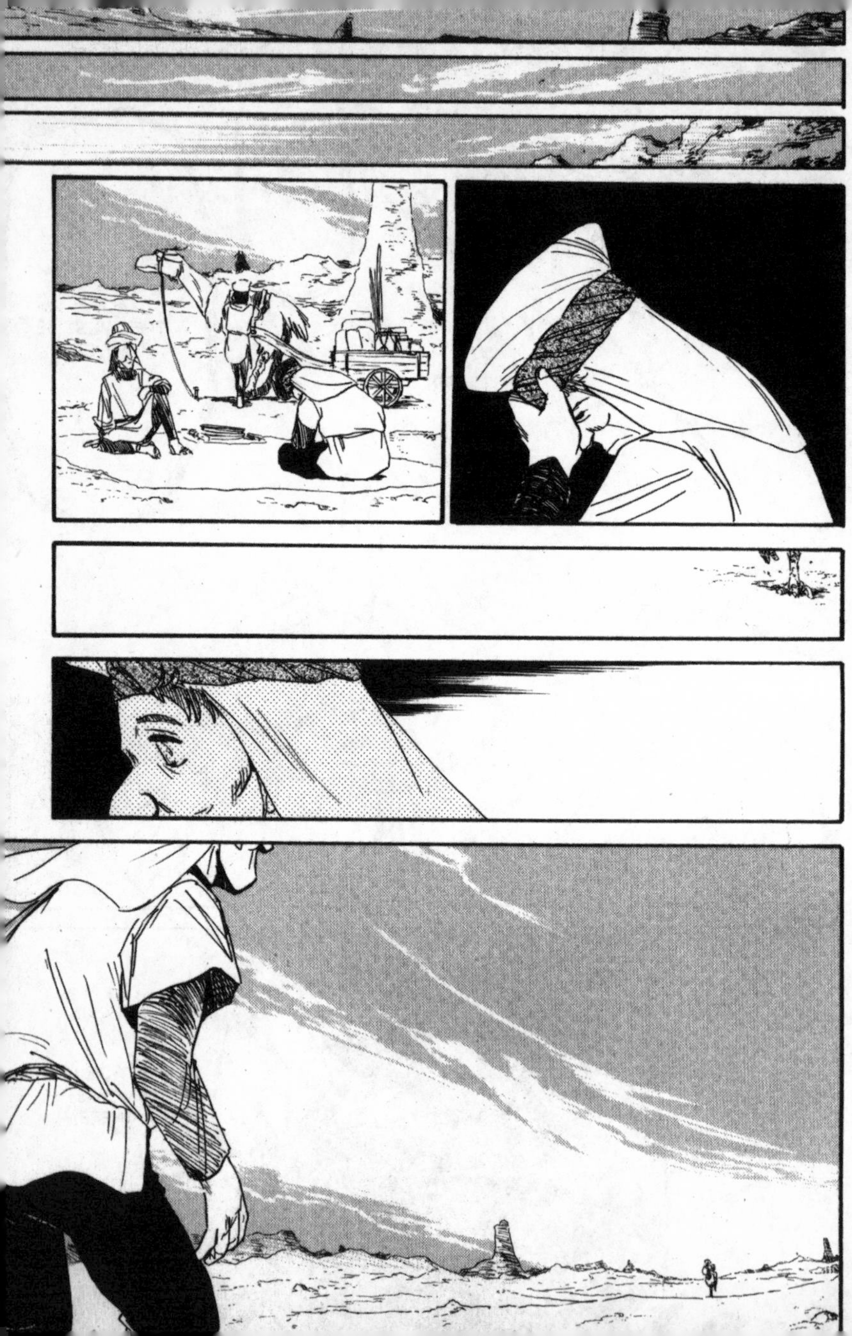

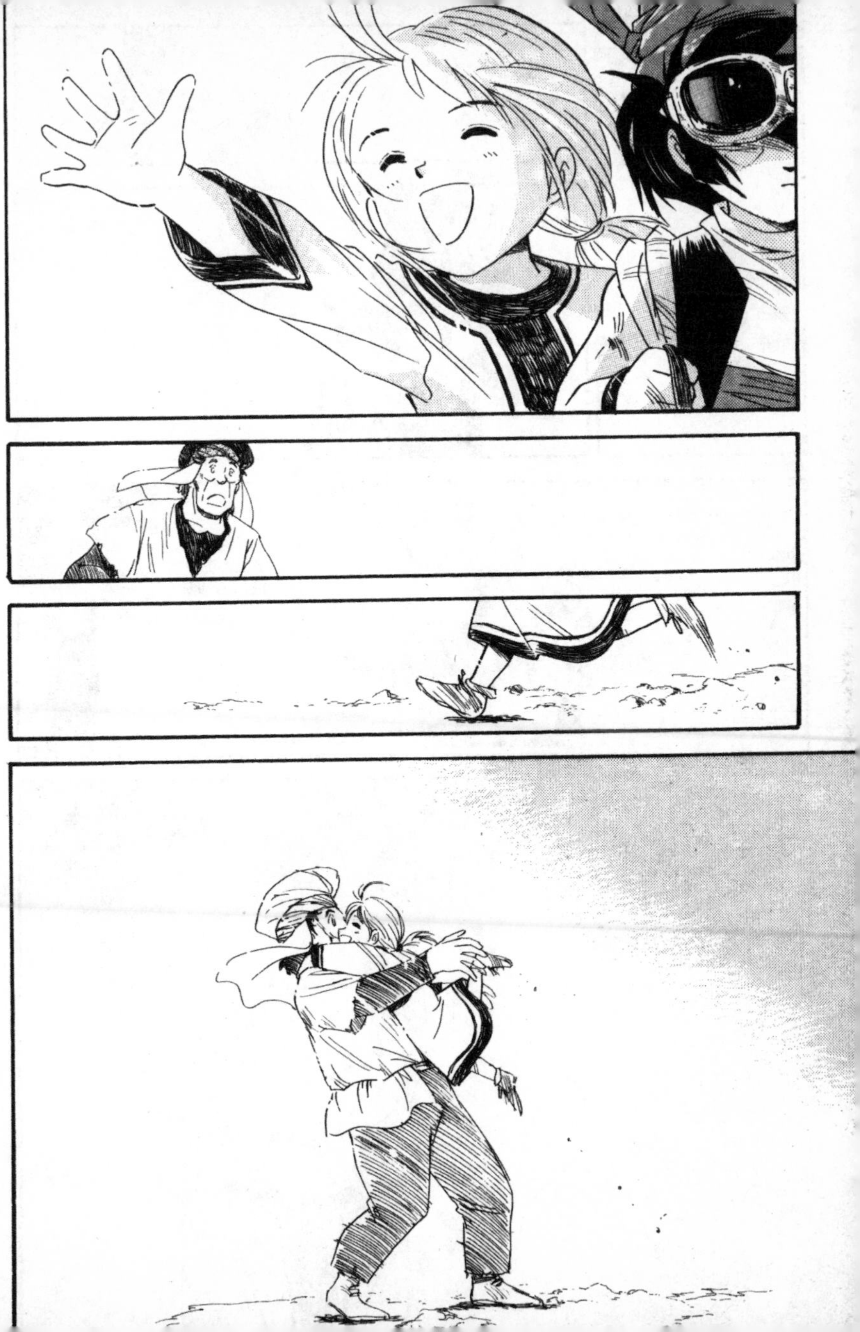

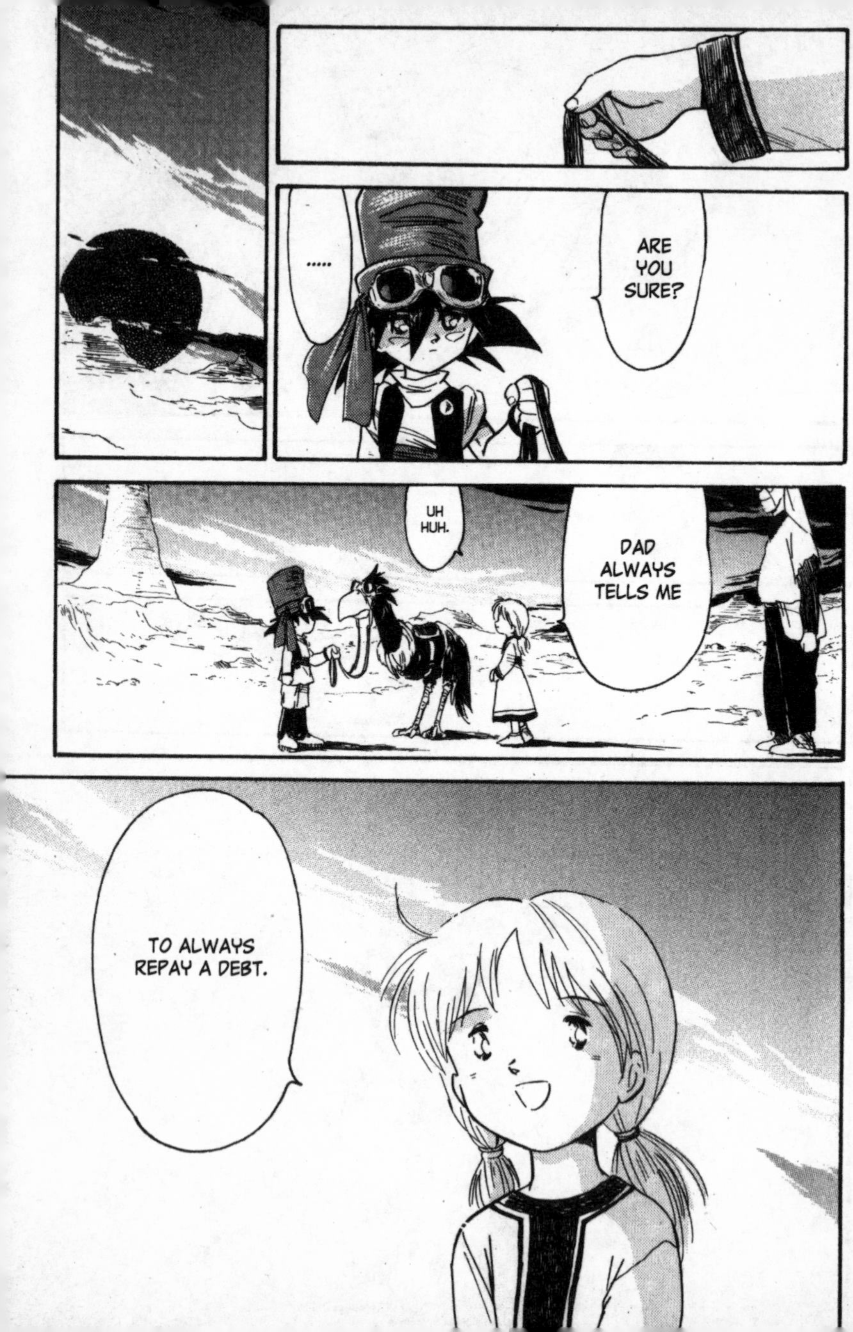

ARE YOU SURE?
.....
DAD ALWAYS TELLS ME
UH HUH.
TO ALWAYS REPAY A DEBT.

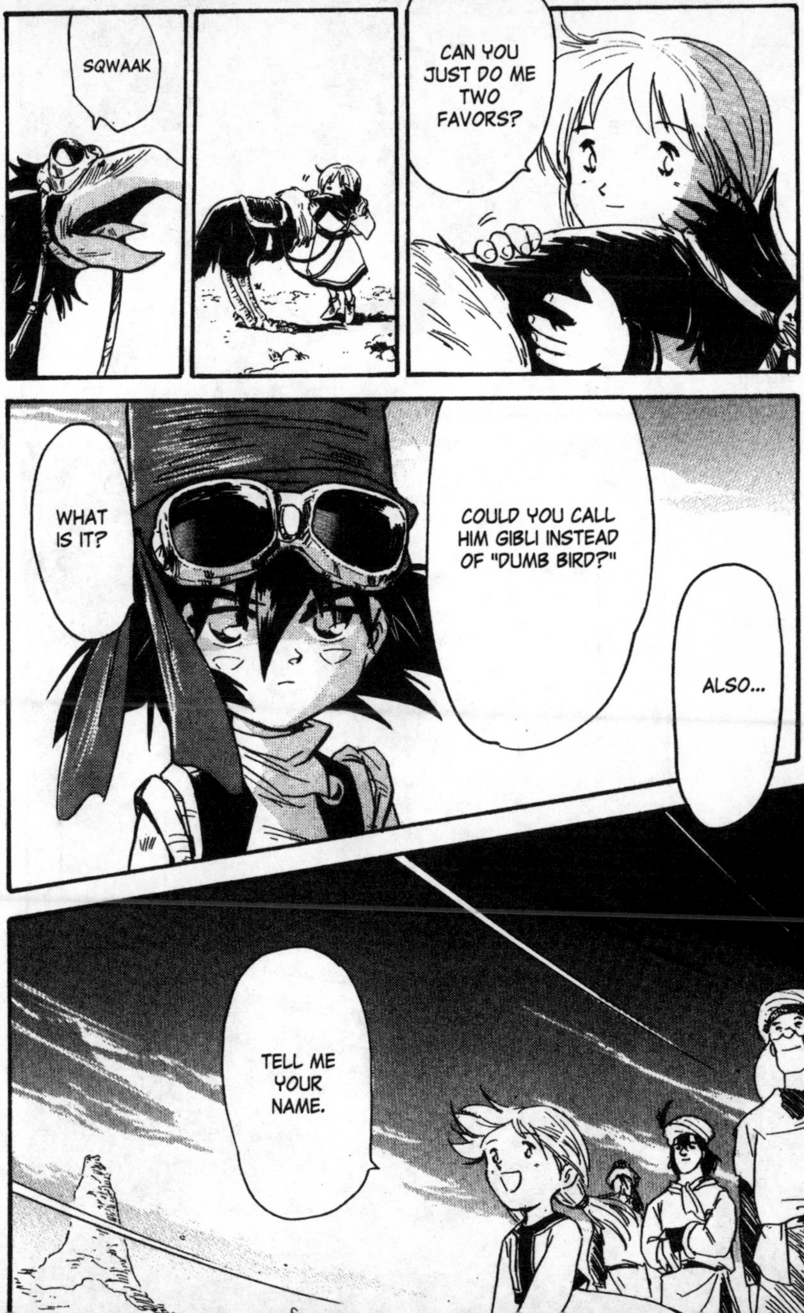
SQWAAK
CAN YOU JUST DO ME TWO FAVORS?
WHAT IS IT?
COULD YOU CALL HIM GIBLI INSTEAD OF "DUMB BIRD?"
ALSO...
TELL ME YOUR NAME.

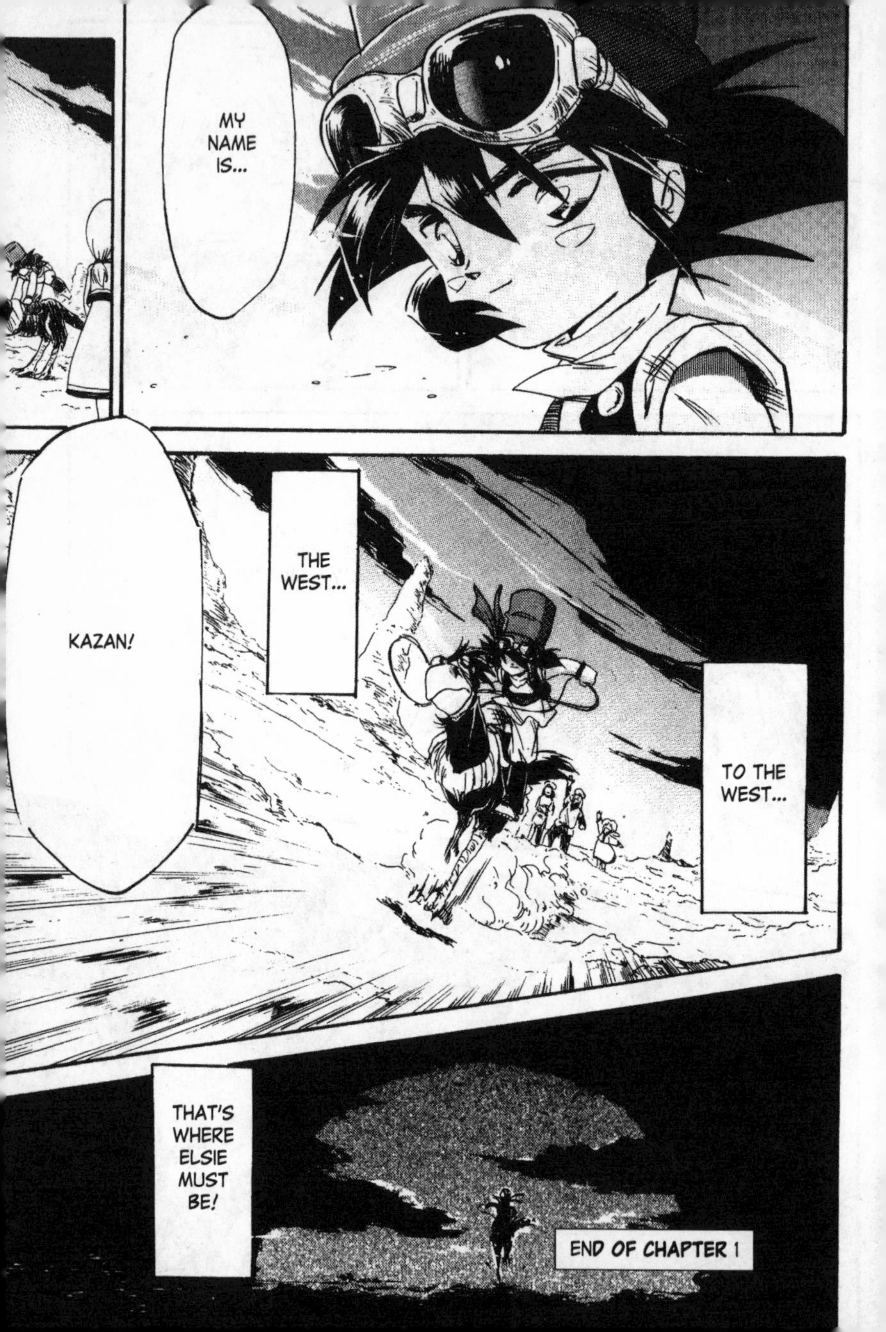

MY NAME IS...
KAZAN!
TO THE WEST...
THE WEST...
THAT'S WHERE ELSIE MUST BE!
END OF CHAPTER 1

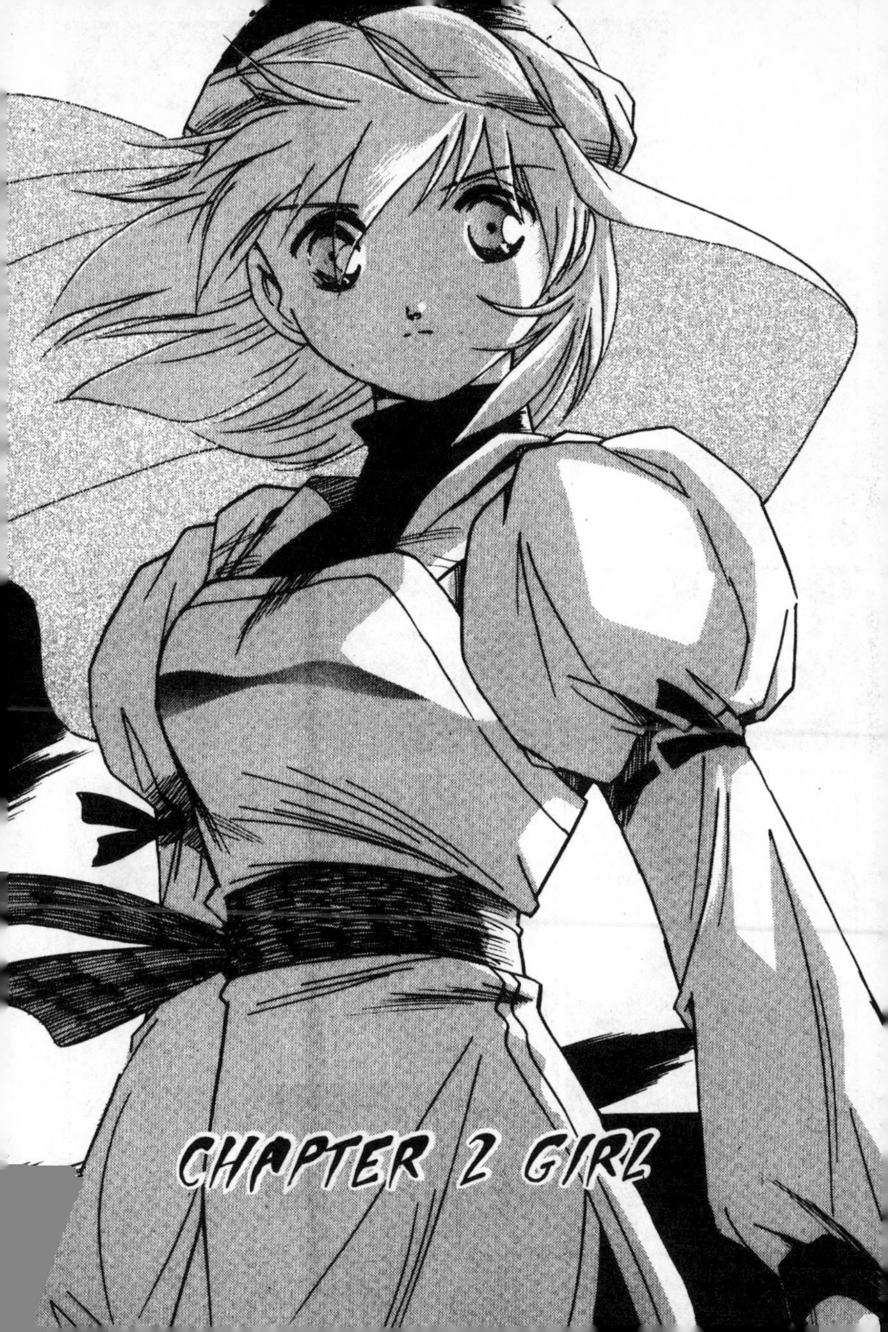
CHAPTER 2 GIRL

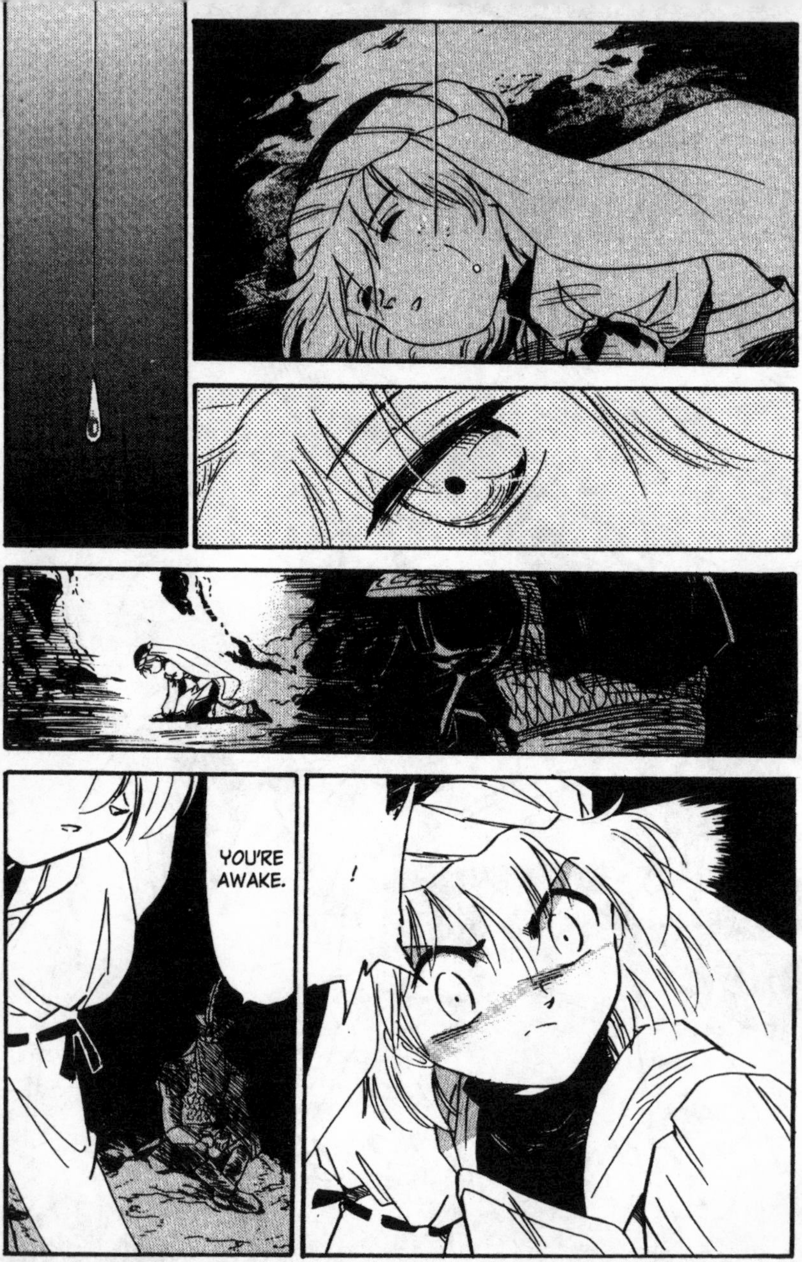

YOU'RE AWAKE.
!

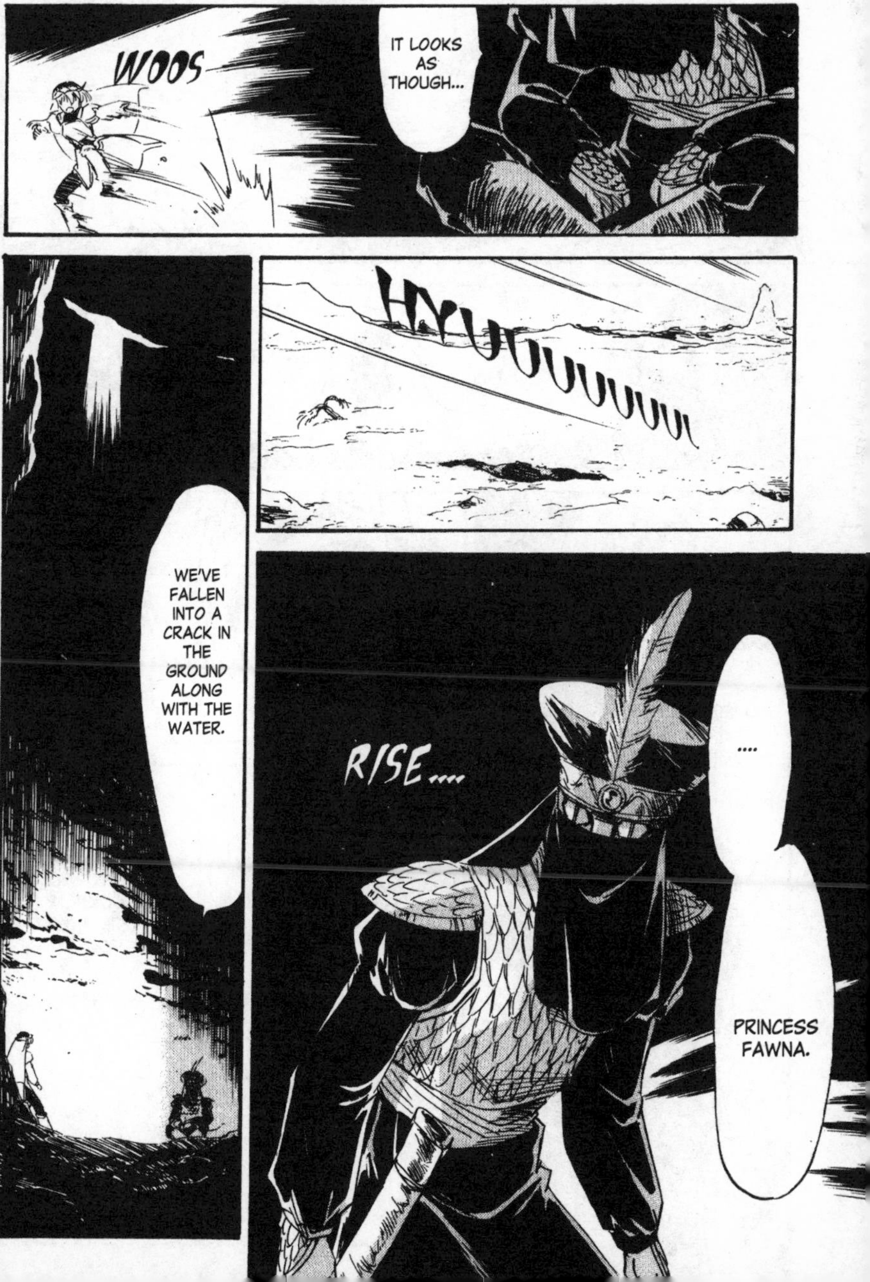
IT LOOKS AS THOUGH...
WOOS
HYUUUUUUUU
WE'VE FALLEN INTO A CRACK IN THE GROUND ALONG WITH THE WATER.
....
RISE....
PRINCESS FAWNA.

DON'T COME ANY CLOSER!!

I WOULD...

LIKE TO ASK YOU SOMETHING.

DO YOU HAPPEN TO KNOW OF A GIRL NAMED ELSIE?

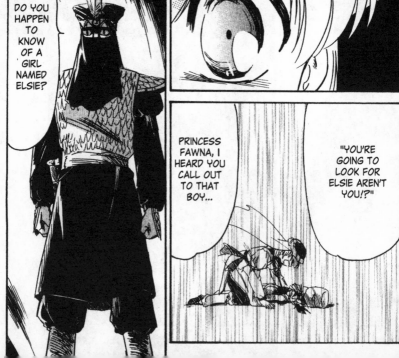

PRINCESS FAWNA, I HEARD YOU CALL OUT TO THAT BOY...

"YOU'RE GOING TO LOOK FOR ELSIE AREN'T YOU!?"

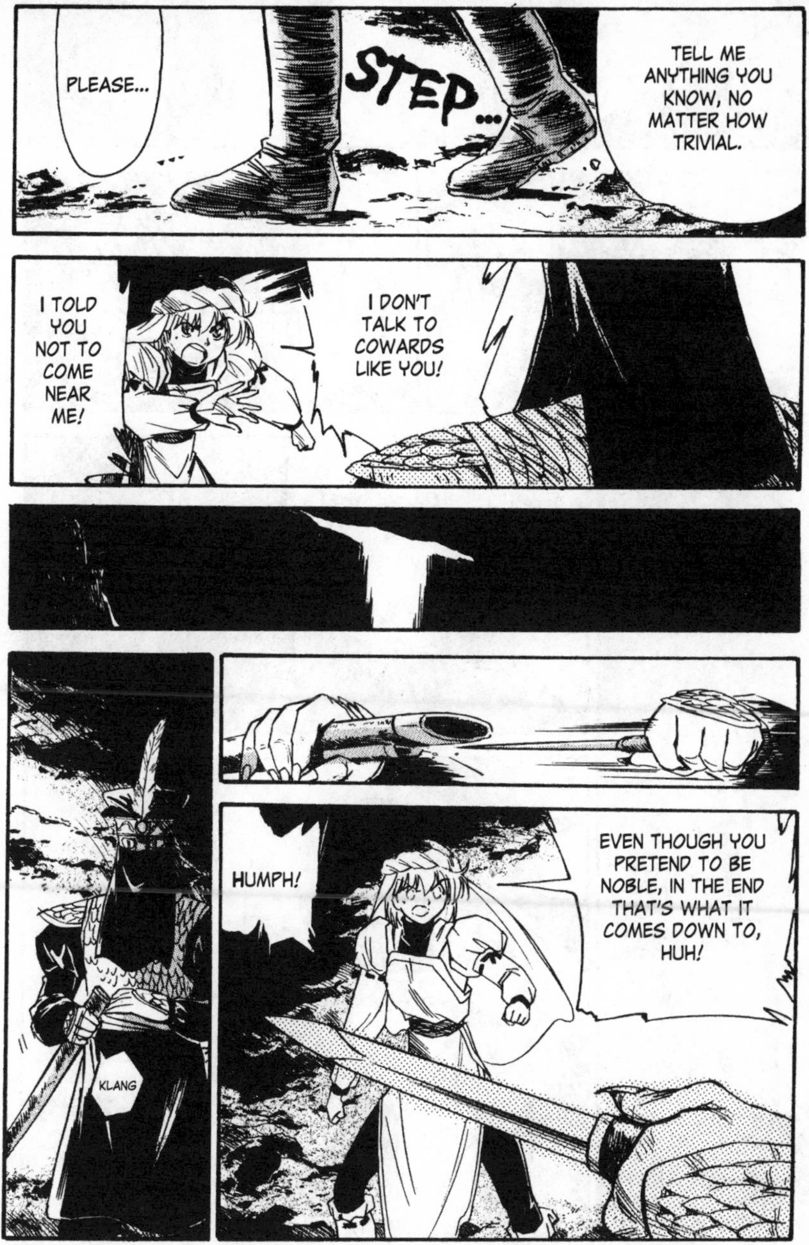

PLEASE...
STEP...
TELL ME ANYTHING YOU KNOW, NO MATTER HOW TRIVIAL.
I TOLD YOU NOT TO COME NEAR ME!
I DON'T TALK TO COWARDS LIKE YOU!
KLANG
HUMPH!
EVEN THOUGH YOU PRETEND TO BE NOBLE, IN THE END THAT'S WHAT IT COMES DOWN TO, HUH!

TINK

THUD

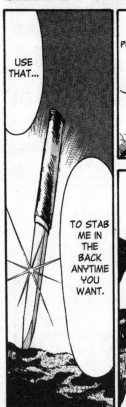

PLEASE...

TELL ME WHAT YOU KNOW...

USE THAT...

TO STAB ME IN THE BACK ANYTIME YOU WANT.

ER...

PUT YOUR HANDS BEHIND YOUR BACK! DON'T MOVE!

KLANG

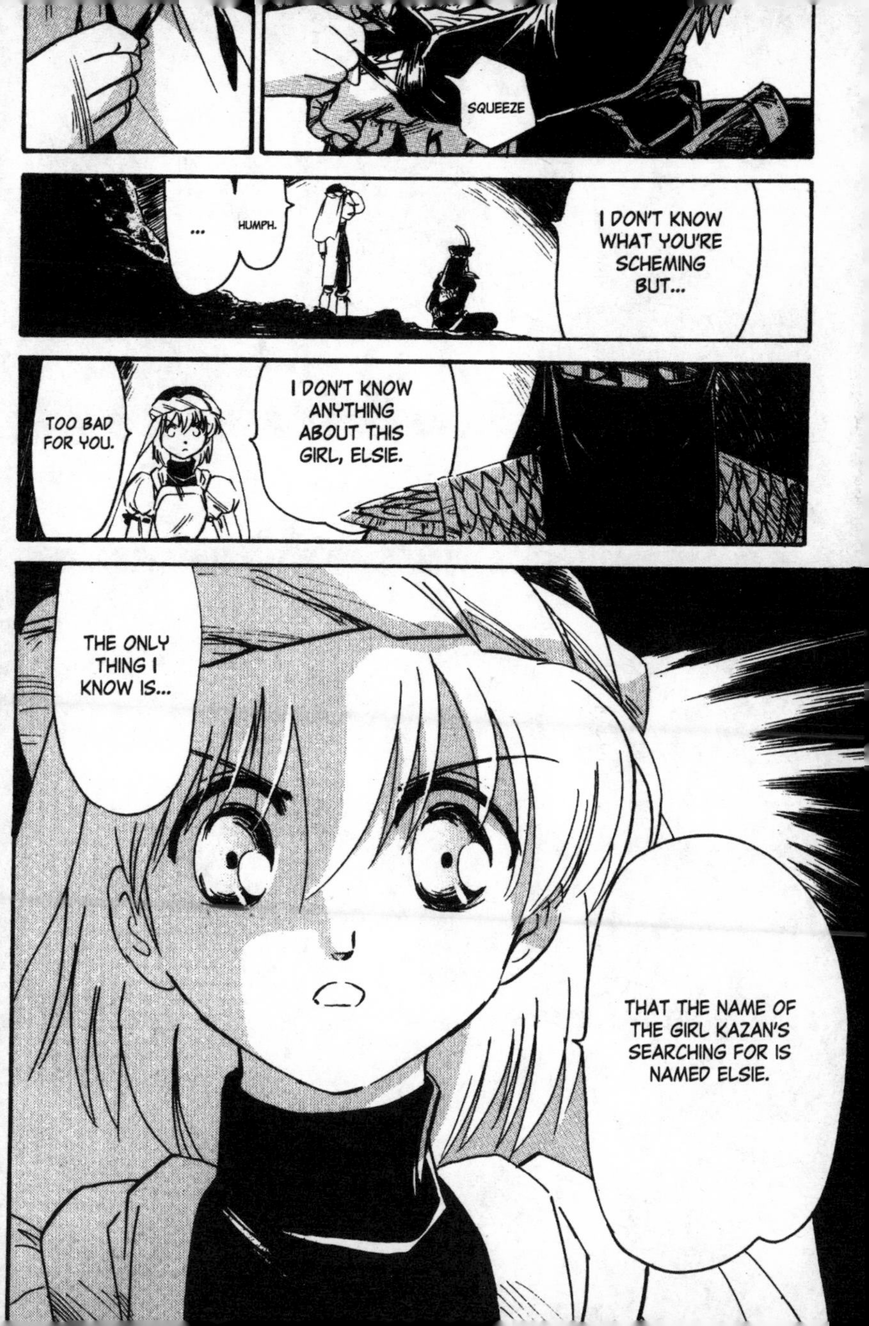
SQUEEZE
I DON'T KNOW WHAT YOU'RE SCHEMING BUT...
HUMPH.
...
I DON'T KNOW ANYTHING ABOUT THIS GIRL, ELSIE.
TOO BAD FOR YOU.
THE ONLY THING I KNOW IS...
THAT THE NAME OF THE GIRL KAZAN'S SEARCHING FOR IS NAMED ELSIE.

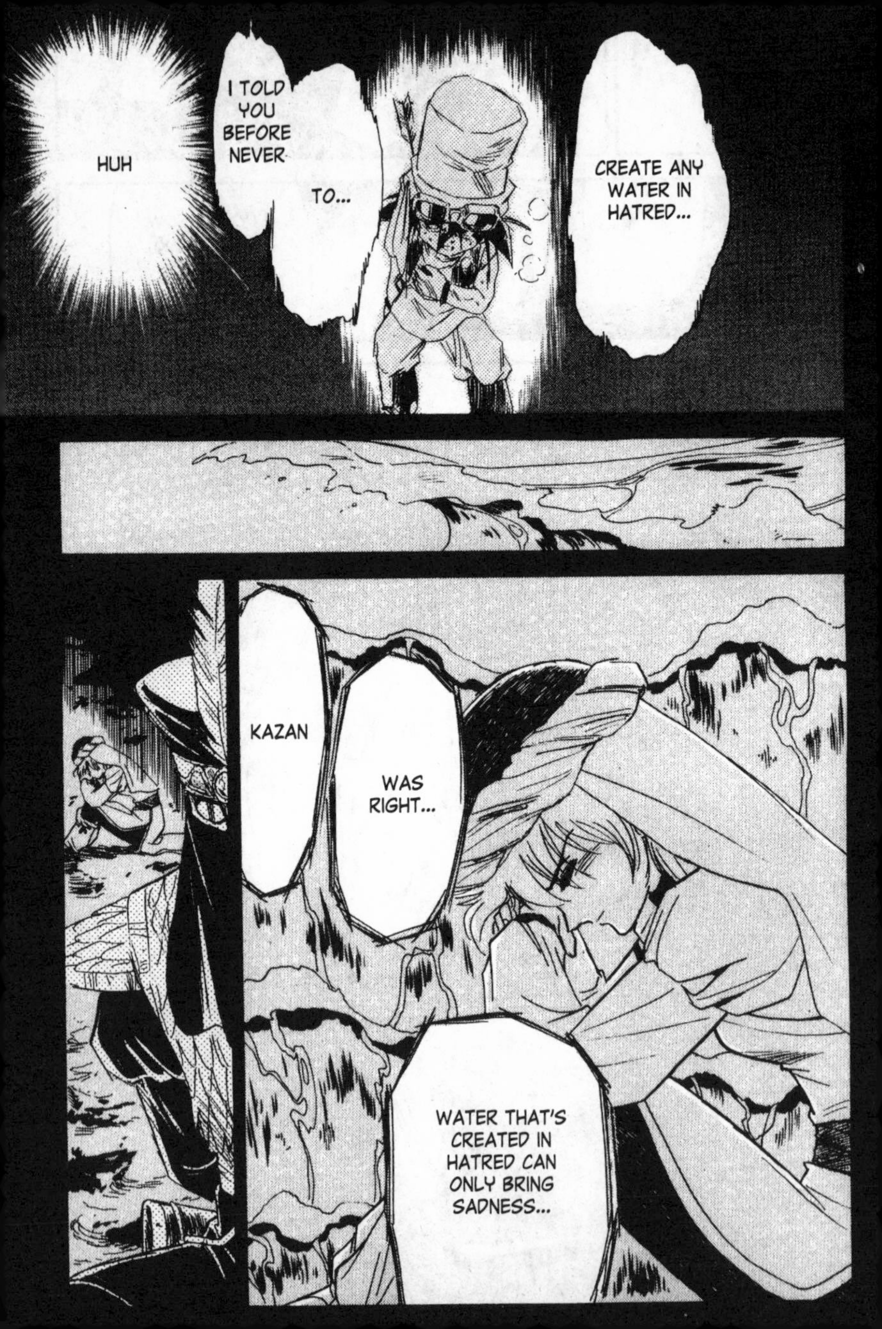
CREATE ANY WATER IN HATRED...
TO...
I TOLD YOU BEFORE NEVER
HUH
WAS RIGHT...
KAZAN
WATER THAT'S CREATED IN HATRED CAN ONLY BRING SADNESS...

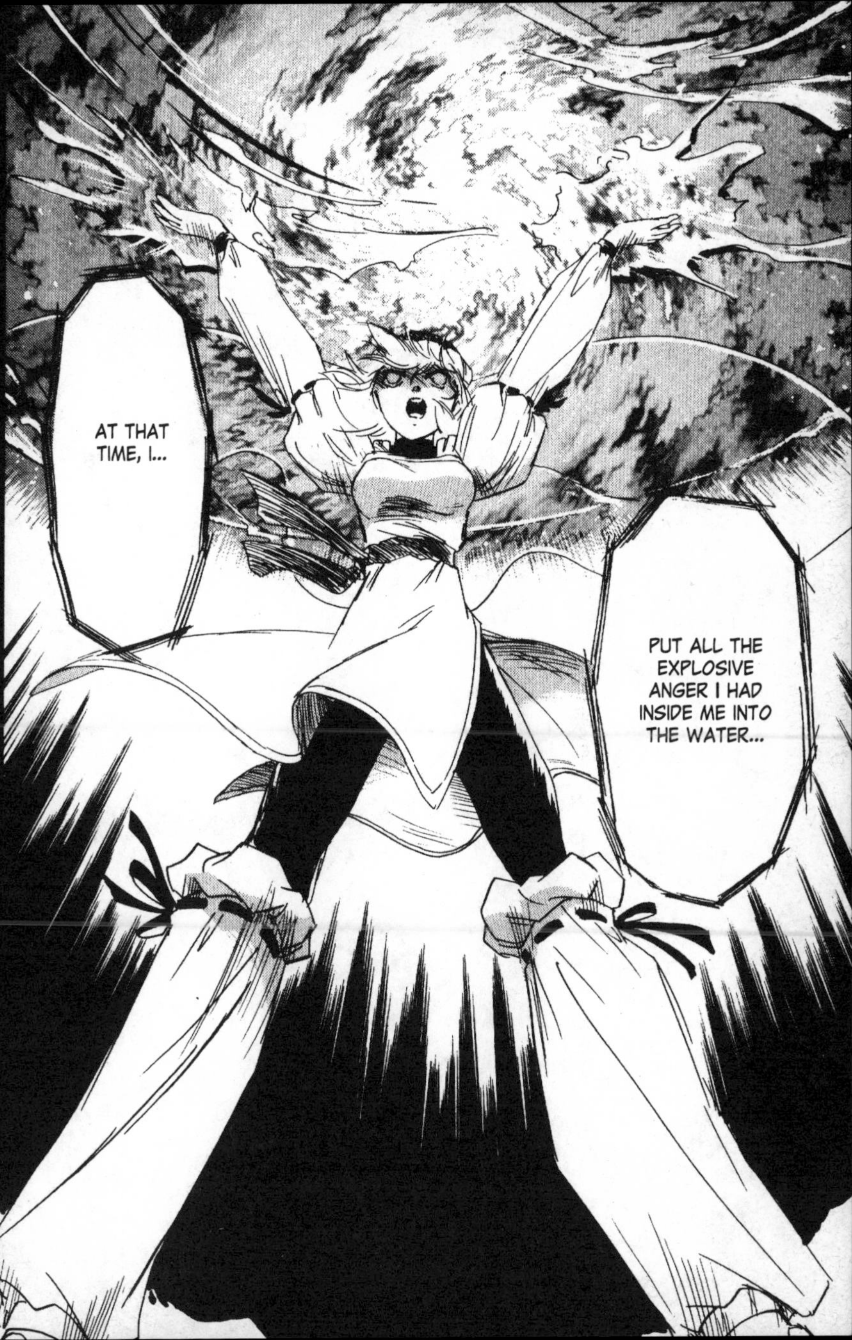
AT THAT TIME, I...
PUT ALL THE EXPLOSIVE ANGER I HAD INSIDE ME INTO THE WATER...

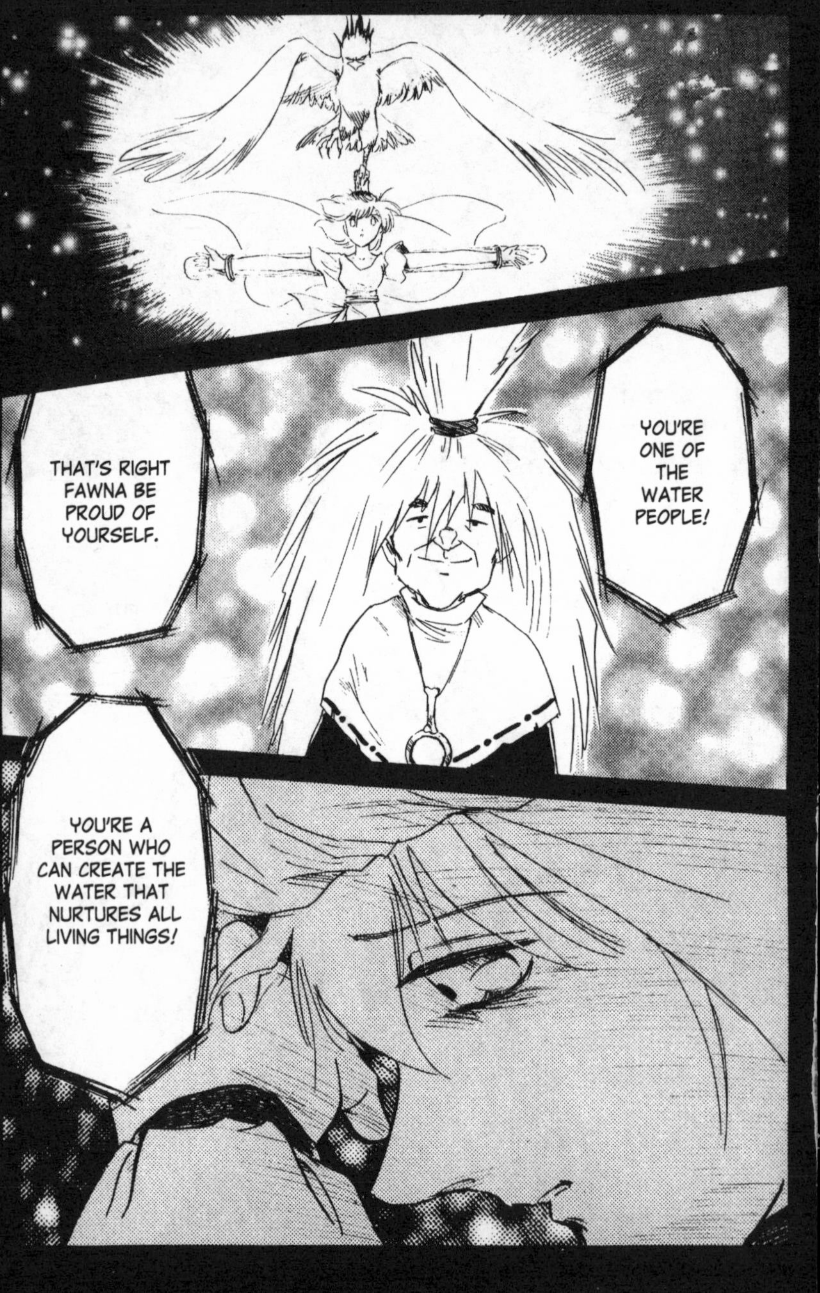
YOU'RE ONE OF THE WATER PEOPLE!
THAT'S RIGHT FAWNA BE PROUD OF YOURSELF.
YOU'RE A PERSON WHO CAN CREATE THE WATER THAT NURTURES ALL LIVING THINGS!

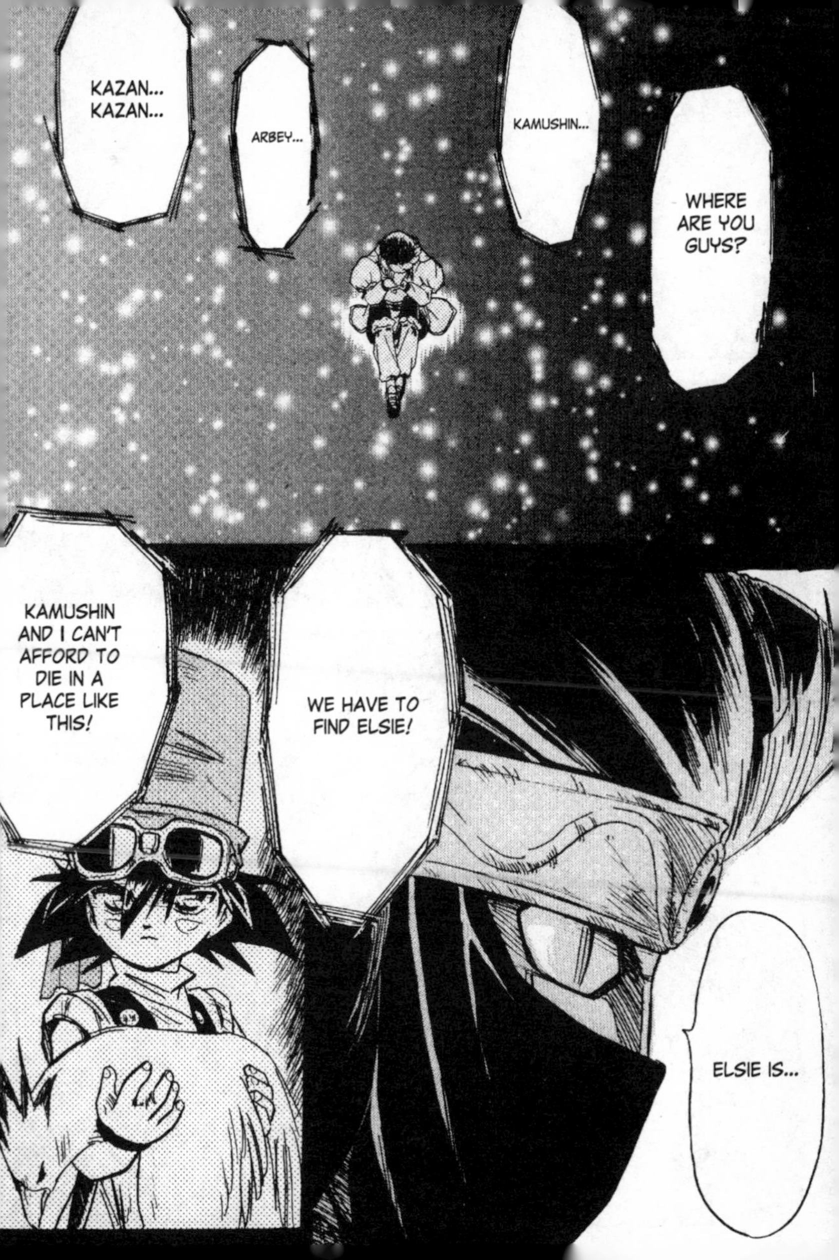
KAZAN... KAZAN...
ARBEY...
KAMUSHIN...
WHERE ARE YOU GUYS?
KAMUSHIN AND I CAN'T AFFORD TO DIE IN A PLACE LIKE THIS!
WE HAVE TO FIND ELSIE!
ELSIE IS...

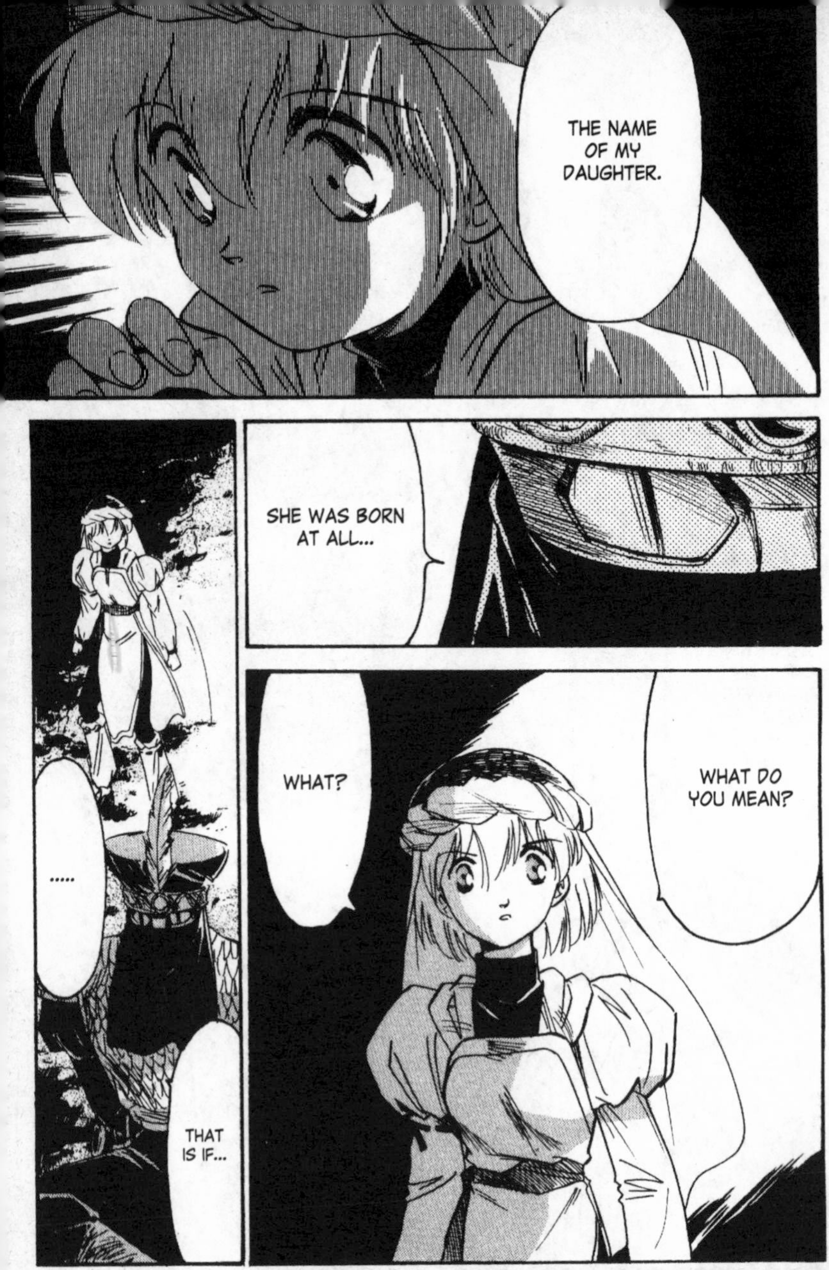
THE NAME OF MY DAUGHTER.
......
THAT IS IF...
SHE WAS BORN AT ALL...
WHAT?
WHAT DO YOU MEAN?

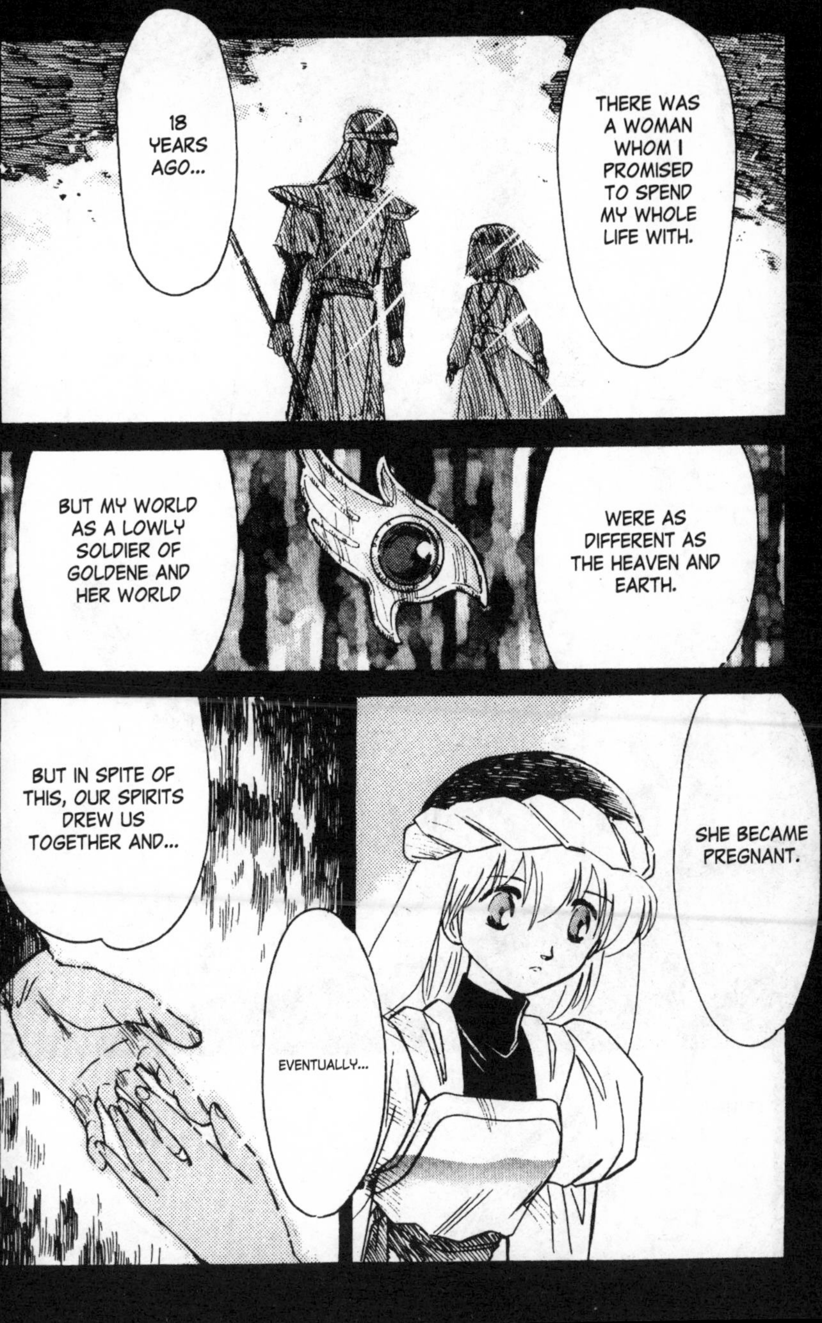
18 YEARS AGO...
THERE WAS A WOMAN WHOM I PROMISED TO SPEND MY WHOLE LIFE WITH.
BUT MY WORLD AS A LOWLY SOLDIER OF GOLDENE AND HER WORLD
WERE AS DIFFERENT AS THE HEAVEN AND EARTH.
BUT IN SPITE OF THIS, OUR SPIRITS DREW US TOGETHER AND...
EVENTUALLY...
SHE BECAME PREGNANT.

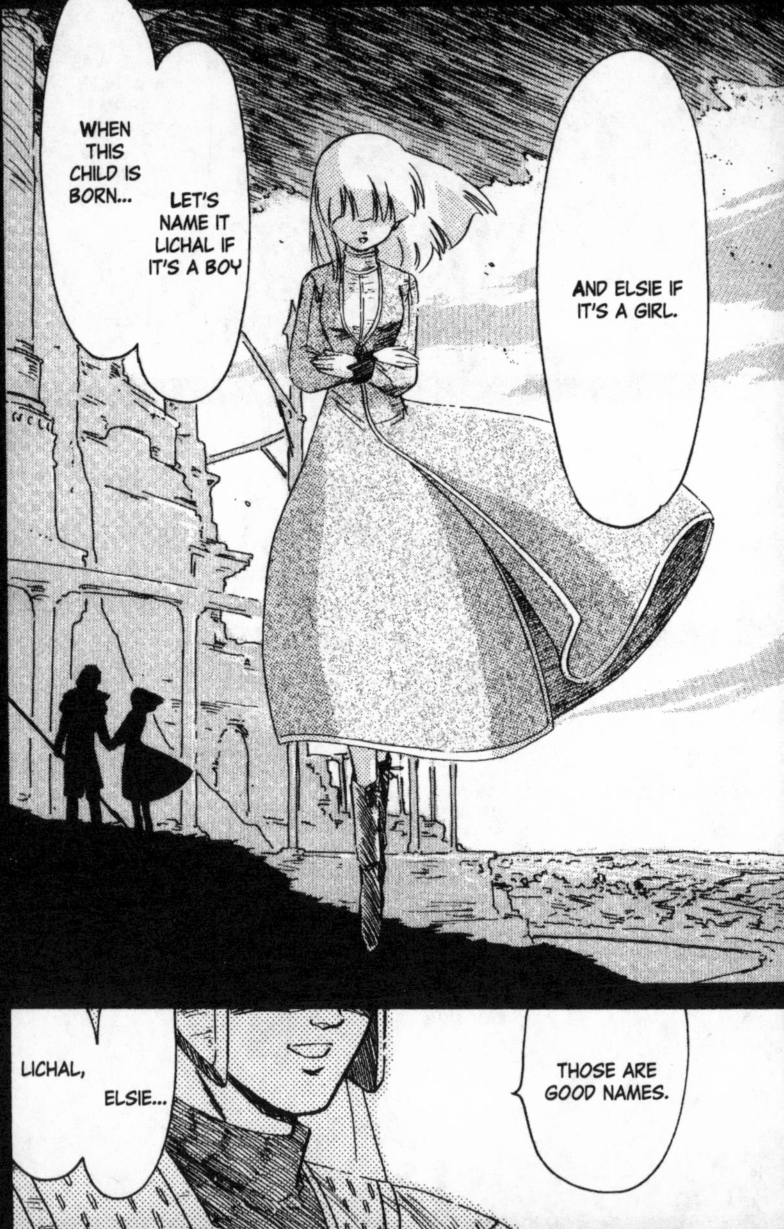

WHEN THIS CHILD IS BORN...
LET'S NAME IT LICHAL IF IT'S A BOY
AND ELSIE IF IT'S A GIRL.
THOSE ARE GOOD NAMES.
LICHAL,
ELSIE...

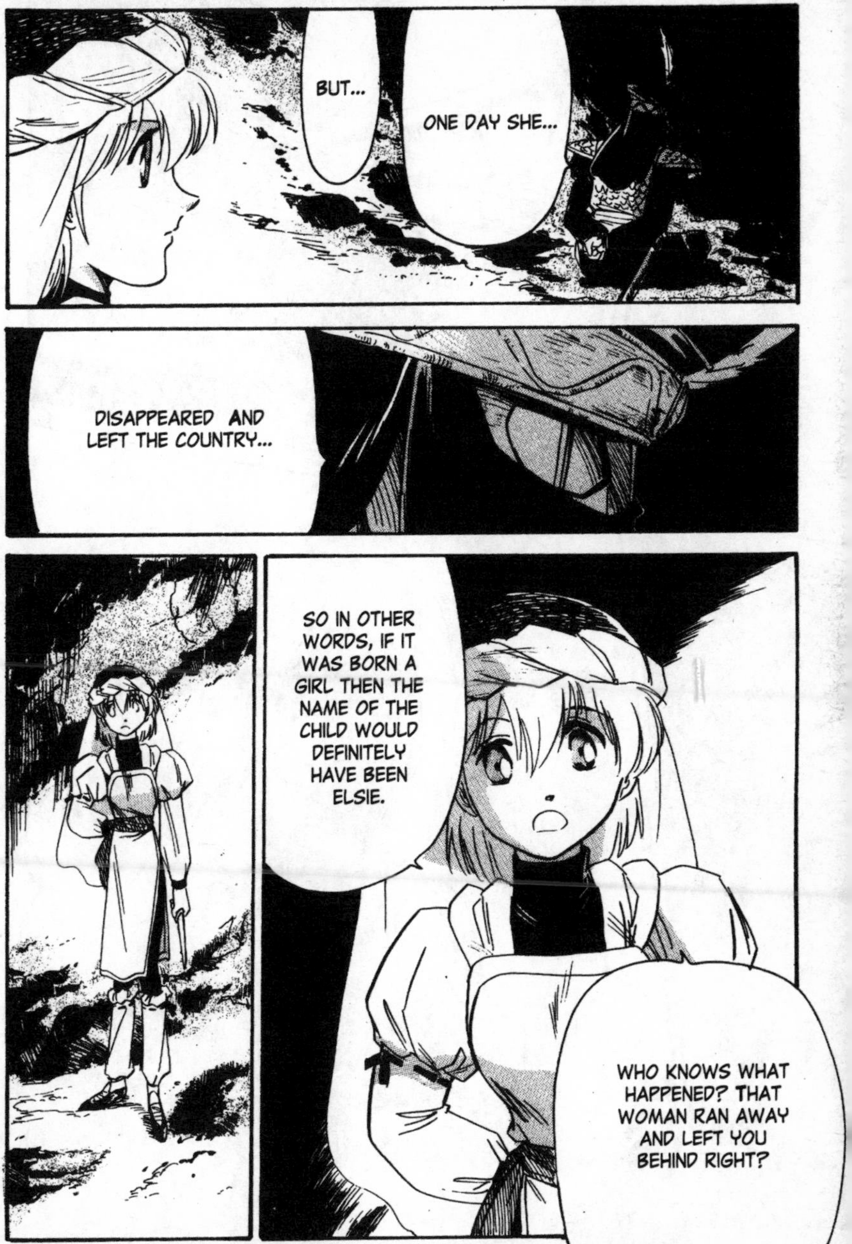
BUT...
ONE DAY SHE...
DISAPPEARED AND LEFT THE COUNTRY...
SO IN OTHER WORDS, IF IT WAS BORN A GIRL THEN THE NAME OF THE CHILD WOULD DEFINITELY HAVE BEEN ELSIE.
WHO KNOWS WHAT HAPPENED? THAT WOMAN RAN AWAY AND LEFT YOU BEHIND RIGHT?

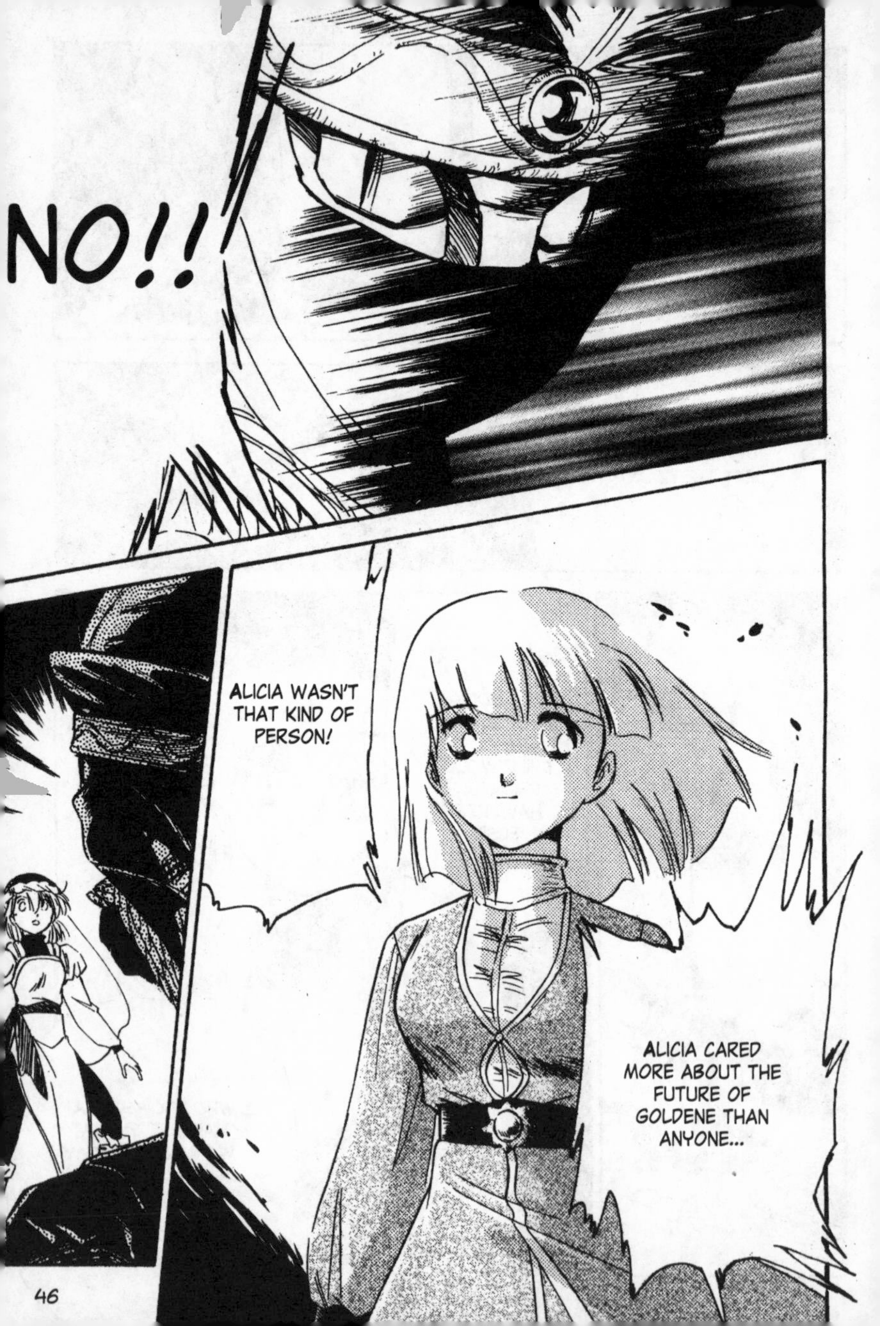
NO!!
ALICIA WASN'T THAT KIND OF PERSON!
ALICIA CARED MORE ABOUT THE FUTURE OF GOLDENE THAN ANYONE...

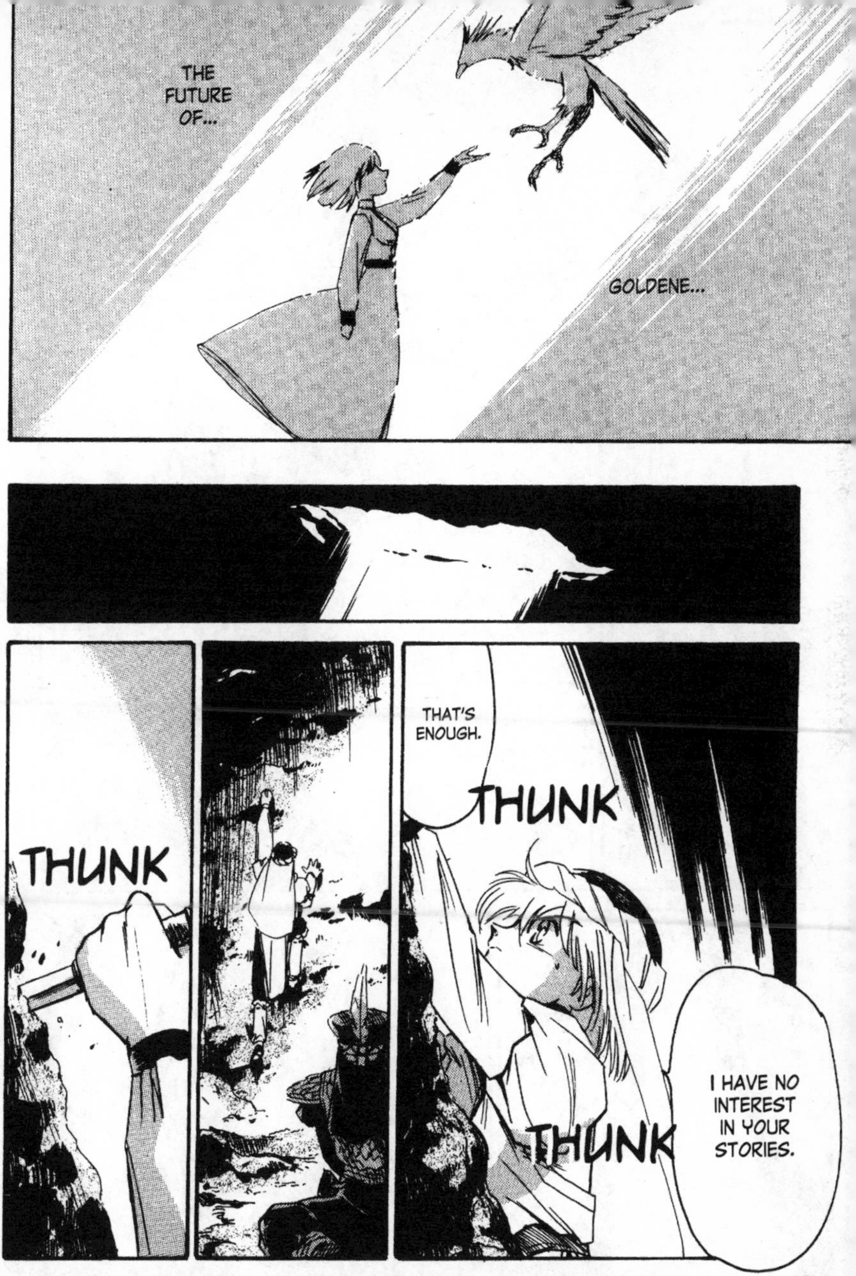
THE FUTURE OF...
GOLDENE...
THAT'S ENOUGH.
THUNK
THUNK
THUNK
I HAVE NO INTEREST IN YOUR STORIES.

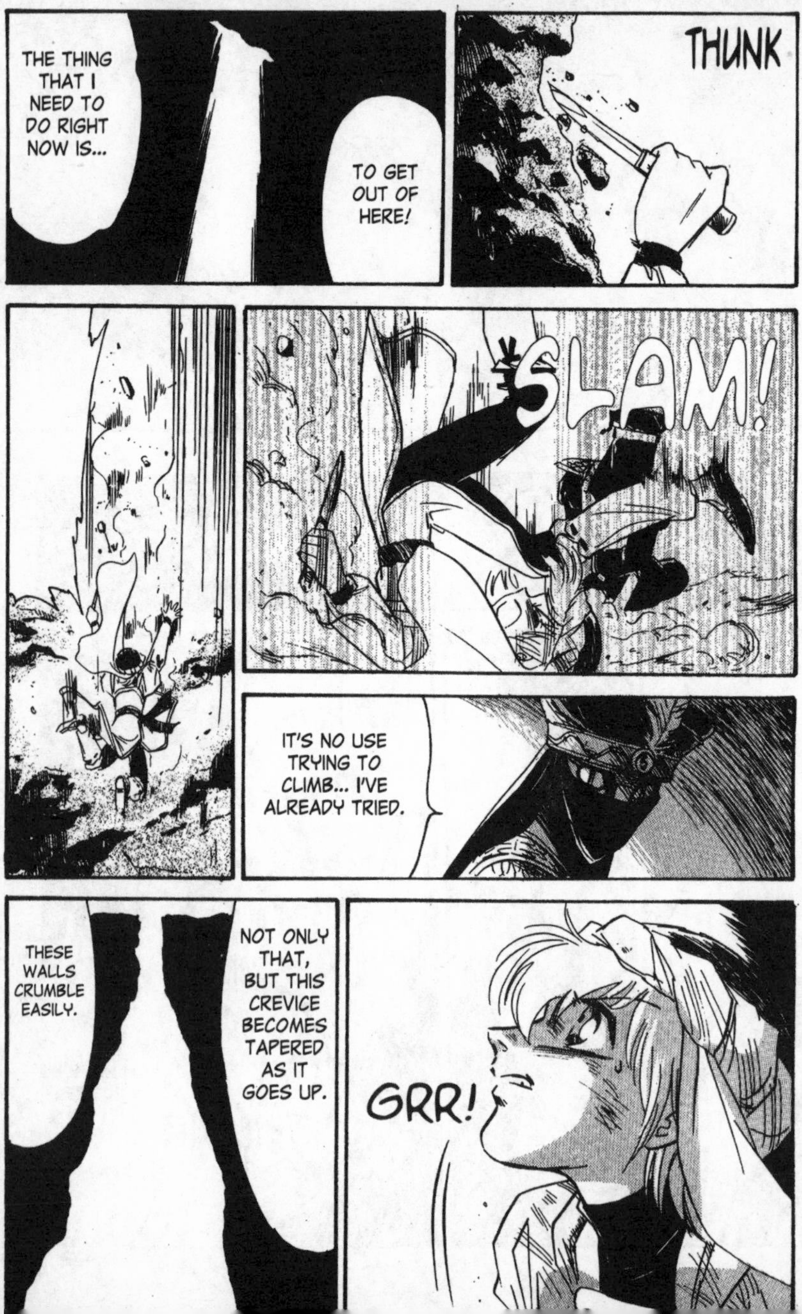
THE THING THAT I NEED TO DO RIGHT NOW IS...
TO GET OUT OF HERE!
THUNK
SLAM!
IT'S NO USE TRYING TO CLIMB... I'VE ALREADY TRIED.
THESE WALLS CRUMBLE EASILY.
NOT ONLY THAT, BUT THIS CREVICE BECOMES TAPERED AS IT GOES UP.
GRR!

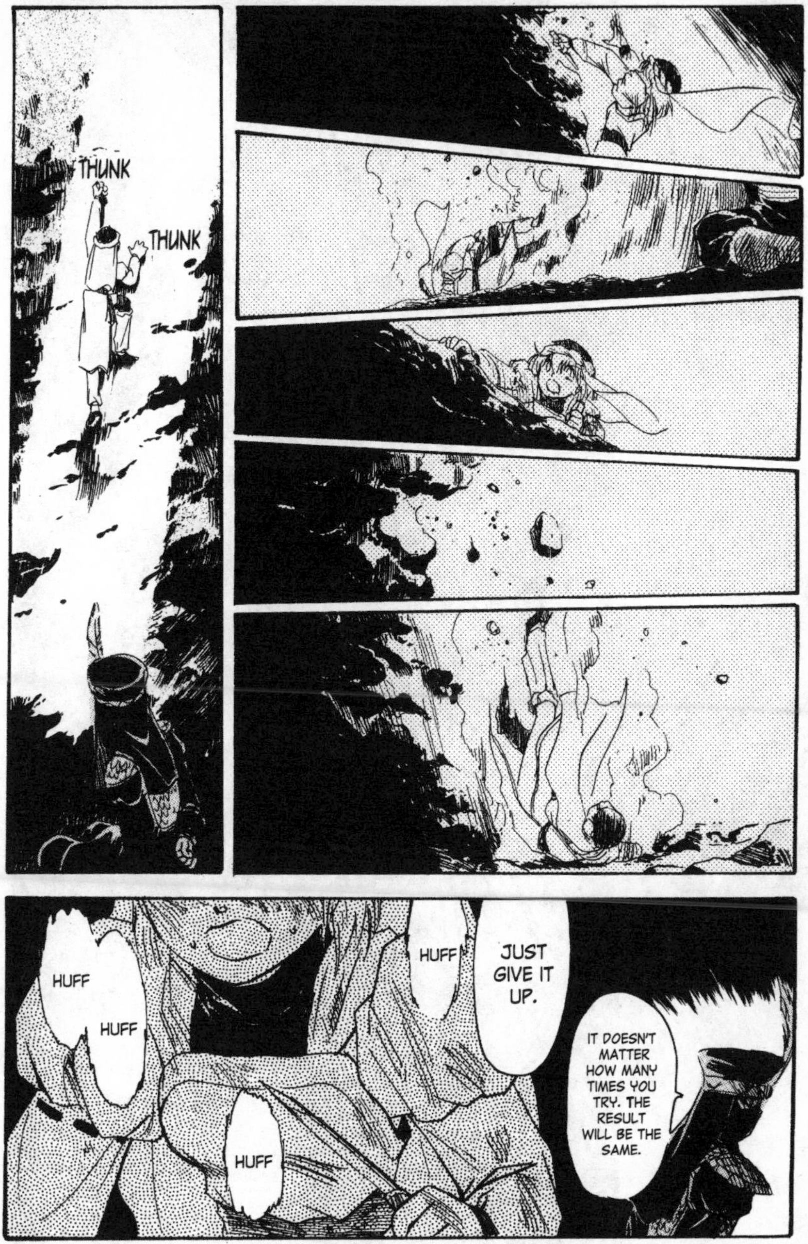
THUNK
THUNK
HUFF
HUFF
HUFF
JUST GIVE IT UP.
IT DOESN'T MATTER HOW MANY TIMES YOU TRY. THE RESULT WILL BE THE SAME.
HUFF

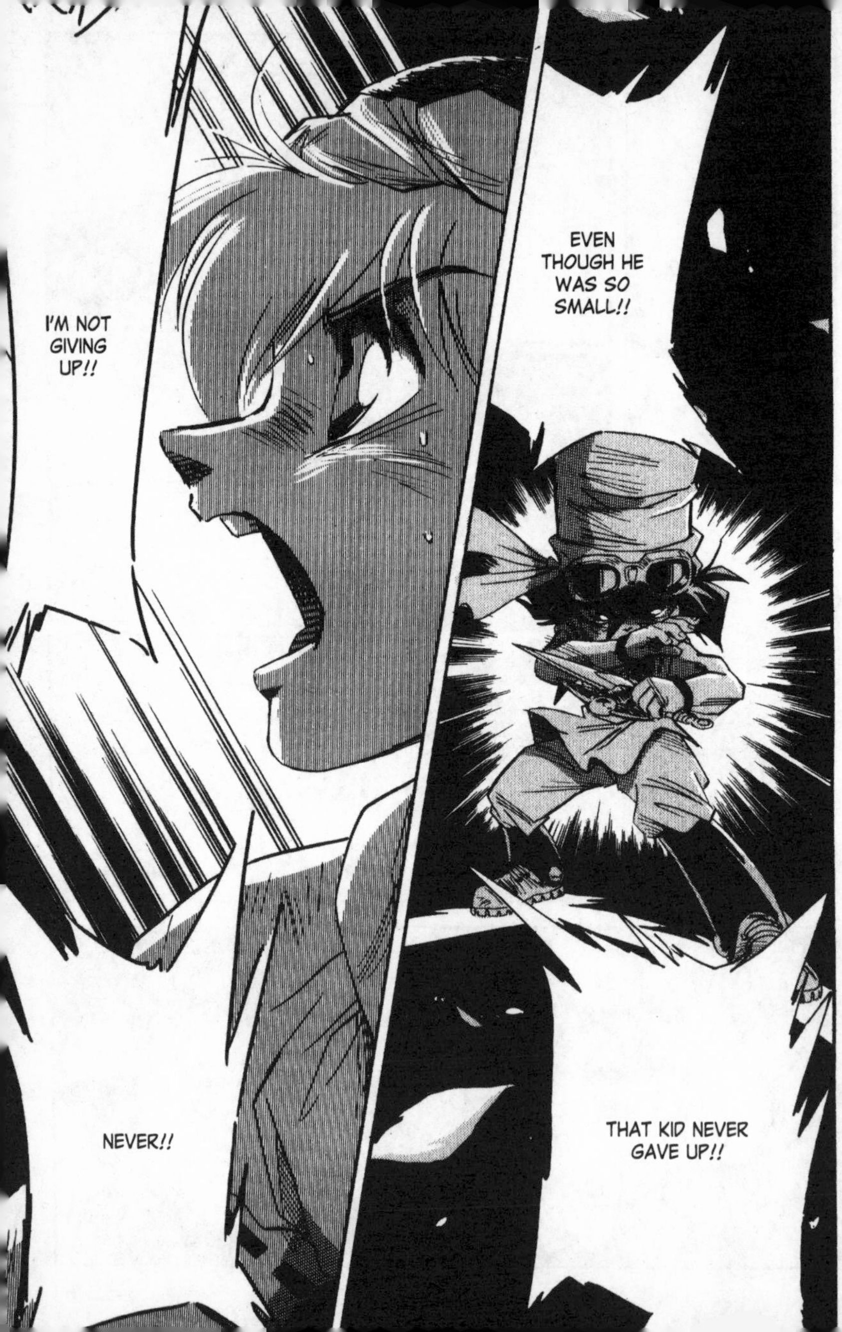
EVEN THOUGH HE WAS SO SMALL!!
THAT KID NEVER GAVE UP!!
I'M NOT GIVING UP!!
NEVER!!

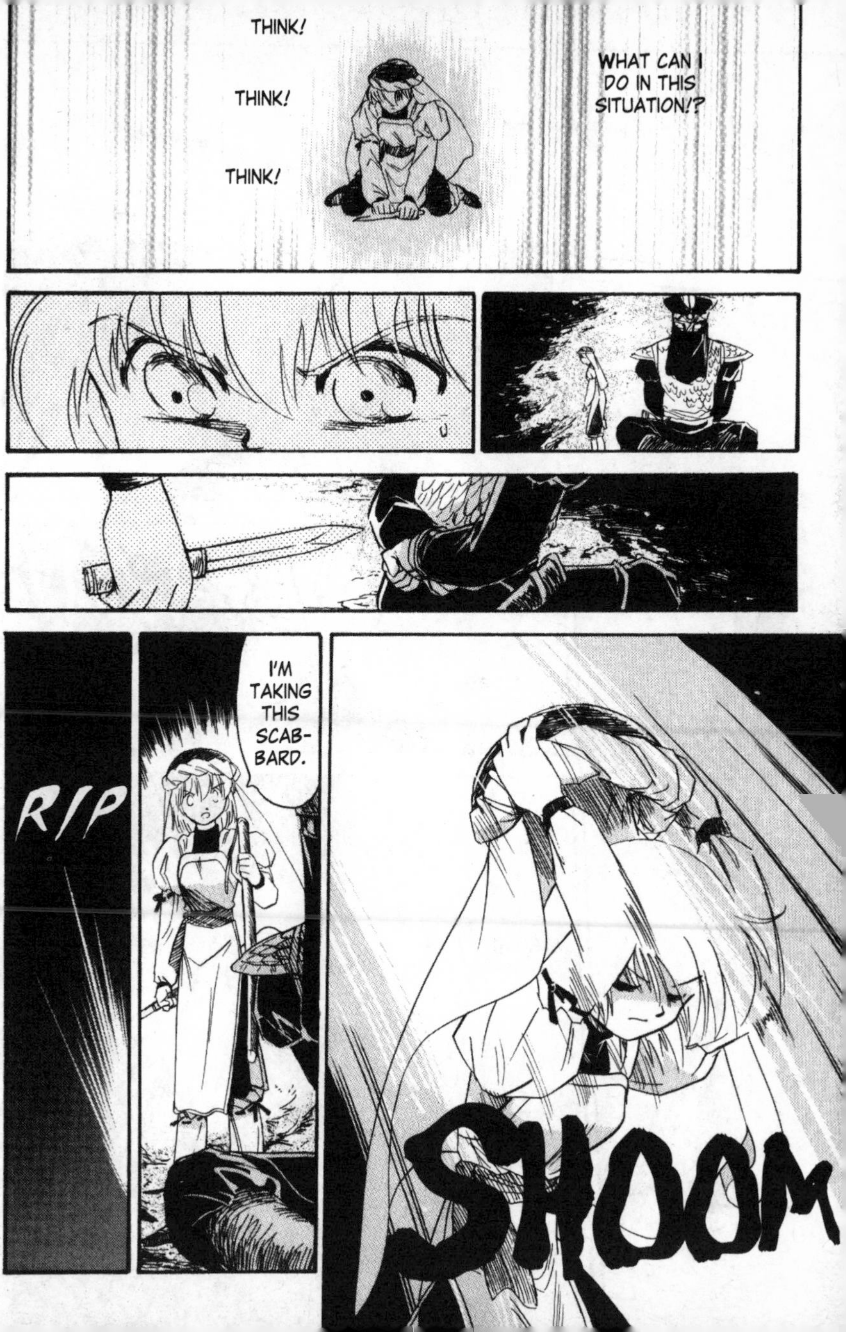
WHAT CAN I DO IN THIS SITUATION!?
THINK!
THINK!
THINK!
I'M TAKING THIS SCAB-BARD.
RIP
SHOOM

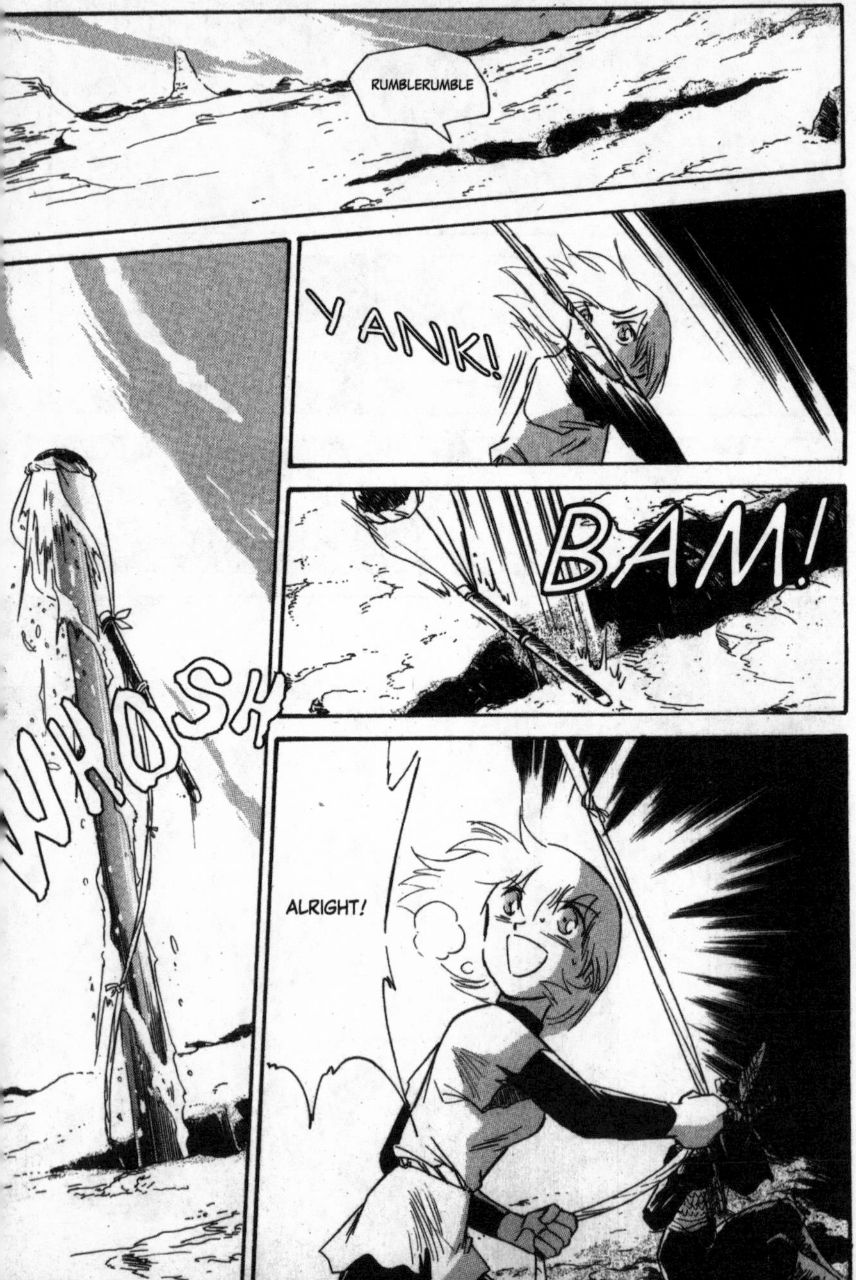
RUMBLERUMBLE
YANK!
BAM!
WHOSH
ALRIGHT!

SHE CUT UP HER CLOTHES WITH THE DAGGER TO MAKE A ROPE... THEN CONNECTED HER HAT TO THE SCABBARD AND USED THE POWER OF THE WATER TO SHOOT IT UPWARDS.

THIS IS A SKILL ONLY POSSIBLE FOR A WATER PERSON!

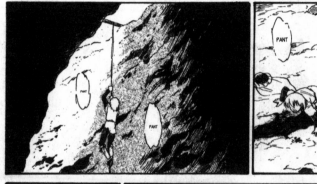

PANT

PANT

PANT

PANT

PANT

PANT

PANT

HEH HEH

HOW ABOUT THAT?

PANT

I CLIMBED IT...

PANT

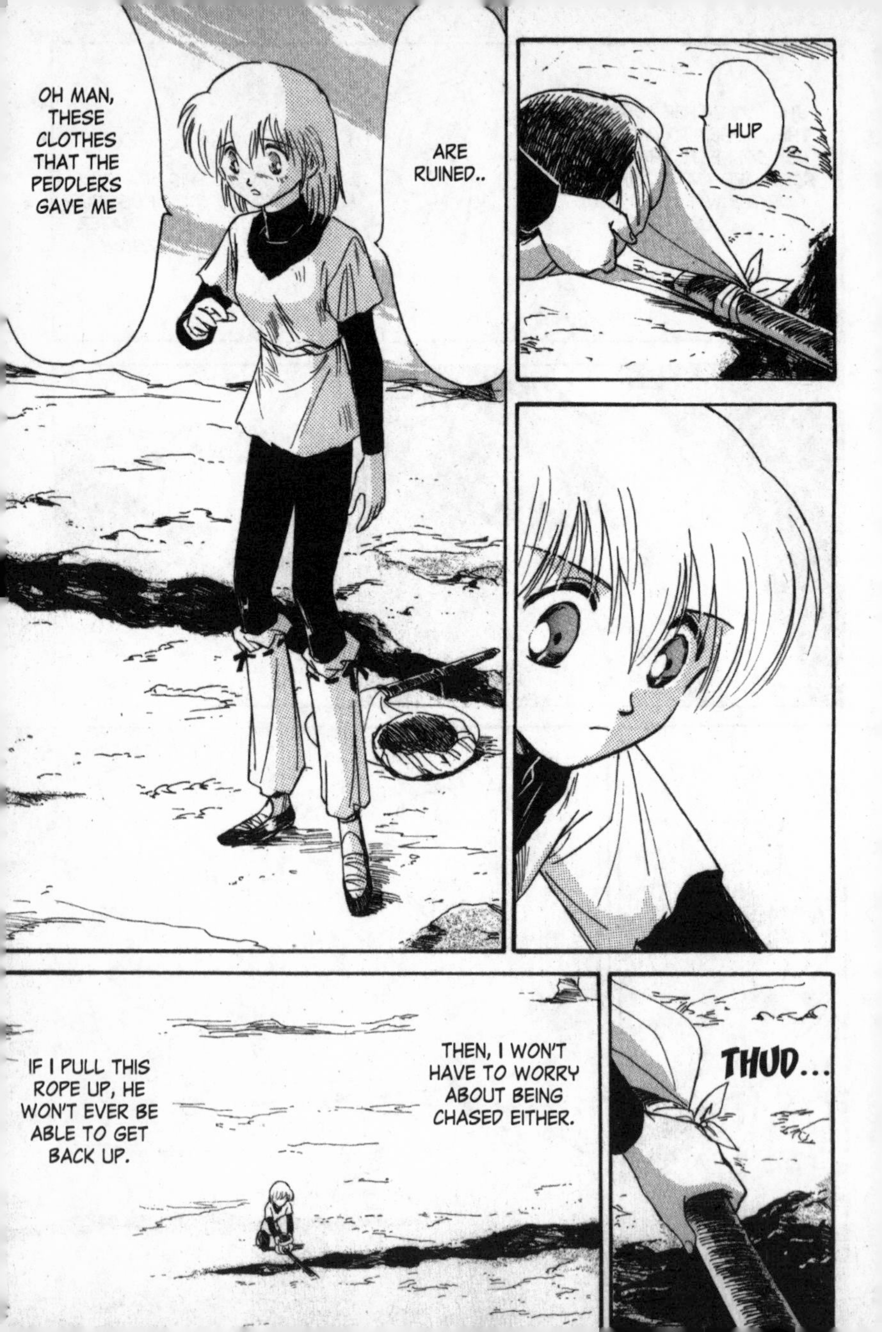
OH MAN, THESE CLOTHES THAT THE PEDDLERS GAVE ME
ARE RUINED..
HUP
THEN, I WON'T HAVE TO WORRY ABOUT BEING CHASED EITHER.
IF I PULL THIS ROPE UP, HE WON'T EVER BE ABLE TO GET BACK UP.
THUD...

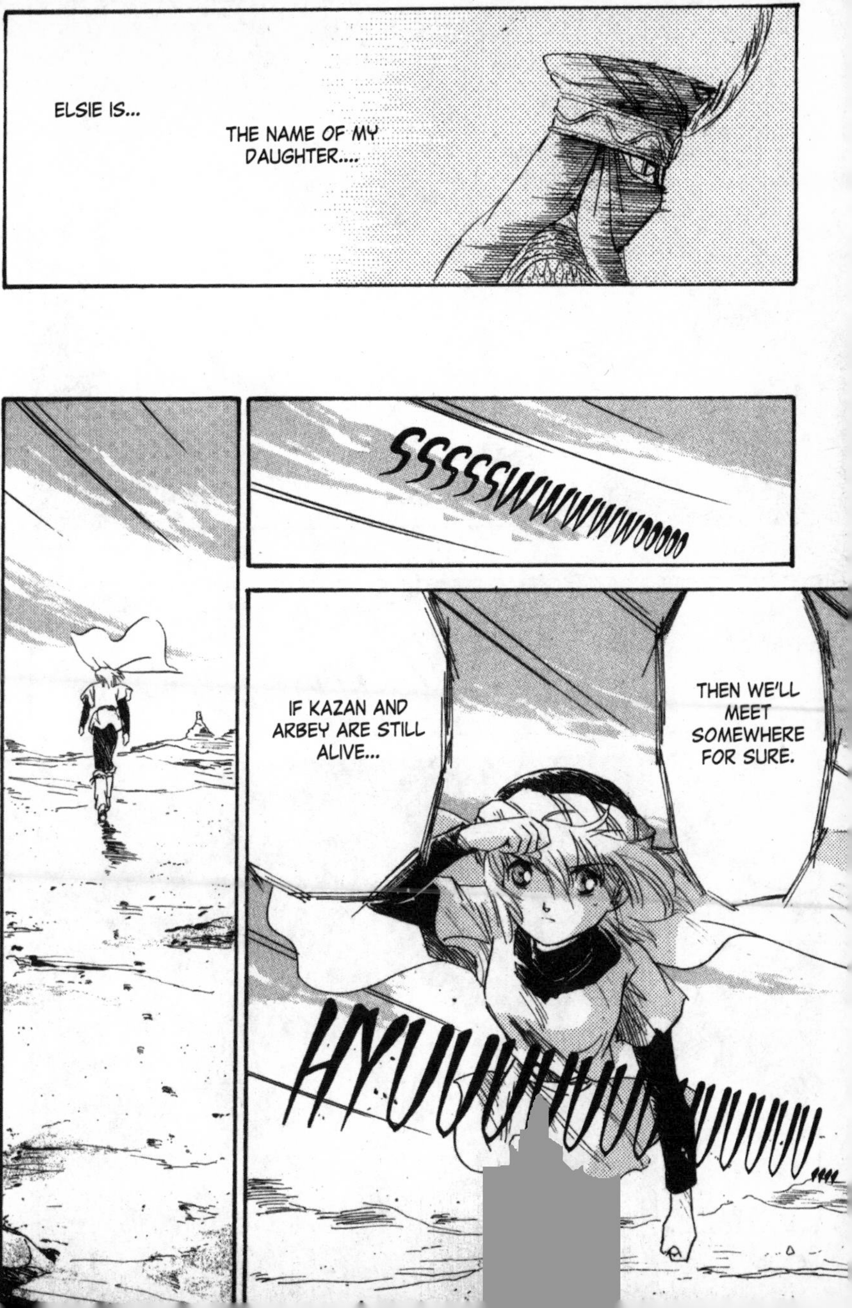
ELSIE IS...
THE NAME OF MY DAUGHTER....
SSSSSWWWWWWOOOOO
IF KAZAN AND ARBEY ARE STILL ALIVE...
THEN WE'LL MEET SOMEWHERE FOR SURE.
HYUUUUUUUUUUUUUUU...

TO GOLDENE!

HYUUUUUUUUUUUUUU

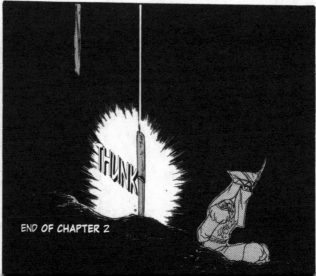

THUNK

END OF CHAPTER 2

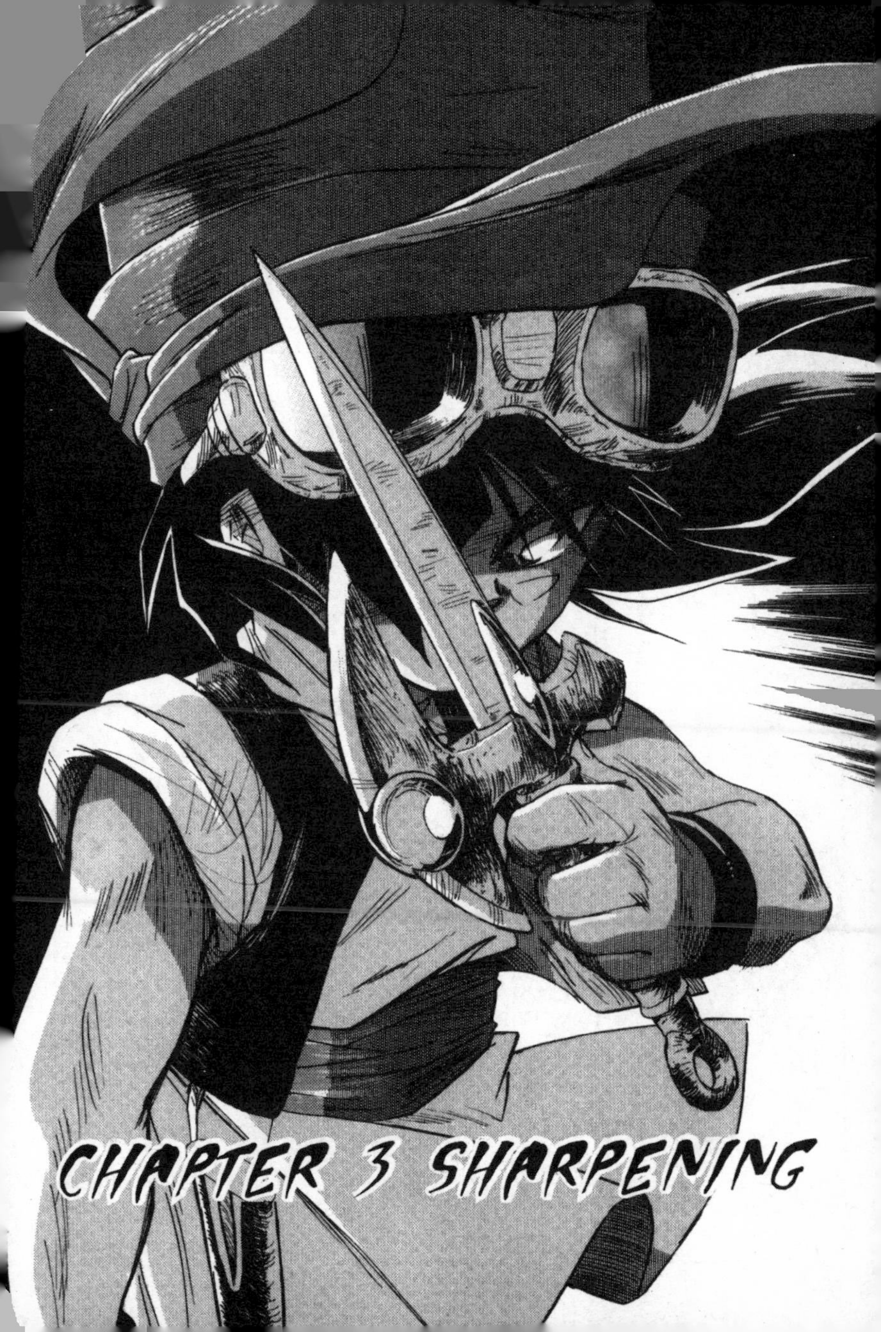
CHAPTER 3 SHARPENING

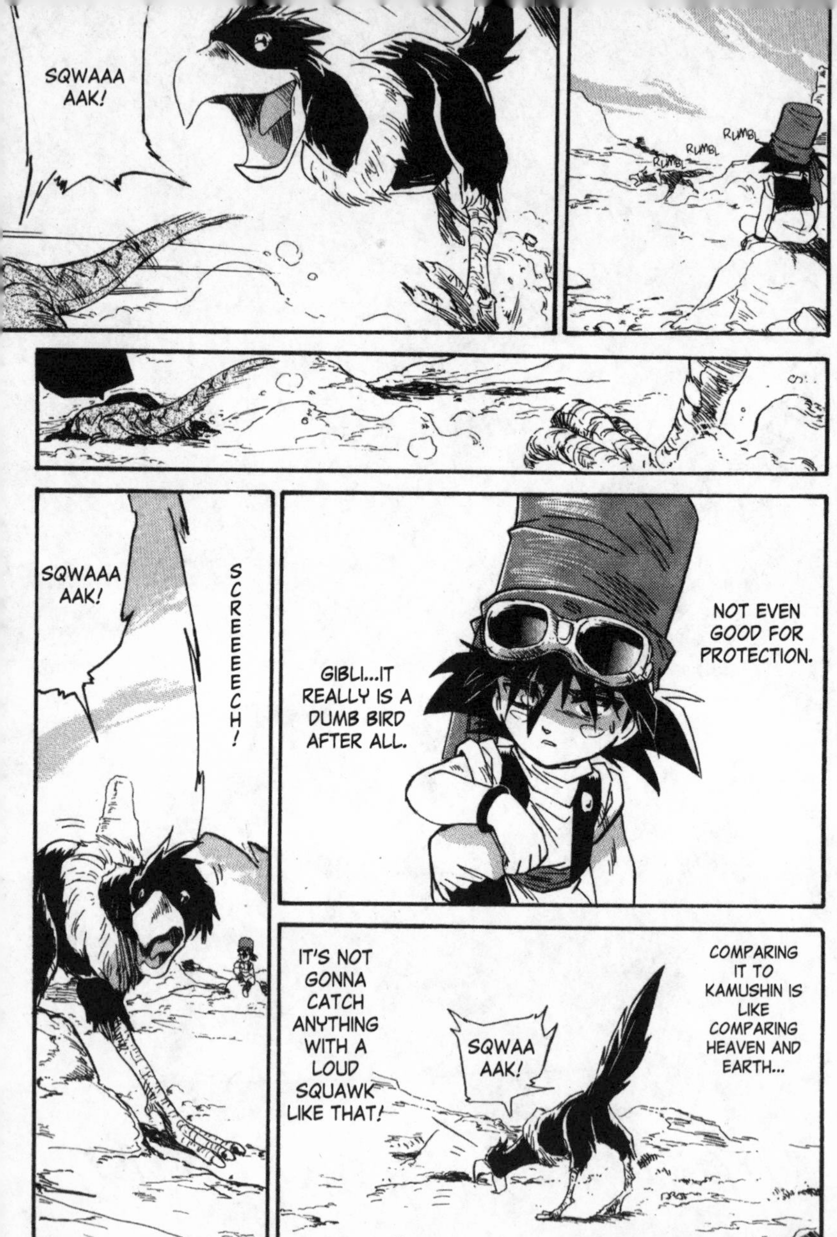
RUMBL
RUMBL
RUMBL
SQWAAA AAK!
NOT EVEN GOOD FOR PROTECTION.
GIBLI...IT REALLY IS A DUMB BIRD AFTER ALL.
SCREEEECH!
SQWAAA AAK!
COMPARING IT TO KAMUSHIN IS LIKE COMPARING HEAVEN AND EARTH...
SQWAA AAK!
IT'S NOT GONNA CATCH ANYTHING WITH A LOUD SQUAWK LIKE THAT!

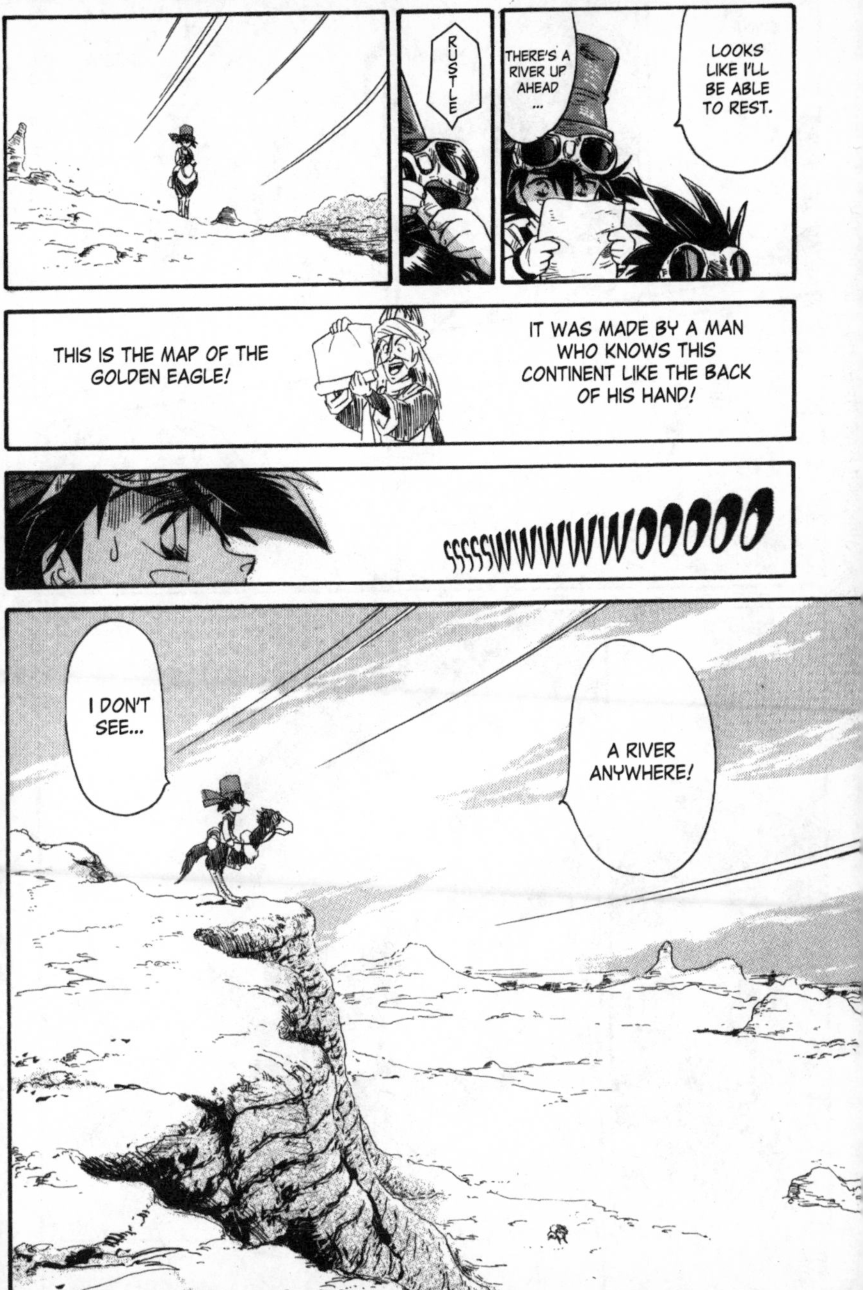
RUSTLE
THERE'S A RIVER UP AHEAD ...
LOOKS LIKE I'LL BE ABLE TO REST.
THIS IS THE MAP OF THE GOLDEN EAGLE!
IT WAS MADE BY A MAN WHO KNOWS THIS CONTINENT LIKE THE BACK OF HIS HAND!
SSSSSWWWWWOOOOO
I DON'T SEE...
A RIVER ANYWHERE!

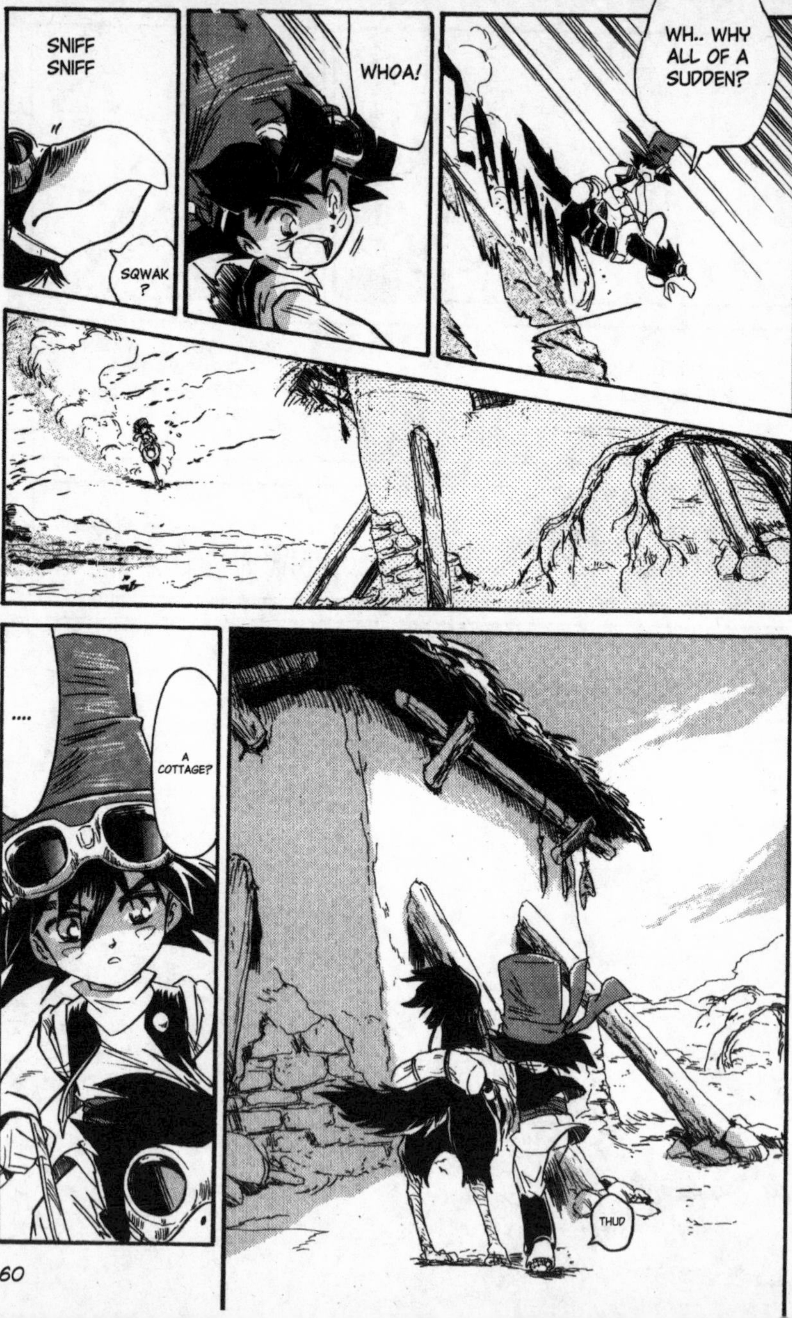
SNIFF SNIFF
SQWAK ?
WHOA!
WH.. WHY ALL OF A SUDDEN?
....
A COTTAGE?
THUD

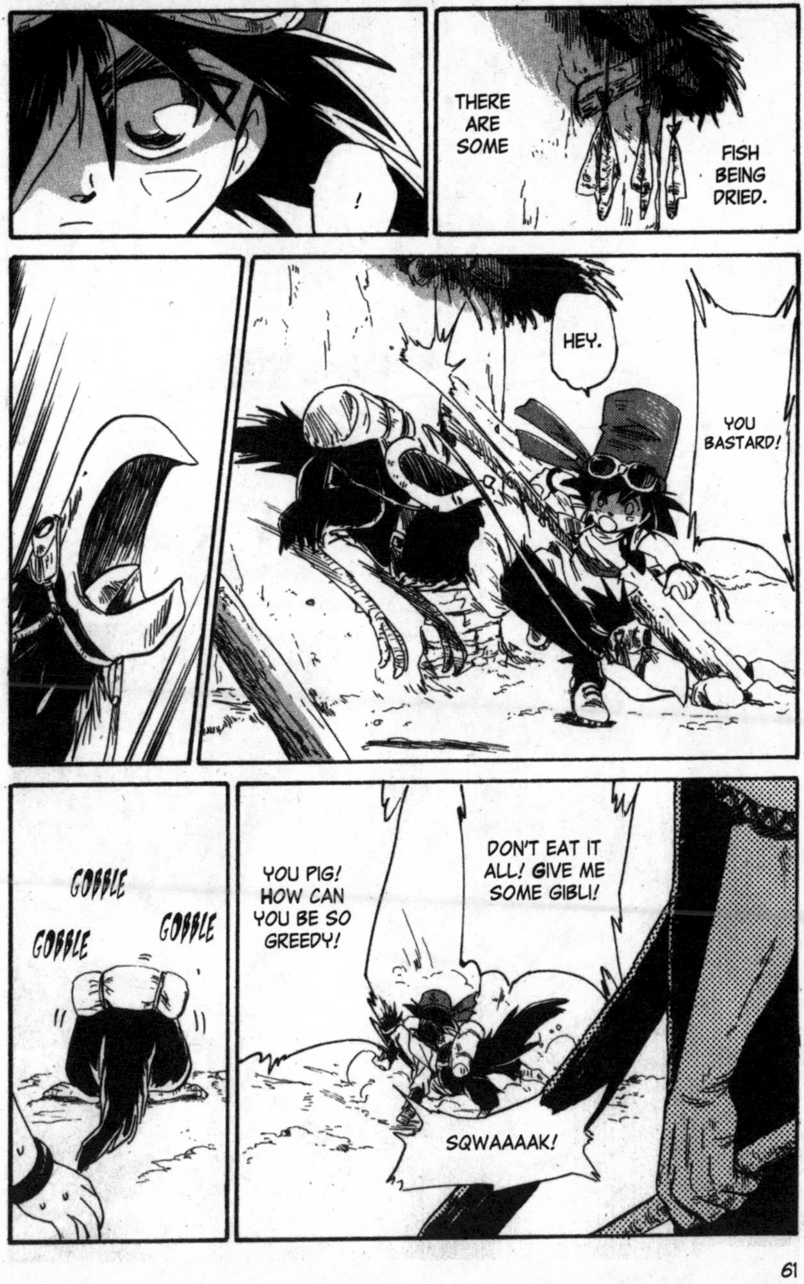
THERE ARE SOME
FISH BEING DRIED.
HEY.
YOU BASTARD!
GOBBLE
GOBBLE
GOBBLE
YOU PIG! HOW CAN YOU BE SO GREEDY!
DON'T EAT IT ALL! GIVE ME SOME GIBLI!
SQWAAAAK!

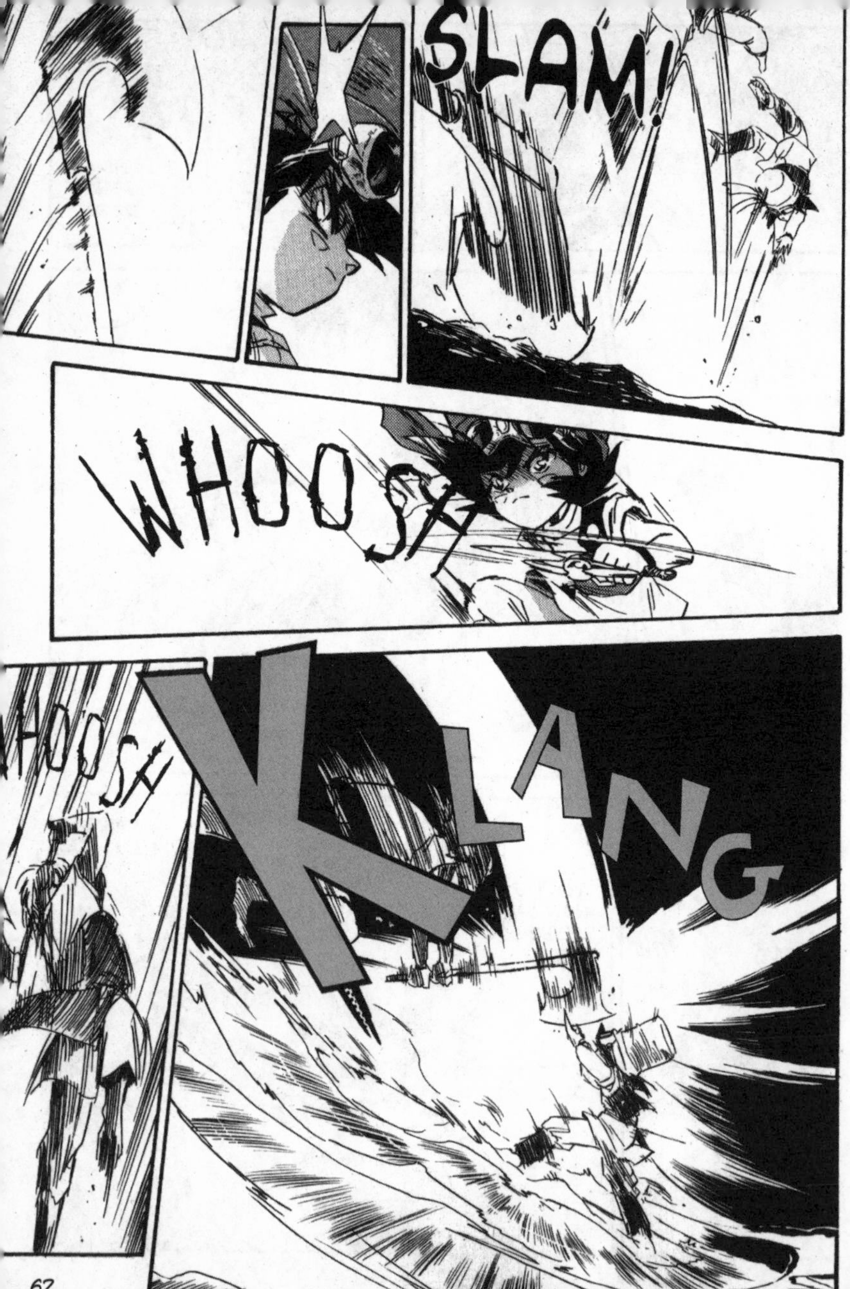
SLAM!
WHOOSH
HOOSH
KLANG

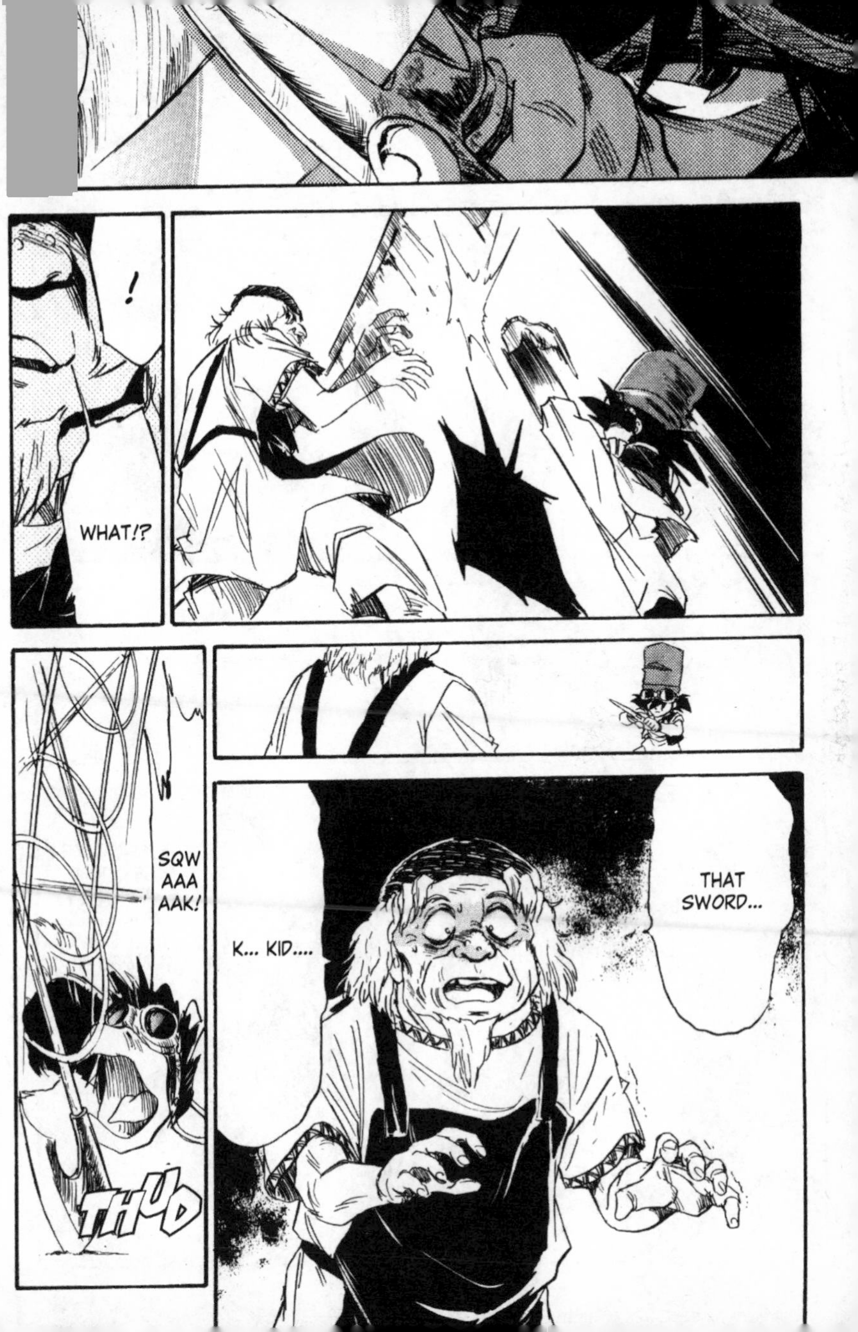
!
WHAT!?
SQW
AAA
AAK!
THUD
THAT
SWORD...
K... KID....

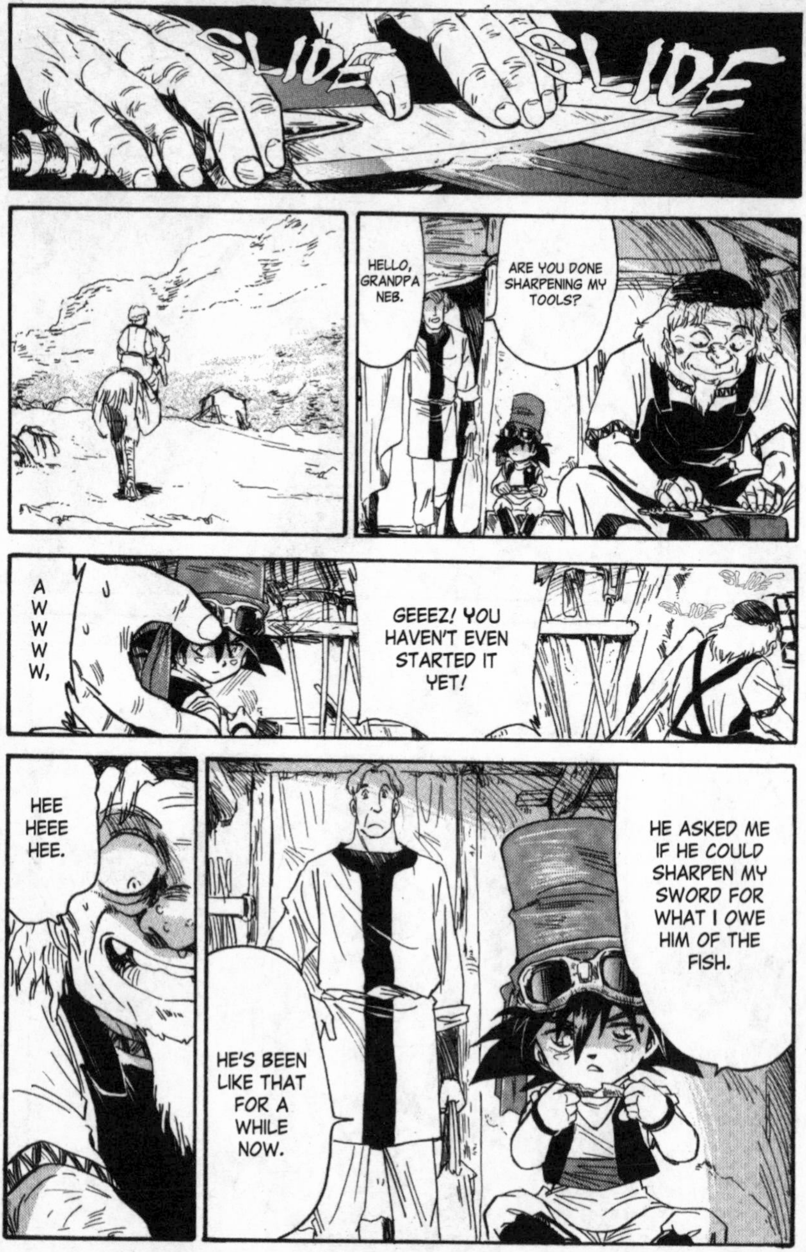
SLIDE SLIDE
HELLO, GRANDPA NEB.
ARE YOU DONE SHARPENING MY TOOLS?
AWWWWW,
GEEEZ! YOU HAVEN'T EVEN STARTED IT YET!
SLIDE
SLIDE
HEE HEEE HEE.
HE ASKED ME IF HE COULD SHARPEN MY SWORD FOR WHAT I OWE HIM OF THE FISH.
HE'S BEEN LIKE THAT FOR A WHILE NOW.

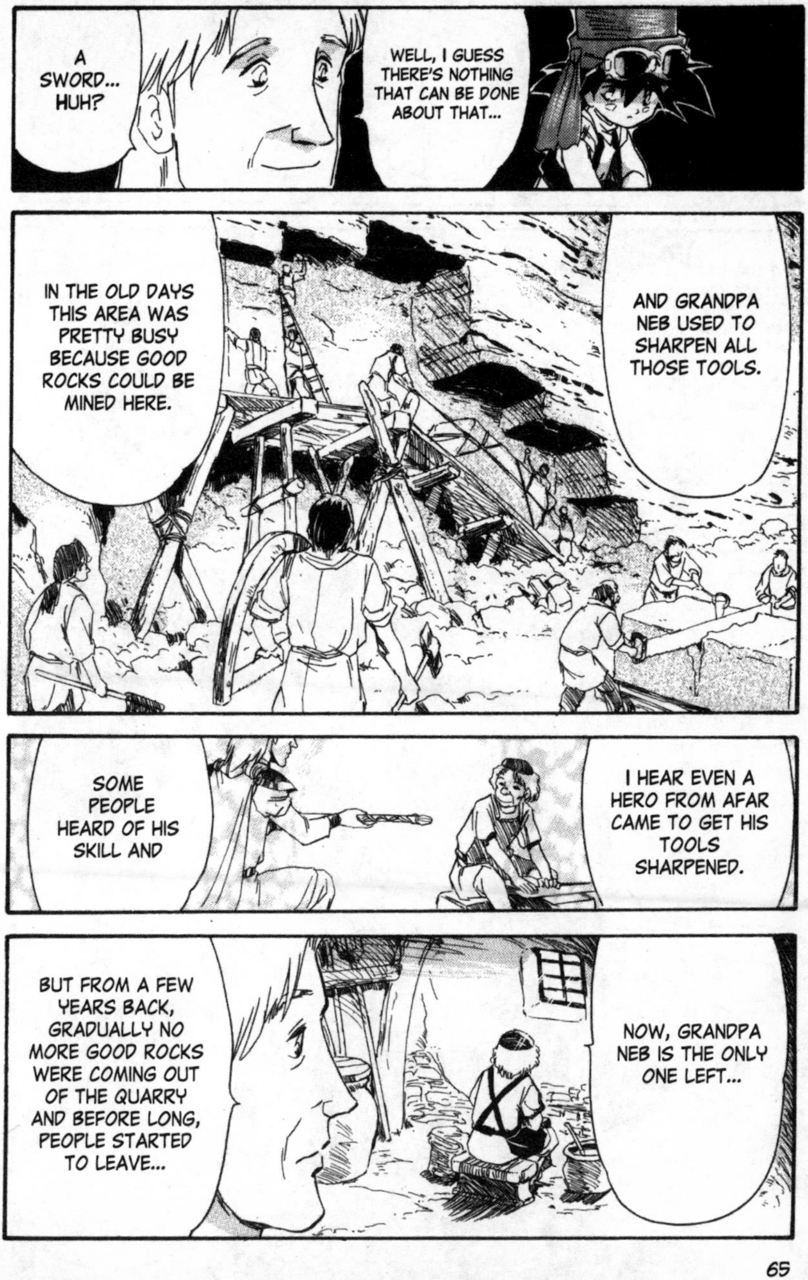
A SWORD... HUH?
WELL, I GUESS THERE'S NOTHING THAT CAN BE DONE ABOUT THAT...
IN THE OLD DAYS THIS AREA WAS PRETTY BUSY BECAUSE GOOD ROCKS COULD BE MINED HERE.
AND GRANDPA NEB USED TO SHARPEN ALL THOSE TOOLS.
SOME PEOPLE HEARD OF HIS SKILL AND
I HEAR EVEN A HERO FROM AFAR CAME TO GET HIS TOOLS SHARPENED.
BUT FROM A FEW YEARS BACK, GRADUALLY NO MORE GOOD ROCKS WERE COMING OUT OF THE QUARRY AND BEFORE LONG, PEOPLE STARTED TO LEAVE...
NOW, GRANDPA NEB IS THE ONLY ONE LEFT...

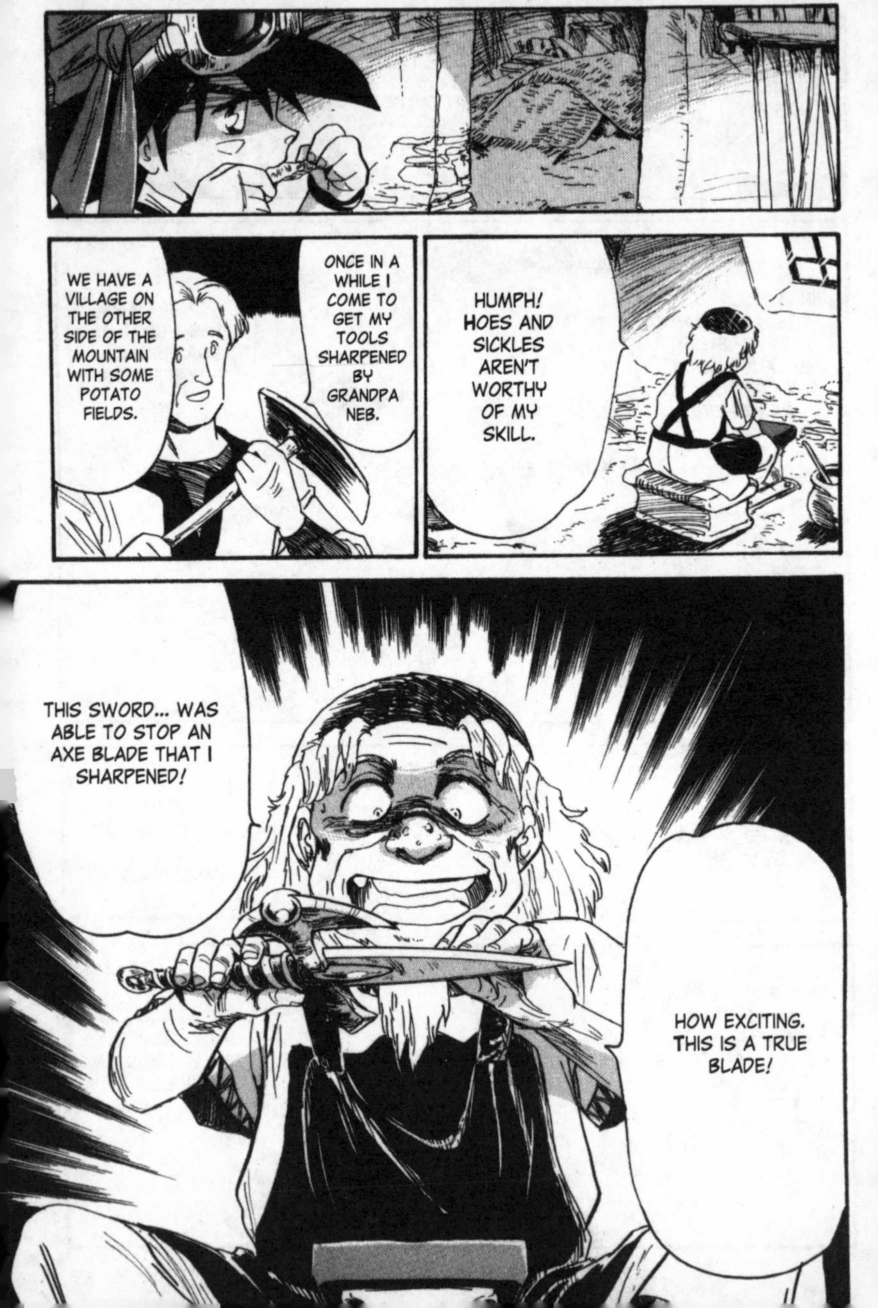
WE HAVE A VILLAGE ON THE OTHER SIDE OF THE MOUNTAIN WITH SOME POTATO FIELDS.
ONCE IN A WHILE I COME TO GET MY TOOLS SHARPENED BY GRANDPA NEB.
HUMPH! HOES AND SICKLES AREN'T WORTHY OF MY SKILL.
THIS SWORD... WAS ABLE TO STOP AN AXE BLADE THAT I SHARPENED!
HOW EXCITING. THIS IS A TRUE BLADE!

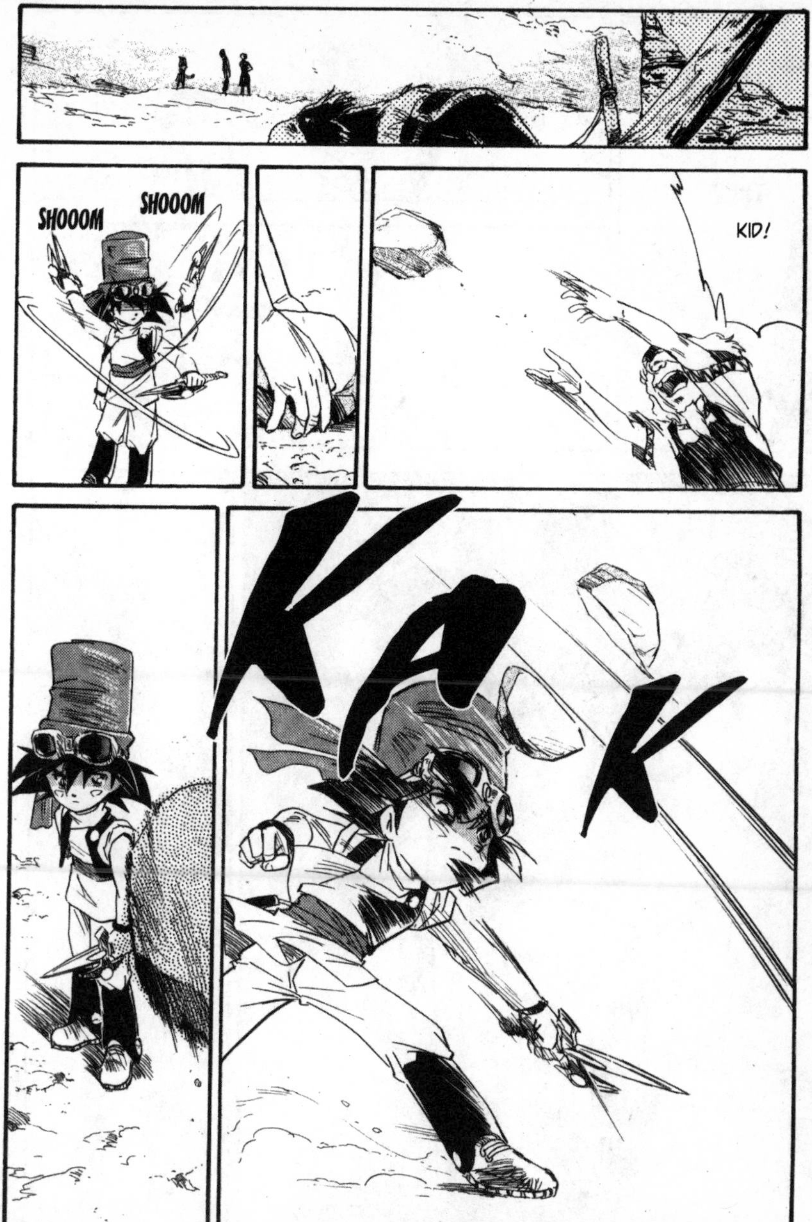
SHOOOM
SHOOOM
KID!
KAK

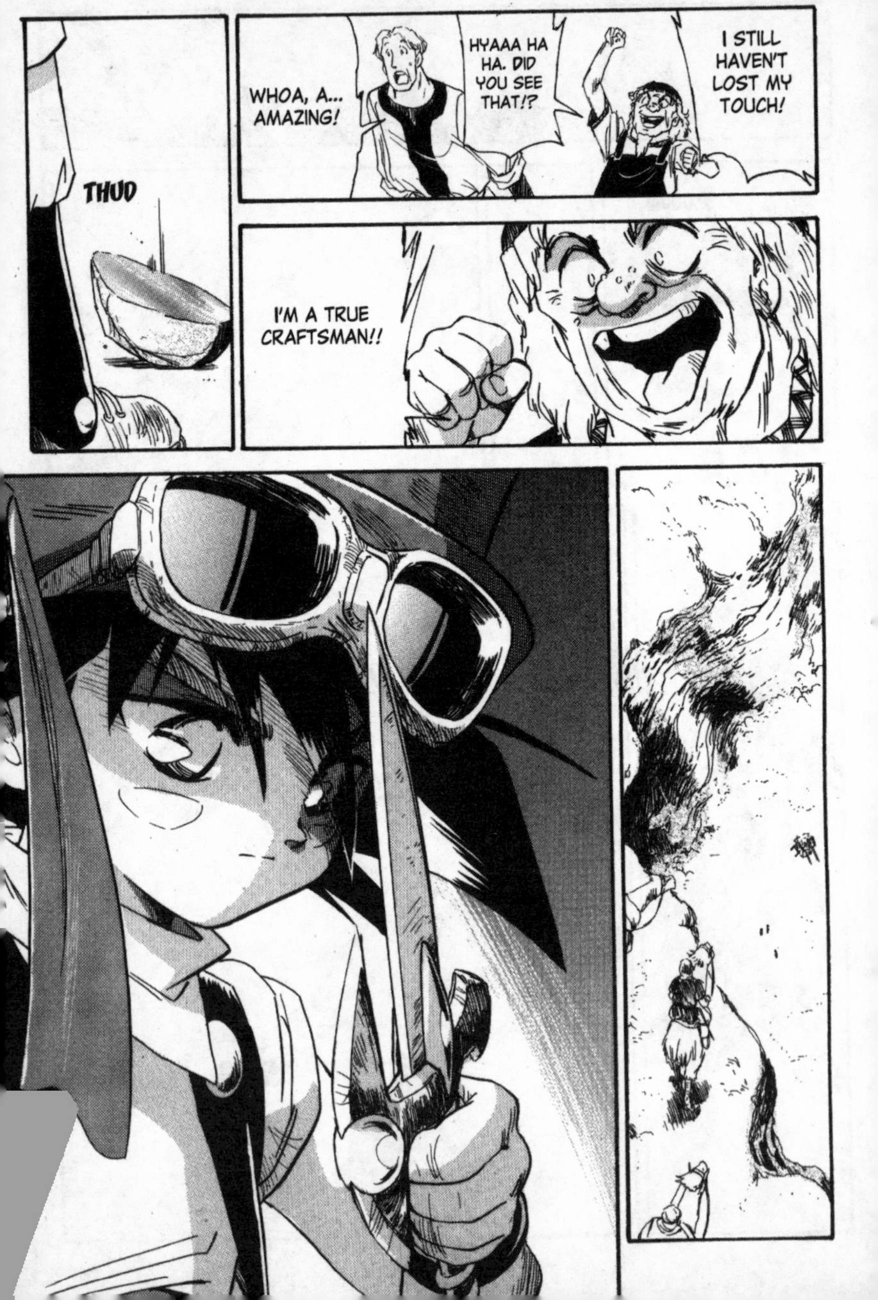
THUD
I STILL HAVEN'T LOST MY TOUCH!
HYAAA HA HA. DID YOU SEE THAT!?
WHOA, A... AMAZING!
I'M A TRUE CRAFTSMAN!!

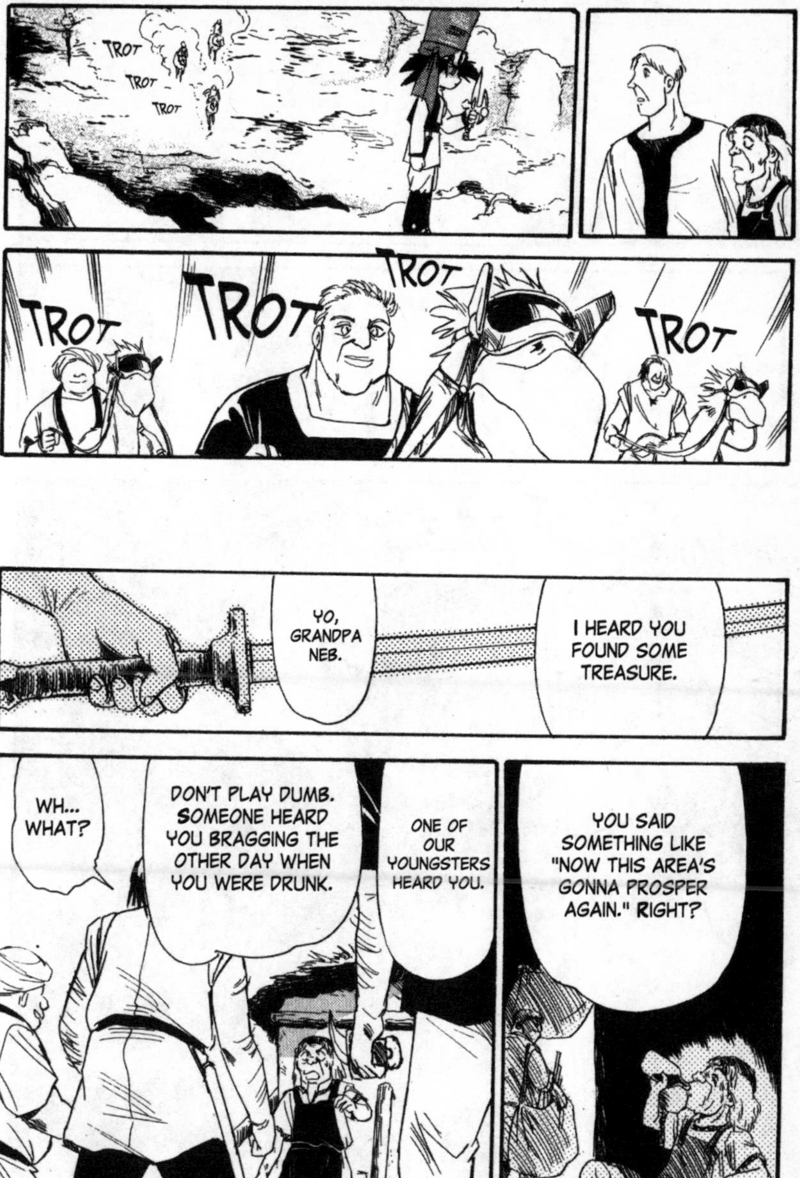

TROT
TROT
TROT
TROT
TROT
TROT
TROT
YO, GRANDPA NEB.
I HEARD YOU FOUND SOME TREASURE.
WH... WHAT?
DON'T PLAY DUMB. SOMEONE HEARD YOU BRAGGING THE OTHER DAY WHEN YOU WERE DRUNK.
ONE OF OUR YOUNGSTERS HEARD YOU.
YOU SAID SOMETHING LIKE "NOW THIS AREA'S GONNA PROSPER AGAIN." RIGHT?

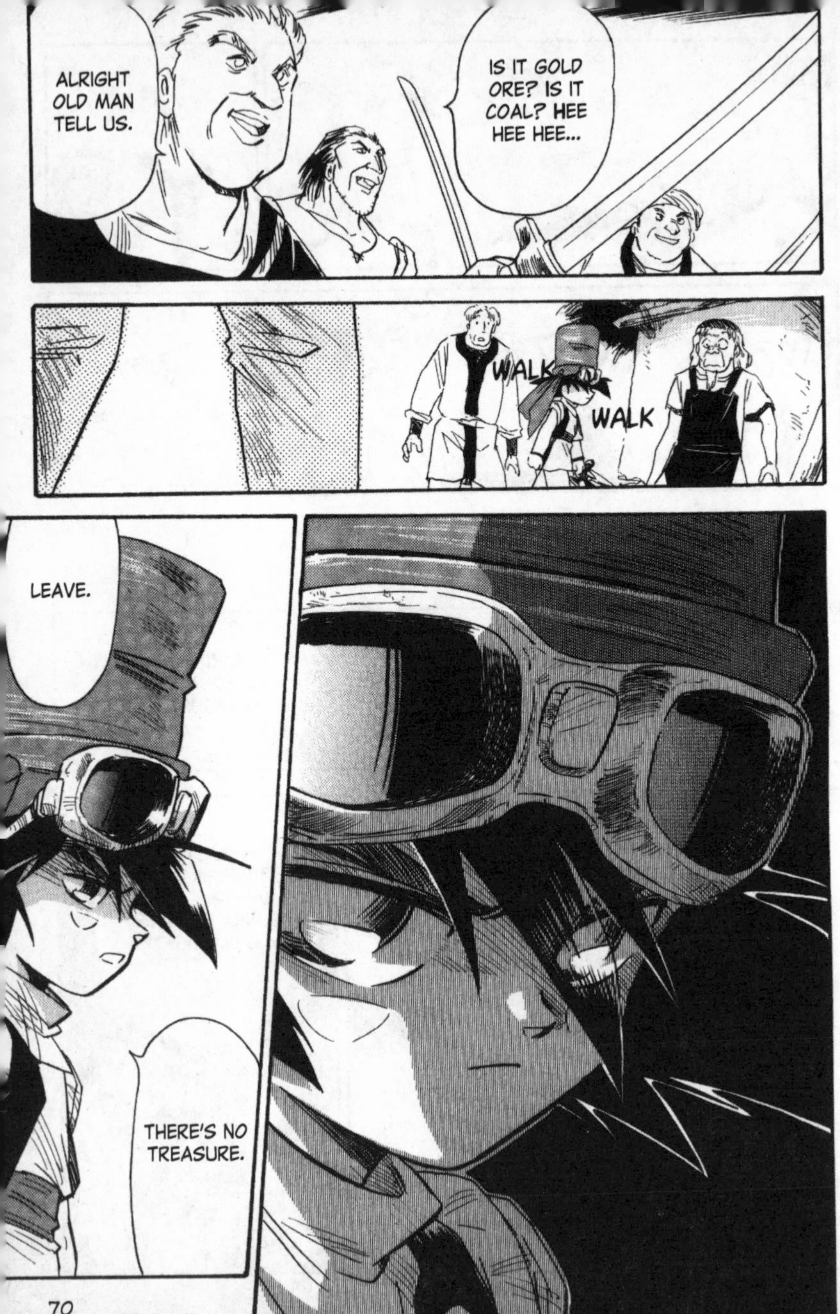

ALRIGHT OLD MAN TELL US.
IS IT GOLD ORE? IS IT COAL? HEE HEE HEE...
WALK
WALK
LEAVE.
THERE'S NO TREASURE.

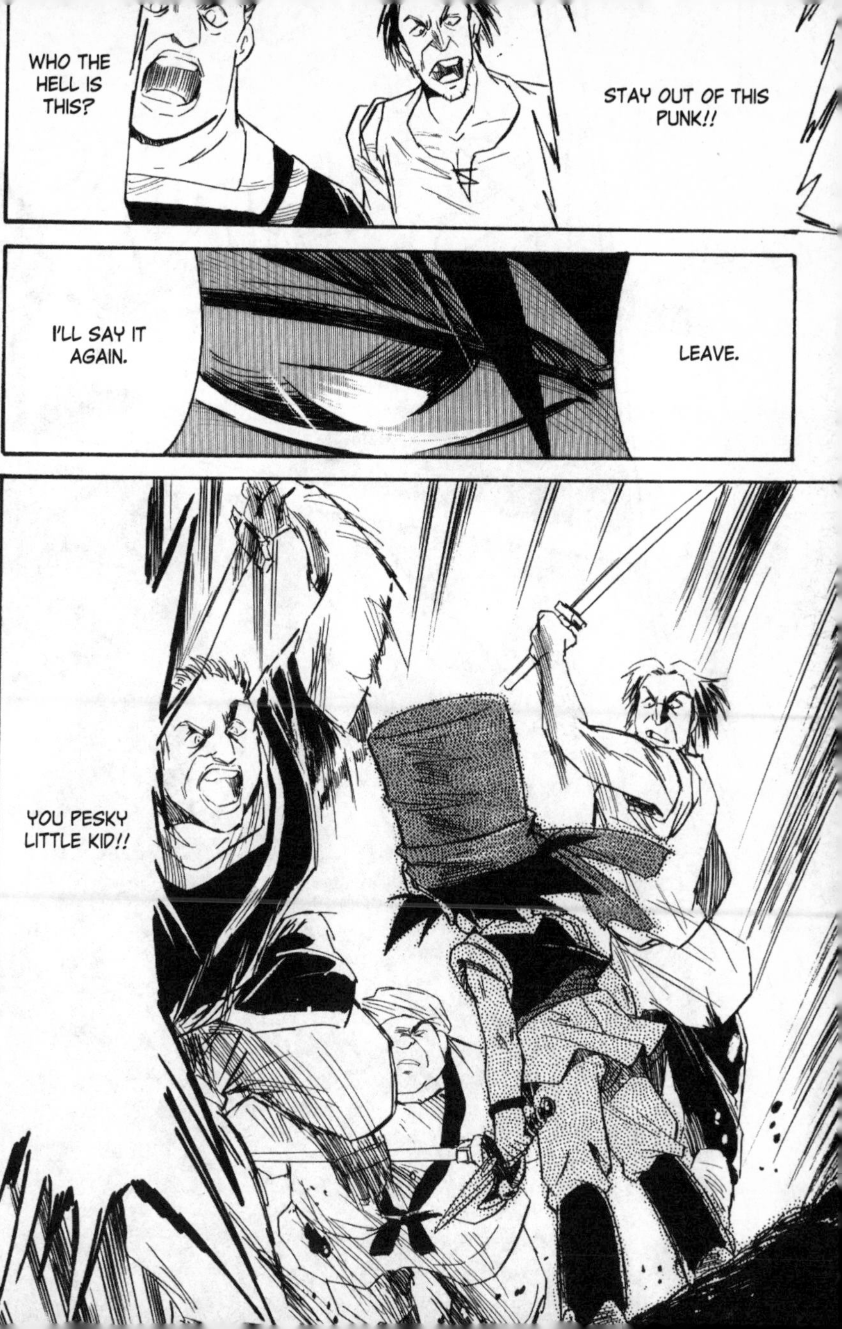
WHO THE HELL IS THIS?
STAY OUT OF THIS PUNK!!
I'LL SAY IT AGAIN.
LEAVE.
YOU PESKY LITTLE KID!!

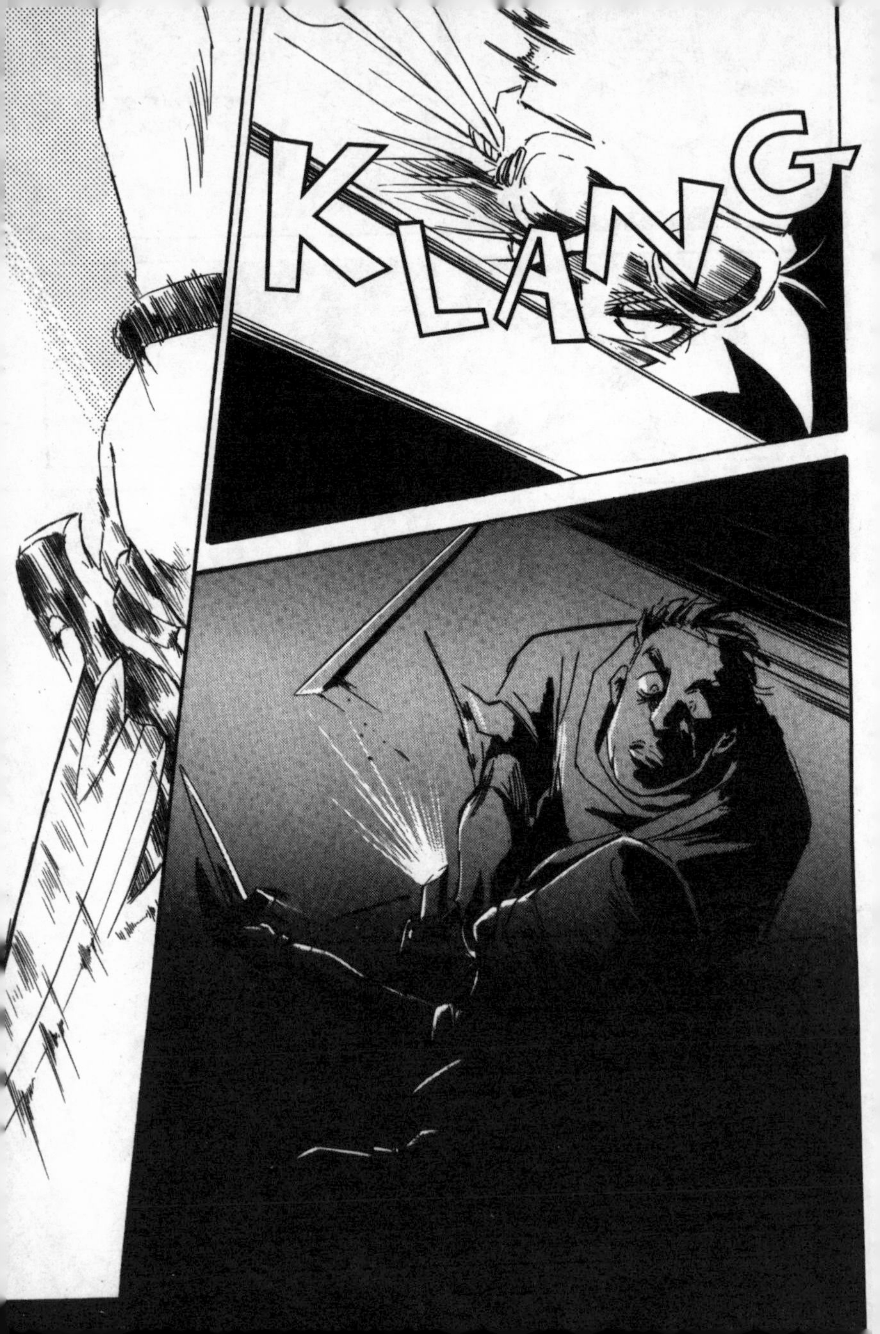
KLANG

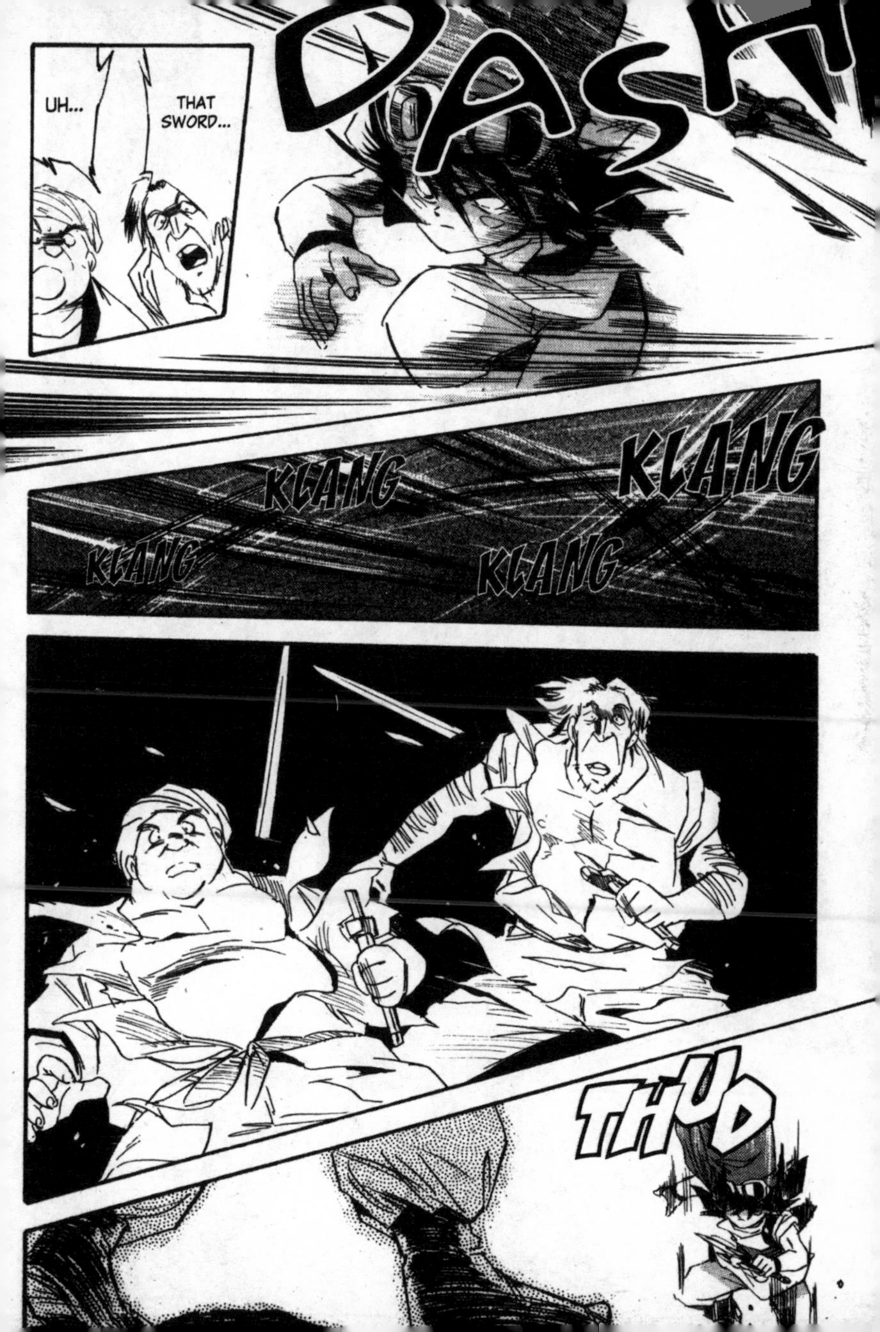

DASH
THAT SWORD...
UH...
KLANG
KLANG
KLANG
KLANG
THUD

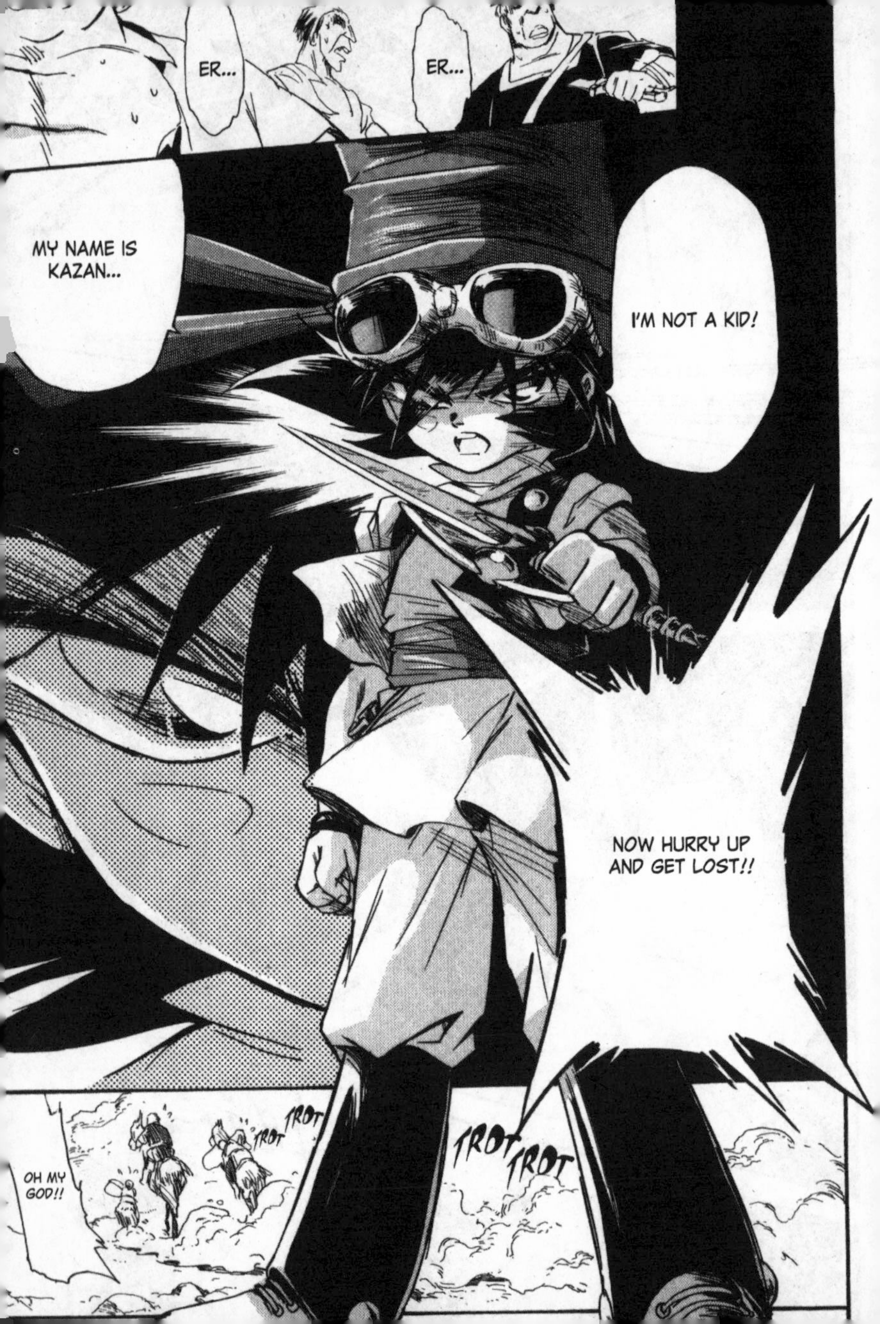
ER...
ER...
I'M NOT A KID!
MY NAME IS KAZAN...
NOW HURRY UP AND GET LOST!!
TROT TROT
TROT TROT
OH MY GOD!!

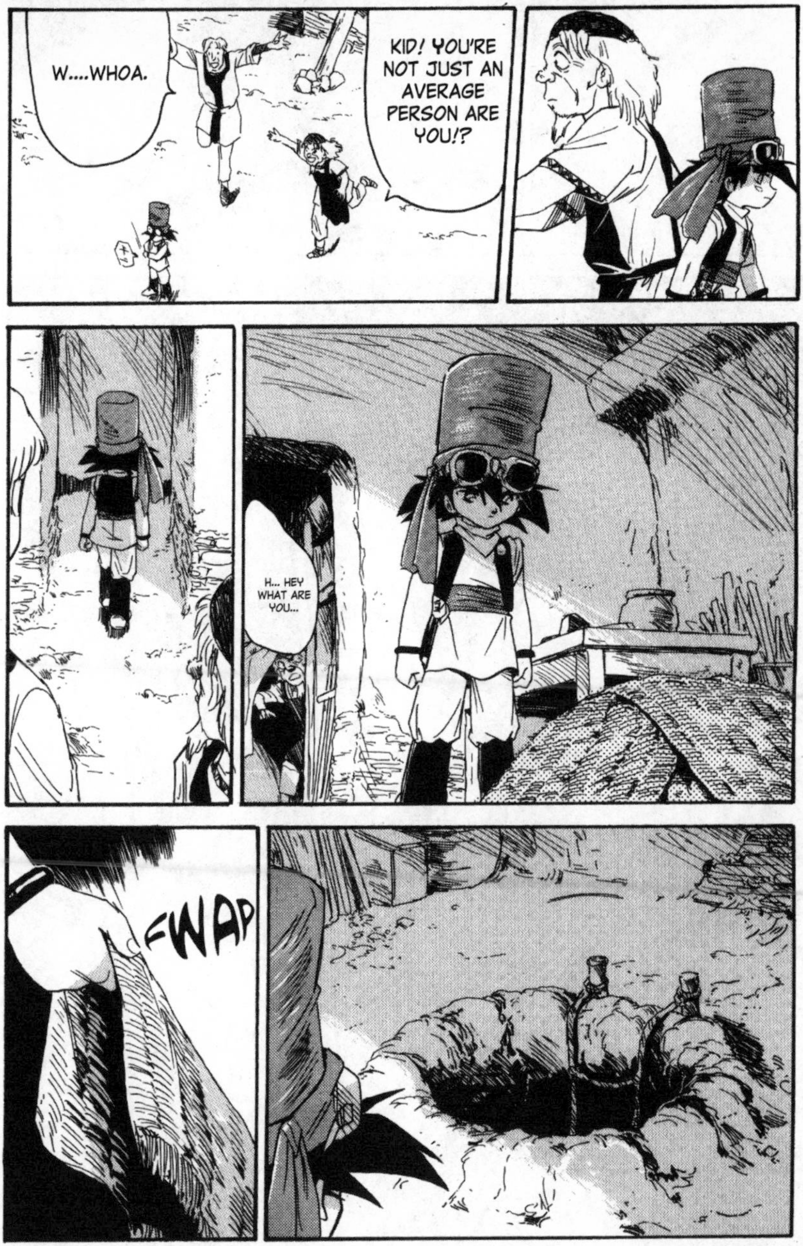
W....WHOA.
KID! YOU'RE NOT JUST AN AVERAGE PERSON ARE YOU!?
H... HEY WHAT ARE YOU...
FWAP

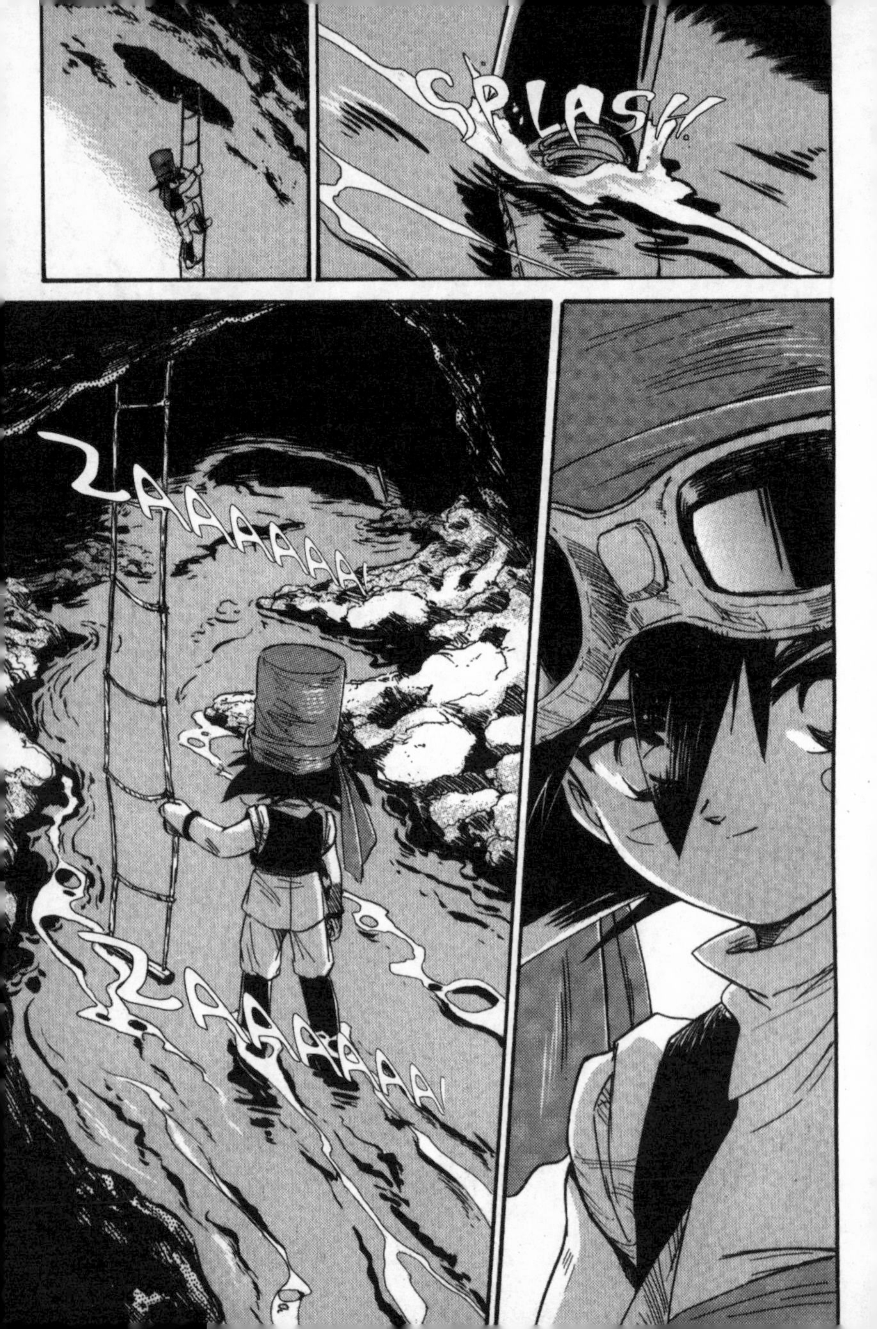
SPLASH!
ZAAAAAAAA!
ZAAAAAAAAA!

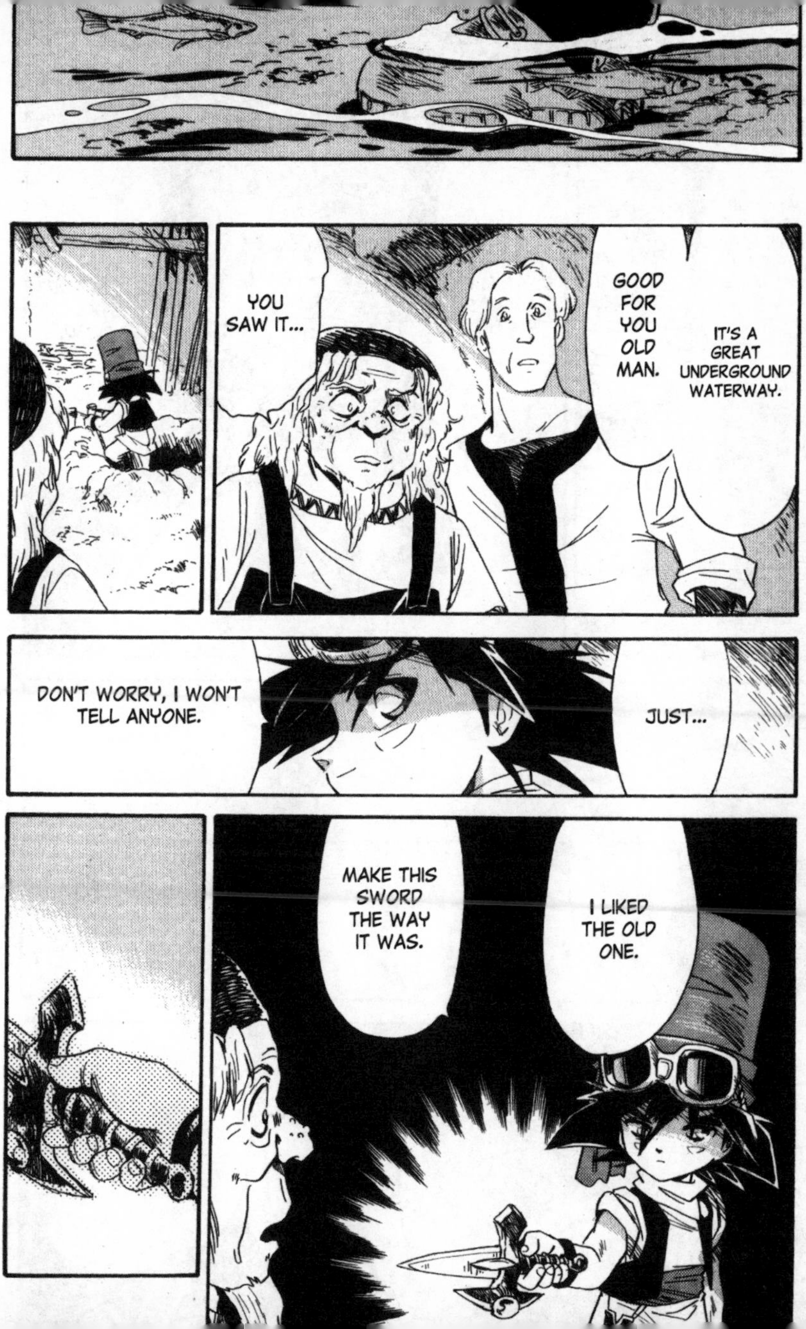

IT'S A GREAT UNDERGROUND WATERWAY.
GOOD FOR YOU OLD MAN.
YOU SAW IT...
JUST...
DON'T WORRY, I WON'T TELL ANYONE.
I LIKED THE OLD ONE.
MAKE THIS SWORD THE WAY IT WAS.

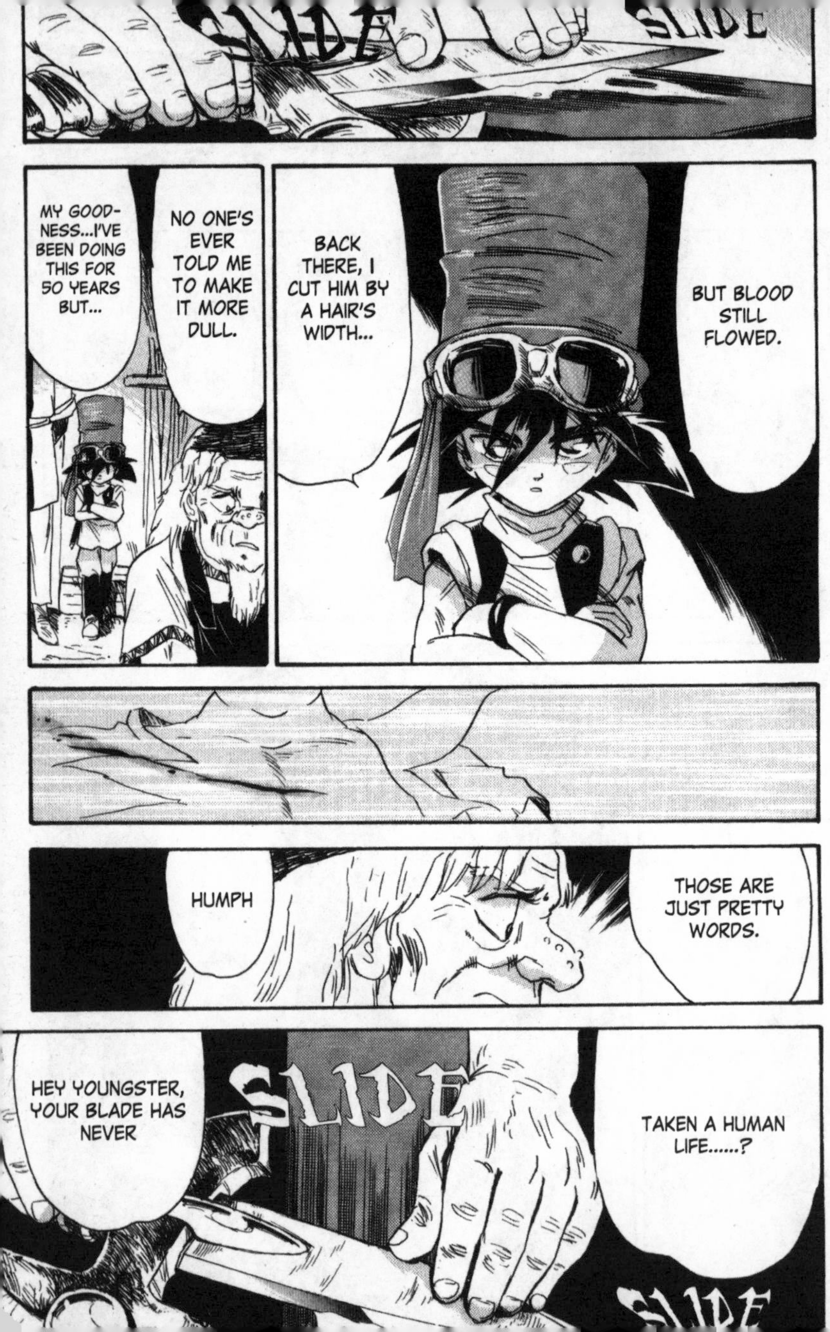
SLIDE
SLIDE
MY GOOD-NESS...I'VE BEEN DOING THIS FOR 50 YEARS BUT...
NO ONE'S EVER TOLD ME TO MAKE IT MORE DULL.
BACK THERE, I CUT HIM BY A HAIR'S WIDTH...
BUT BLOOD STILL FLOWED.
HUMPH
THOSE ARE JUST PRETTY WORDS.
HEY YOUNGSTER, YOUR BLADE HAS NEVER
SLIDE
TAKEN A HUMAN LIFE......?
SLIDE

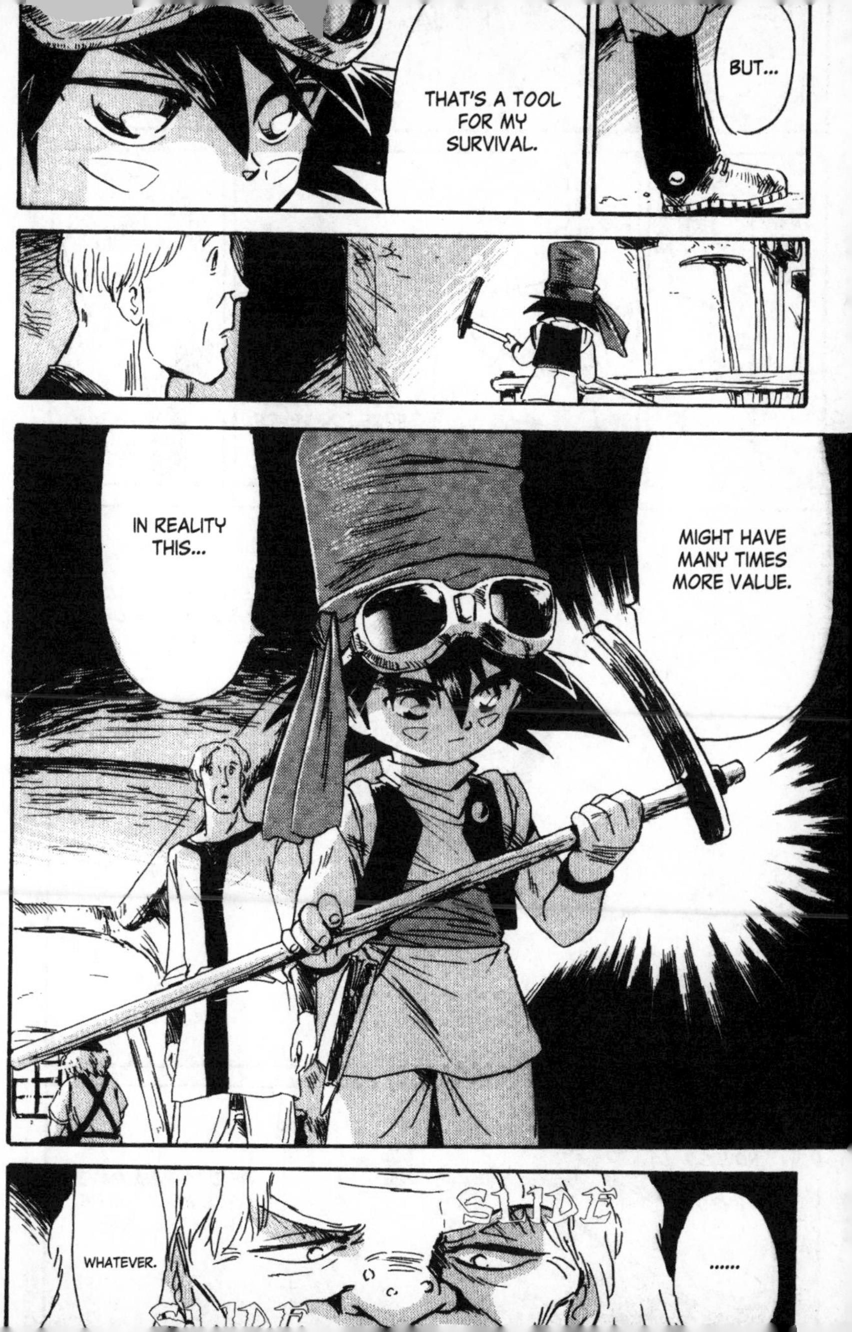
THAT'S A TOOL FOR MY SURVIVAL.
BUT...
IN REALITY THIS...
MIGHT HAVE MANY TIMES MORE VALUE.
WHATEVER.
SLIDE
......

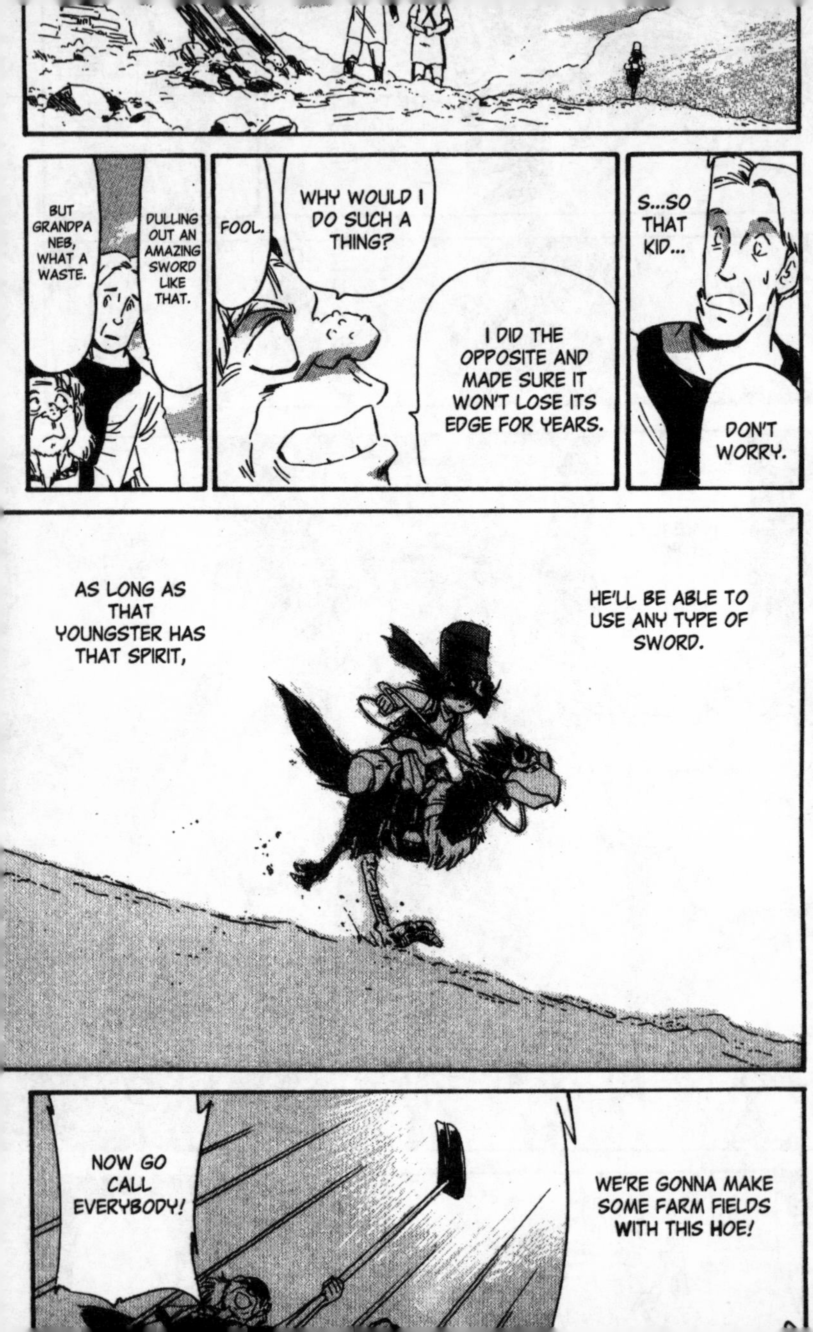

BUT GRANDPA NEB, WHAT A WASTE.
DULLING OUT AN AMAZING SWORD LIKE THAT.
FOOL.
WHY WOULD I DO SUCH A THING?
I DID THE OPPOSITE AND MADE SURE IT WON'T LOSE ITS EDGE FOR YEARS.
S...SO THAT KID...
DON'T WORRY.
AS LONG AS THAT YOUNGSTER HAS THAT SPIRIT,
HE'LL BE ABLE TO USE ANY TYPE OF SWORD.
NOW GO CALL EVERYBODY!
WE'RE GONNA MAKE SOME FARM FIELDS WITH THIS HOE!

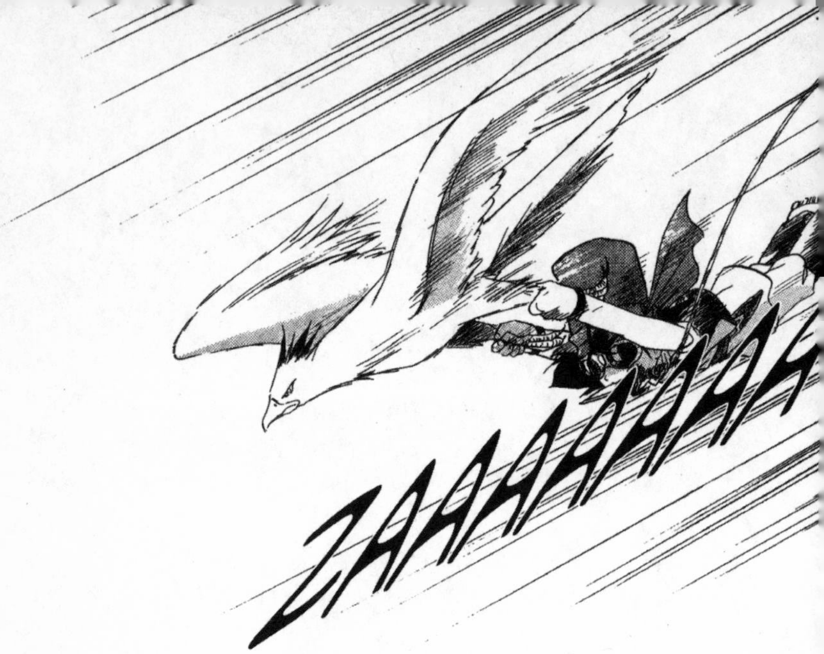
ZAAAAAAA

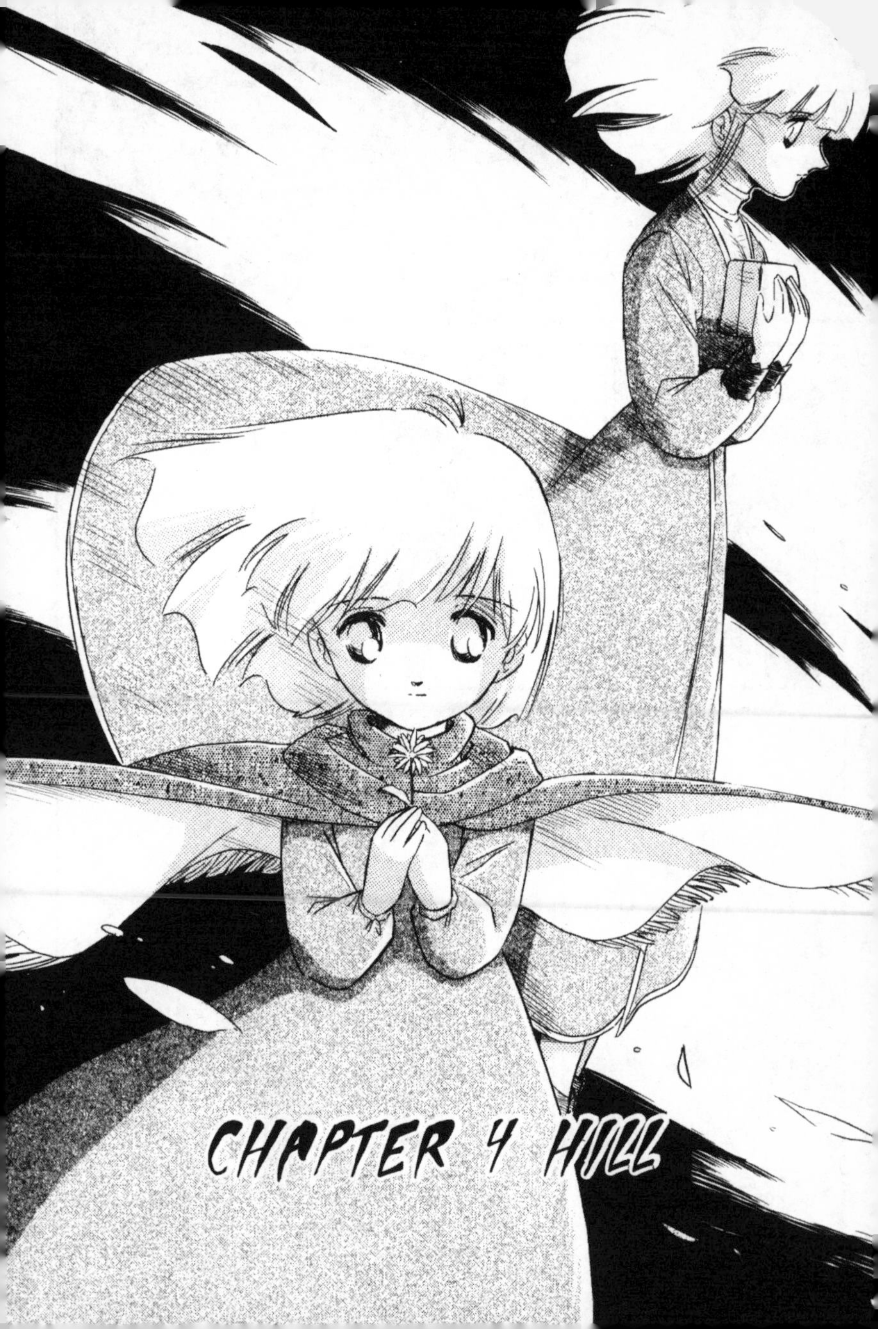
CHAPTER 4 HILL

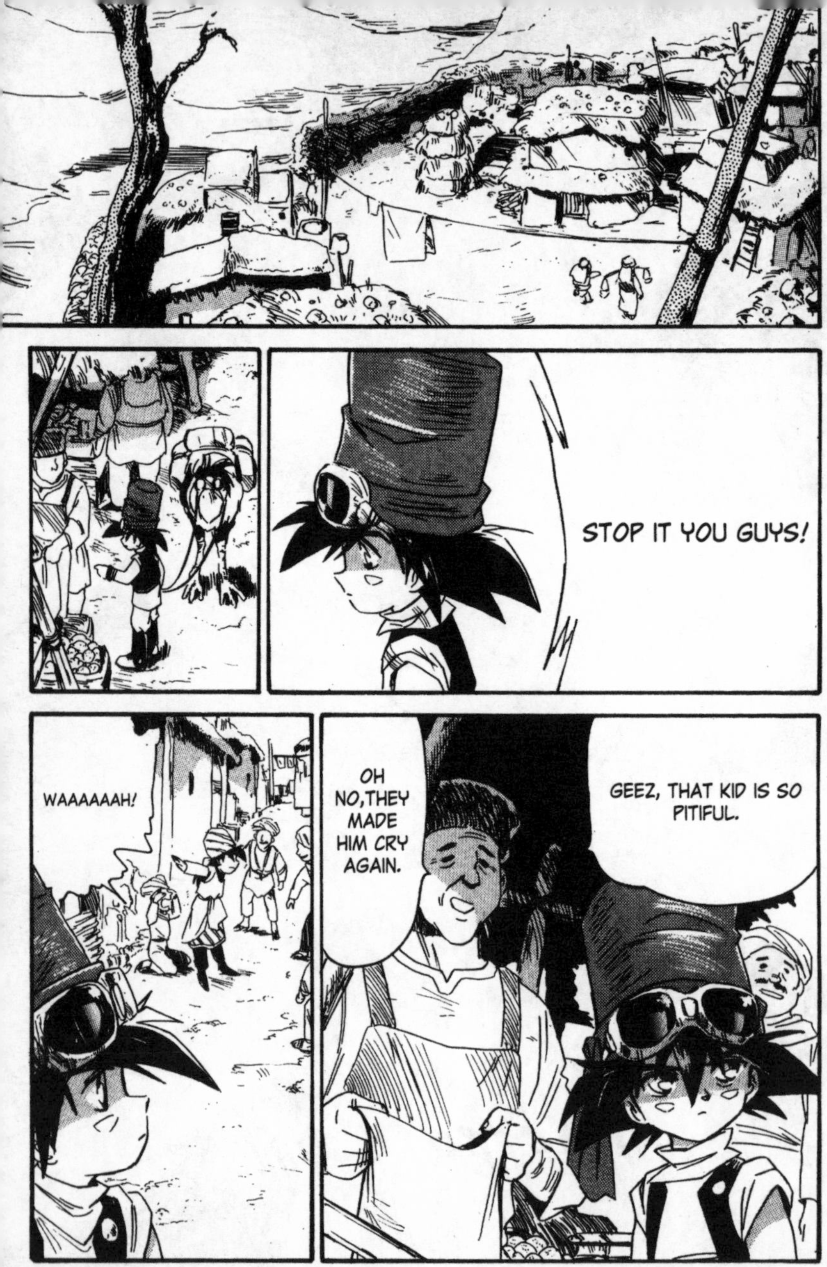
STOP IT YOU GUYS!
WAAAAAAH!
OH NO,THEY MADE HIM CRY AGAIN.
GEEZ, THAT KID IS SO PITIFUL.

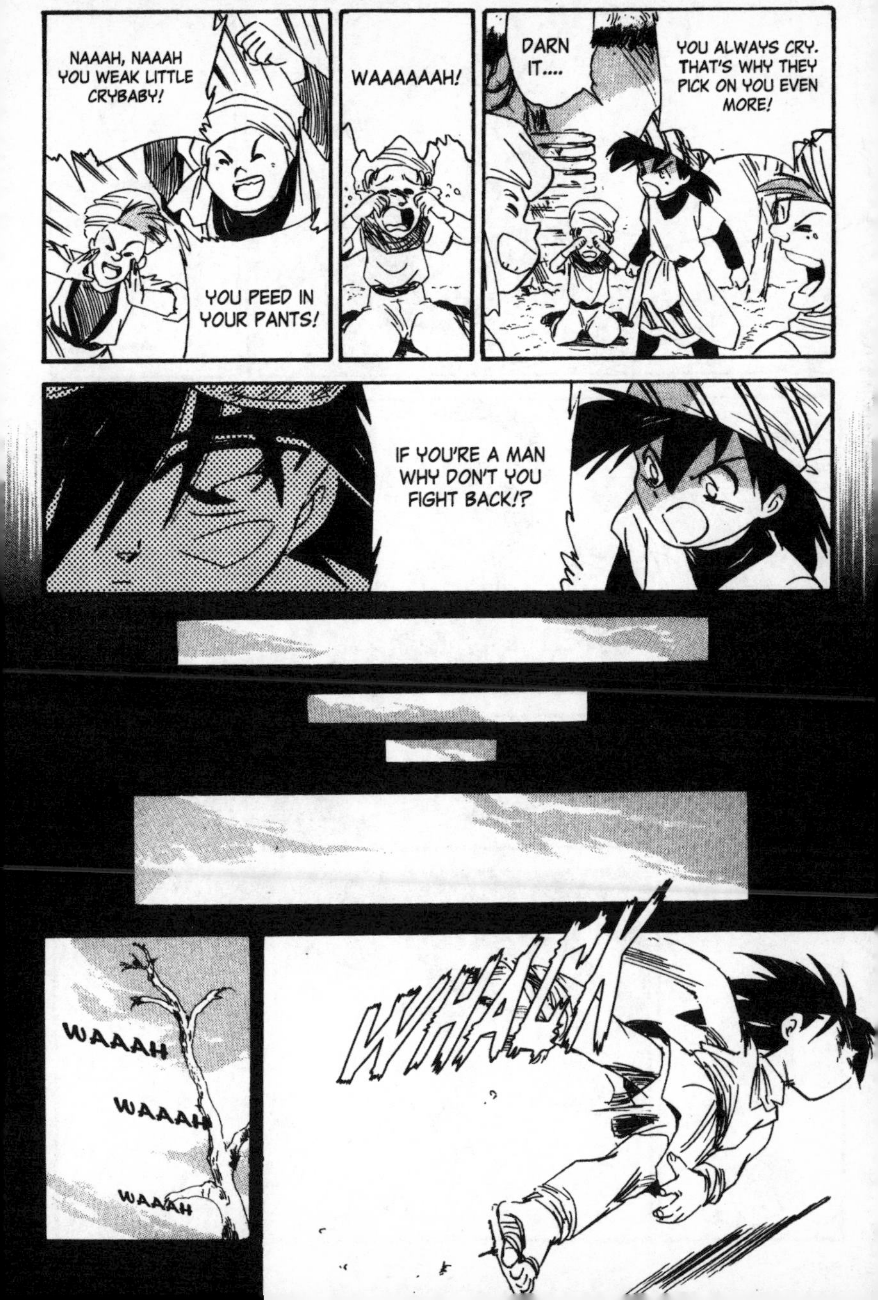

NAAAH, NAAAH YOU WEAK LITTLE CRYBABY!
YOU PEED IN YOUR PANTS!
WAAAAAAH!
DARN IT....
YOU ALWAYS CRY. THAT'S WHY THEY PICK ON YOU EVEN MORE!
IF YOU'RE A MAN WHY DON'T YOU FIGHT BACK!?
WAAAH
WAAAH
WAAAH
WHACK

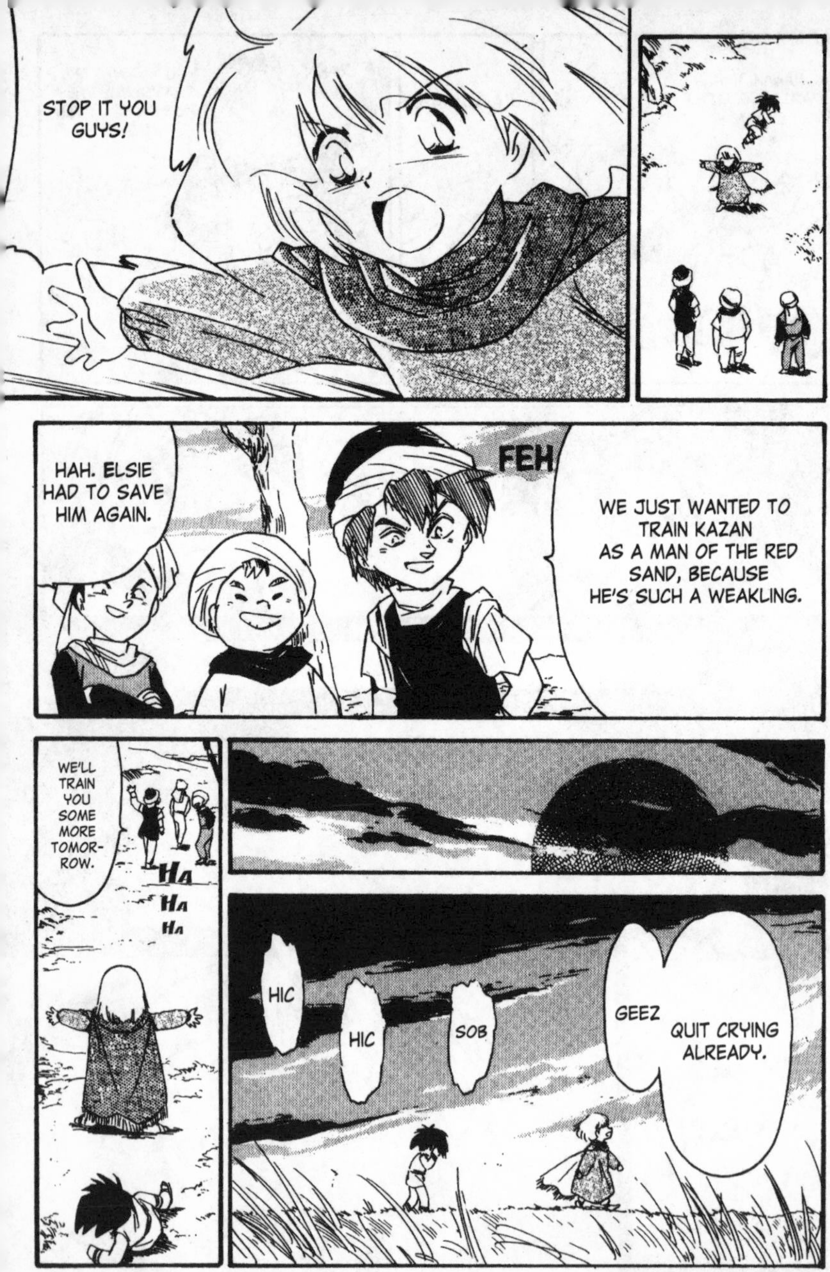

STOP IT YOU GUYS!
HAH. ELSIE HAD TO SAVE HIM AGAIN.
FEH
WE JUST WANTED TO TRAIN KAZAN AS A MAN OF THE RED SAND, BECAUSE HE'S SUCH A WEAKLING.
WE'LL TRAIN YOU SOME MORE TOMOR-ROW.
HA HA HA
HIC
HIC
SOB
GEEZ
QUIT CRYING ALREADY.

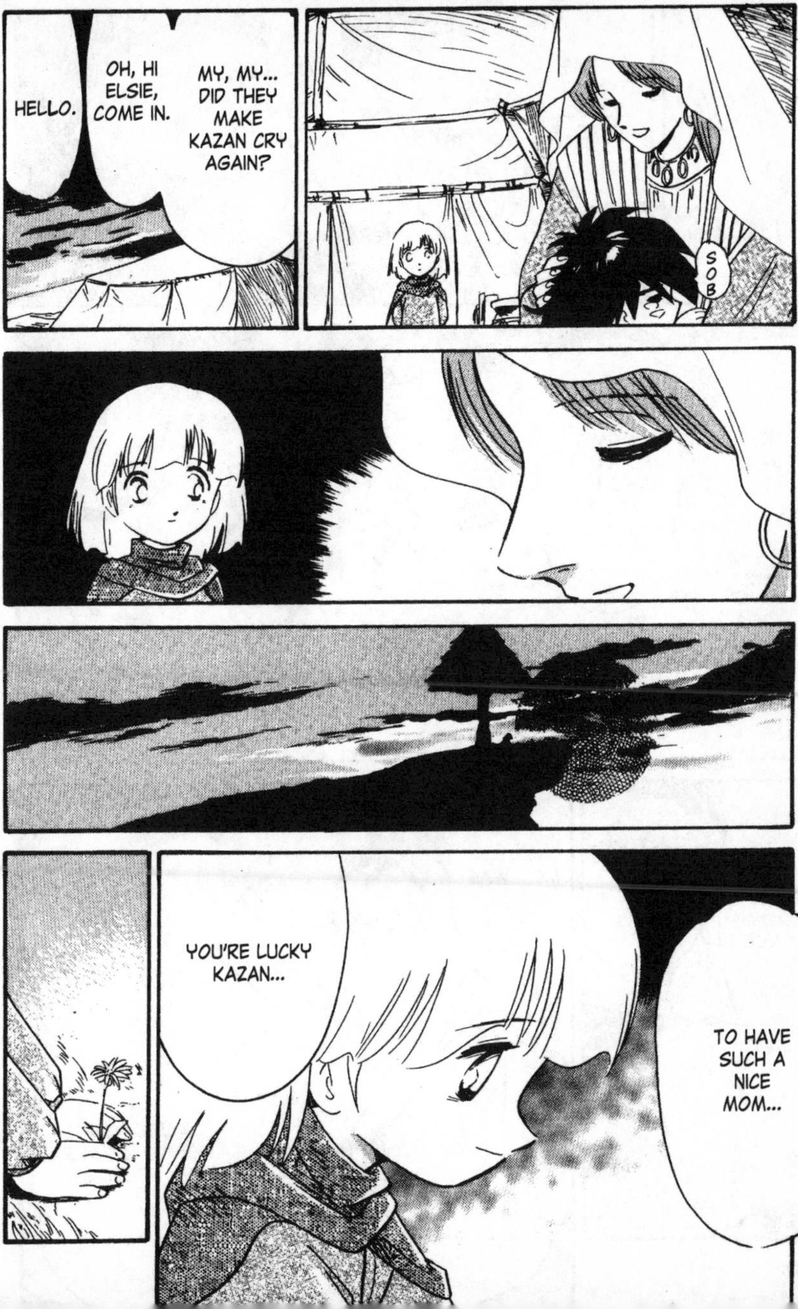
MY, MY... DID THEY MAKE KAZAN CRY AGAIN?
OH, HI ELSIE, COME IN.
HELLO.
SOB
TO HAVE SUCH A NICE MOM...
YOU'RE LUCKY KAZAN...

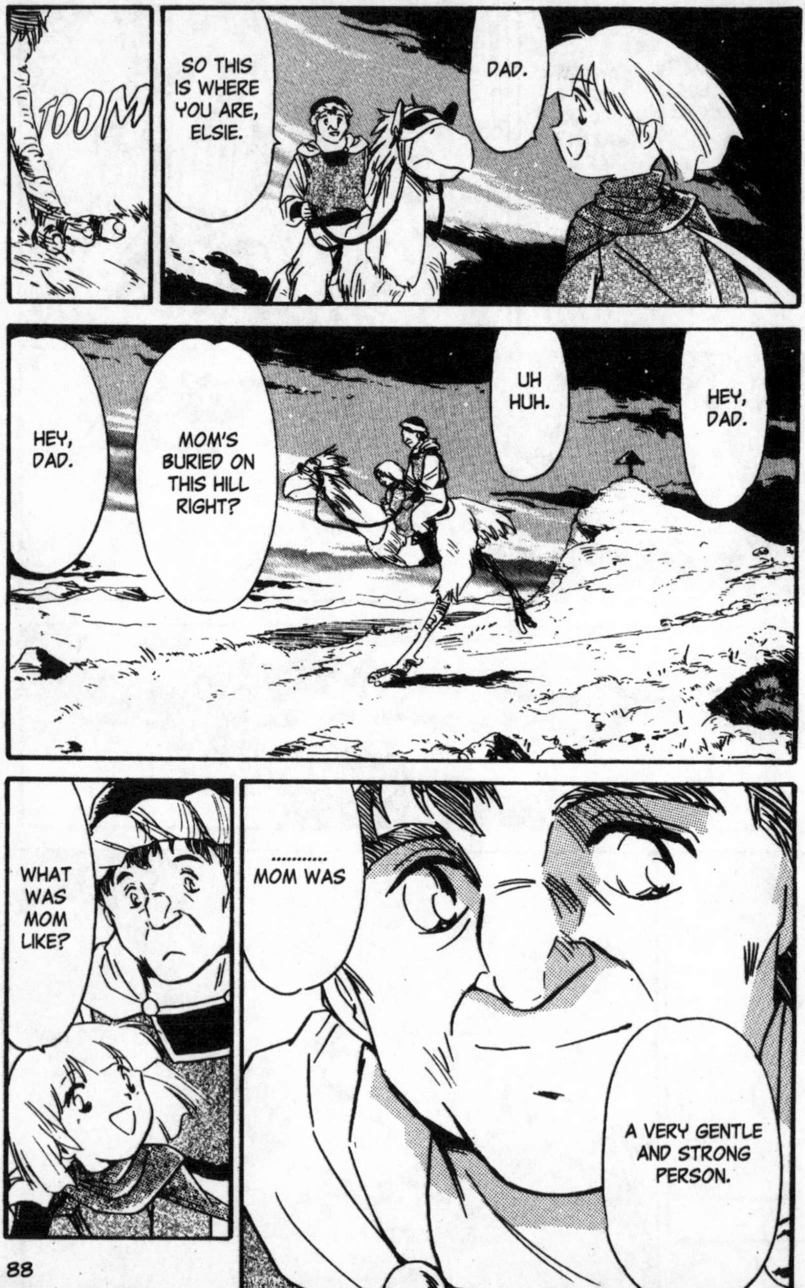
TOOM
SO THIS IS WHERE YOU ARE, ELSIE.
DAD.
HEY, DAD.
UH HUH.
MOM'S BURIED ON THIS HILL RIGHT?
HEY, DAD.
WHAT WAS MOM LIKE?
.... MOM WAS
A VERY GENTLE AND STRONG PERSON.

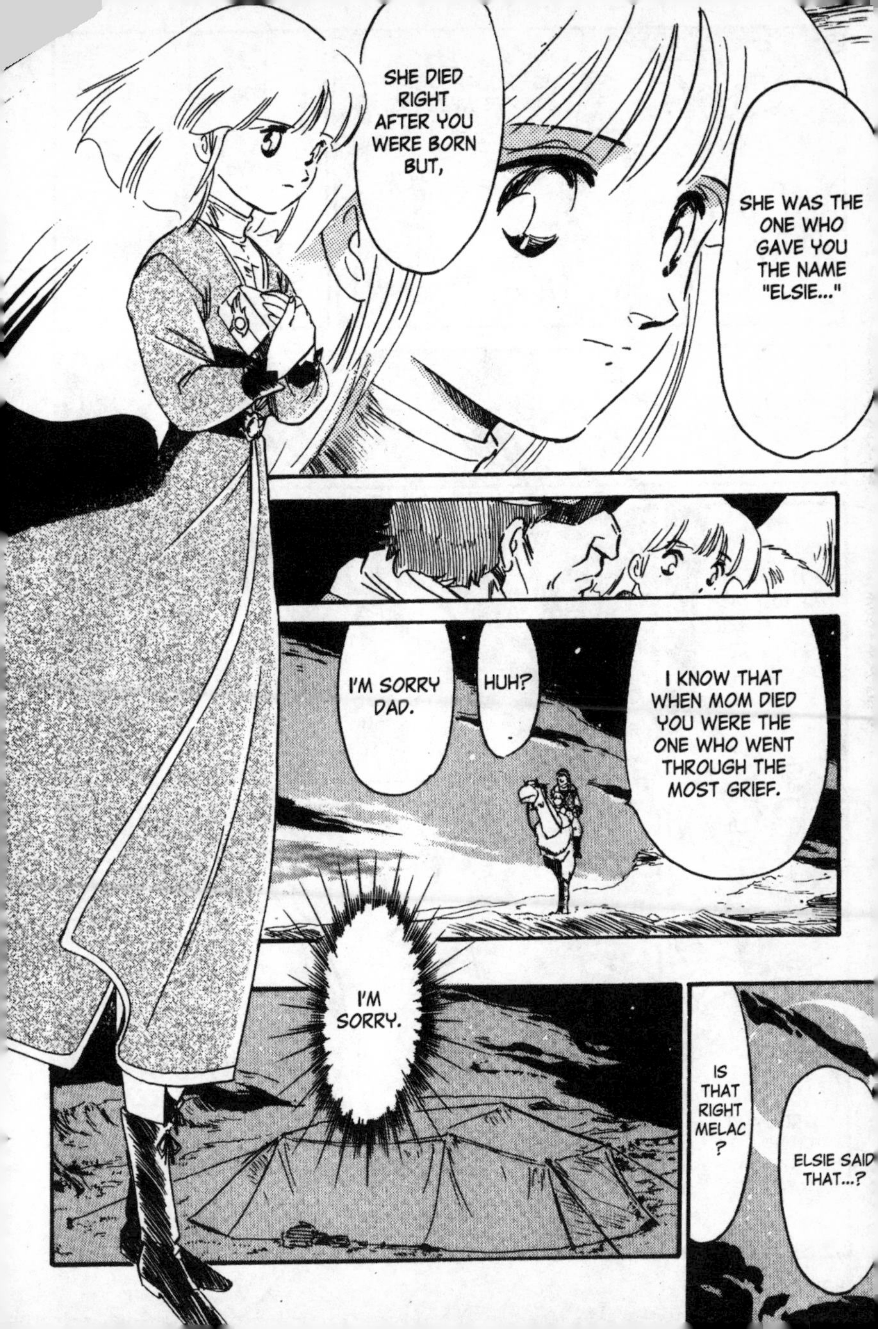
SHE WAS THE ONE WHO GAVE YOU THE NAME "ELSIE..."
SHE DIED RIGHT AFTER YOU WERE BORN BUT,
I KNOW THAT WHEN MOM DIED YOU WERE THE ONE WHO WENT THROUGH THE MOST GRIEF.
HUH?
I'M SORRY DAD.
I'M SORRY.
ELSIE SAID THAT...?
IS THAT RIGHT MELAC ?

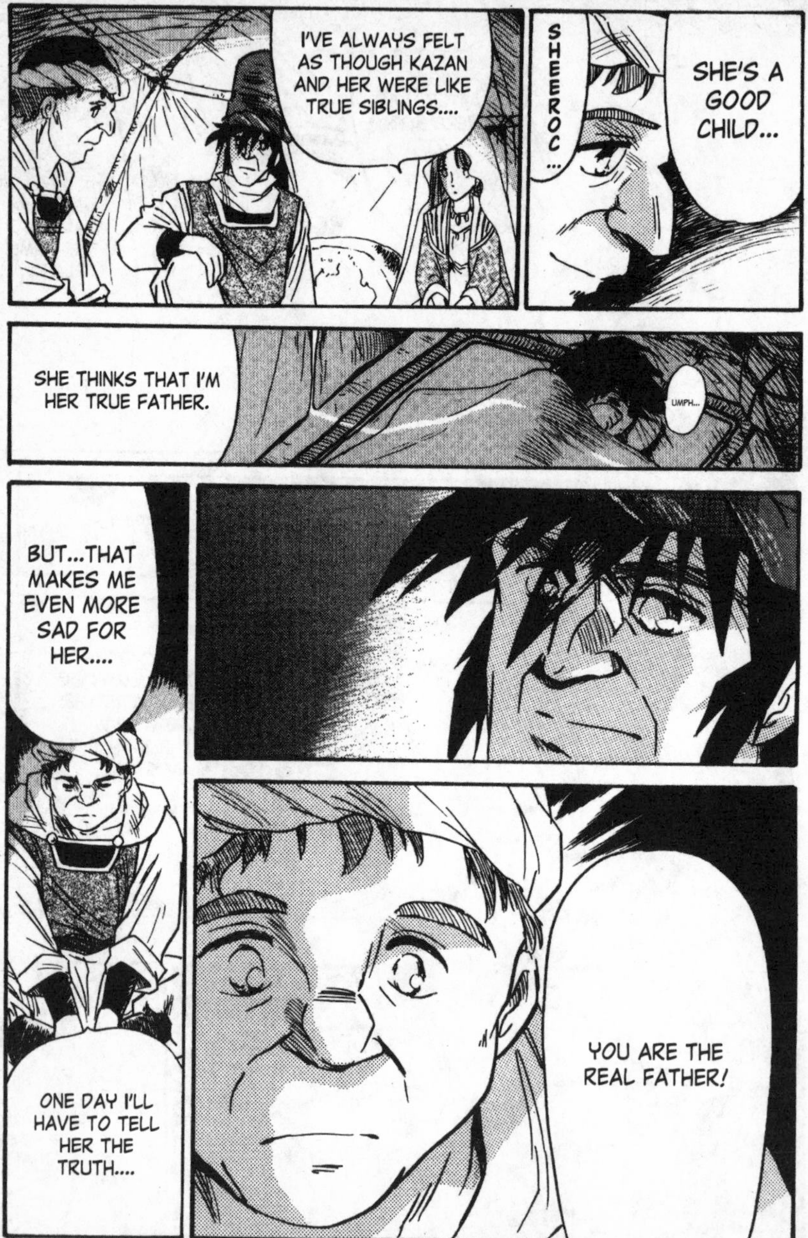
I'VE ALWAYS FELT AS THOUGH KAZAN AND HER WERE LIKE TRUE SIBLINGS....
SHEEROC...
SHE'S A GOOD CHILD...
SHE THINKS THAT I'M HER TRUE FATHER.
UMPH...
BUT...THAT MAKES ME EVEN MORE SAD FOR HER....
ONE DAY I'LL HAVE TO TELL HER THE TRUTH....
YOU ARE THE REAL FATHER!

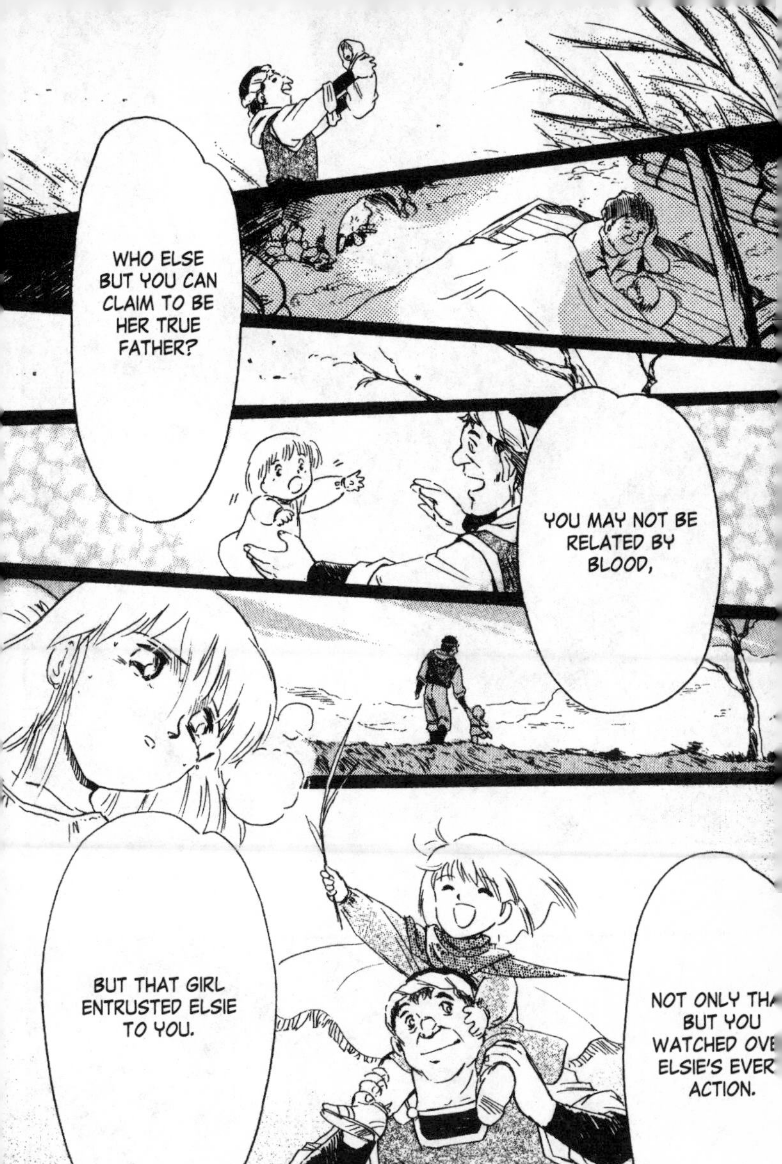

WHO ELSE BUT YOU CAN CLAIM TO BE HER TRUE FATHER?
YOU MAY NOT BE RELATED BY BLOOD,
BUT THAT GIRL ENTRUSTED ELSIE TO YOU.
NOT ONLY THA BUT YOU WATCHED OVE ELSIE'S EVER ACTION.

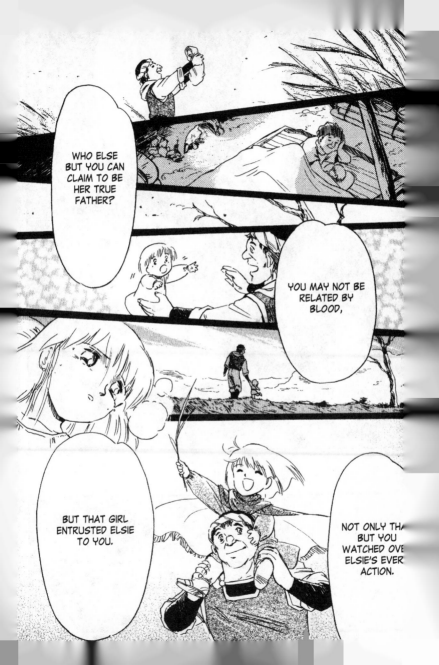

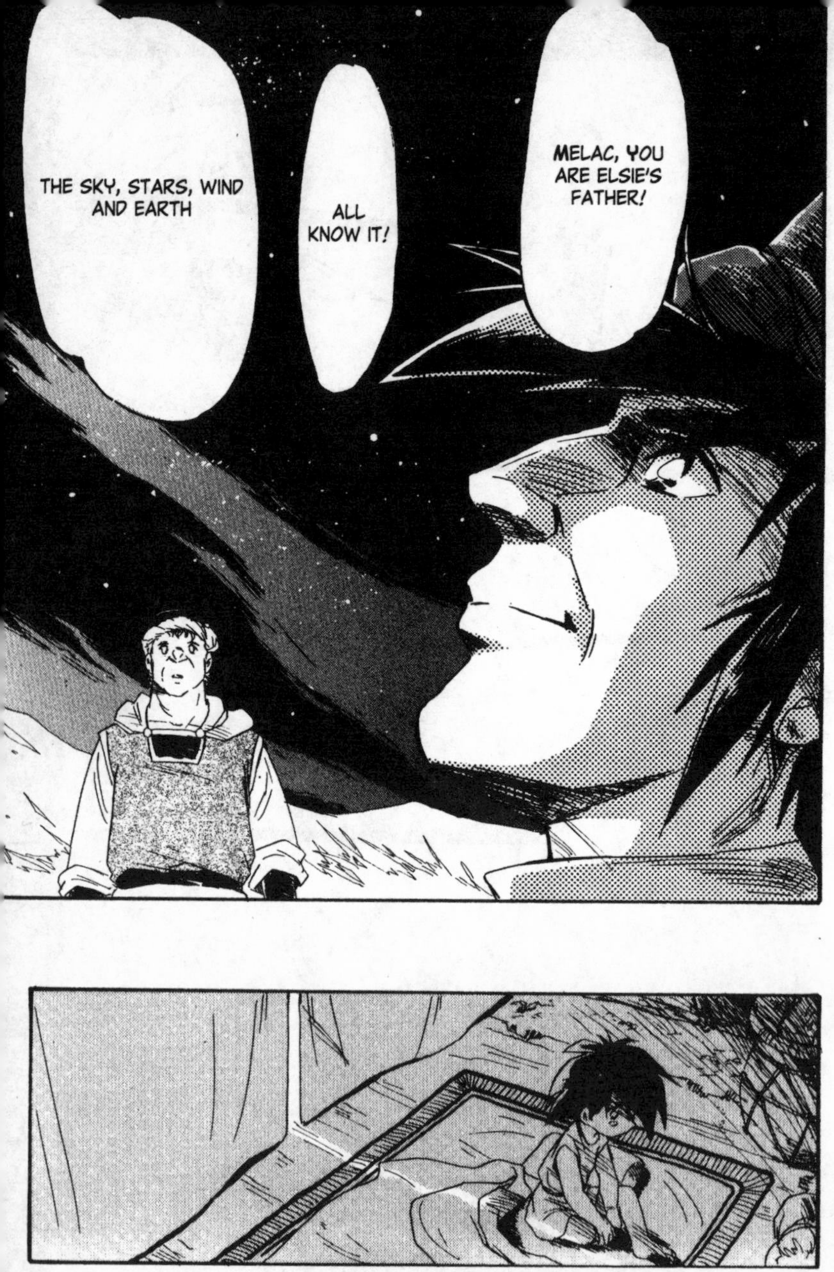

MELAC, YOU ARE ELSIE'S FATHER!
ALL KNOW IT!
THE SKY, STARS, WIND AND EARTH

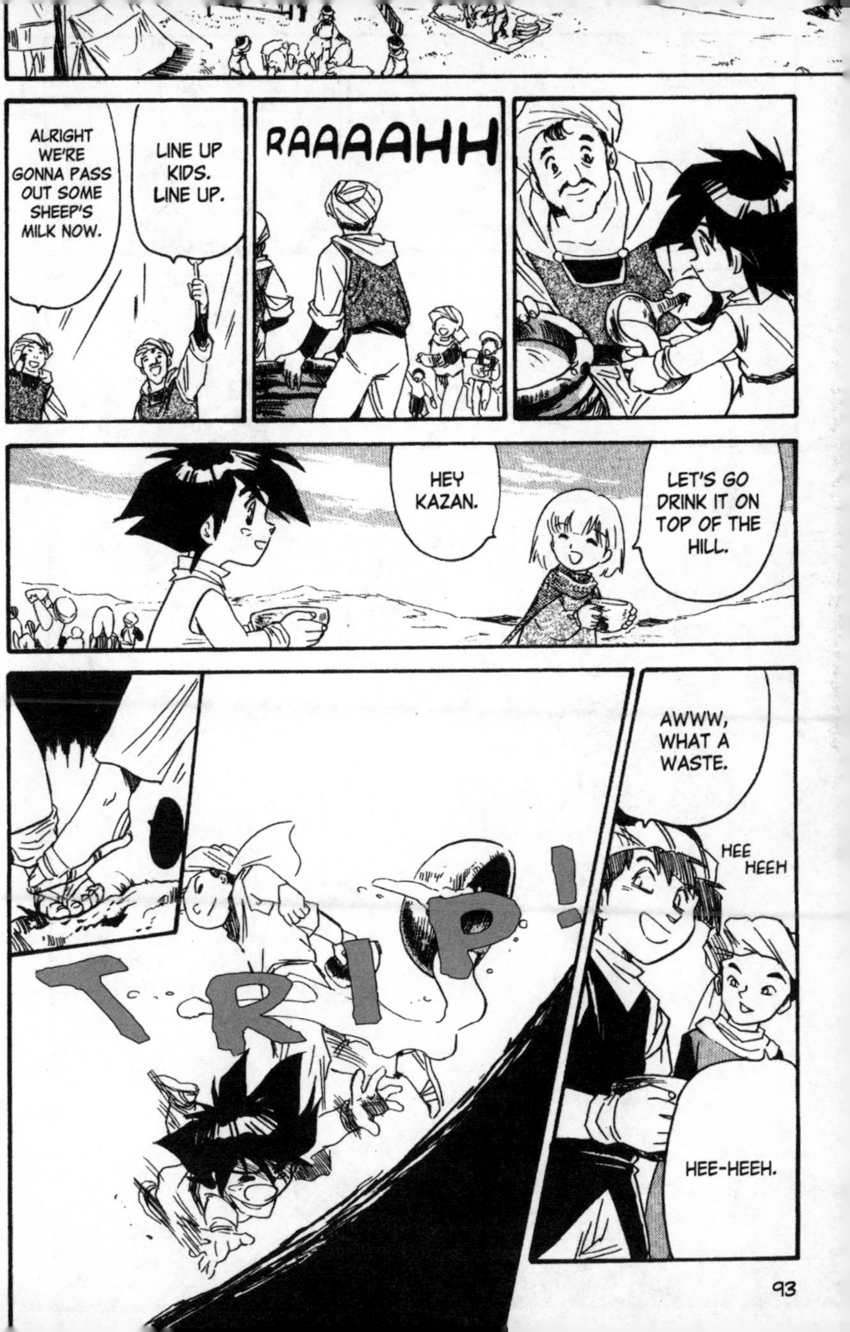
ALRIGHT WE'RE GONNA PASS OUT SOME SHEEP'S MILK NOW.
LINE UP KIDS. LINE UP.
RAAAAHH
HEY KAZAN.
LET'S GO DRINK IT ON TOP OF THE HILL.
AWWW, WHAT A WASTE.
HEE HEEH
HEE-HEEH.
TRIP!

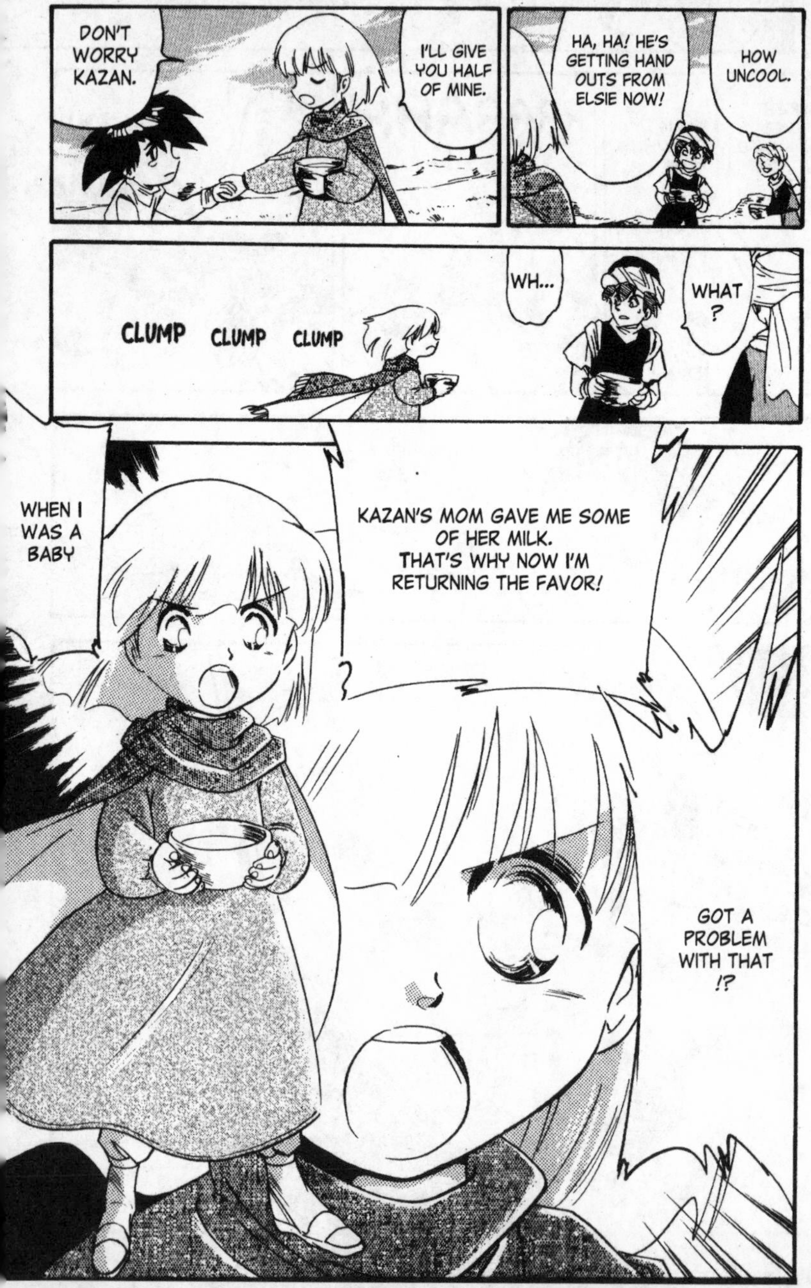

DON'T WORRY KAZAN.
I'LL GIVE YOU HALF OF MINE.
HA, HA! HE'S GETTING HAND OUTS FROM ELSIE NOW!
HOW UNCOOL.
CLUMP CLUMP CLUMP
WH...
WHAT ?
WHEN I WAS A BABY
KAZAN'S MOM GAVE ME SOME OF HER MILK.
THAT'S WHY NOW I'M RETURNING THE FAVOR!
GOT A PROBLEM WITH THAT !?

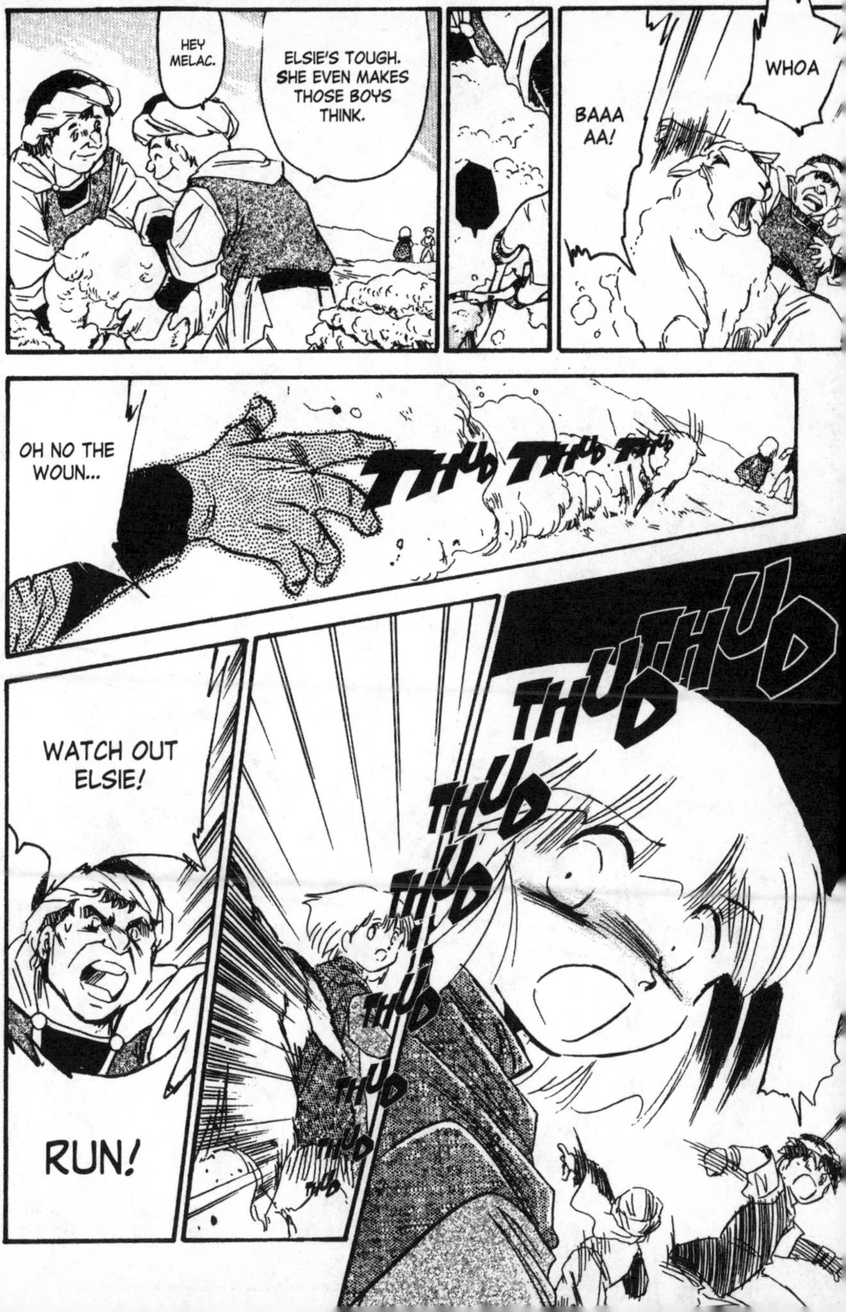
HEY MELAC.
ELSIE'S TOUGH. SHE EVEN MAKES THOSE BOYS THINK.
BAAA AA!
WHOA
OH NO THE WOUN...
THUD THUD THUD
WATCH OUT ELSIE!
RUN!
THUD THUD THUD THUD THUD THUD THUD THUD

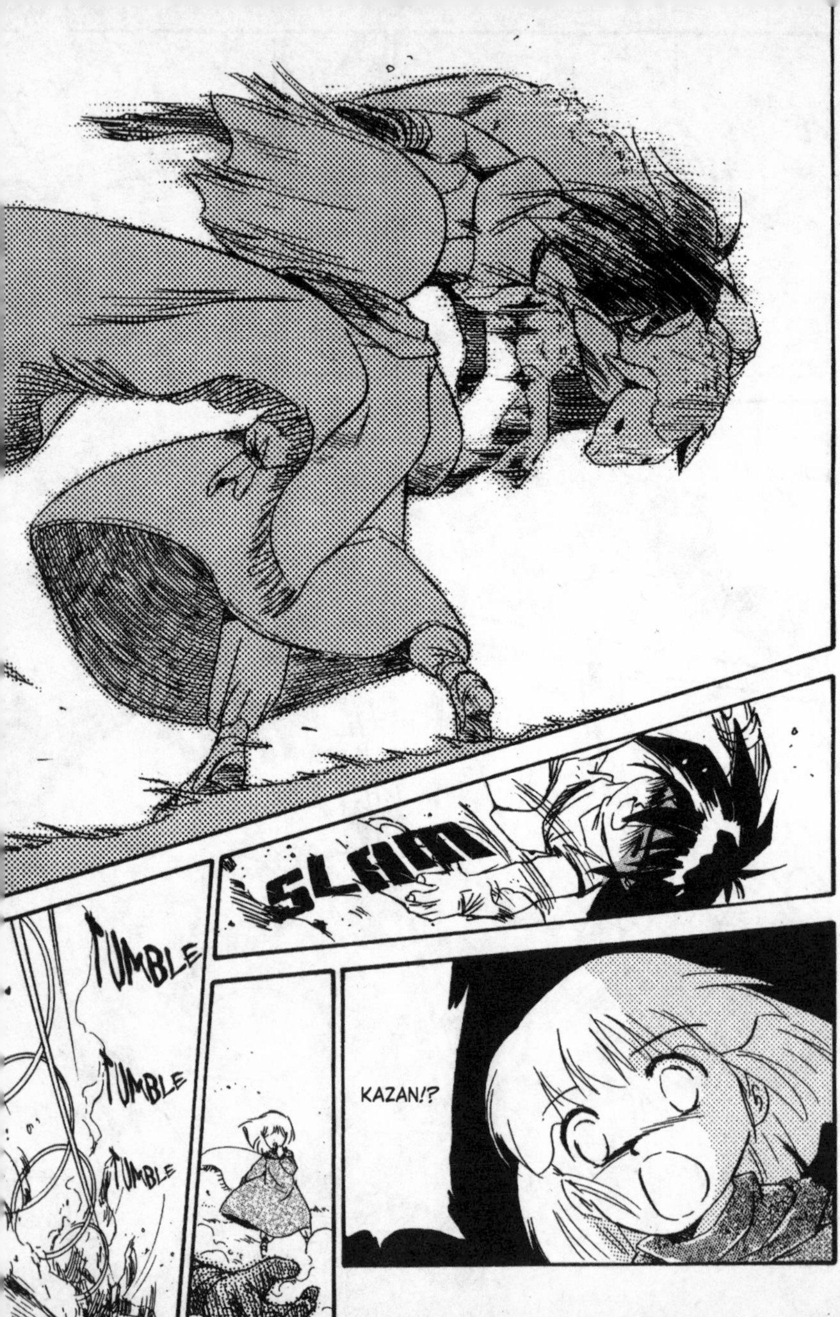
SLAM
TUMBLE
TUMBLE
TUMBLE
KAZAN!?

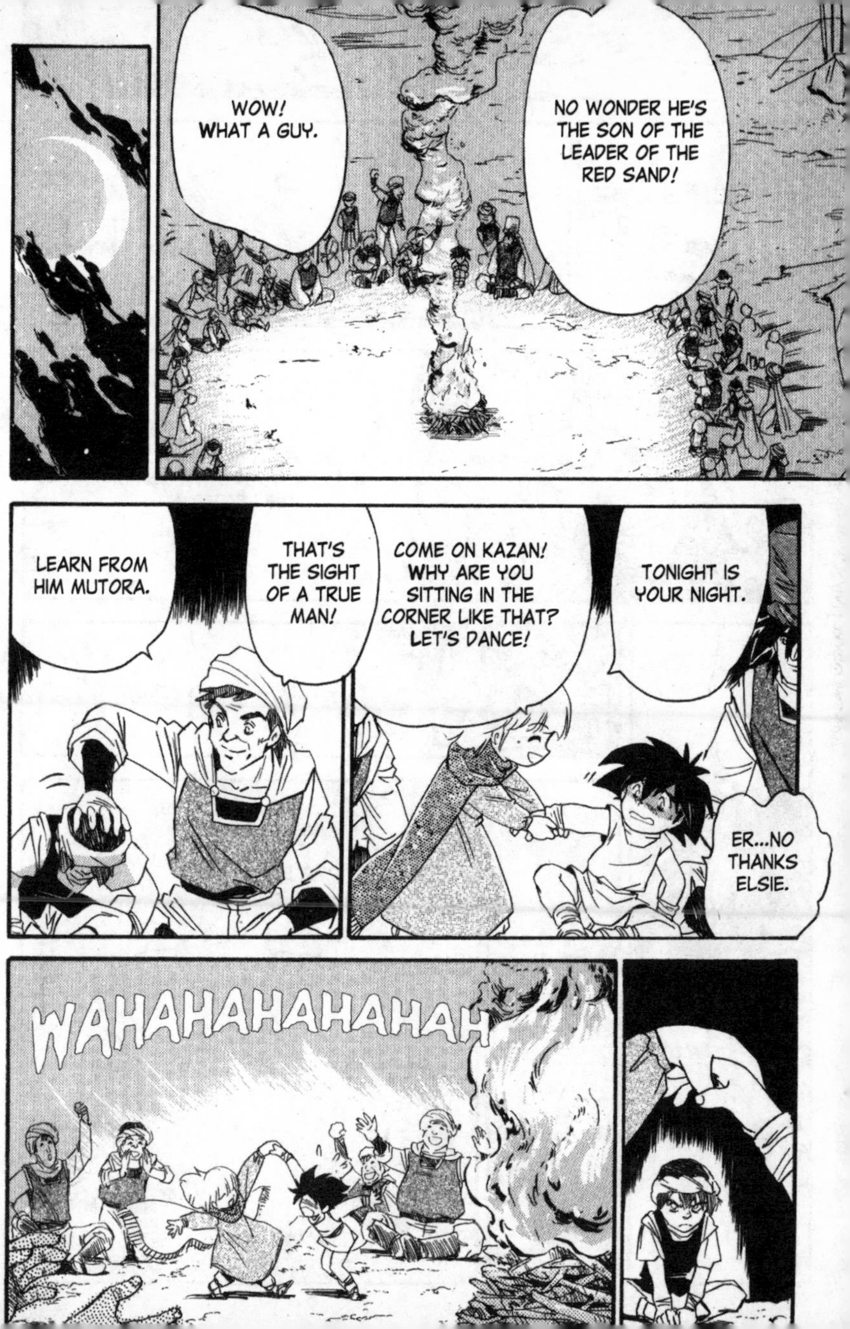
WOW! WHAT A GUY.
NO WONDER HE'S THE SON OF THE LEADER OF THE RED SAND!
LEARN FROM HIM MUTORA.
THAT'S THE SIGHT OF A TRUE MAN!
COME ON KAZAN! WHY ARE YOU SITTING IN THE CORNER LIKE THAT? LET'S DANCE!
TONIGHT IS YOUR NIGHT.
ER...NO THANKS ELSIE.
WAHAHAHAHAHAHAH

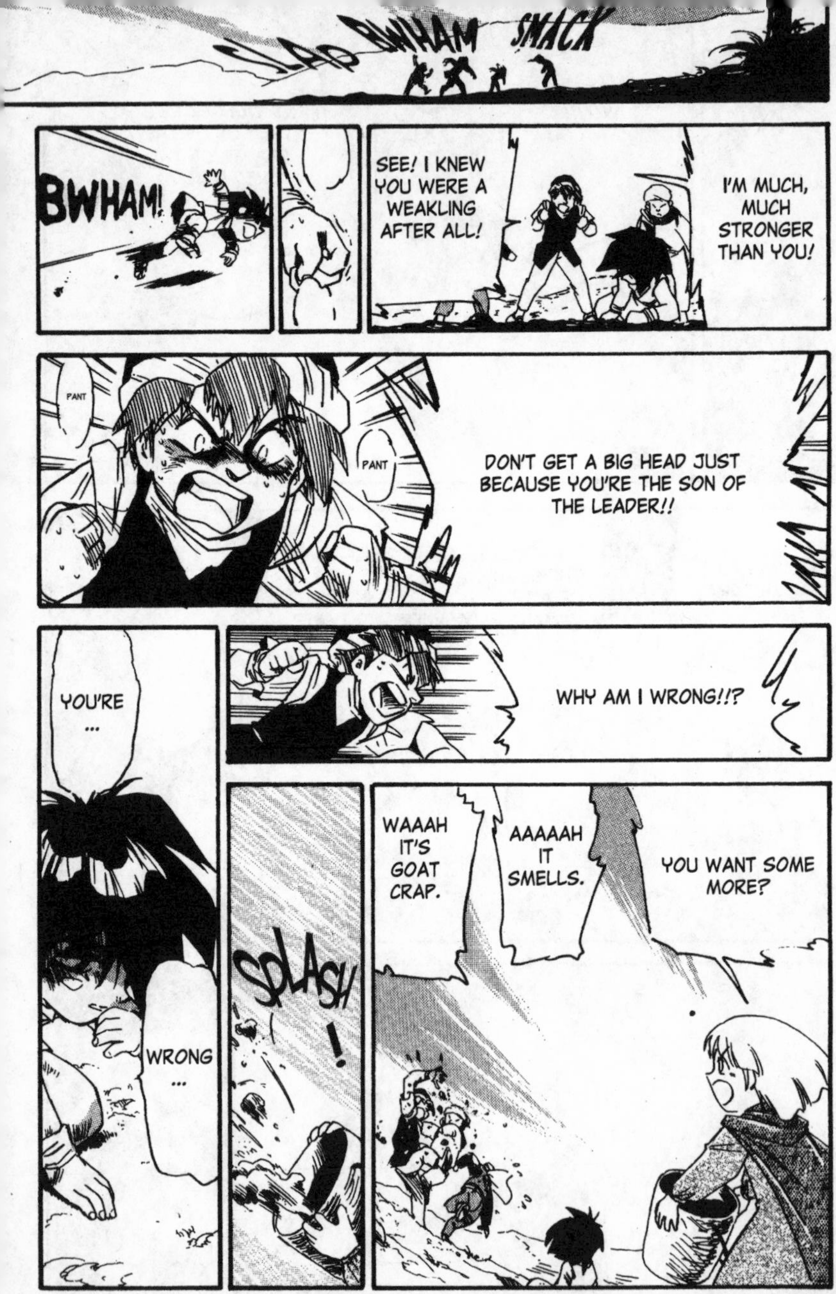

SLAP
BWHAM
SMACK
BWHAM!
SEE! I KNEW YOU WERE A WEAKLING AFTER ALL!
I'M MUCH, MUCH STRONGER THAN YOU!
PANT
PANT
DON'T GET A BIG HEAD JUST BECAUSE YOU'RE THE SON OF THE LEADER!!
YOU'RE ...
WHY AM I WRONG!!?
WRONG ...
SPLASH !
WAAAH IT'S GOAT CRAP.
AAAAAH IT SMELLS.
YOU WANT SOME MORE?

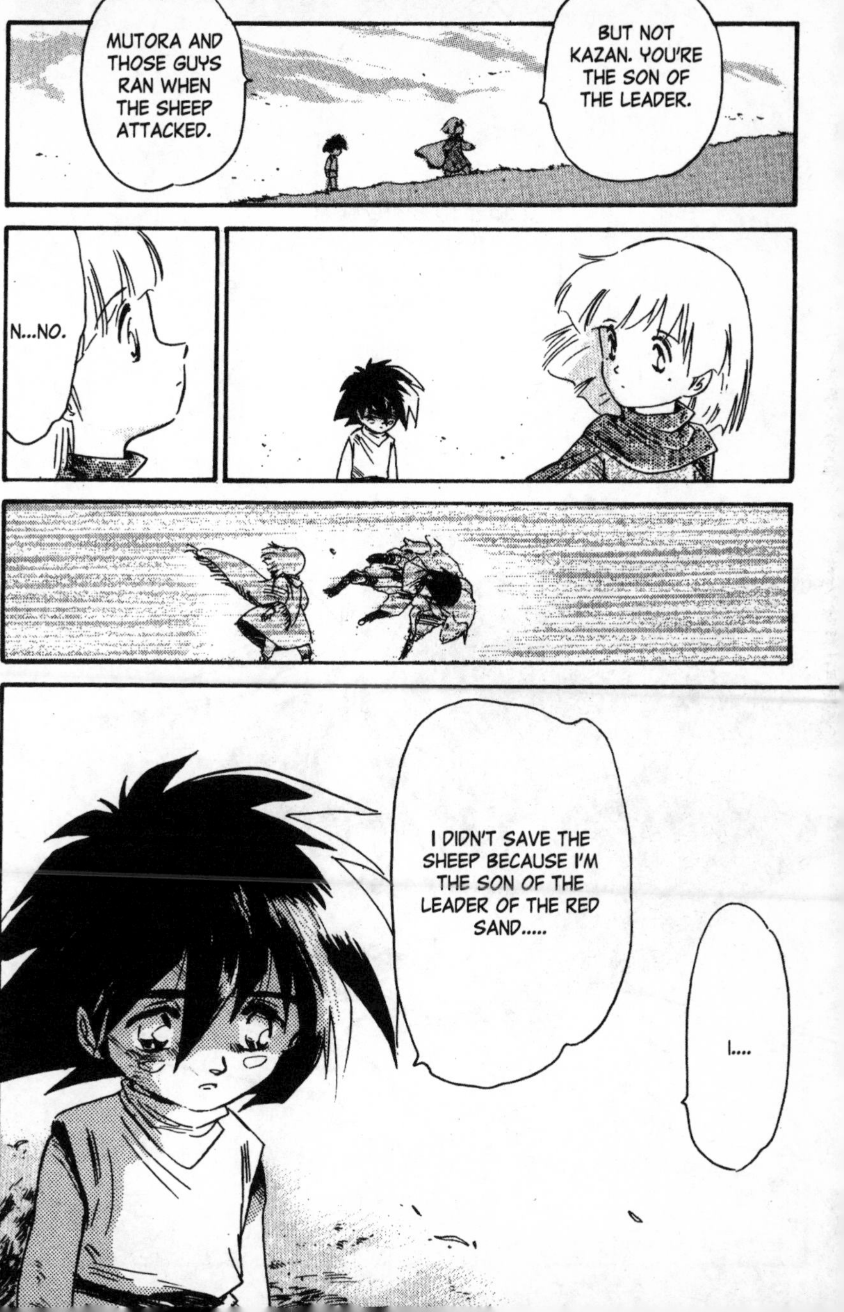

MUTORA AND THOSE GUYS RAN WHEN THE SHEEP ATTACKED.
BUT NOT KAZAN. YOU'RE THE SON OF THE LEADER.
N...NO.
I DIDN'T SAVE THE SHEEP BECAUSE I'M THE SON OF THE LEADER OF THE RED SAND.....
I....

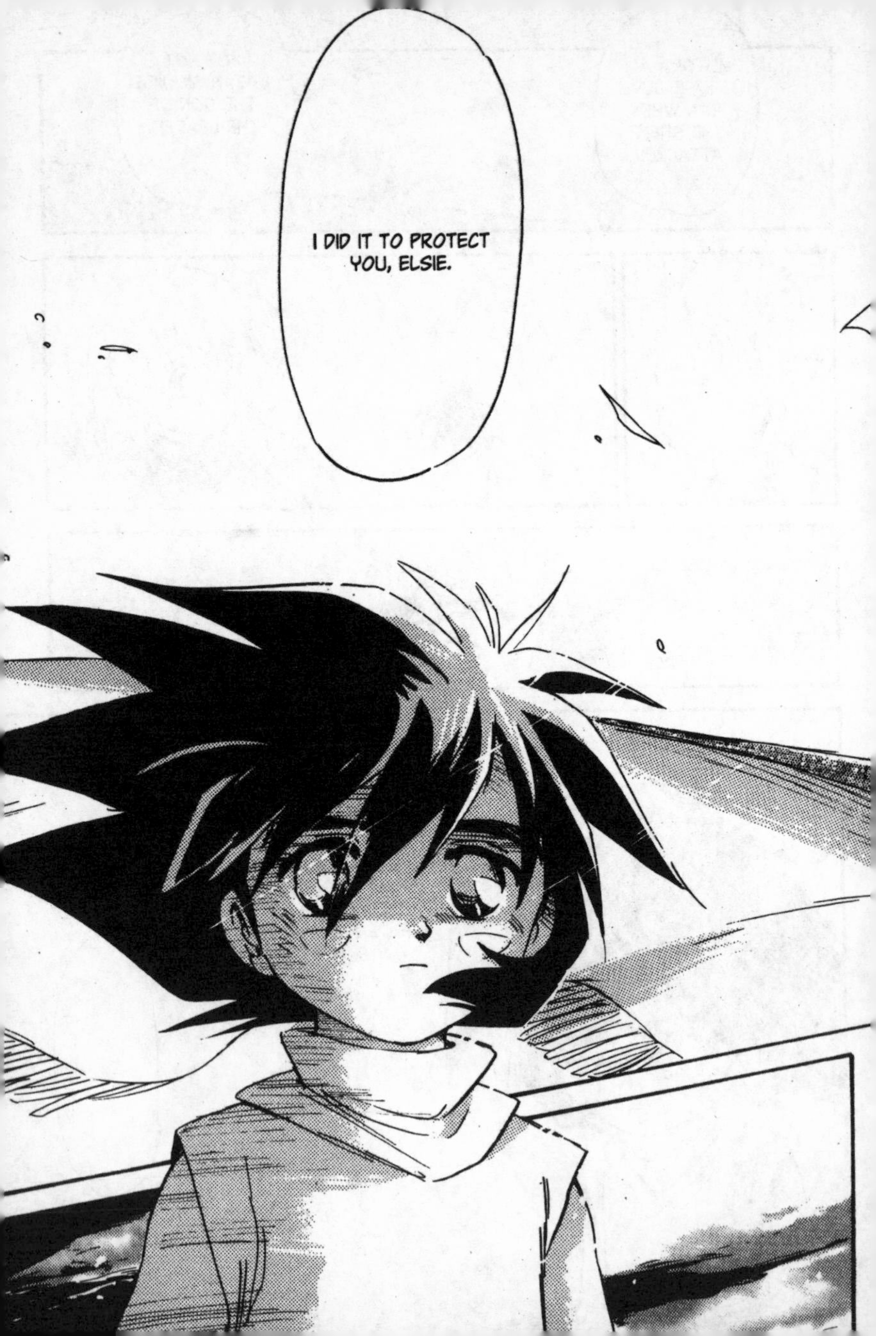
I DID IT TO PROTECT YOU, ELSIE.

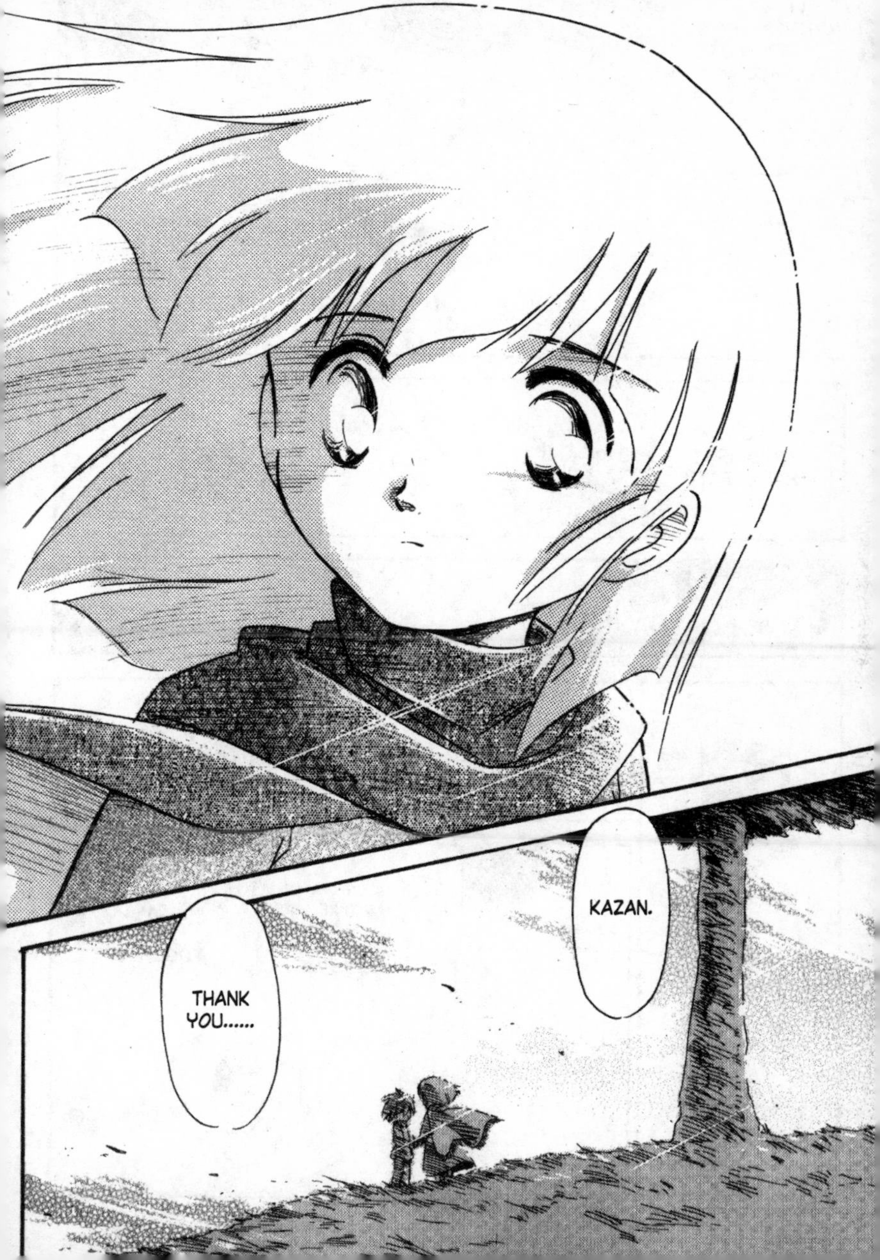
KAZAN.
THANK YOU......

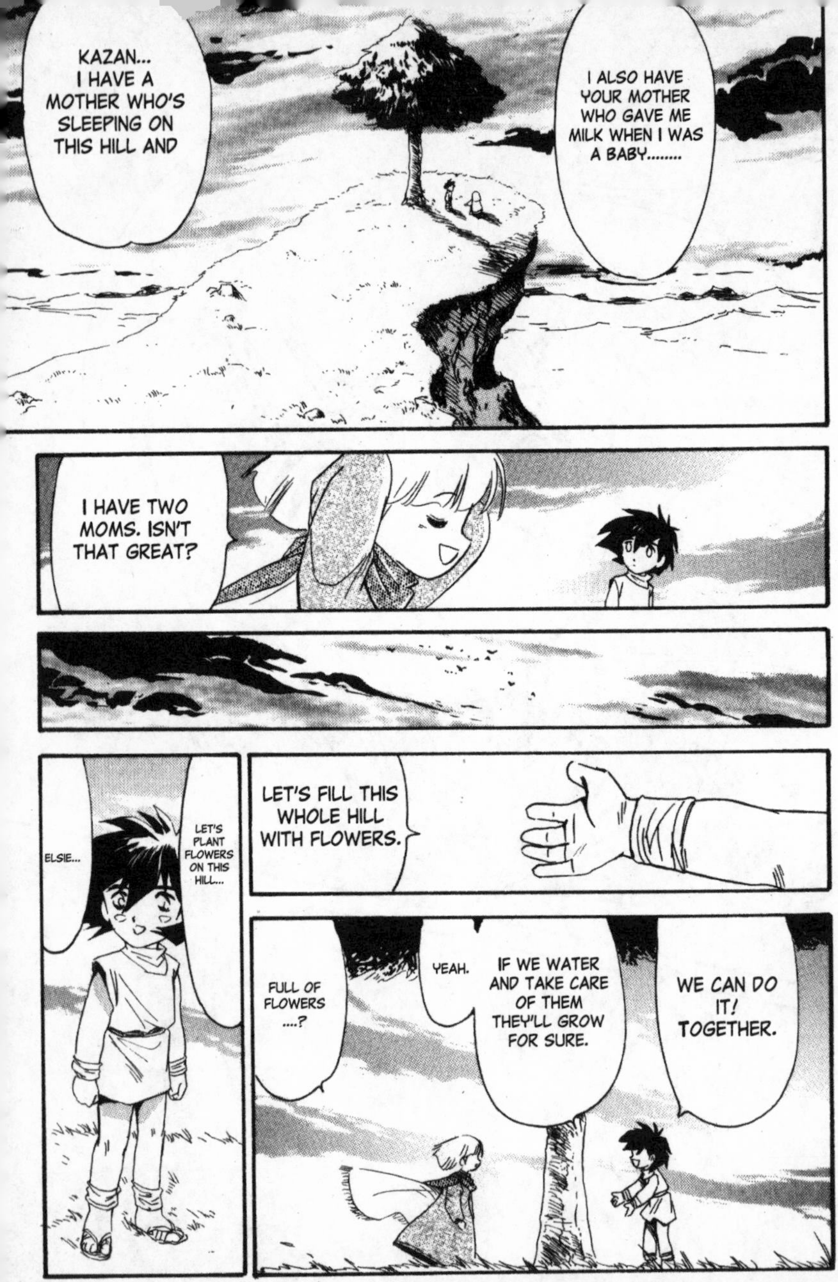
KAZAN... I HAVE A MOTHER WHO'S SLEEPING ON THIS HILL AND
I ALSO HAVE YOUR MOTHER WHO GAVE ME MILK WHEN I WAS A BABY........
I HAVE TWO MOMS. ISN'T THAT GREAT?
LET'S FILL THIS WHOLE HILL WITH FLOWERS.
LET'S PLANT FLOWERS ON THIS HILL...
ELSIE...
WE CAN DO IT! TOGETHER.
IF WE WATER AND TAKE CARE OF THEM THEY'LL GROW FOR SURE.
YEAH.
FULL OF FLOWERS ....?

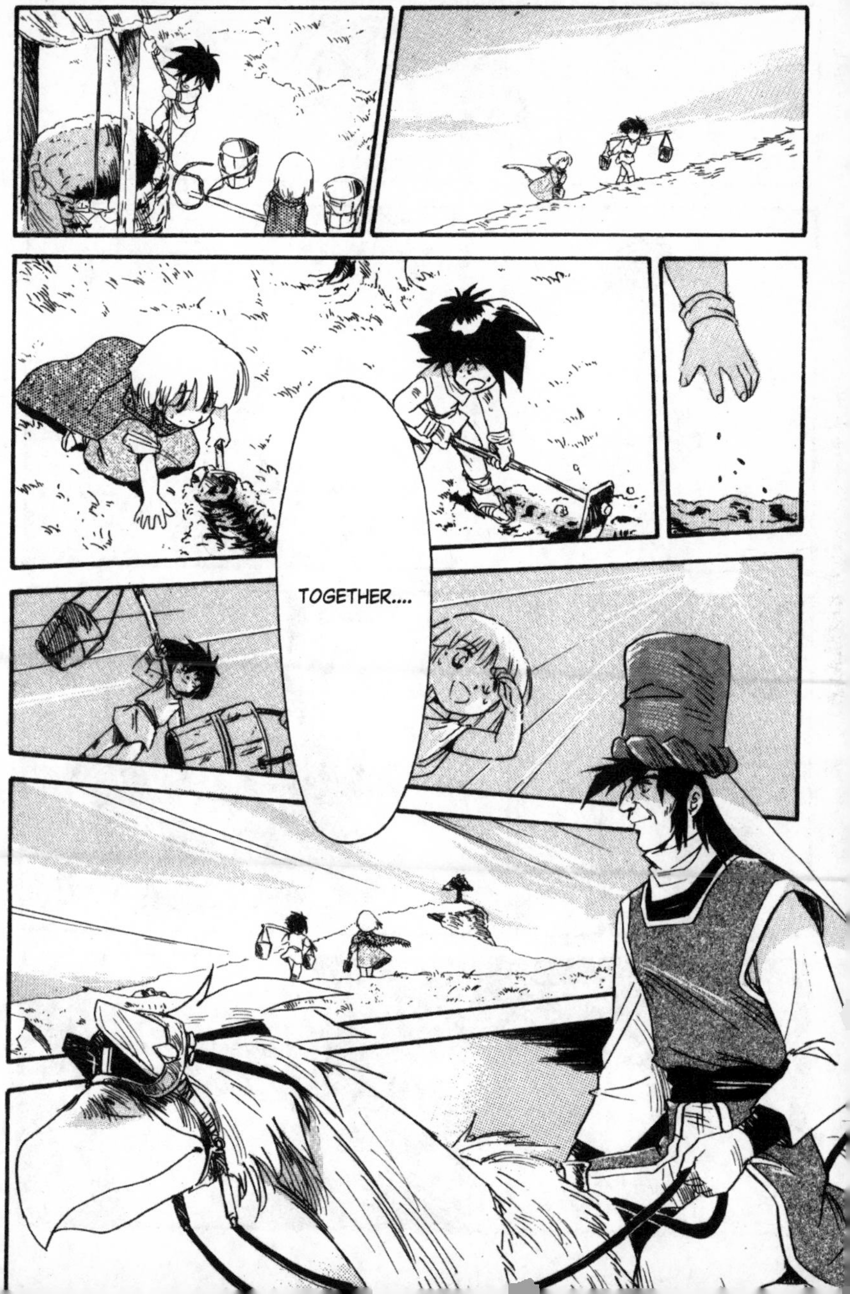
TOGETHER....

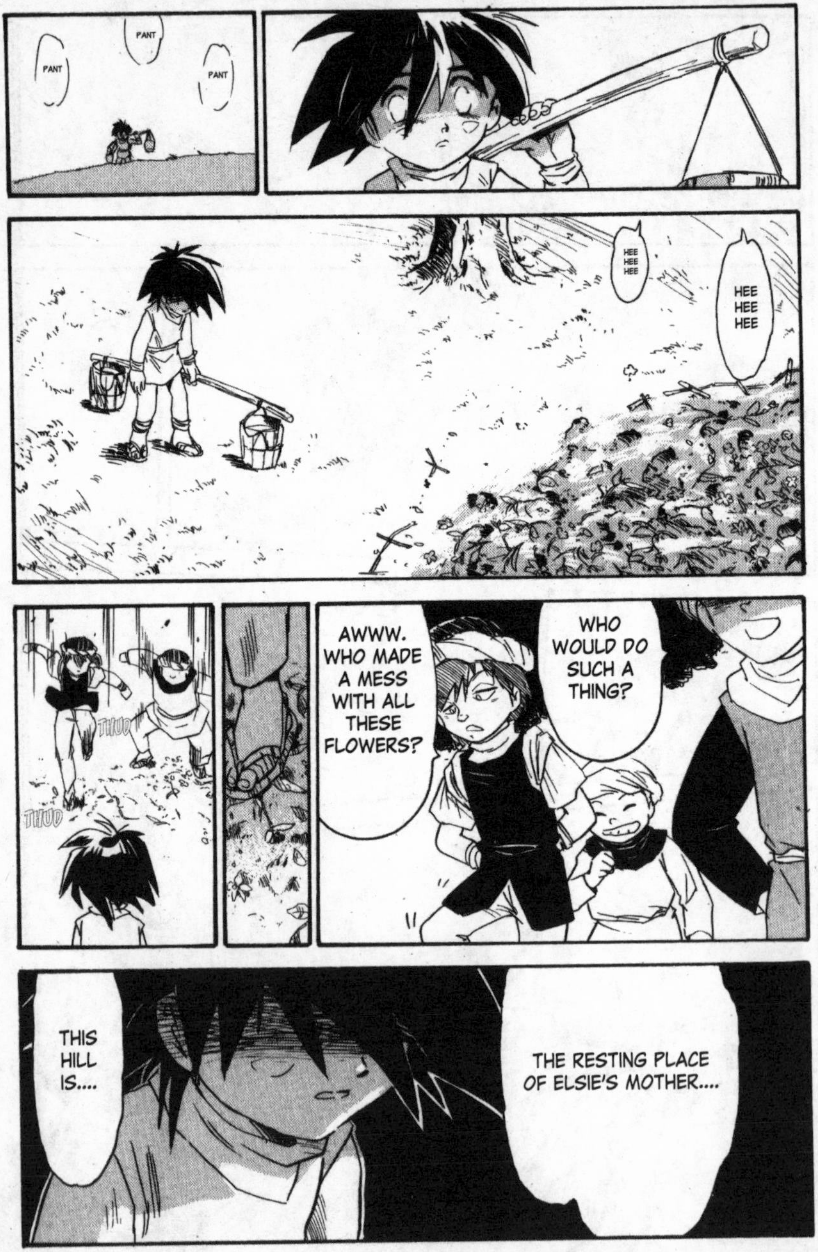
PANT
PANT
PANT
HEE HEE HEE
HEE HEE HEE
THUD
THUD
AWWW. WHO MADE A MESS WITH ALL THESE FLOWERS?
WHO WOULD DO SUCH A THING?
THIS HILL IS....
THE RESTING PLACE OF ELSIE'S MOTHER....

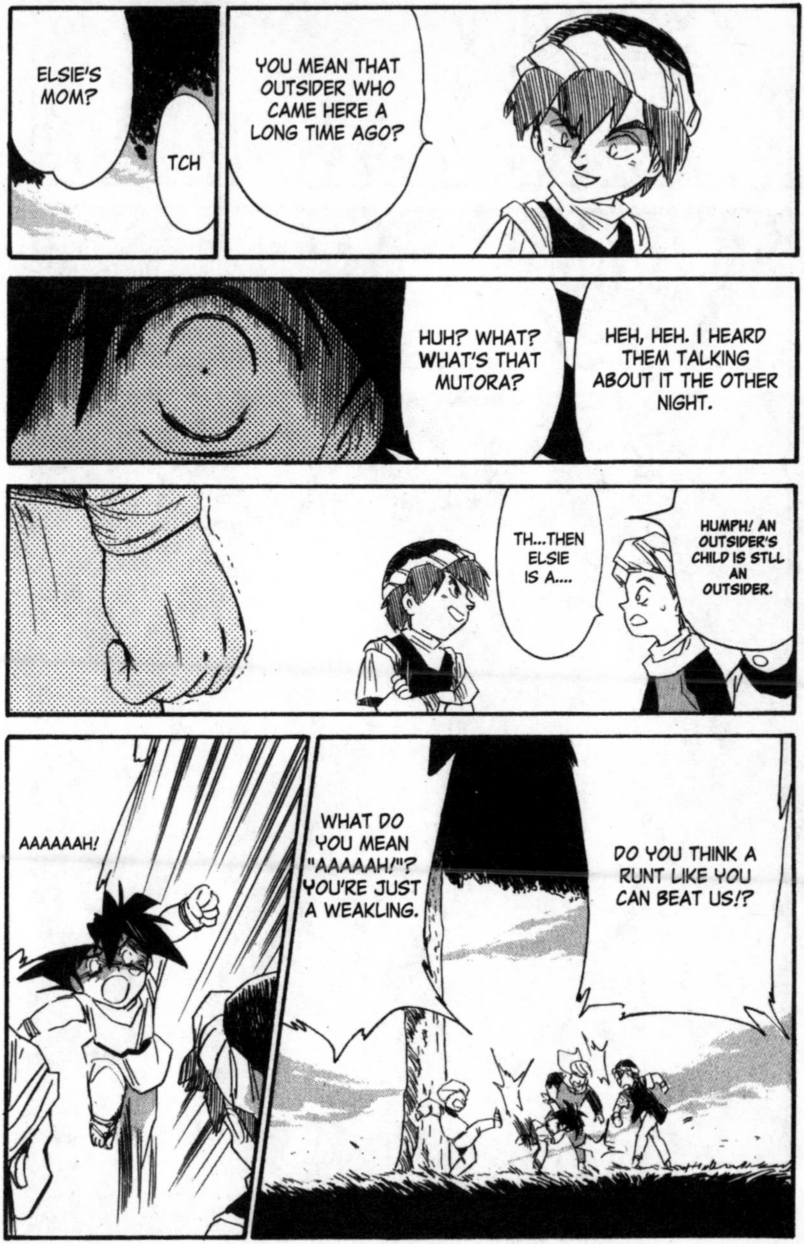

ELSIE'S MOM?
TCH
YOU MEAN THAT OUTSIDER WHO CAME HERE A LONG TIME AGO?
HUH? WHAT? WHAT'S THAT MUTORA?
HEH, HEH. I HEARD THEM TALKING ABOUT IT THE OTHER NIGHT.
TH...THEN ELSIE IS A....
HUMPH! AN OUTSIDER'S CHILD IS STLL AN OUTSIDER.
AAAAAAH!
WHAT DO YOU MEAN "AAAAAH!"? YOU'RE JUST A WEAKLING.
DO YOU THINK A RUNT LIKE YOU CAN BEAT US!?

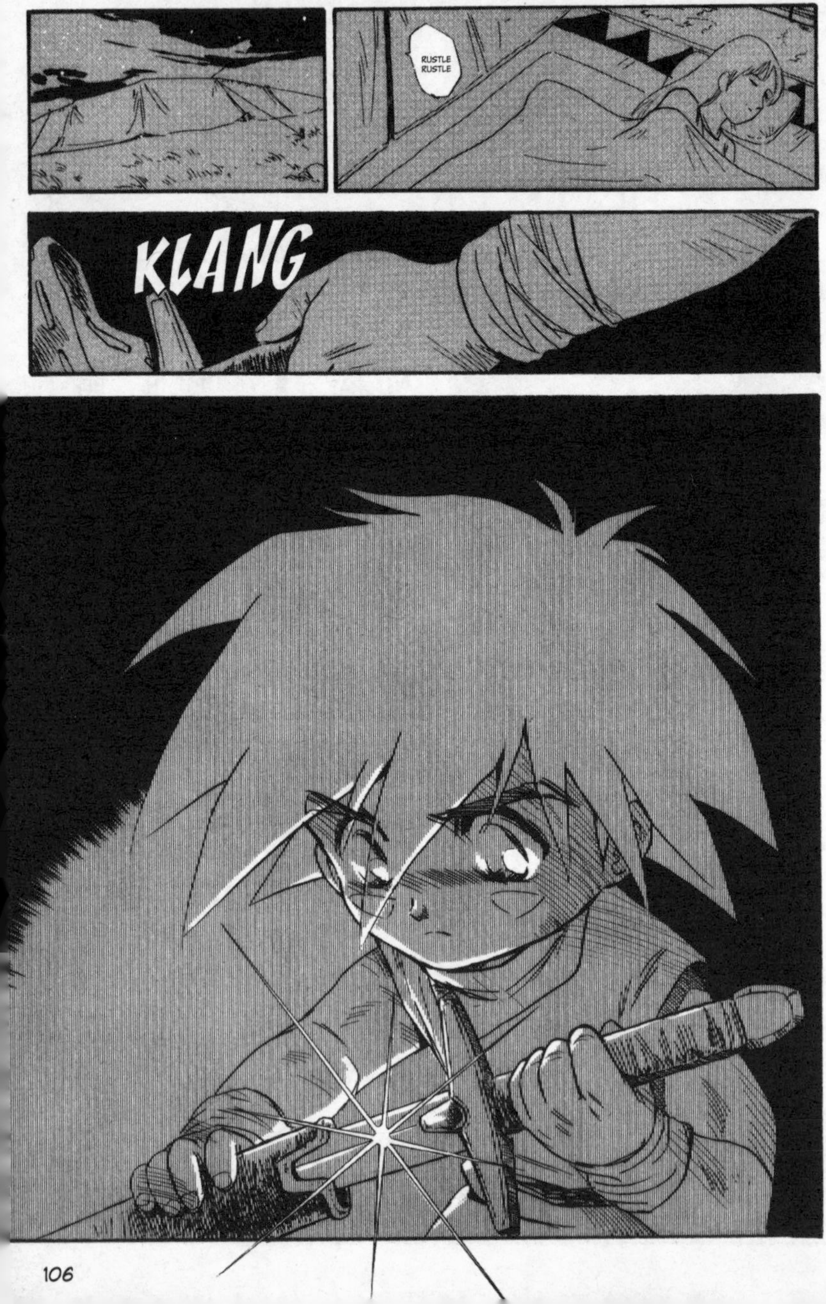
RUSTLE
RUSTLE
KLANG

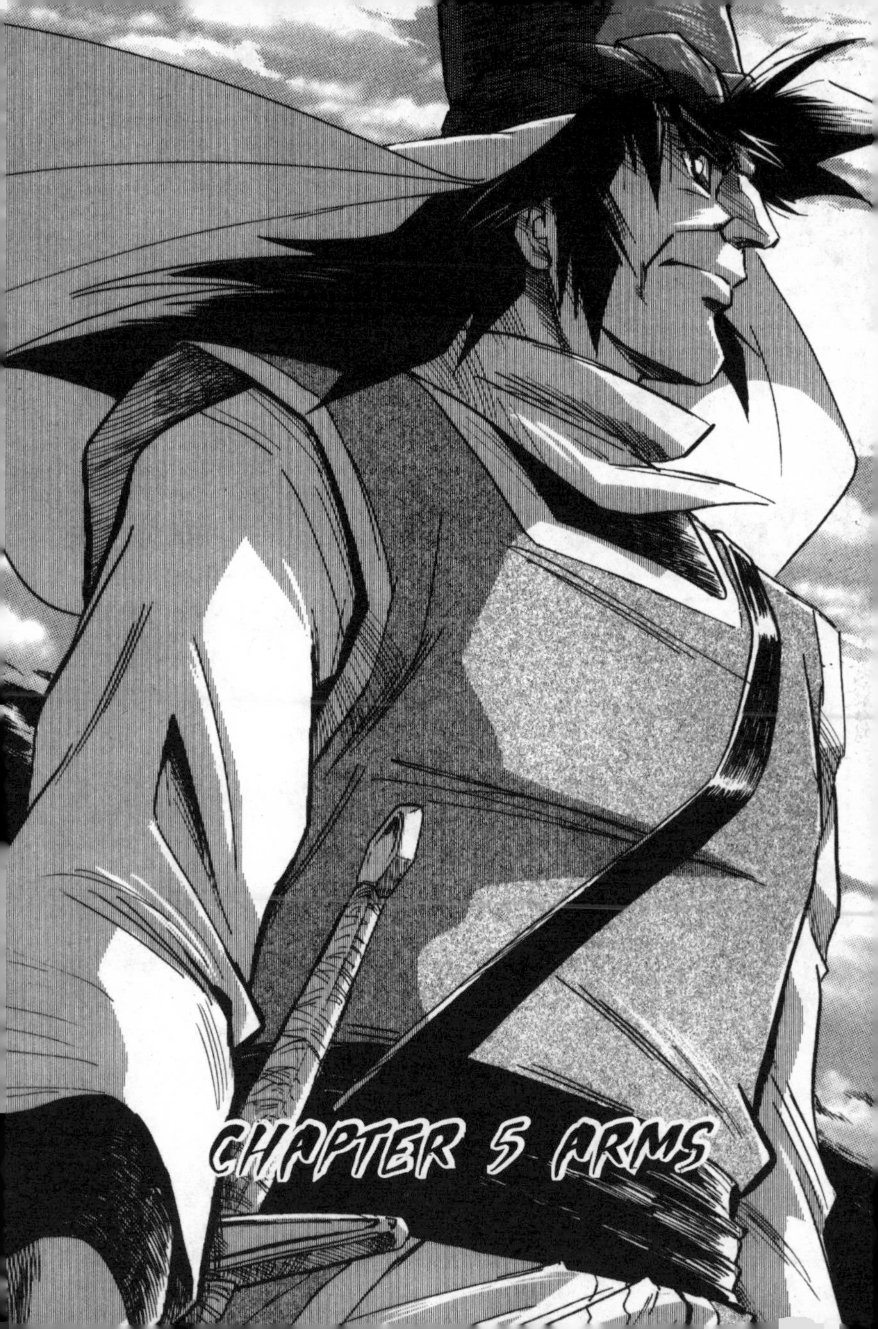
CHAPTER 5 ARMS

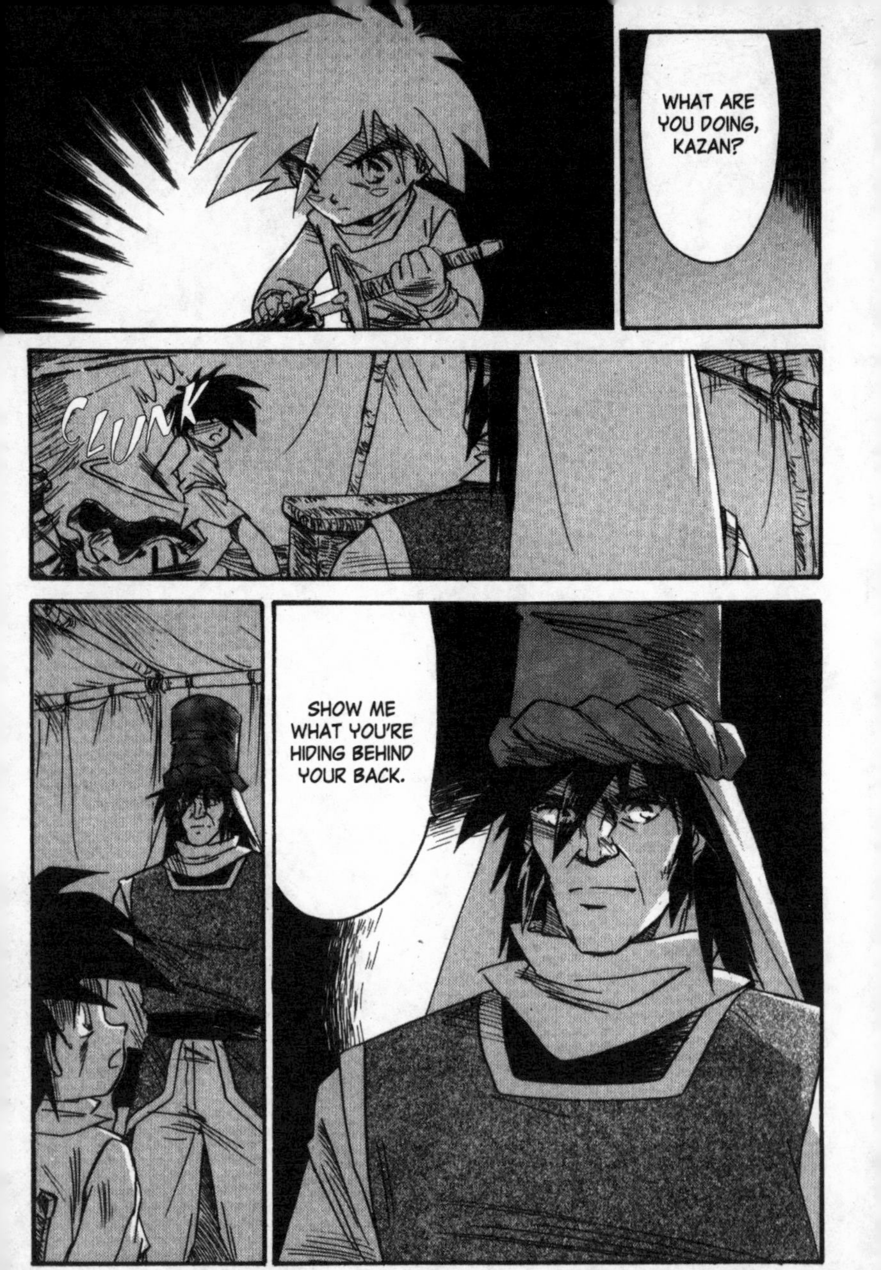
WHAT ARE YOU DOING, KAZAN?
CLUNK
SHOW ME WHAT YOU'RE HIDING BEHIND YOUR BACK.

SHAKE SHAKE SHAKE

D...DAD

PLEASE GIVE THIS...TO ME.

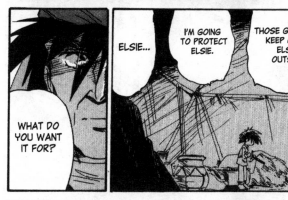

ELSIE...

I'M GOING TO PROTECT ELSIE.

THOSE GUYS...THEY KEEP CALLING ELSIE AN OUTSIDER...

WHAT DO YOU WANT IT FOR?

BECAUSE I'M

WEAK SO....

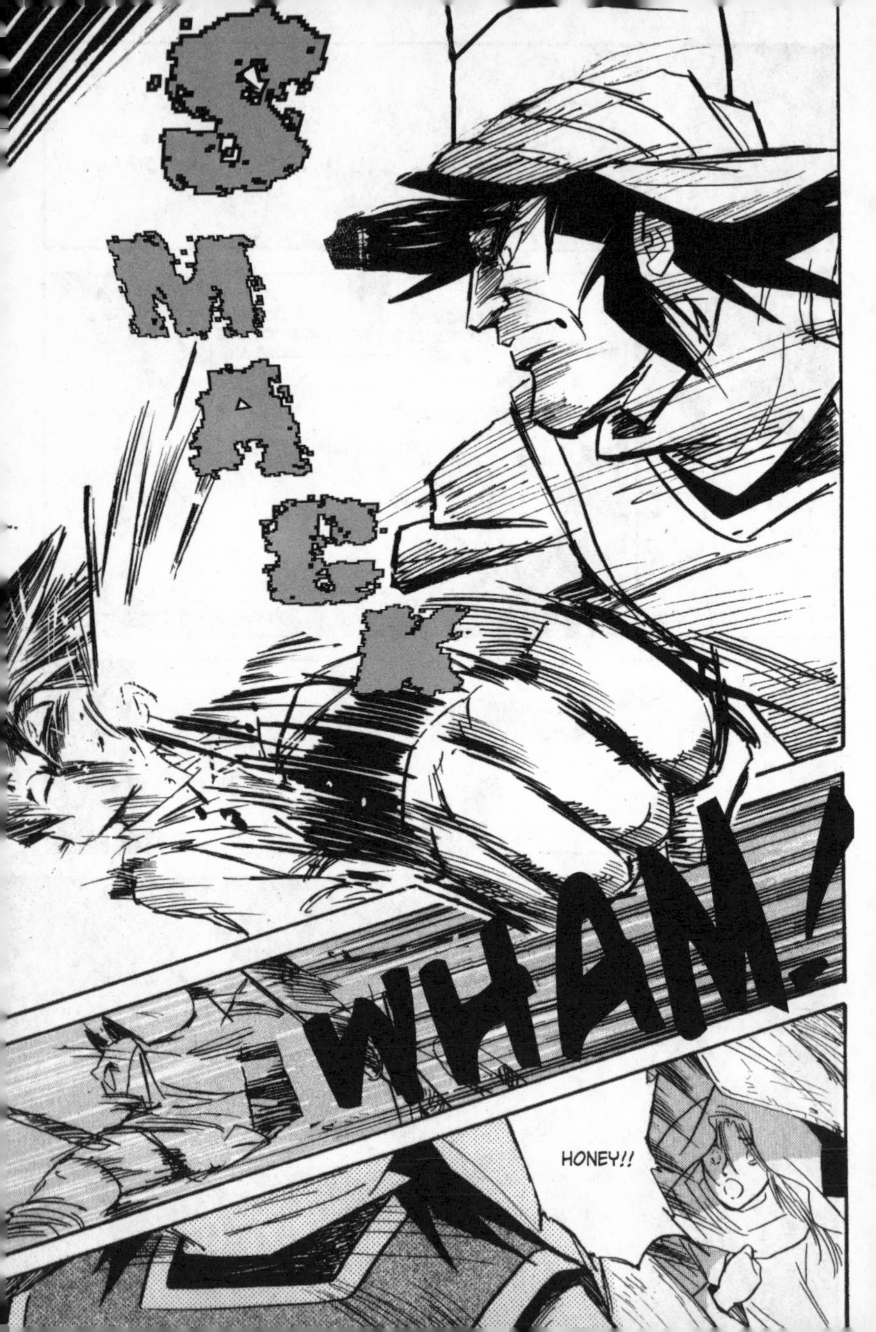
SMACK
WHAM!
HONEY!!

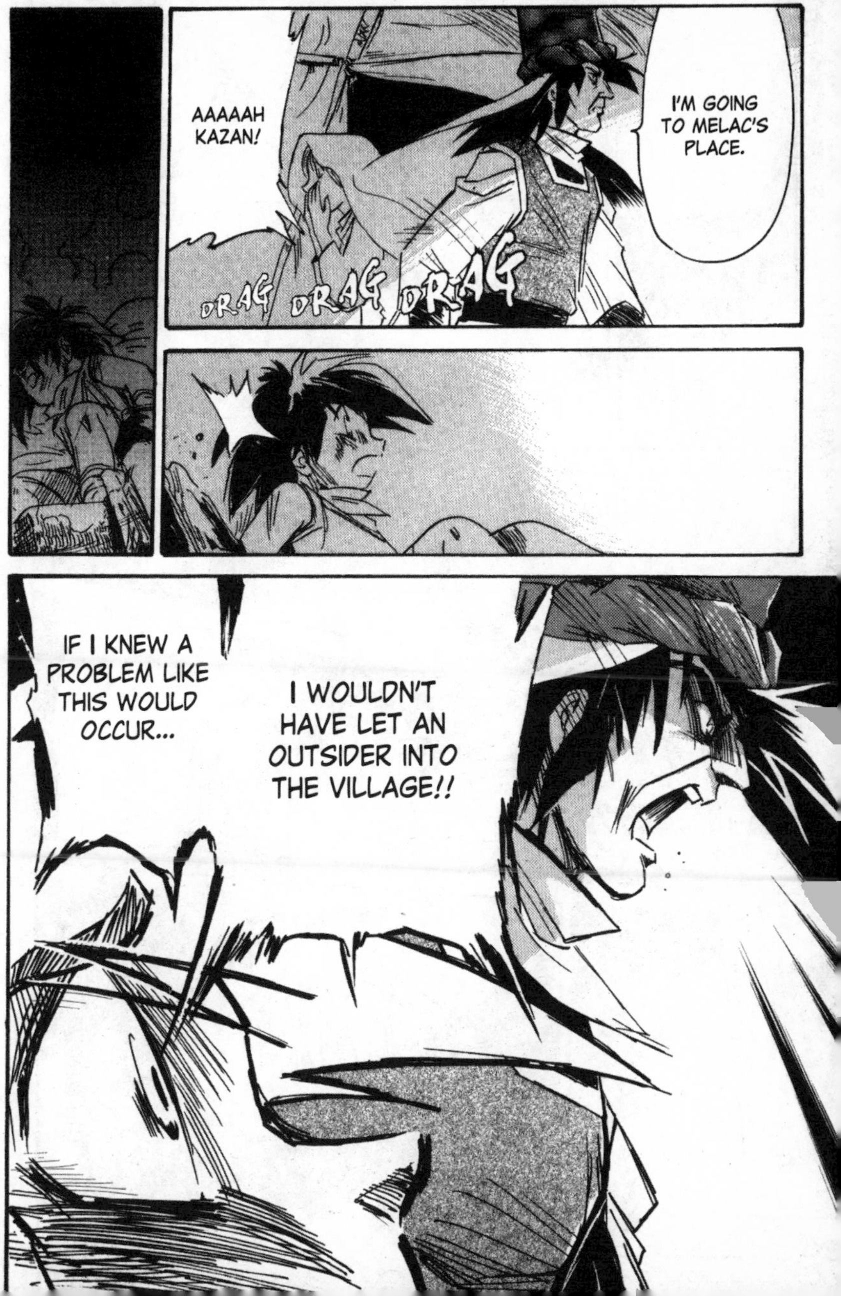
I'M GOING TO MELAC'S PLACE.
AAAAAH KAZAN!
DRAG DRAG DRAG
I WOULDN'T HAVE LET AN OUTSIDER INTO THE VILLAGE!!
IF I KNEW A PROBLEM LIKE THIS WOULD OCCUR...

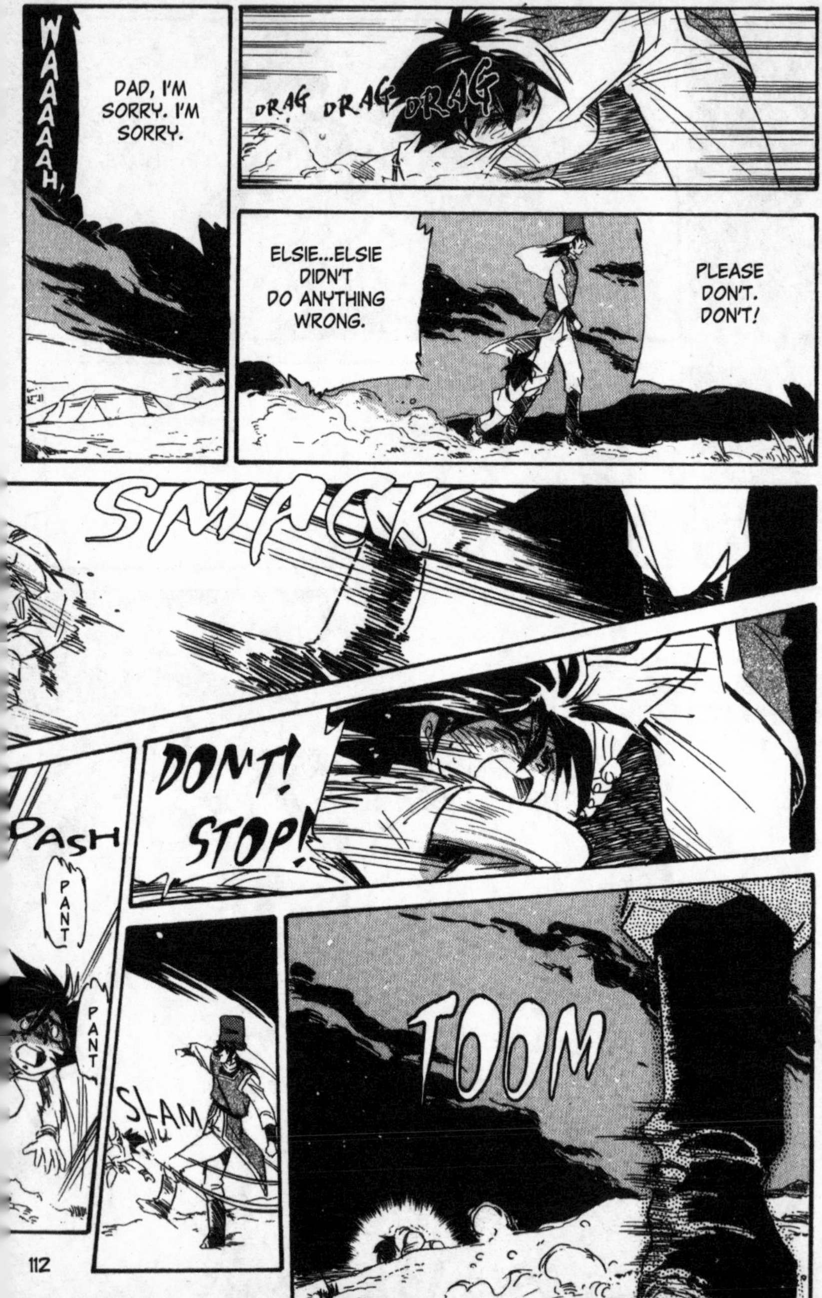
WAAAAAAH,
DAD, I'M SORRY. I'M SORRY.
DRAG DRAG DRAG
ELSIE...ELSIE DIDN'T DO ANYTHING WRONG.
PLEASE DON'T. DON'T!
SMACK
DON'T! STOP!
PASH
PANT
PANT
SLAM
TOOM

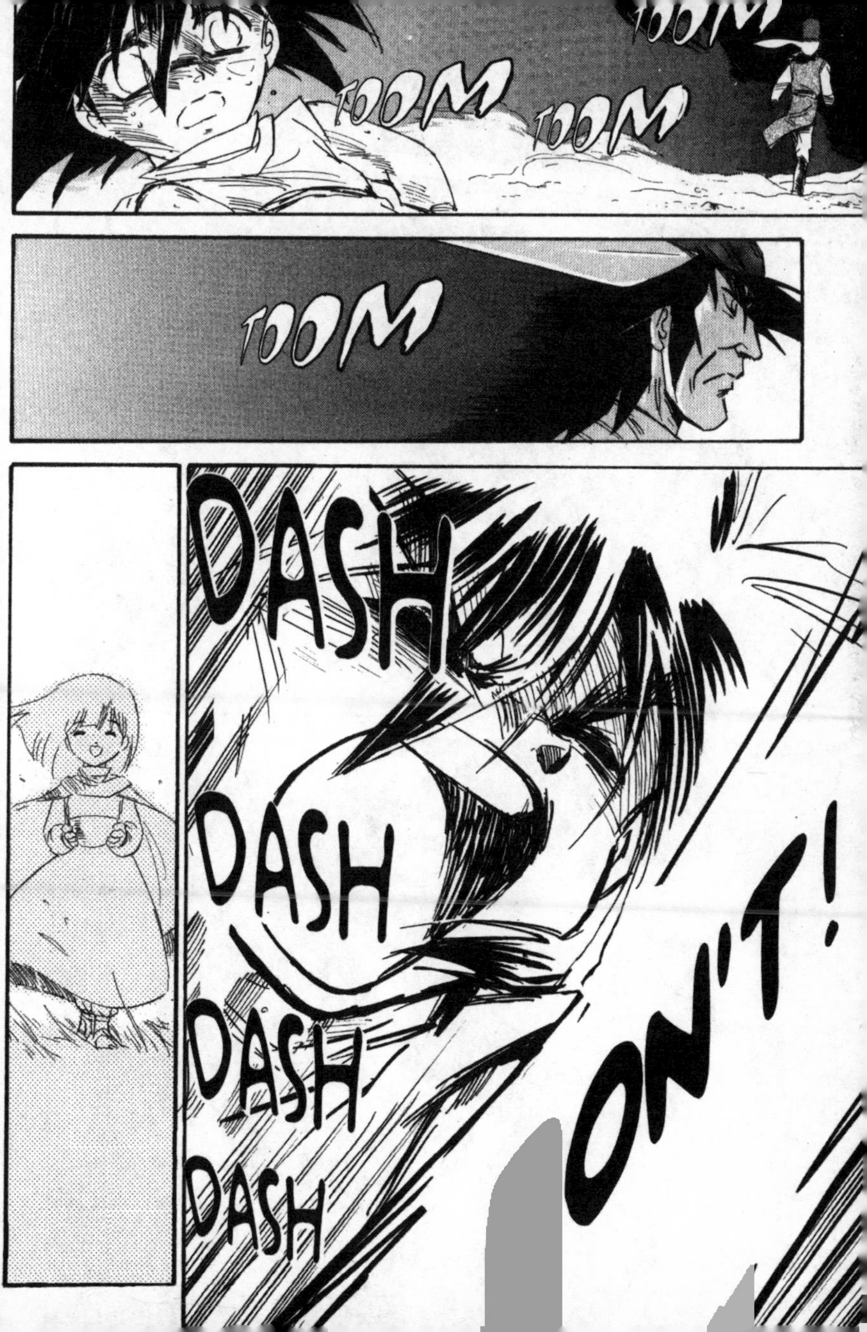
TOOM
TOOM
TOOM
TOOM
DASH
DASH
DASH
DASH
ON'T!

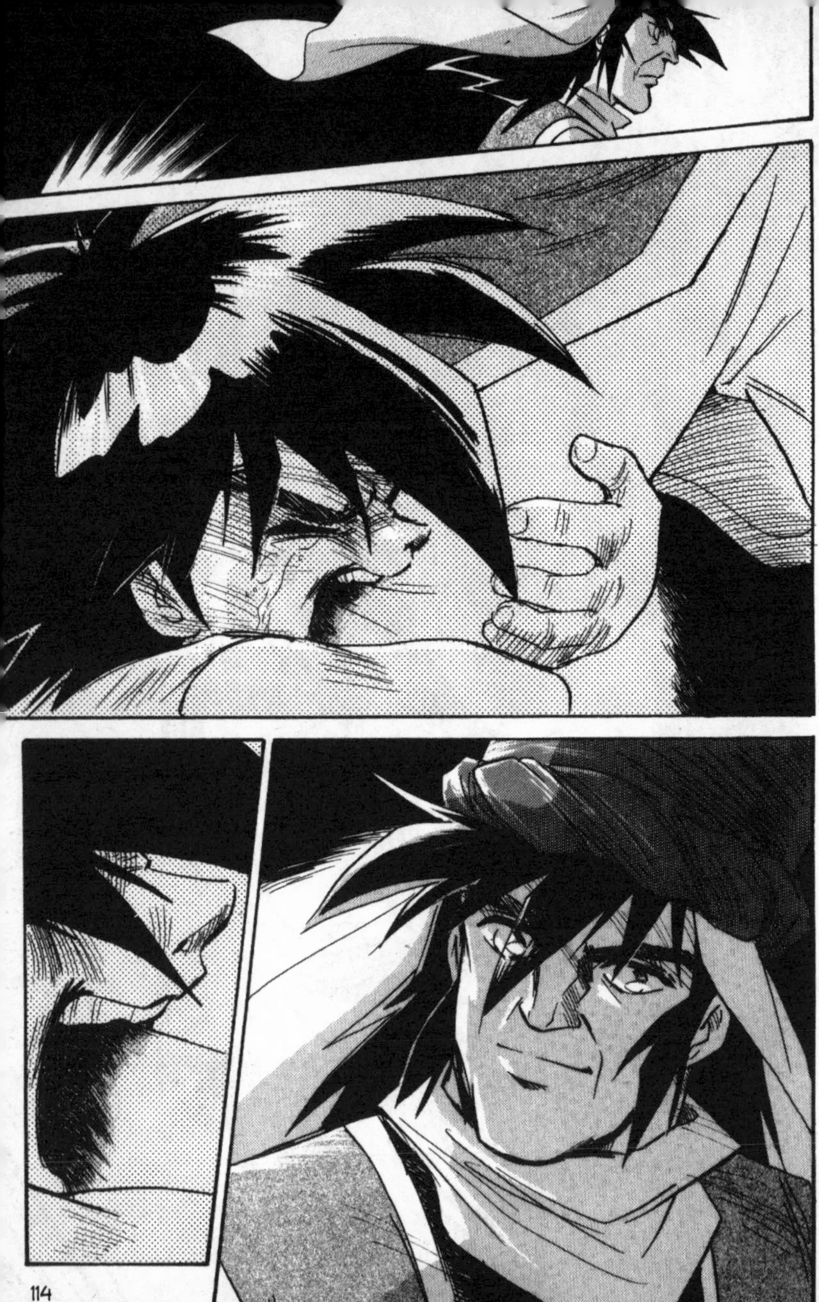

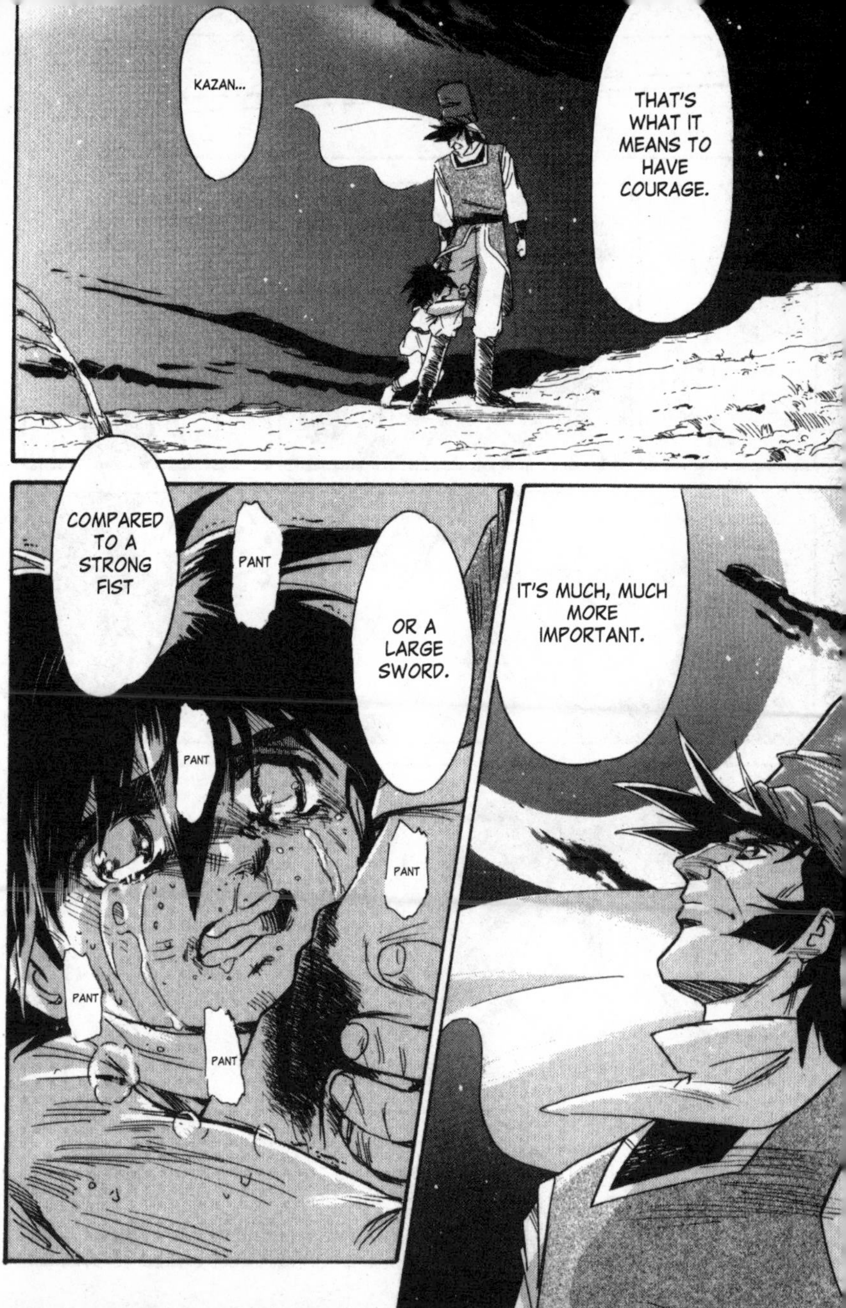
THAT'S WHAT IT MEANS TO HAVE COURAGE.
KAZAN...
COMPARED TO A STRONG FIST
PANT
OR A LARGE SWORD.
PANT
PANT
PANT
PANT
IT'S MUCH, MUCH MORE IMPORTANT.

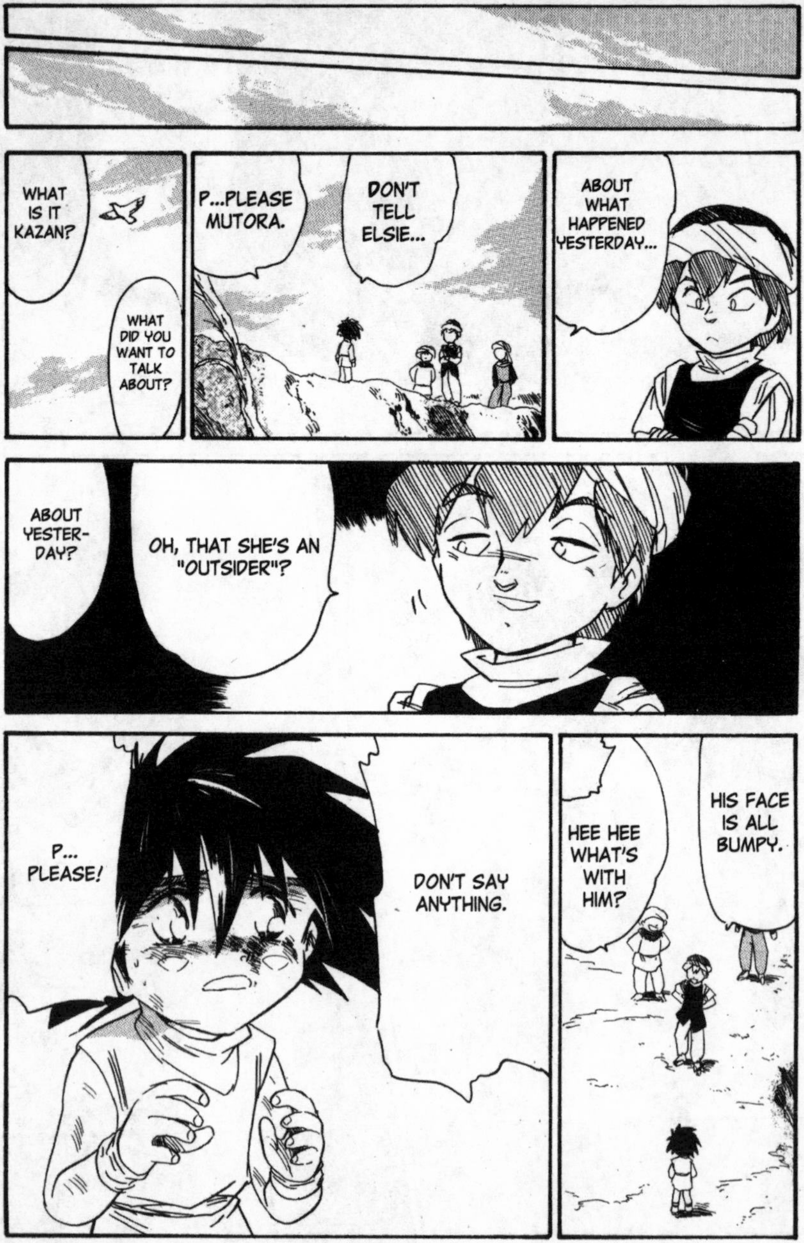
WHAT IS IT KAZAN?
WHAT DID YOU WANT TO TALK ABOUT?
P...PLEASE MUTORA.
DON'T TELL ELSIE...
ABOUT WHAT HAPPENED YESTERDAY...
ABOUT YESTER-DAY?
OH, THAT SHE'S AN "OUTSIDER"?
P... PLEASE!
DON'T SAY ANYTHING.
HEE HEE WHAT'S WITH HIM?
HIS FACE IS ALL BUMPY.

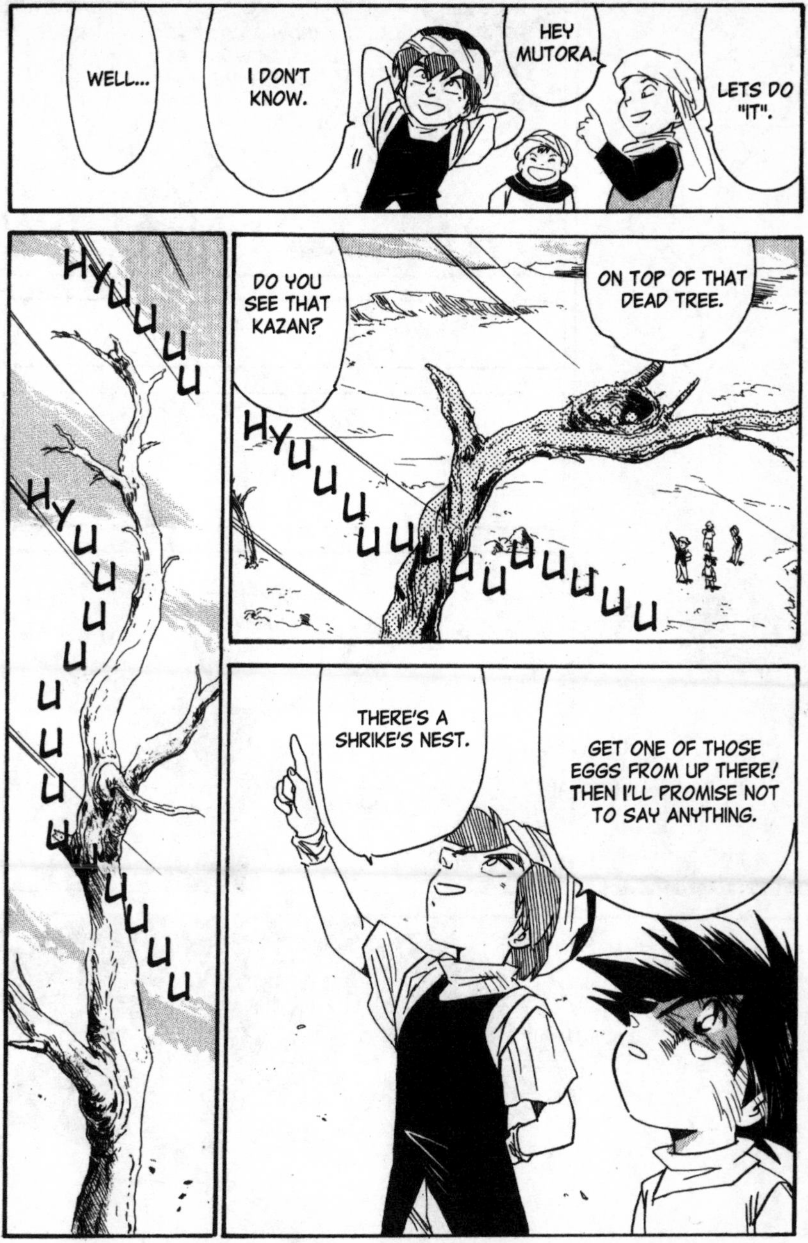
LETS DO "IT".
HEY MUTORA.
I DON'T KNOW.
WELL...
DO YOU SEE THAT KAZAN?
ON TOP OF THAT DEAD TREE.
HYUUUUUUUUUUUUUUUU
HYUUUUU
HYUUUUUUUUUUUUUU
THERE'S A SHRIKE'S NEST.
GET ONE OF THOSE EGGS FROM UP THERE! THEN I'LL PROMISE NOT TO SAY ANYTHING.

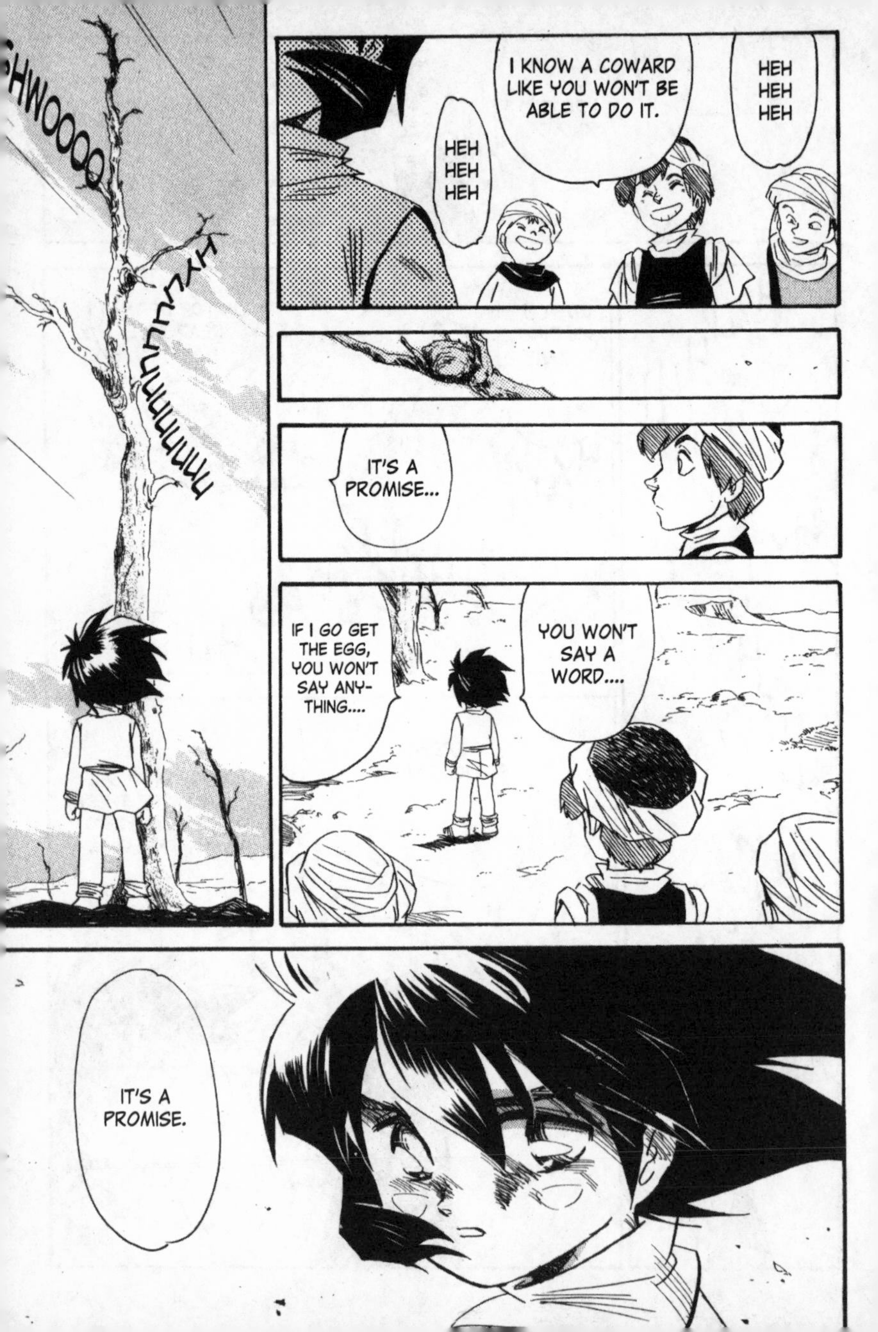
SHWOOOOO
HYUNNNNNNNNNNN
HEH HEH HEH
I KNOW A COWARD LIKE YOU WON'T BE ABLE TO DO IT.
HEH HEH HEH
IT'S A PROMISE...
IF I GO GET THE EGG, YOU WON'T SAY ANY-THING....
YOU WON'T SAY A WORD....
IT'S A PROMISE.

H..HEY MUTORA, HE'S REALLY CLIMBING IT.

WH..WHAT ARE WE GONNA DO?

ZAP

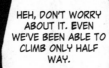

HEH, DON'T WORRY ABOUT IT. EVEN WE'VE BEEN ABLE TO CLIMB ONLY HALF WAY.

SOONER OR LATER HE'LL START CRYING.

DASH

PANT

PANT

PANT

ARE YOU GUYS PICKING ON KAZAN AGAIN!?

WHOA ELSIE, THAT'S WHERE YOU'RE WRONG.

IT WAS HIS IDEA TO GO GET THE SHRIKE'S EGG.

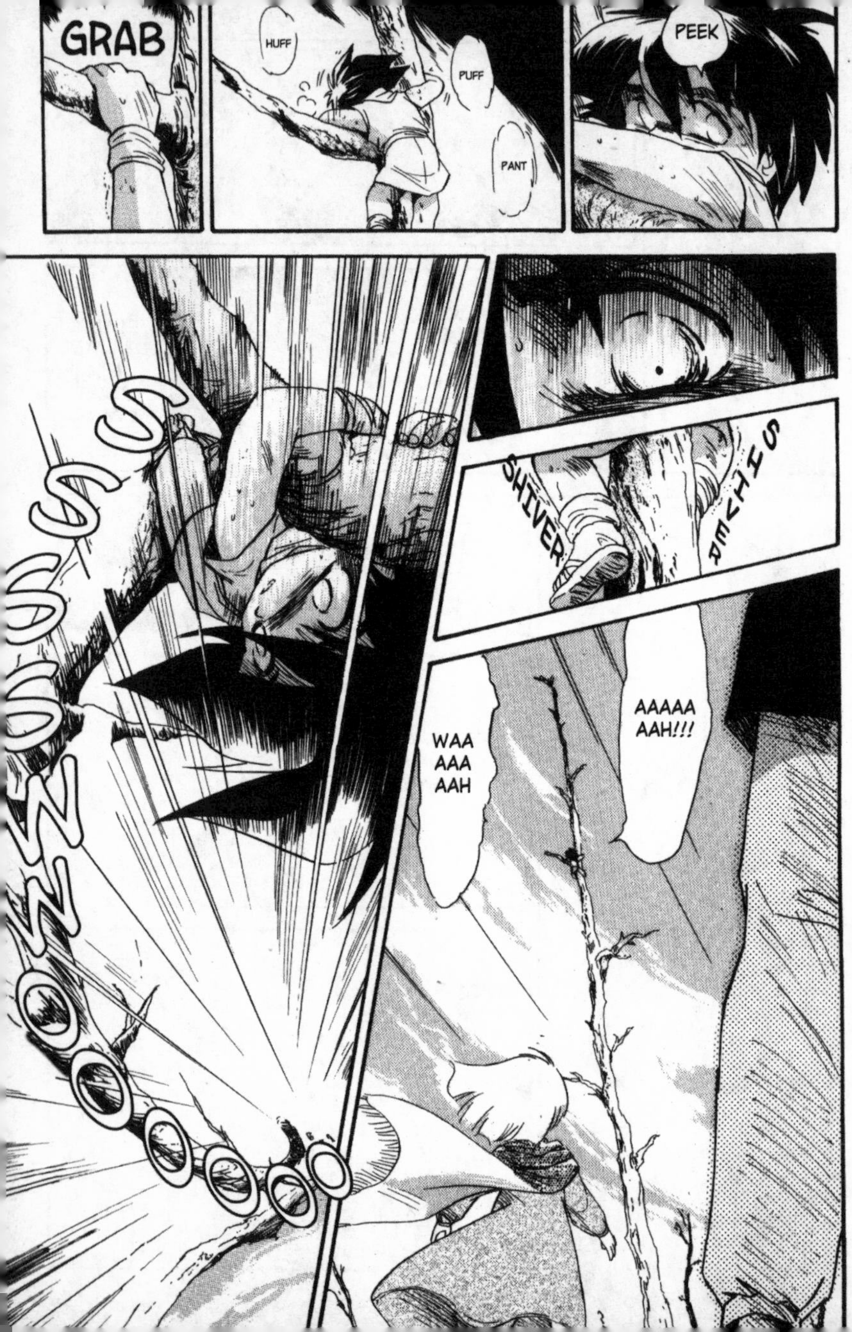
PEEK
HUFF
PUFF
PANT
GRAB
SHIVER
SHIVER
AAAAA AAH!!!
WAA AAA AAH
SSSSWOOOOOO

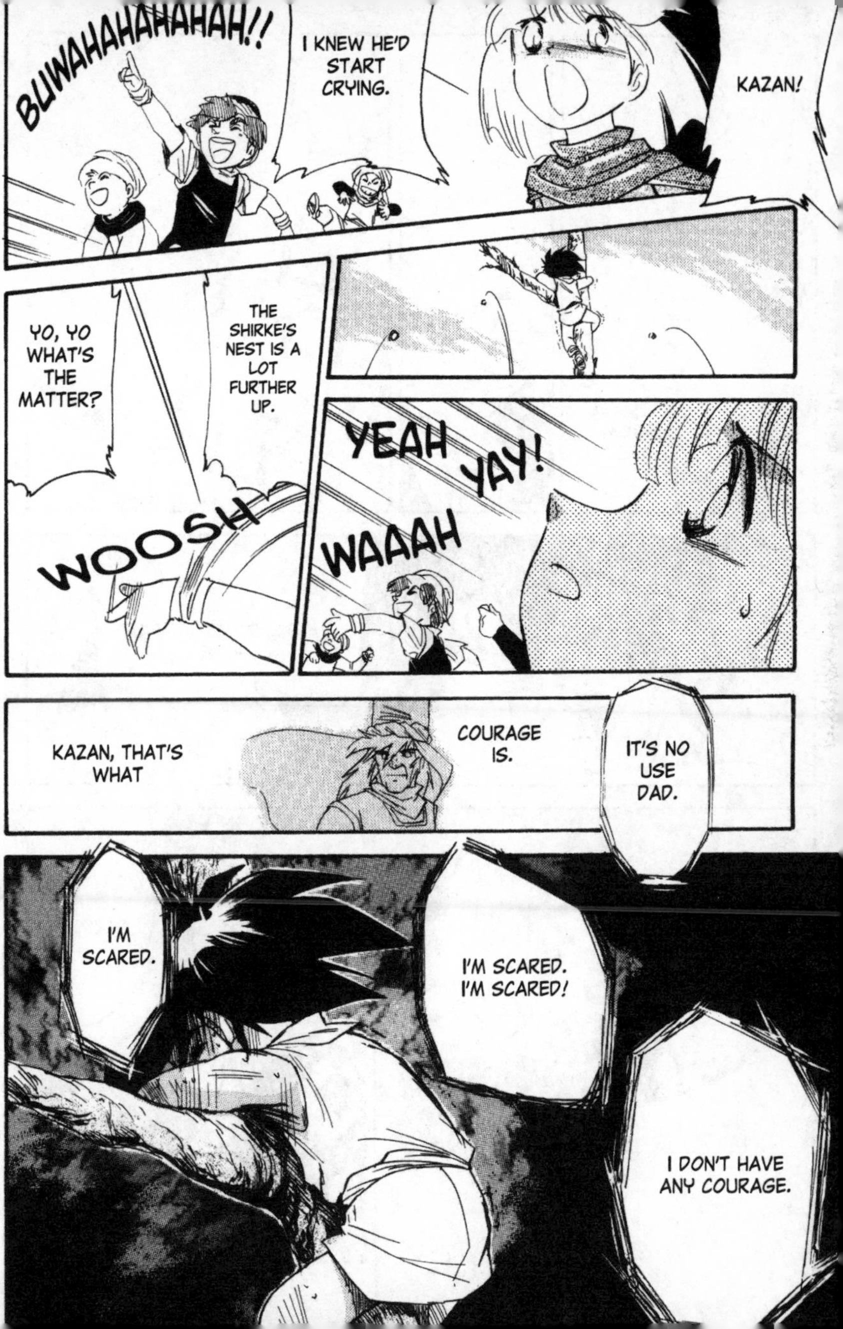
BUWAHAHAHAHAH!!
I KNEW HE'D START CRYING.
KAZAN!
YO, YO WHAT'S THE MATTER?
THE SHIRKE'S NEST IS A LOT FURTHER UP.
WOOSH
YEAH
YAY!
WAAAH
KAZAN, THAT'S WHAT
COURAGE IS.
IT'S NO USE DAD.
I'M SCARED.
I'M SCARED. I'M SCARED!
I DON'T HAVE ANY COURAGE.

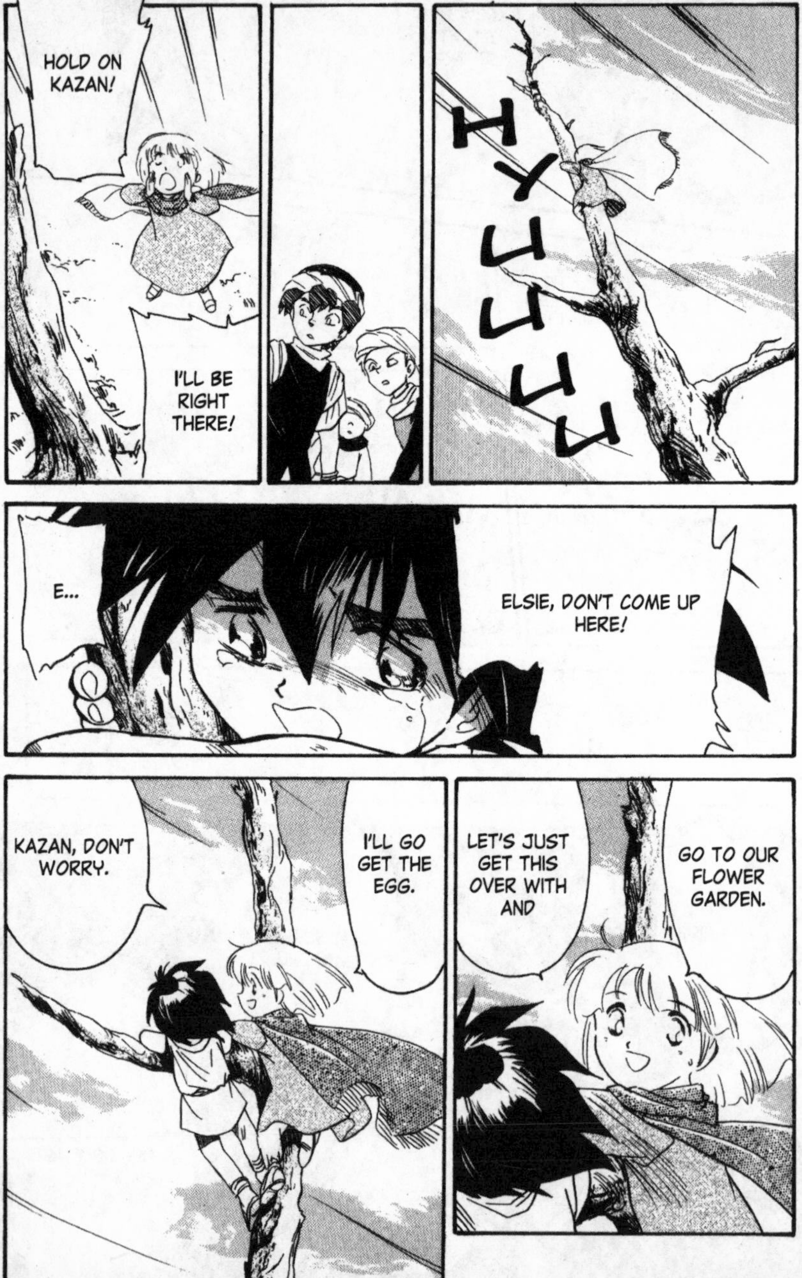
HOLD ON KAZAN!
I'LL BE RIGHT THERE!
E...
ELSIE, DON'T COME UP HERE!
KAZAN, DON'T WORRY.
I'LL GO GET THE EGG.
LET'S JUST GET THIS OVER WITH AND
GO TO OUR FLOWER GARDEN.

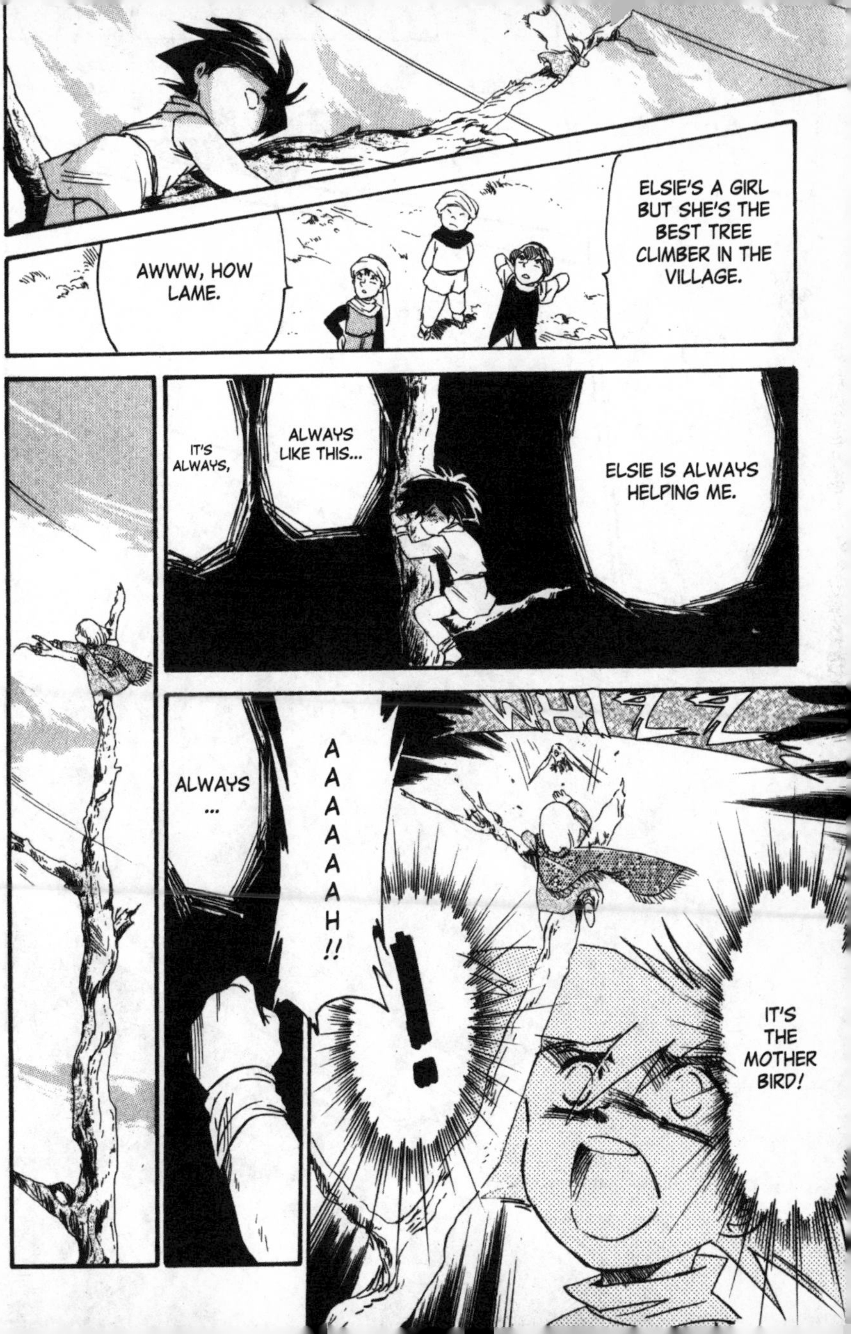
ELSIE'S A GIRL BUT SHE'S THE BEST TREE CLIMBER IN THE VILLAGE.
AWWW, HOW LAME.
ELSIE IS ALWAYS HELPING ME.
ALWAYS LIKE THIS...
IT'S ALWAYS,
ALWAYS ...
AAAAAAAH!!
!
IT'S THE MOTHER BIRD!

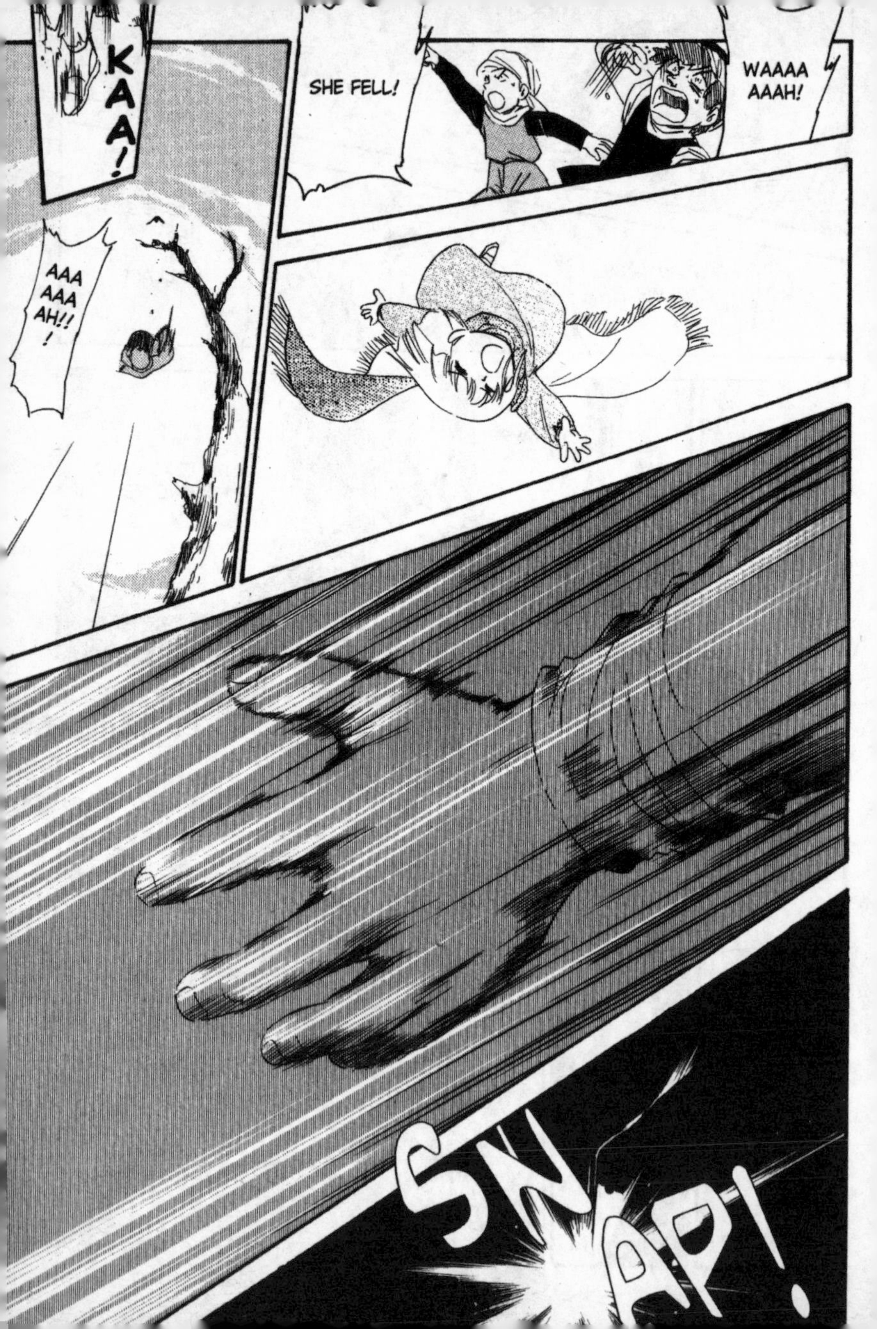

WAAAA AAAH!
SHE FELL!
KAA!
AAA AAA AH!!!
SNAP!

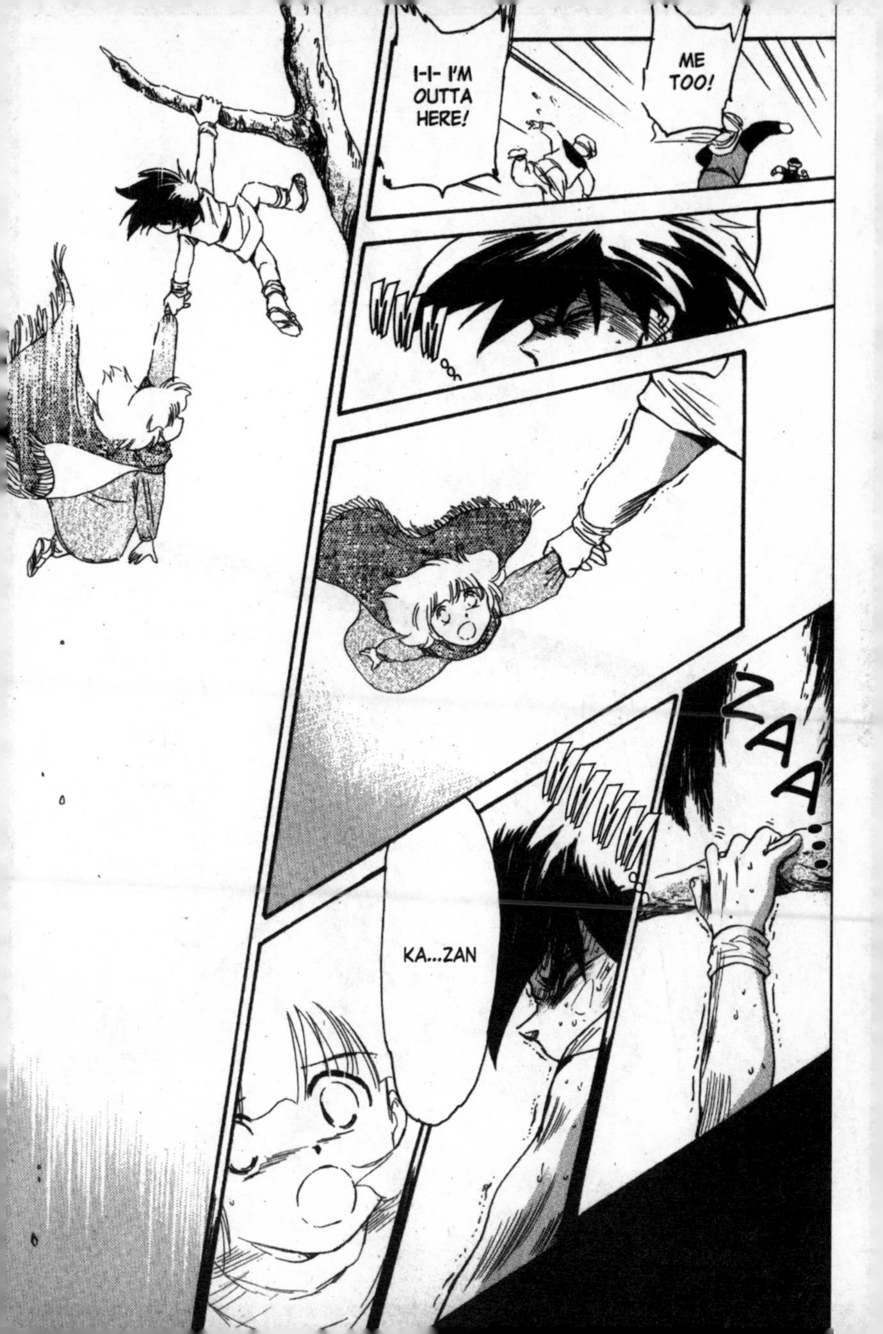

ME TOO!
I-I- I'M OUTTA HERE!
ZAA...
KA...ZAN

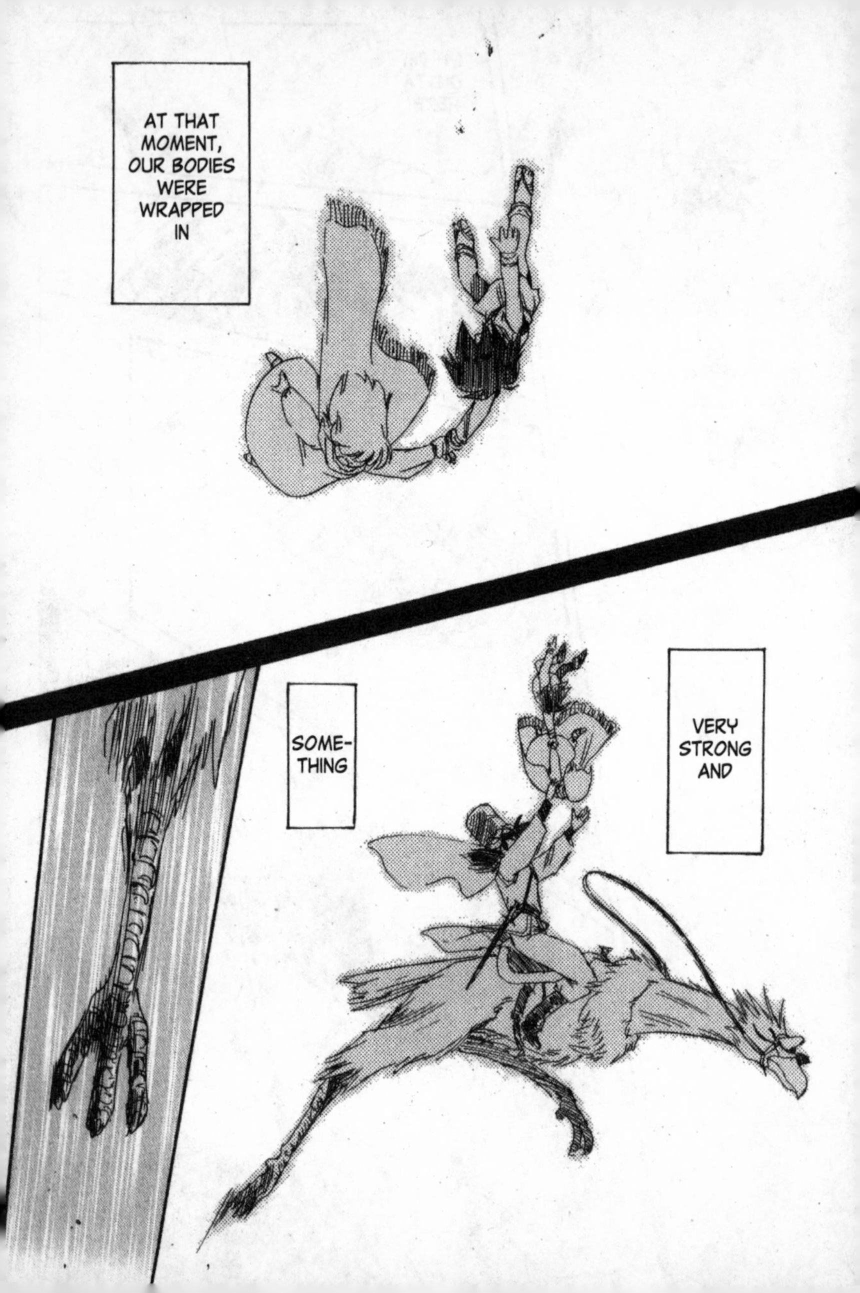
AT THAT MOMENT, OUR BODIES WERE WRAPPED IN
VERY STRONG AND
SOME-THING

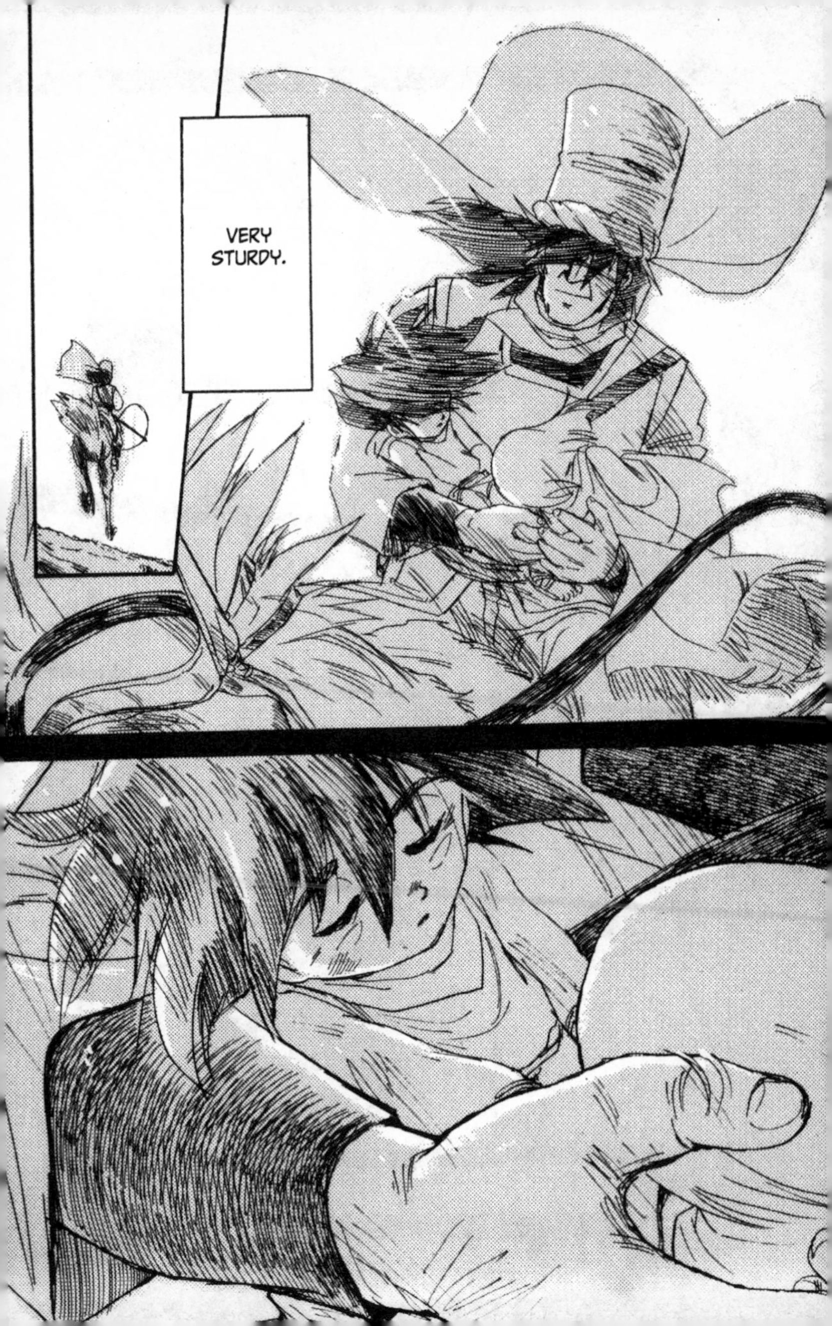
VERY
STURDY.

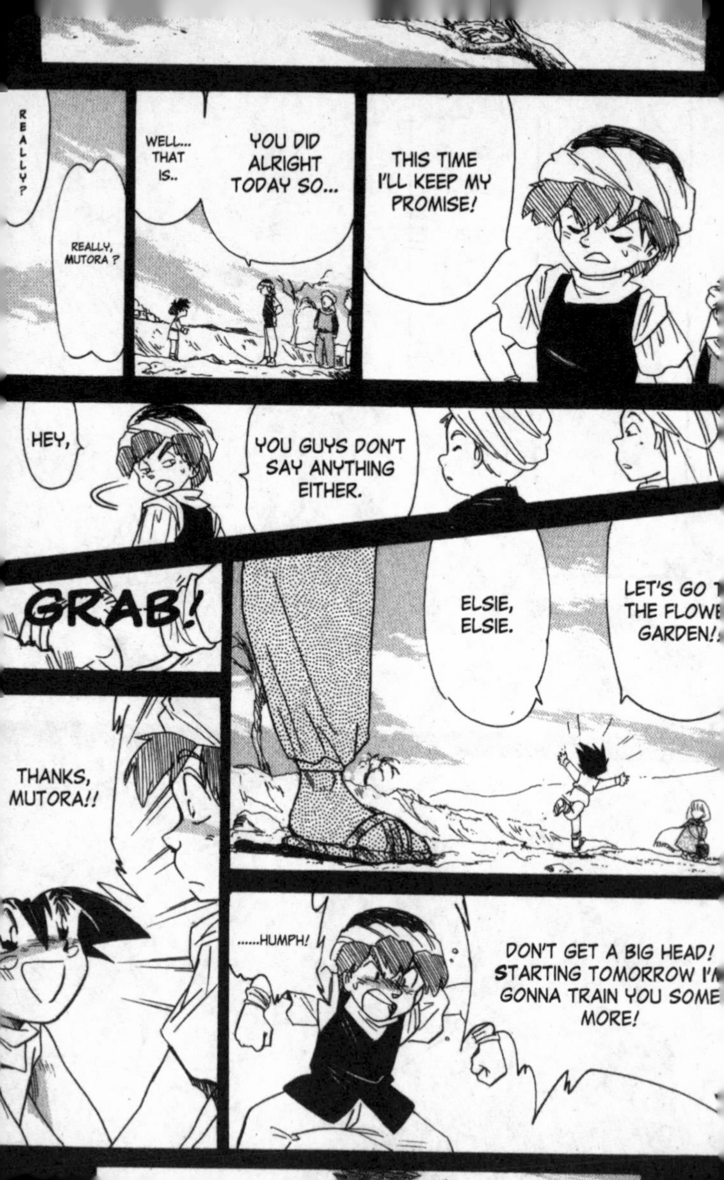
THIS TIME I'LL KEEP MY PROMISE!
YOU DID ALRIGHT TODAY SO...
WELL... THAT IS..
REALLY?
REALLY, MUTORA?
HEY,
YOU GUYS DON'T SAY ANYTHING EITHER.
ELSIE, ELSIE.
GRAB!
THANKS, MUTORA!!
DON'T GET A BIG HEAD! STARTING TOMORROW I'M GONNA TRAIN YOU SOME MORE!
......HUMPH!

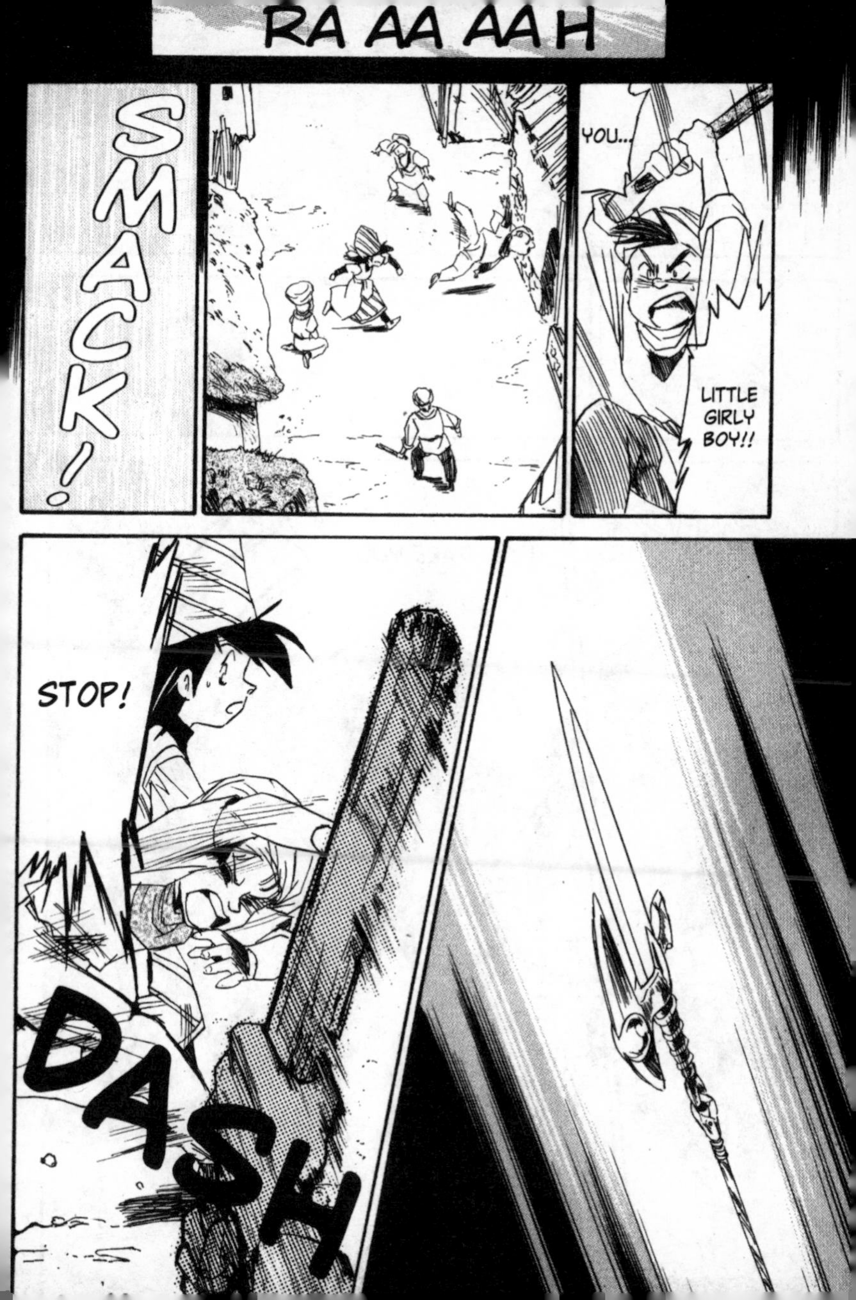
RA AA AA H
SMACK!
YOU...
LITTLE GIRLY BOY!!
STOP!
DASH

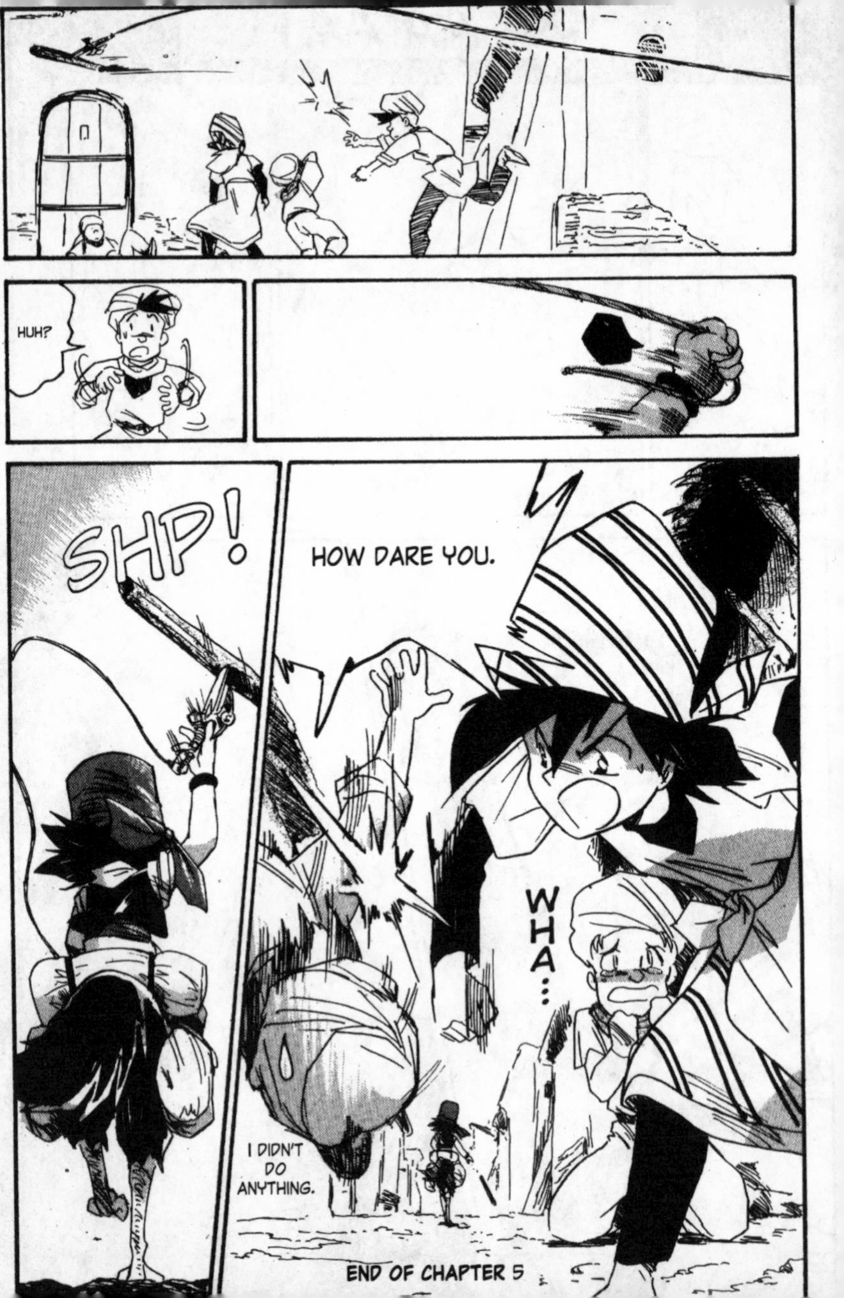

HUH?
SHP!
HOW DARE YOU.
WHA...
I DIDN'T DO ANYTHING.
END OF CHAPTER 5

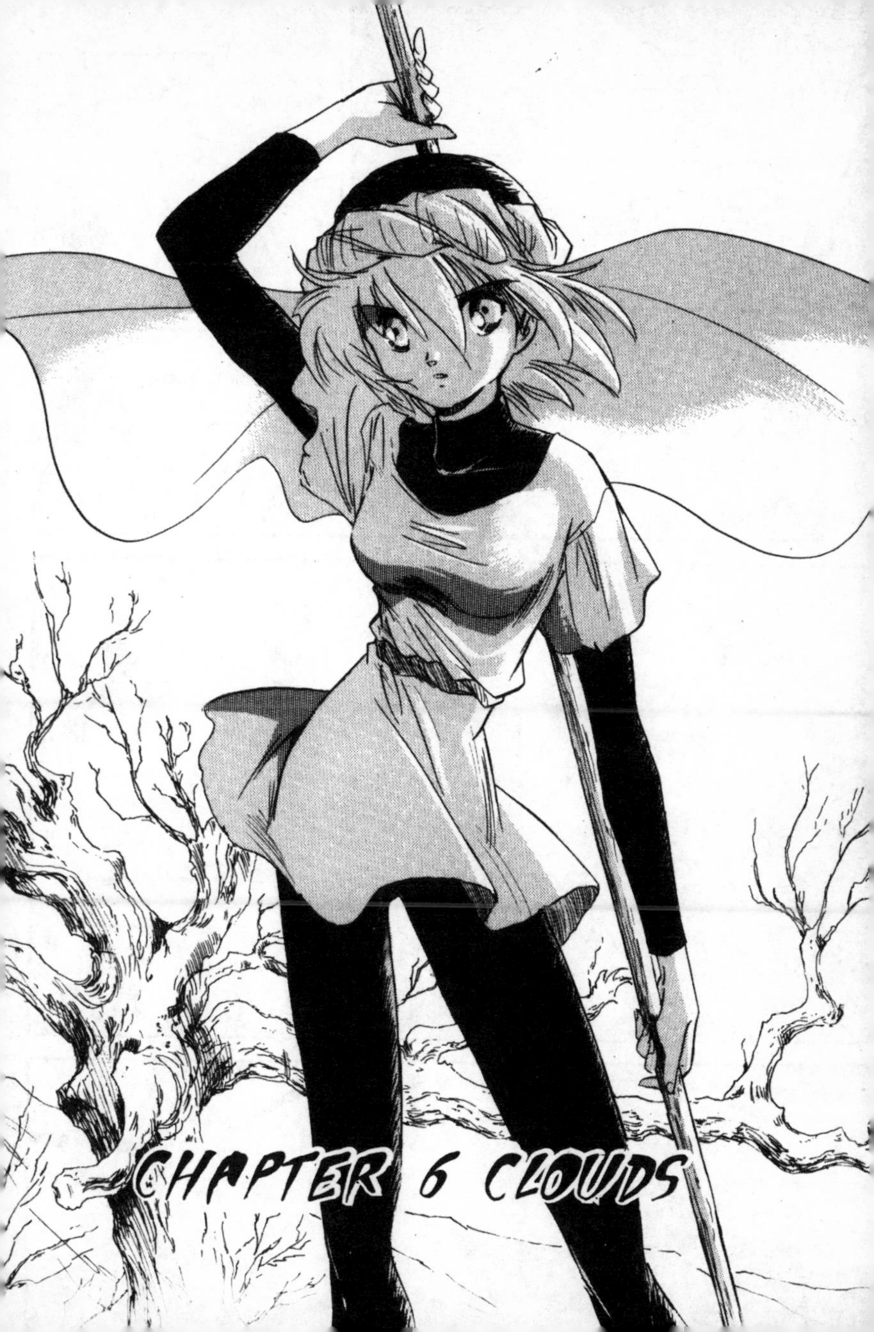
CHAPTER 6 CLOUDS

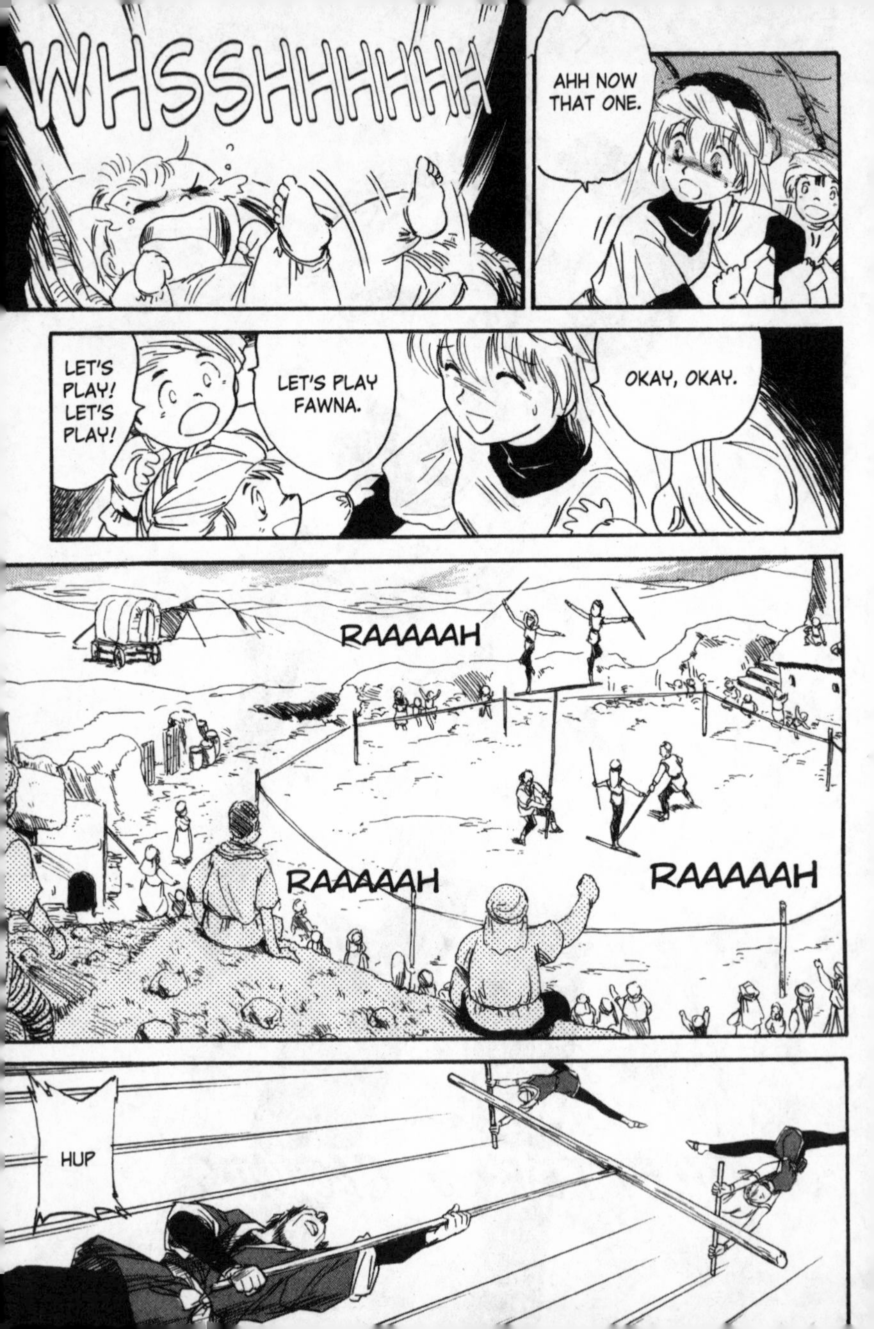
WHSSHHHHHH
AHH NOW THAT ONE.
LET'S PLAY! LET'S PLAY!
LET'S PLAY FAWNA.
OKAY, OKAY.
RAAAAAH
RAAAAAH
RAAAAAH
HUP

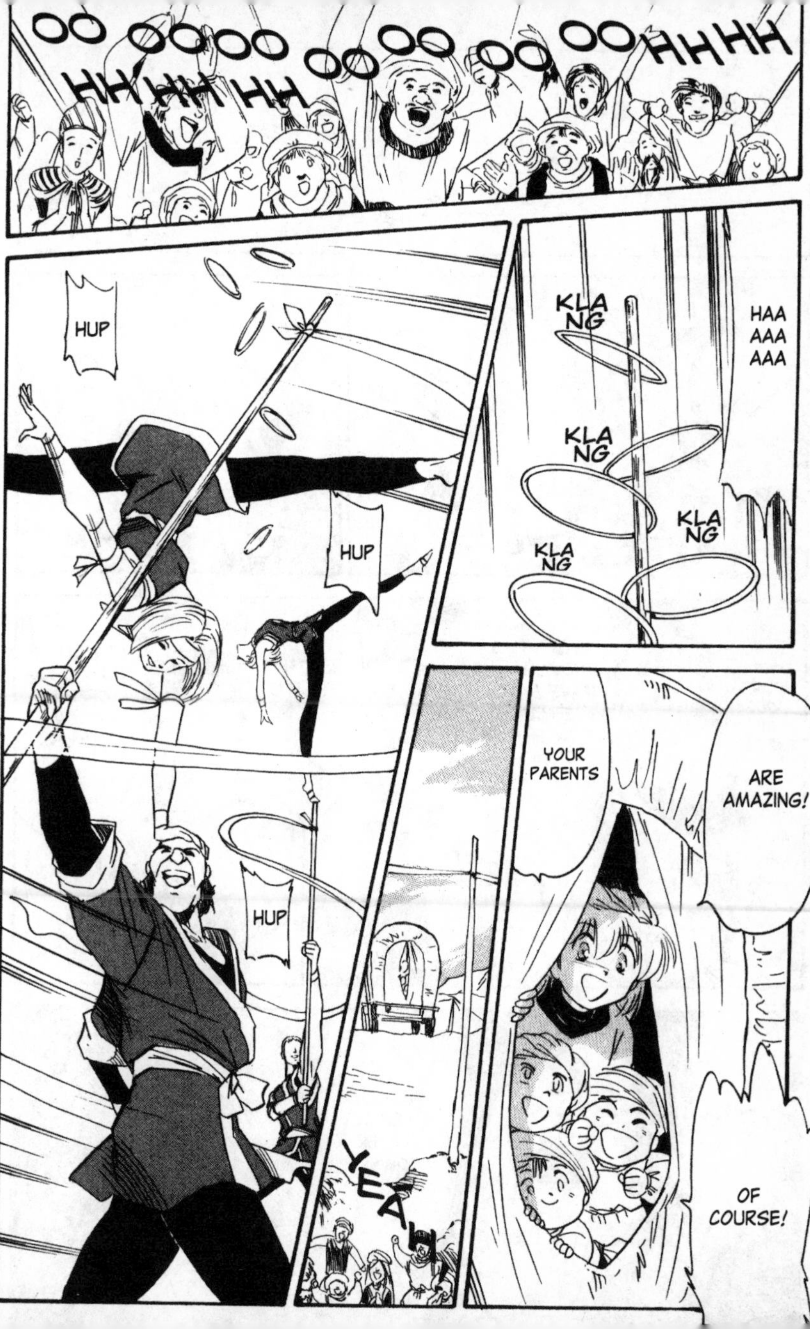

OO OOOOO OO OO OO OO AHHH
HH HH HH
HUP
HUP
HUP
KLANG
KLANG
KLANG
KLANG
HAA AAA AAA
YEAH
YOUR PARENTS
ARE AMAZING!
OF COURSE!

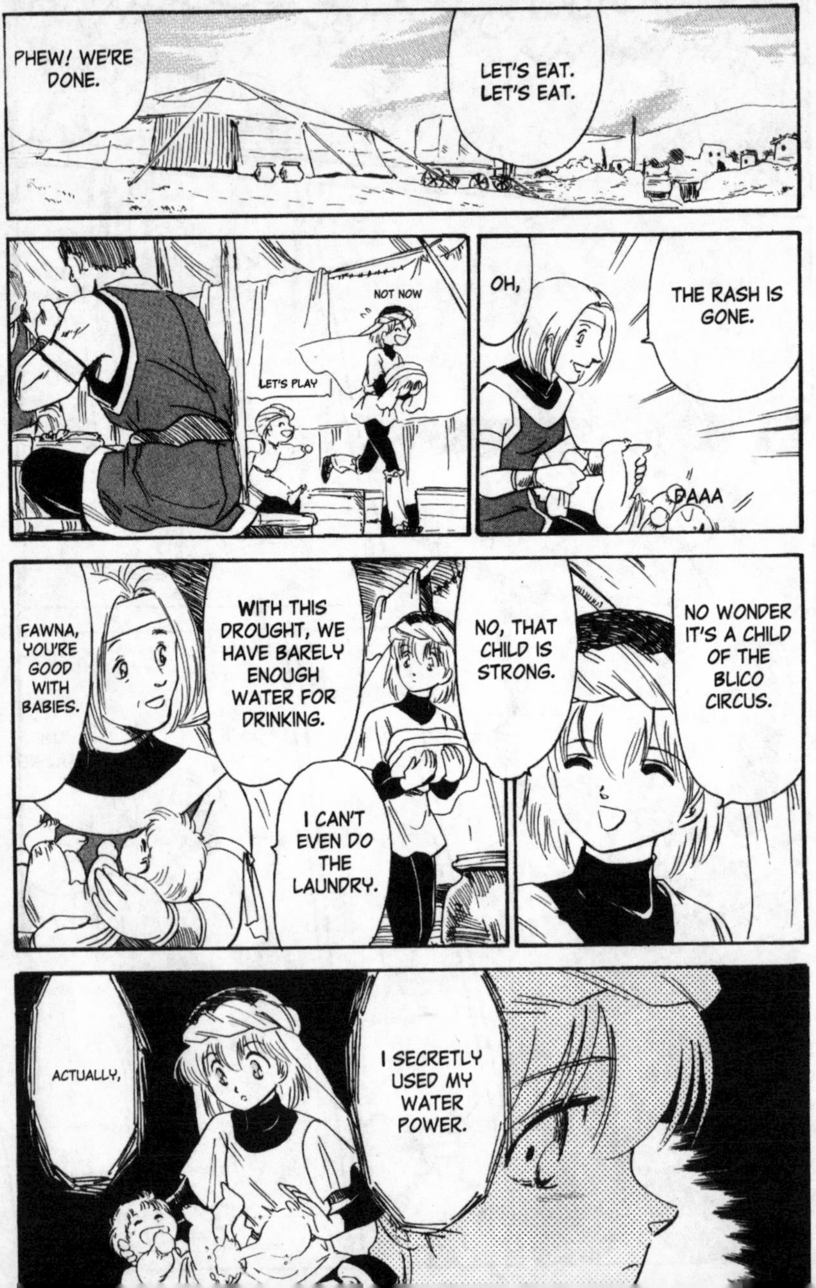
PHEW! WE'RE DONE.
LET'S EAT. LET'S EAT.
LET'S PLAY
NOT NOW
OH,
THE RASH IS GONE.
DAAA
FAWNA, YOU'RE GOOD WITH BABIES.
WITH THIS DROUGHT, WE HAVE BARELY ENOUGH WATER FOR DRINKING.
I CAN'T EVEN DO THE LAUNDRY.
NO, THAT CHILD IS STRONG.
NO WONDER IT'S A CHILD OF THE BLICO CIRCUS.
ACTUALLY,
I SECRETLY USED MY WATER POWER.

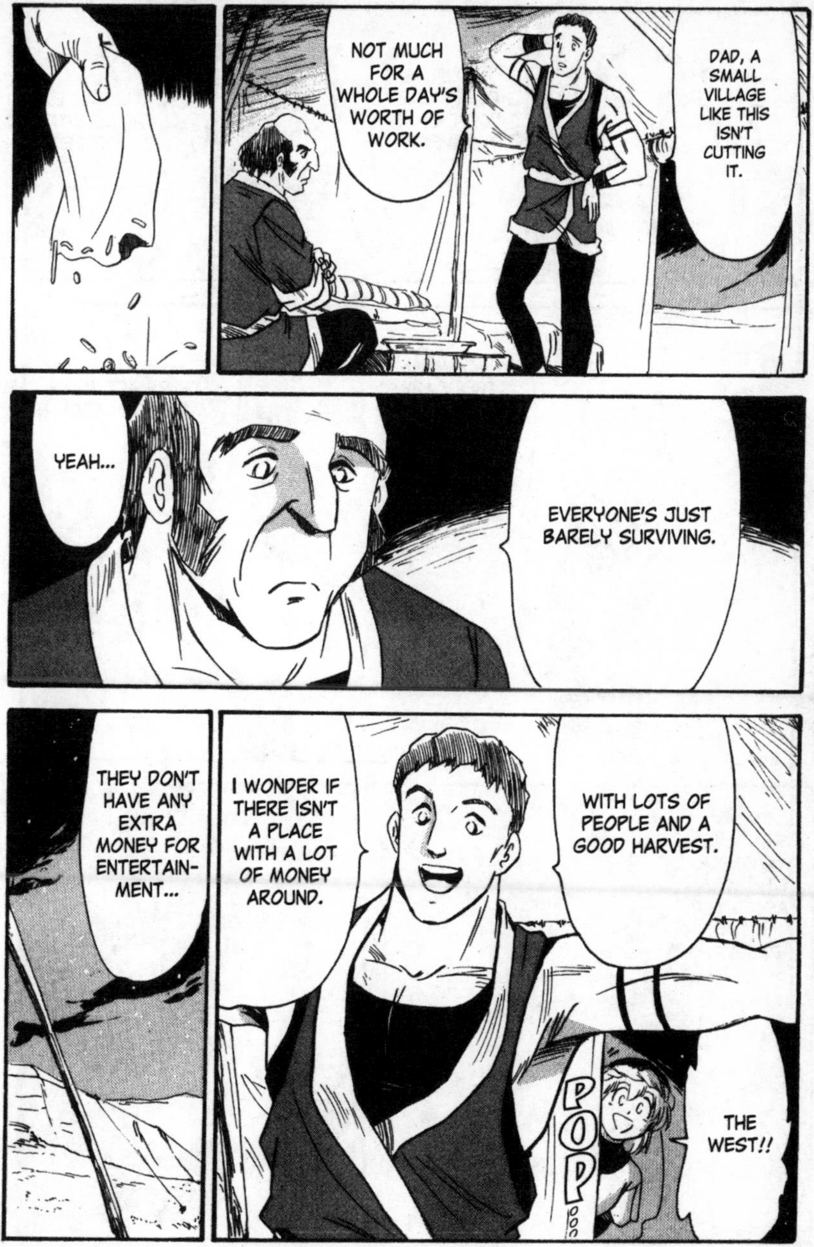
NOT MUCH FOR A WHOLE DAY'S WORTH OF WORK.
DAD, A SMALL VILLAGE LIKE THIS ISN'T CUTTING IT.
YEAH...
EVERYONE'S JUST BARELY SURVIVING.
THEY DON'T HAVE ANY EXTRA MONEY FOR ENTERTAIN-MENT...
I WONDER IF THERE ISN'T A PLACE WITH A LOT OF MONEY AROUND.
WITH LOTS OF PEOPLE AND A GOOD HARVEST.
POP
THE WEST!!

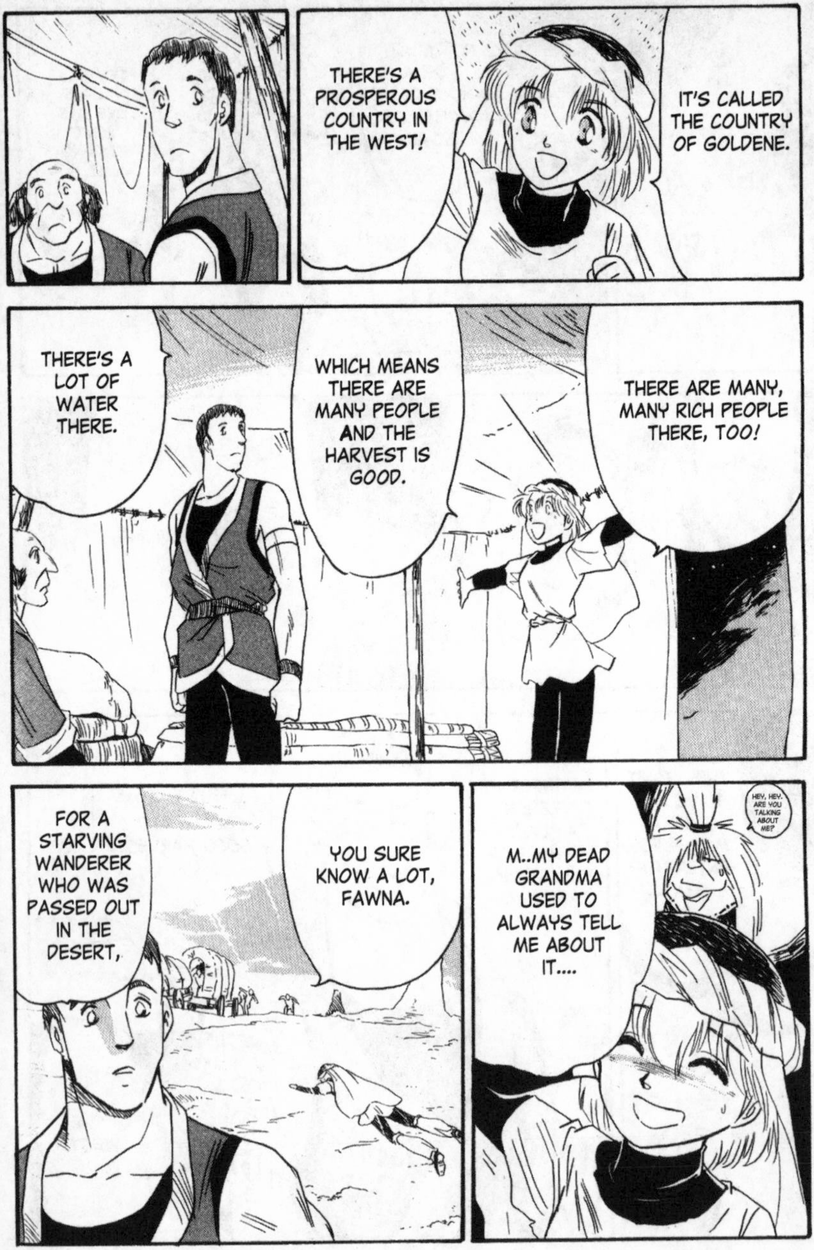
THERE'S A PROSPEROUS COUNTRY IN THE WEST!
IT'S CALLED THE COUNTRY OF GOLDENE.
THERE'S A LOT OF WATER THERE.
WHICH MEANS THERE ARE MANY PEOPLE AND THE HARVEST IS GOOD.
THERE ARE MANY, MANY RICH PEOPLE THERE, TOO!
FOR A STARVING WANDERER WHO WAS PASSED OUT IN THE DESERT,
YOU SURE KNOW A LOT, FAWNA.
M..MY DEAD GRANDMA USED TO ALWAYS TELL ME ABOUT IT....
HEY, HEY. ARE YOU TALKING ABOUT ME?

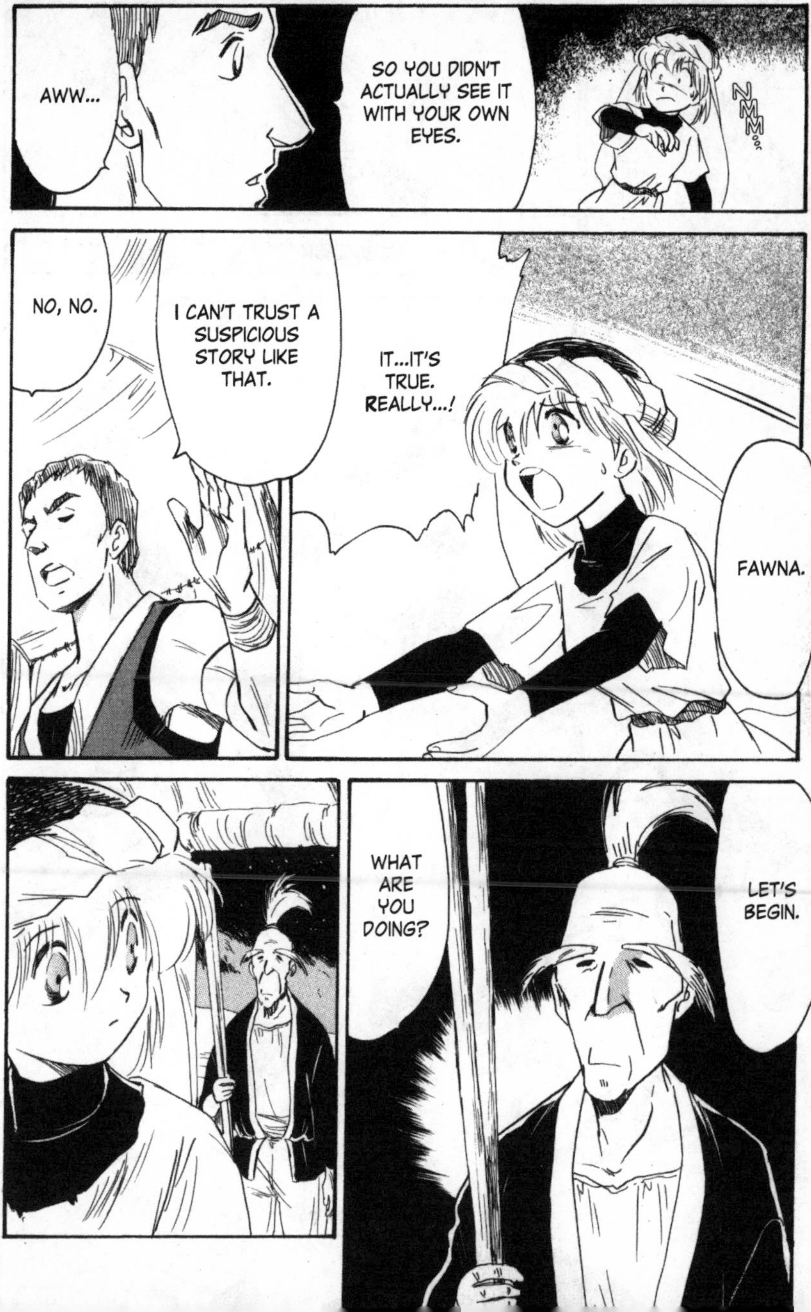
AWW...
SO YOU DIDN'T ACTUALLY SEE IT WITH YOUR OWN EYES.
NMM...
NO, NO.
I CAN'T TRUST A SUSPICIOUS STORY LIKE THAT.
IT...IT'S TRUE. REALLY...!
FAWNA.
WHAT ARE YOU DOING?
LET'S BEGIN.

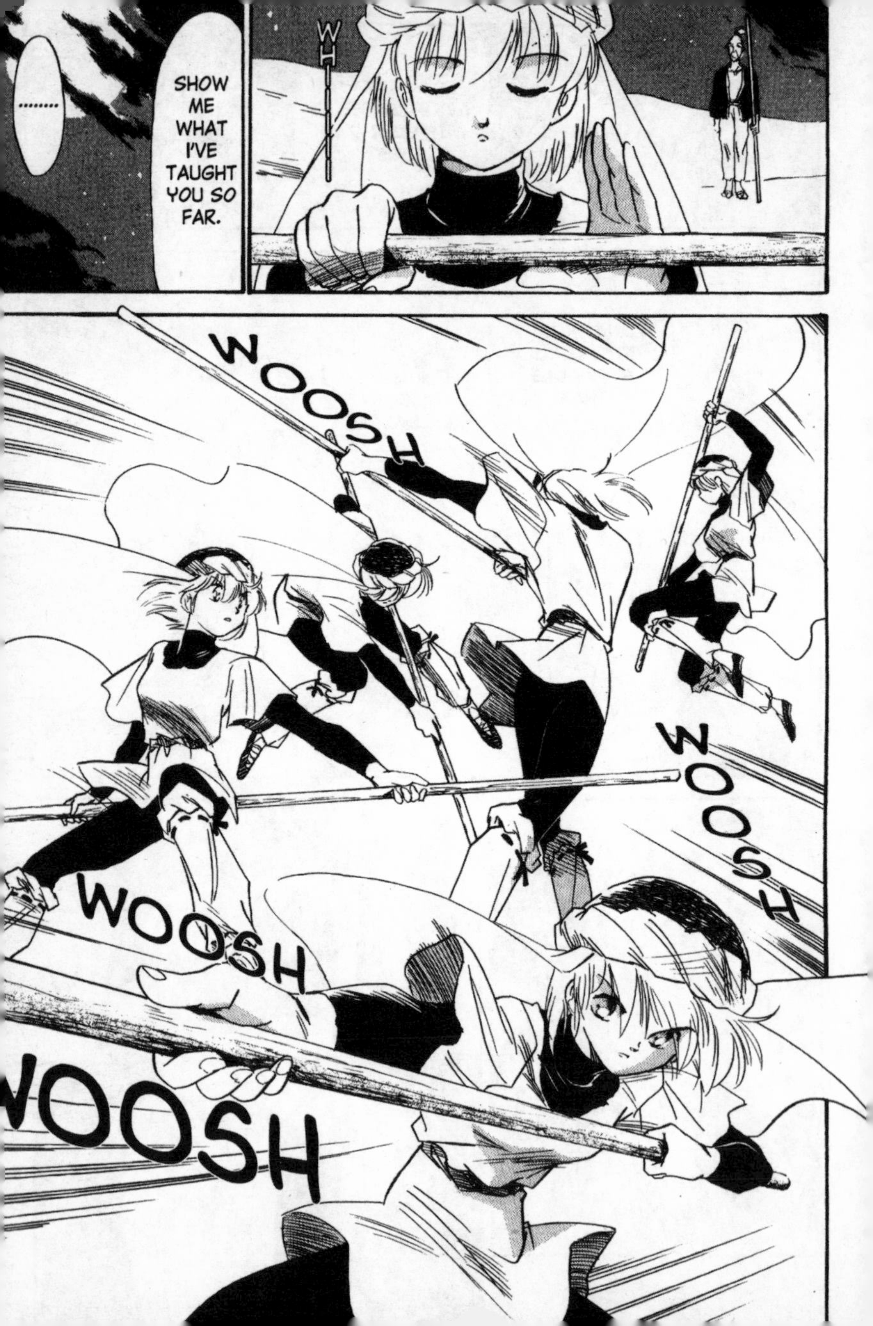

SHOW ME WHAT I'VE TAUGHT YOU SO FAR.
....
WHHH
WOOSH
WOOSH
WOOSH
WOOSH

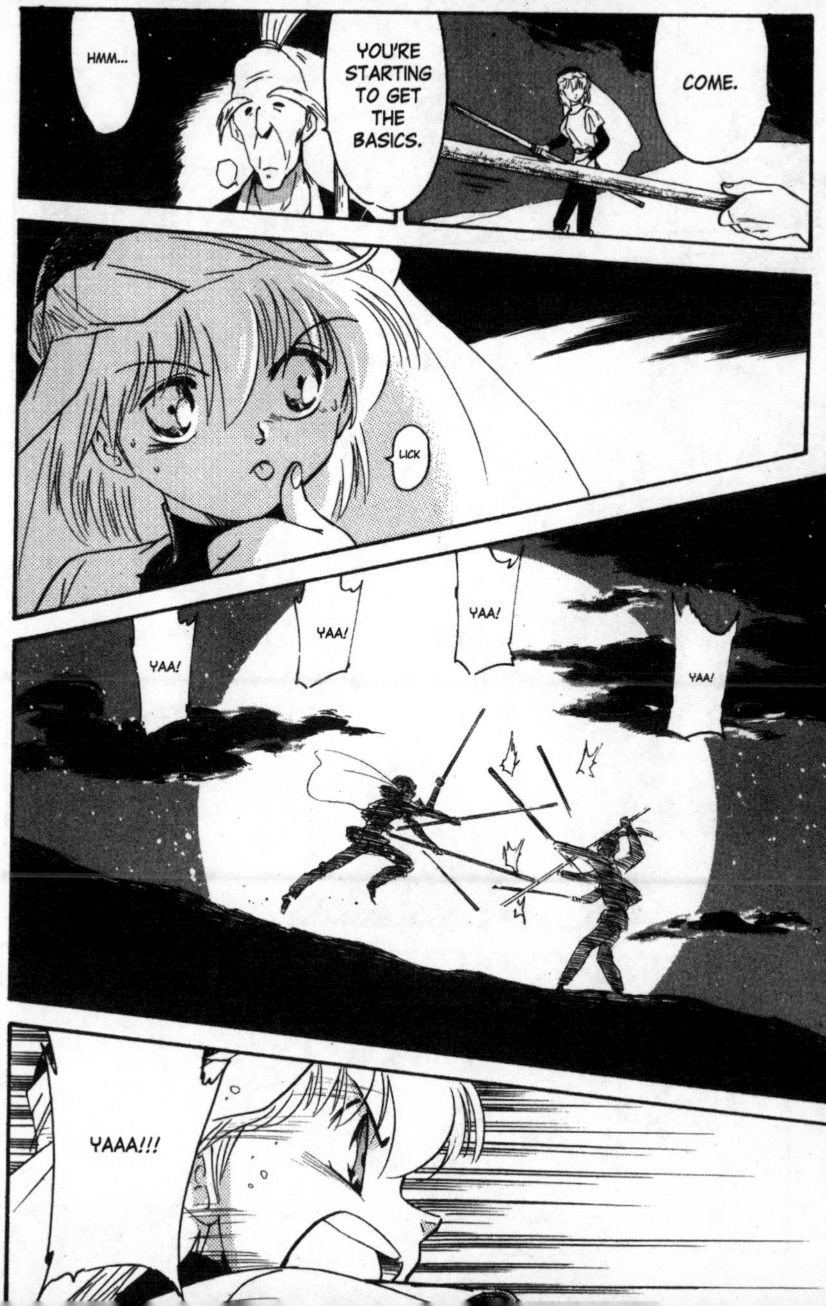
COME.
YOU'RE STARTING TO GET THE BASICS.
HMM...
LICK
YAA!
YAA!
YAA!
YAA!
YAAA!!!

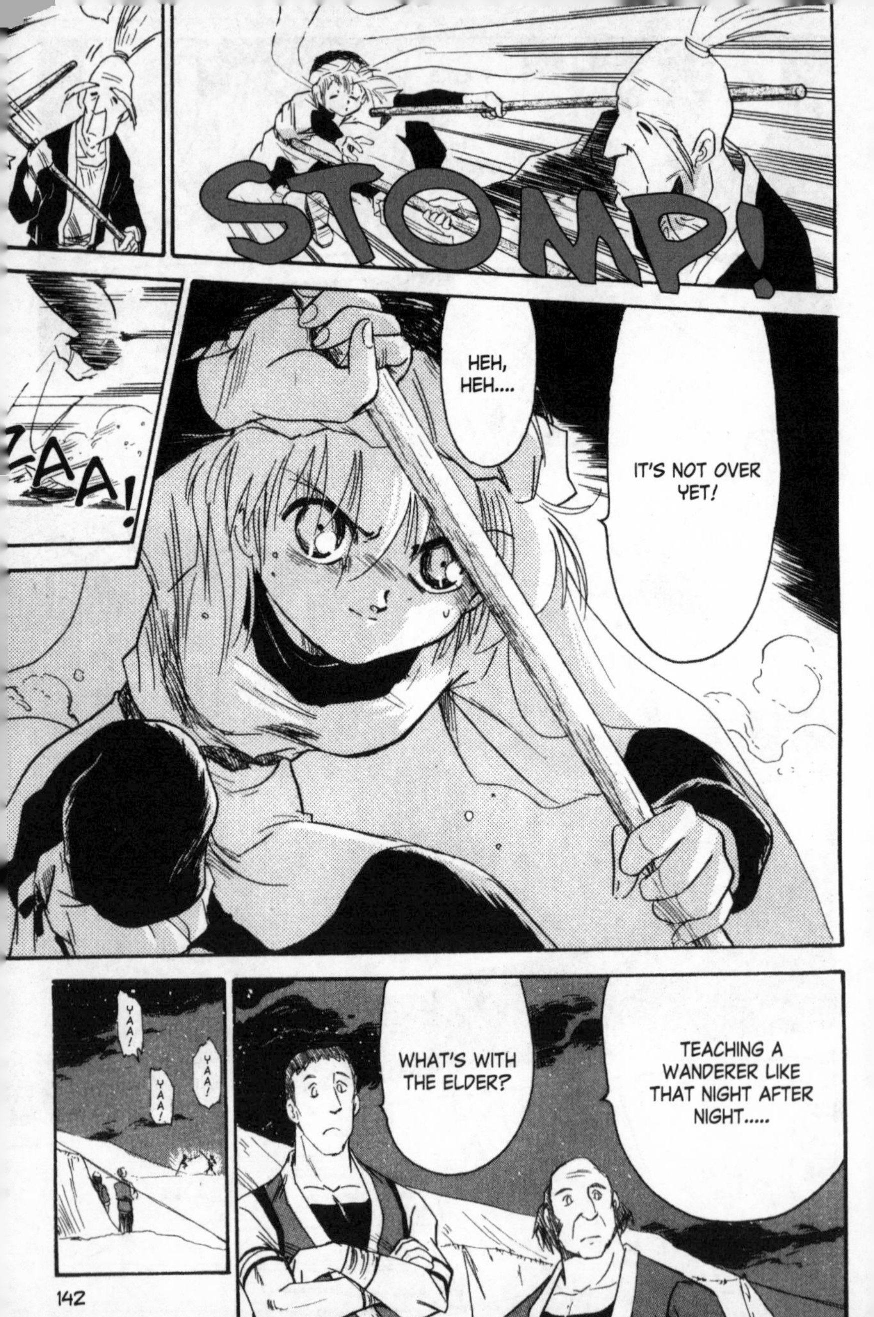

STOMP!
ZAA!
HEH, HEH....
IT'S NOT OVER YET!
YAA!
YAA!
YAA!
WHAT'S WITH THE ELDER?
TEACHING A WANDERER LIKE THAT NIGHT AFTER NIGHT.....

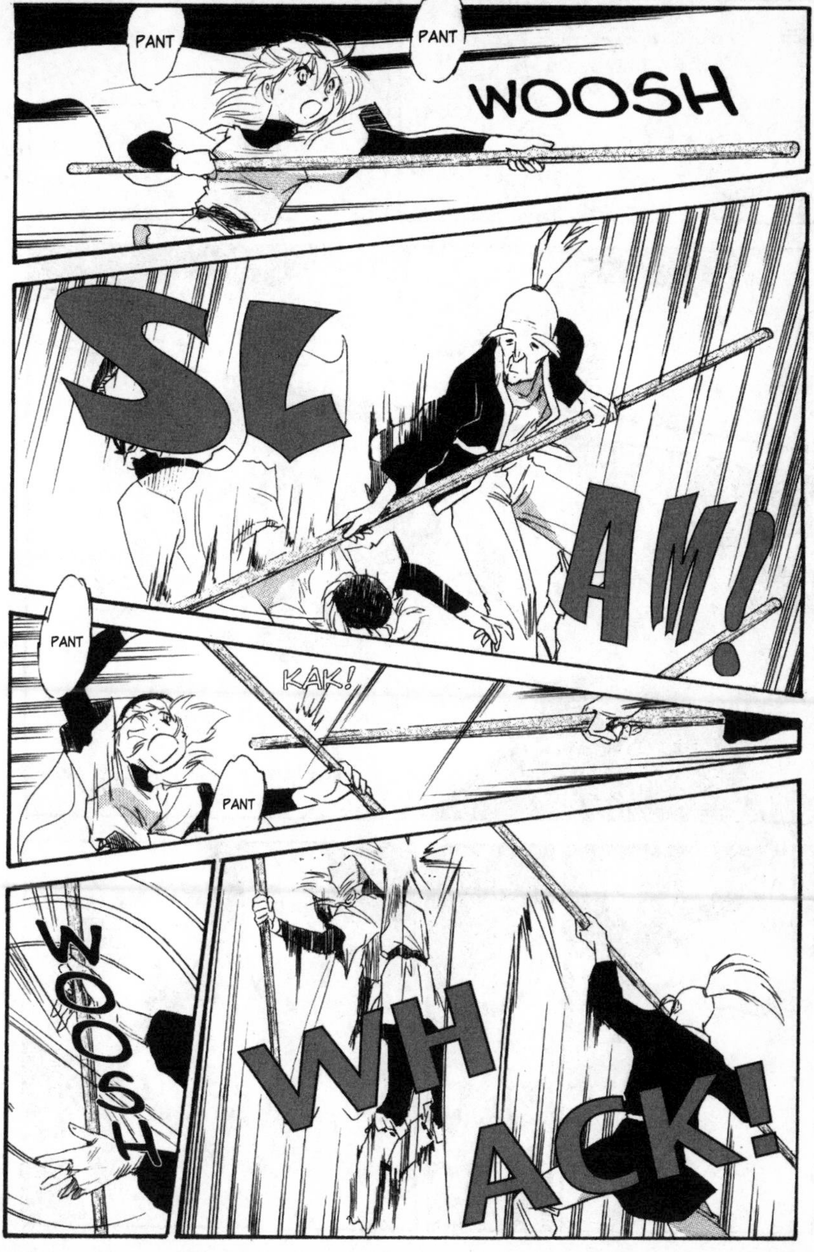
PANT
PANT
WOOSH
SLAM!
PANT
KAK!
PANT
WOOSH
WHACK!

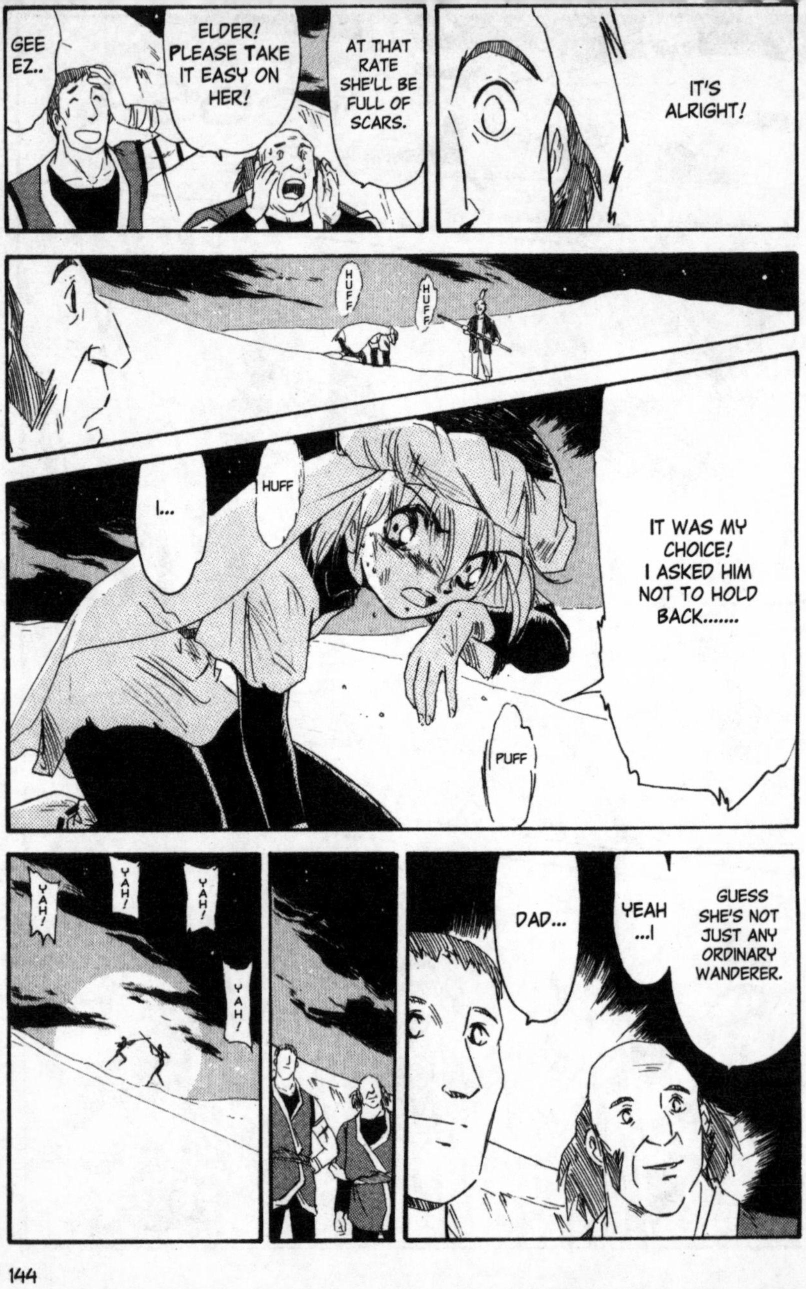

GEE EZ..
ELDER! PLEASE TAKE IT EASY ON HER!
AT THAT RATE SHE'LL BE FULL OF SCARS.
IT'S ALRIGHT!
HUFF
HUFF
I...
HUFF
IT WAS MY CHOICE! I ASKED HIM NOT TO HOLD BACK.......
PUFF
YAH!
YAH!
YAH!
YAH!
DAD...
YEAH ...I
GUESS SHE'S NOT JUST ANY ORDINARY WANDERER.

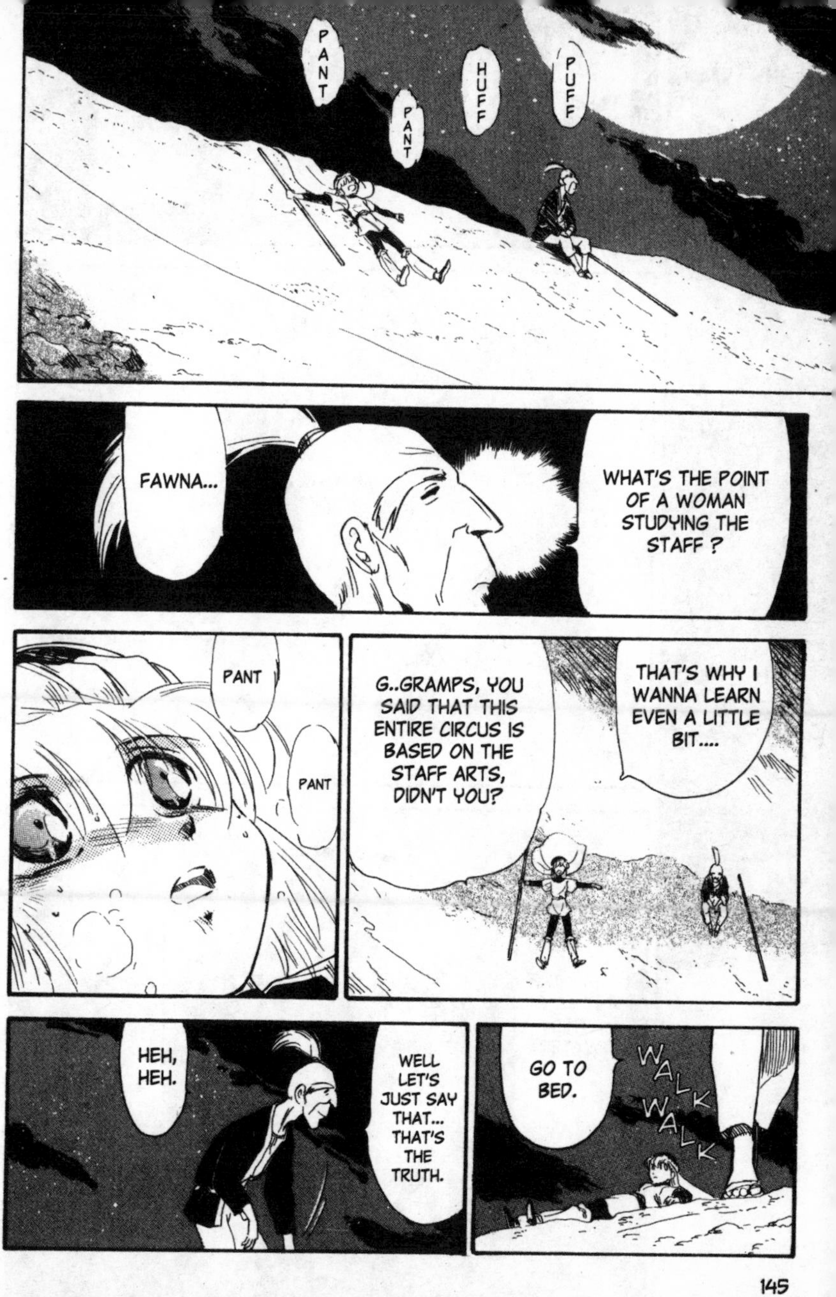
PANT
PANT
HUFF
PUFF
FAWNA...
WHAT'S THE POINT OF A WOMAN STUDYING THE STAFF ?
PANT
PANT
G..GRAMPS, YOU SAID THAT THIS ENTIRE CIRCUS IS BASED ON THE STAFF ARTS, DIDN'T YOU?
THAT'S WHY I WANNA LEARN EVEN A LITTLE BIT....
HEH, HEH.
WELL LET'S JUST SAY THAT... THAT'S THE TRUTH.
GO TO BED.
WALK WALK

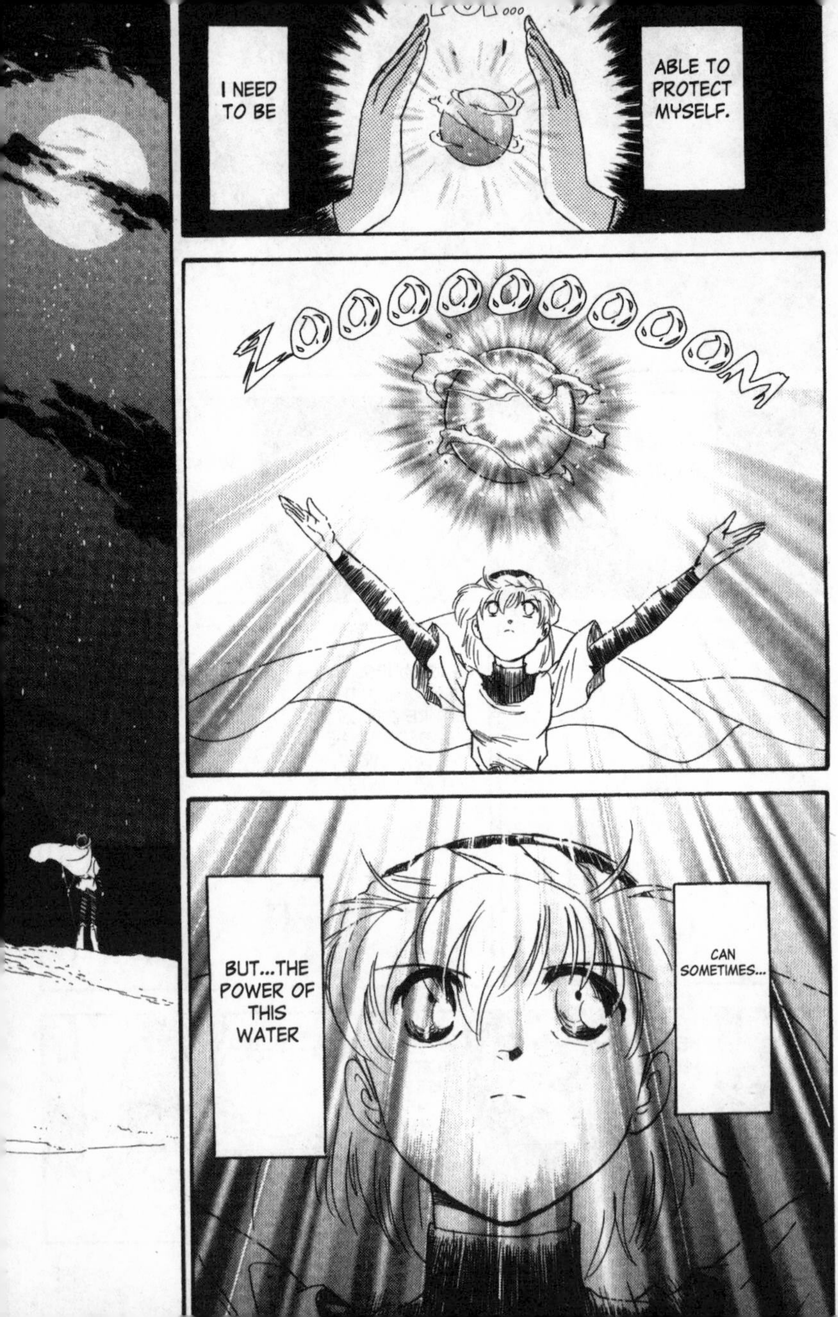
I NEED TO BE
ABLE TO PROTECT MYSELF.
ZOOOOOOOOOOM
BUT...THE POWER OF THIS WATER
CAN SOMETIMES...

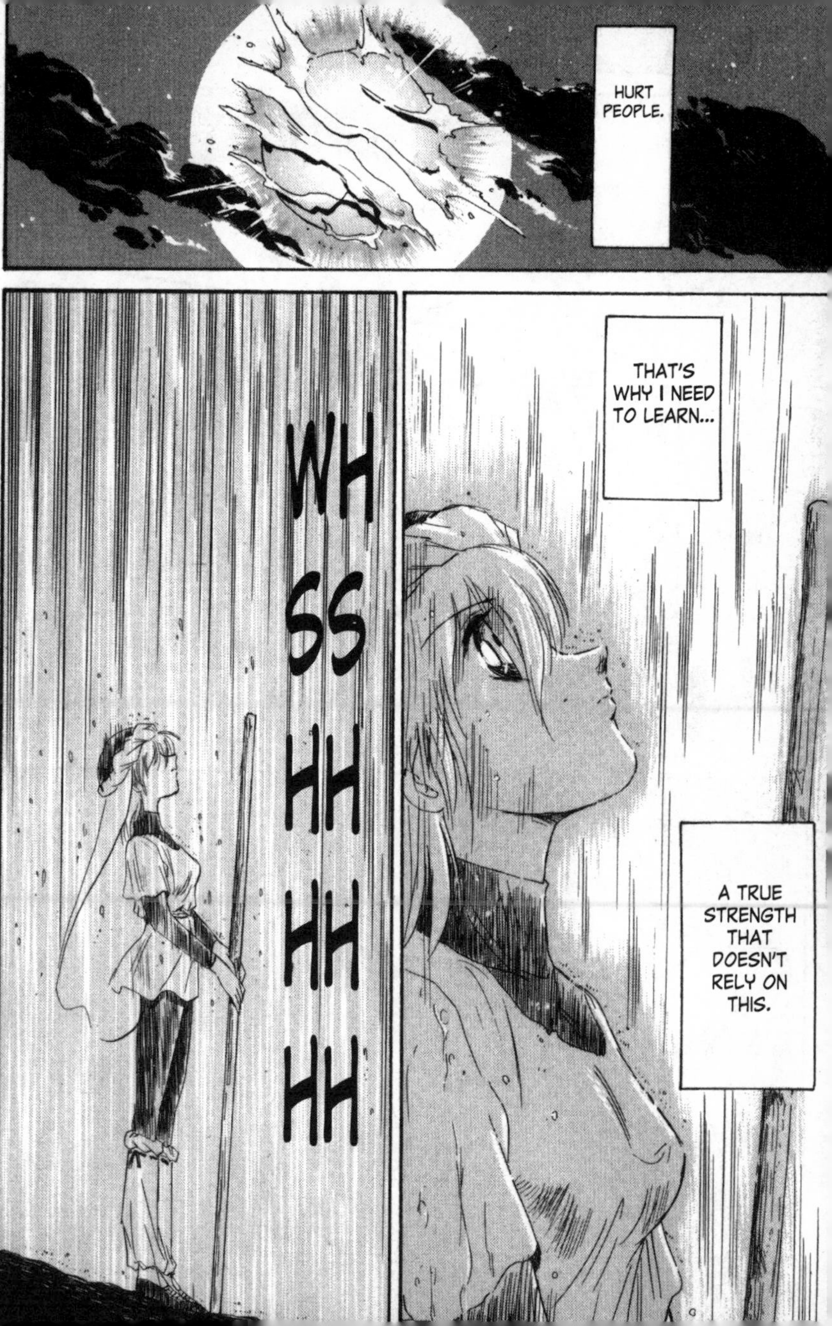
HURT PEOPLE.
THAT'S WHY I NEED TO LEARN...
A TRUE STRENGTH THAT DOESN'T RELY ON THIS.
WHSSHHHHHH

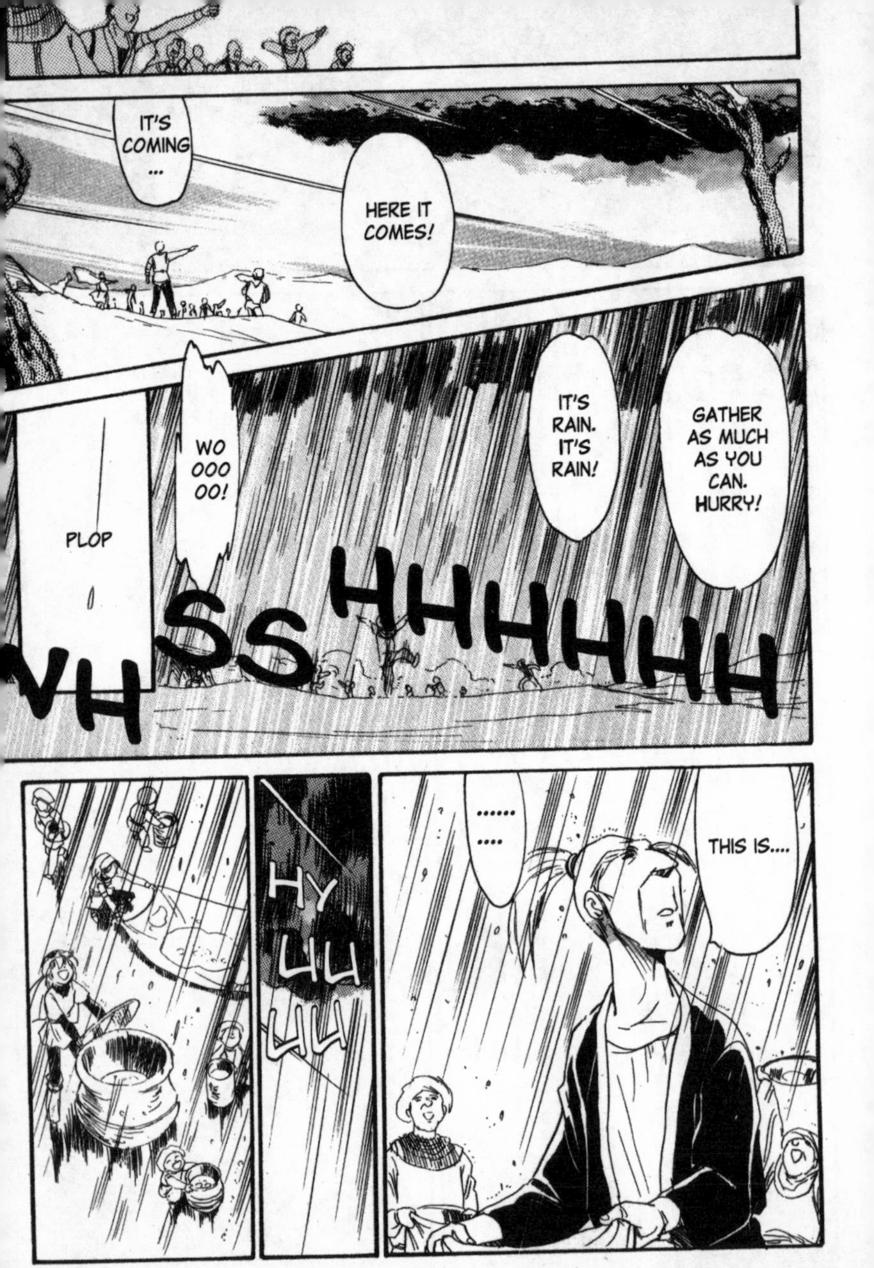
IT'S COMING ...
HERE IT COMES!
GATHER AS MUCH AS YOU CAN. HURRY!
IT'S RAIN. IT'S RAIN!
WO OOO OO!
PLOP
WHSSHHHHHHH
THIS IS....
....
HYUUUU

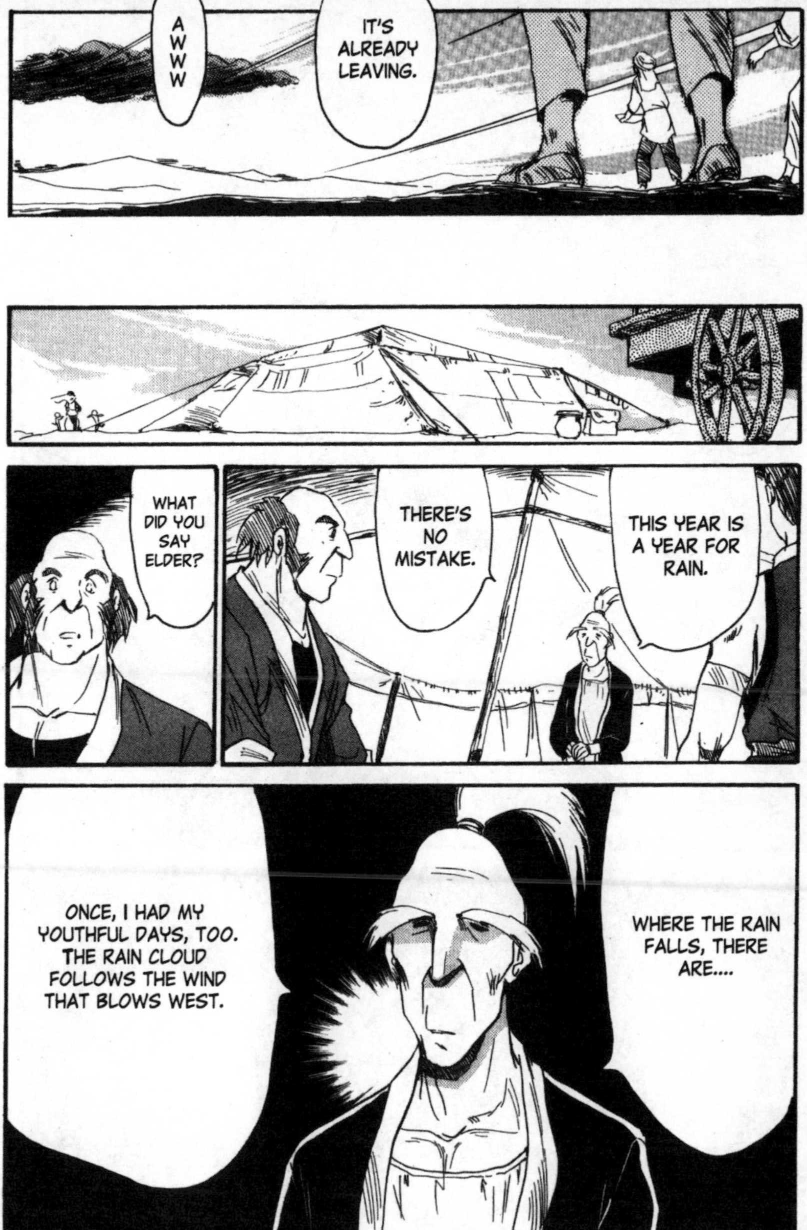
IT'S ALREADY LEAVING.
AWWW
THIS YEAR IS A YEAR FOR RAIN.
THERE'S NO MISTAKE.
WHAT DID YOU SAY ELDER?
WHERE THE RAIN FALLS, THERE ARE....
ONCE, I HAD MY YOUTHFUL DAYS, TOO. THE RAIN CLOUD FOLLOWS THE WIND THAT BLOWS WEST.

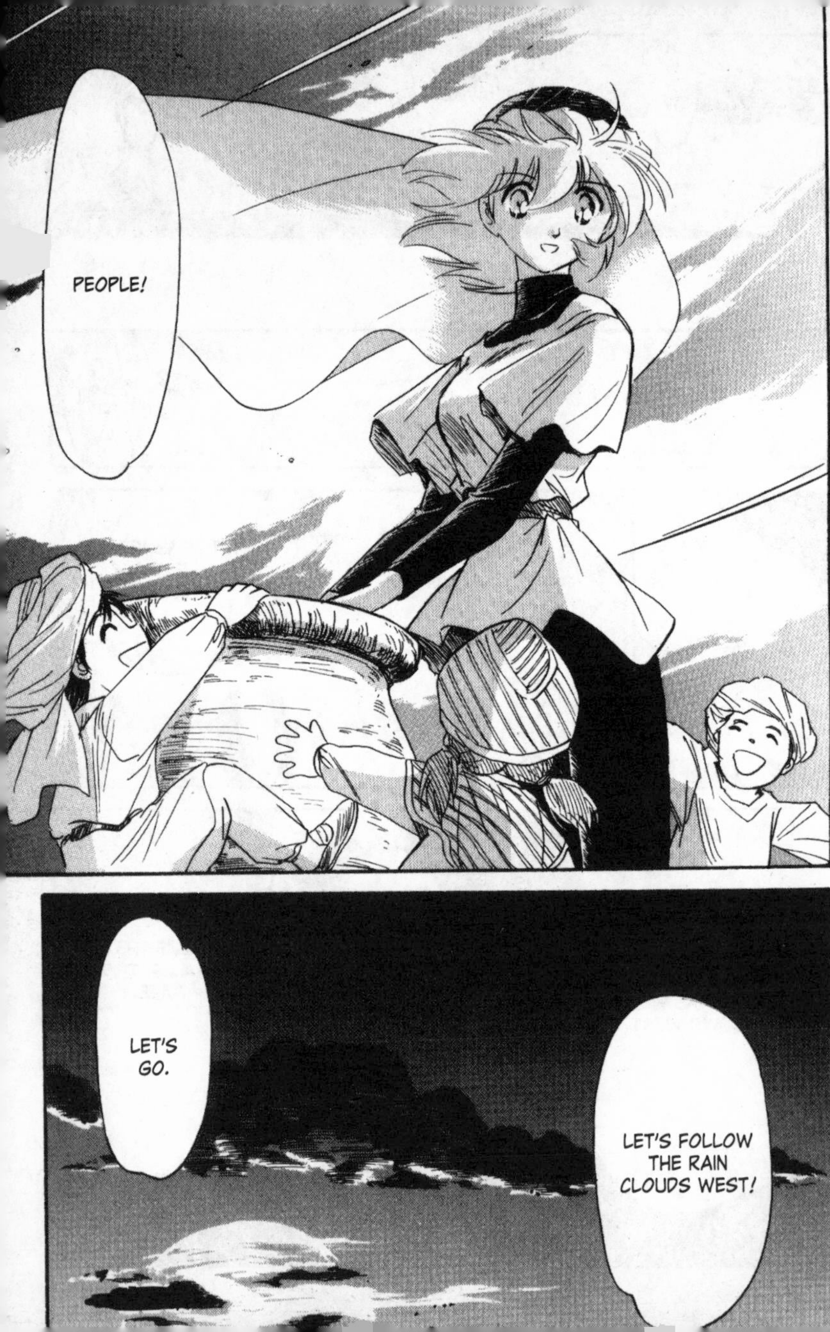
PEOPLE!
LET'S FOLLOW THE RAIN CLOUDS WEST!
LET'S GO.

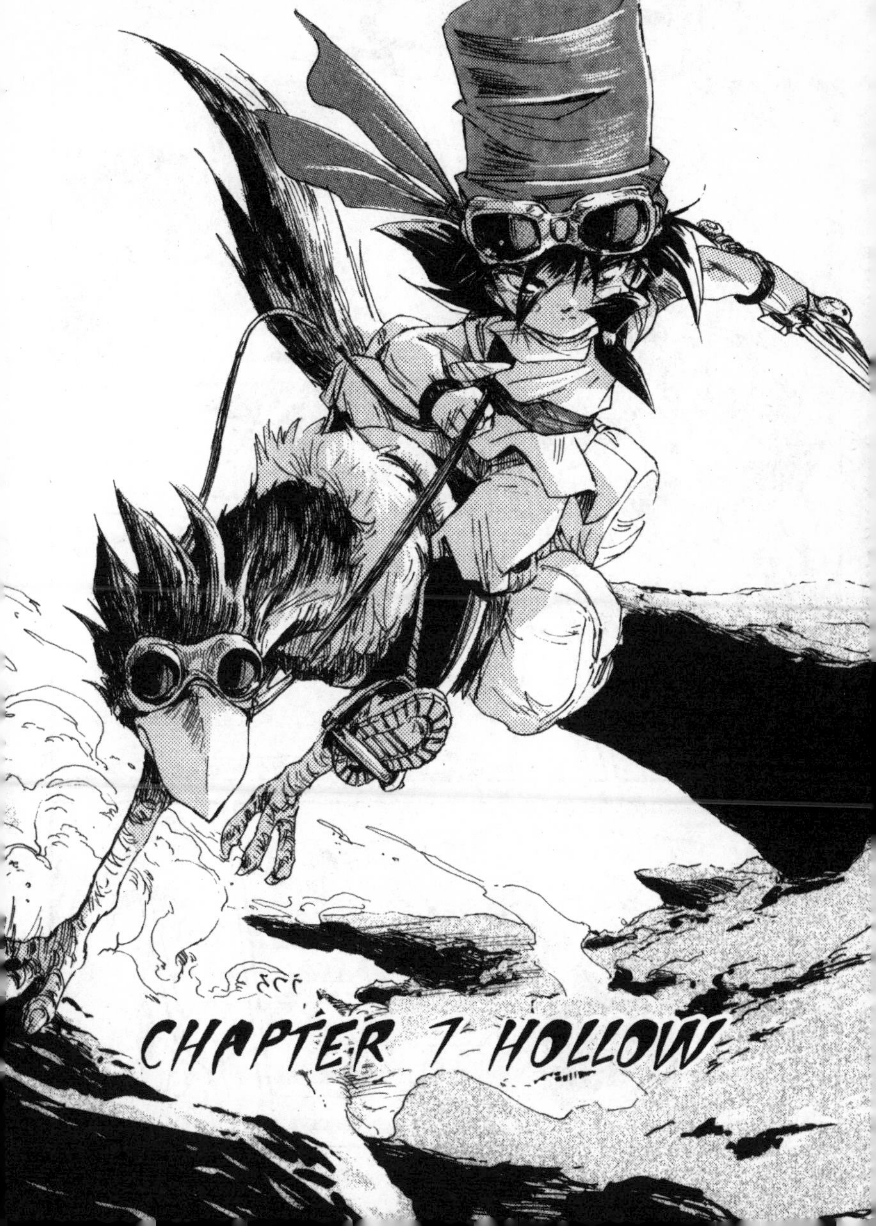
CHAPTER 7 HOLLOW

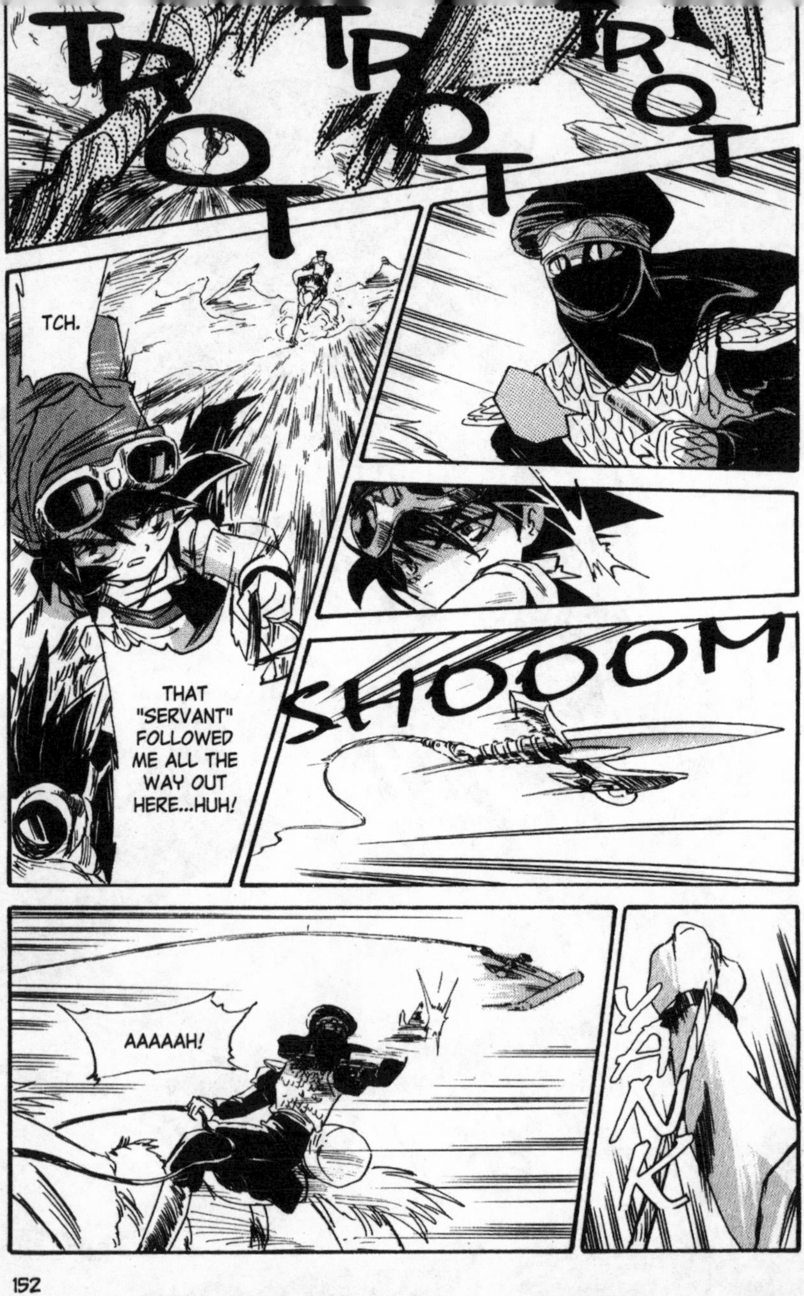
TROT
TROT
TROT
TCH.
THAT "SERVANT" FOLLOWED ME ALL THE WAY OUT HERE...HUH!
SHOOOM
AAAAAH!
YANK

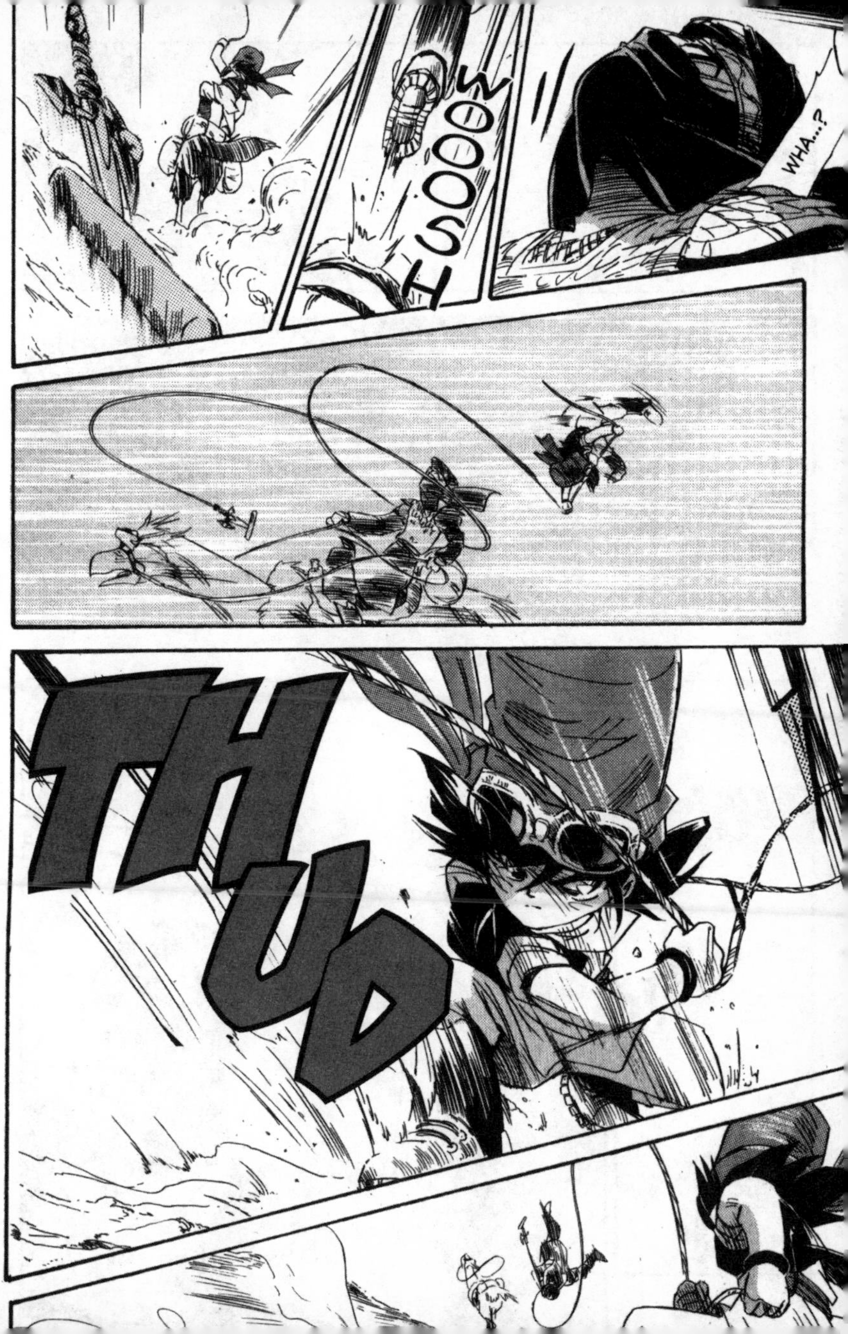
WHA...?
WOOOOSH
THUD

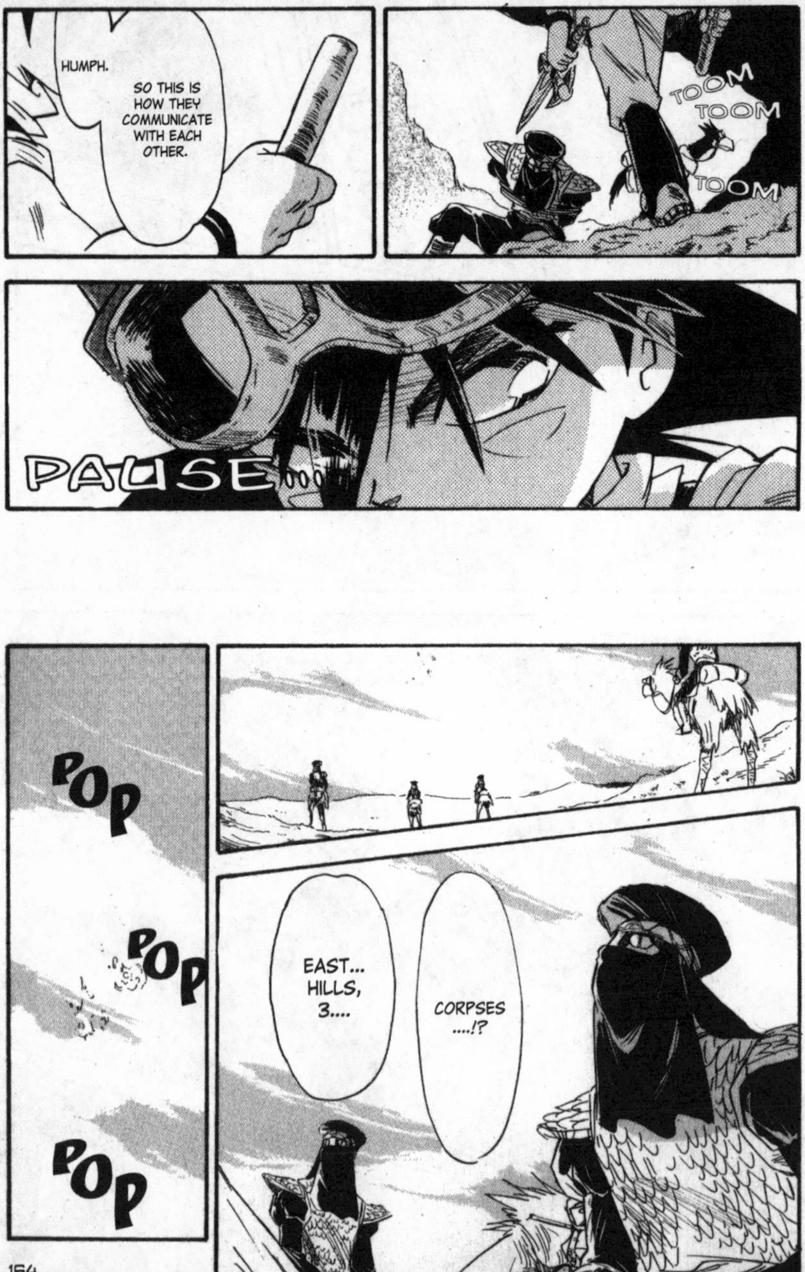
HUMPH.
SO THIS IS HOW THEY COMMUNICATE WITH EACH OTHER.
TOOM
TOOM
TOOM
PAUSE...
POP
POP
POP
EAST... HILLS, 3....
CORPSES ....!?

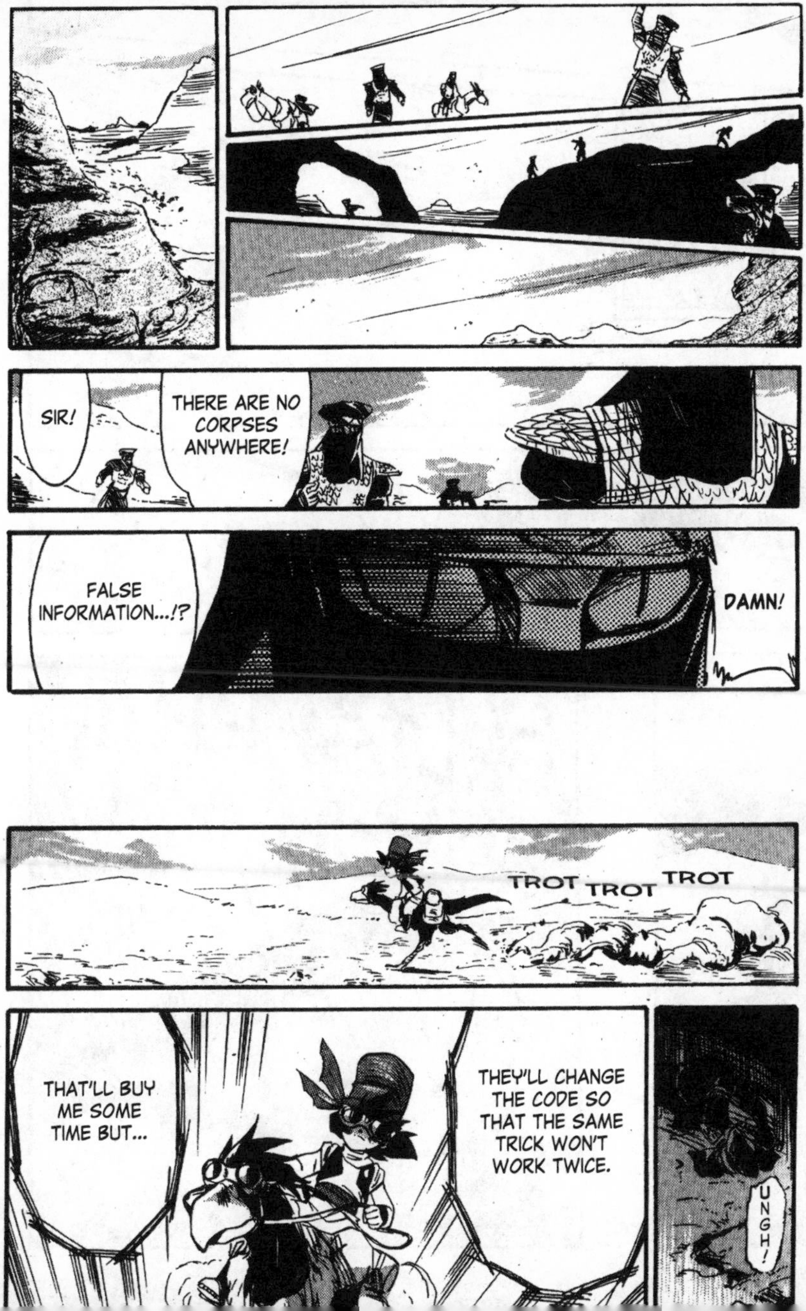
SIR!
THERE ARE NO CORPSES ANYWHERE!
FALSE INFORMATION...!?
DAMN!
TROT TROT TROT
THAT'LL BUY ME SOME TIME BUT...
THEY'LL CHANGE THE CODE SO THAT THE SAME TRICK WON'T WORK TWICE.
UNGH!

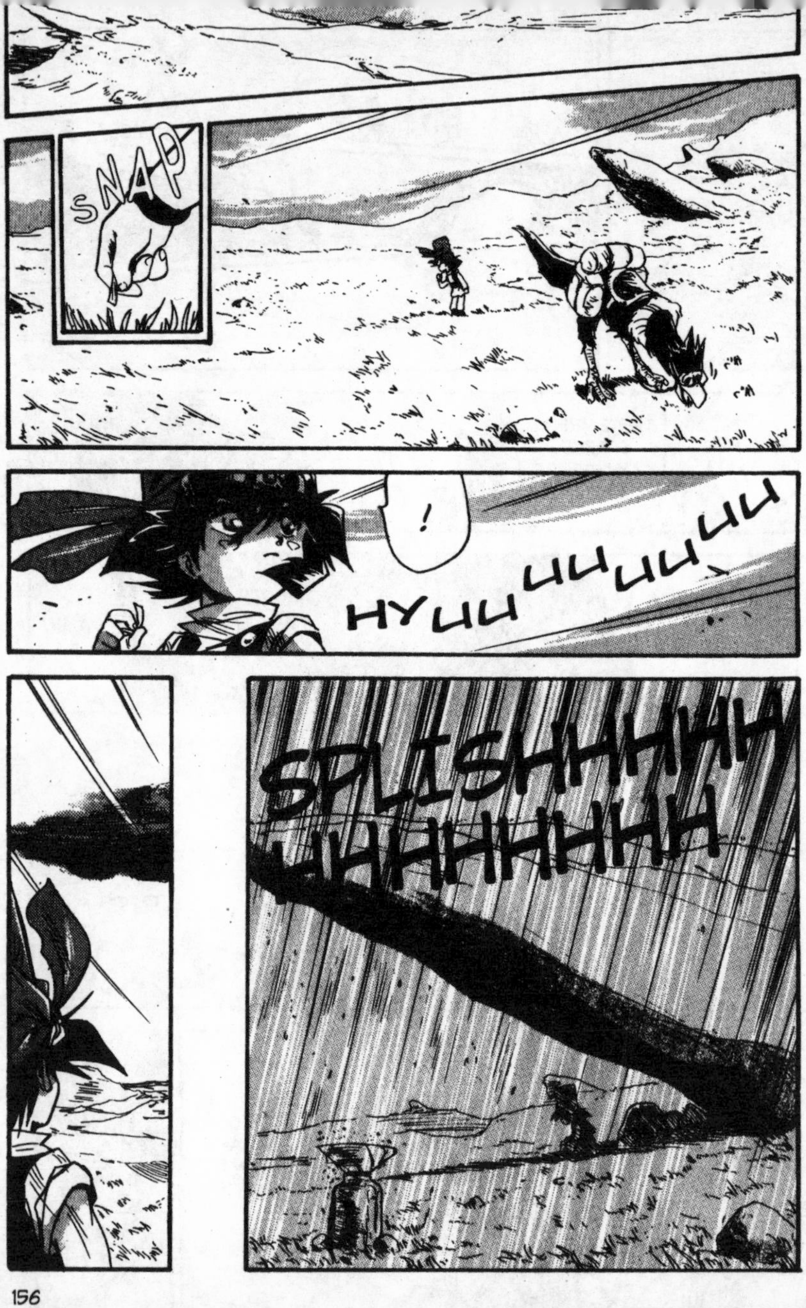
SNAP
!
HYUUUUUUUUUU
SPLISHHHHHHHHHHHHHHHH

THIS IS THE ONLY AREA WITH GRASS GROWING.

NOT ONLY THAT BUT THE GRASS IS STILL YOUNG...THERE MUST HAVE BEEN SOME RAIN THAT PASSED THROUGH HERE A COUPLE OF TIMES.

RUMBLE RUMBLE RUMBLE

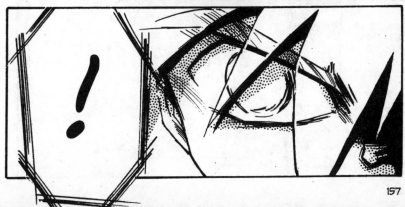

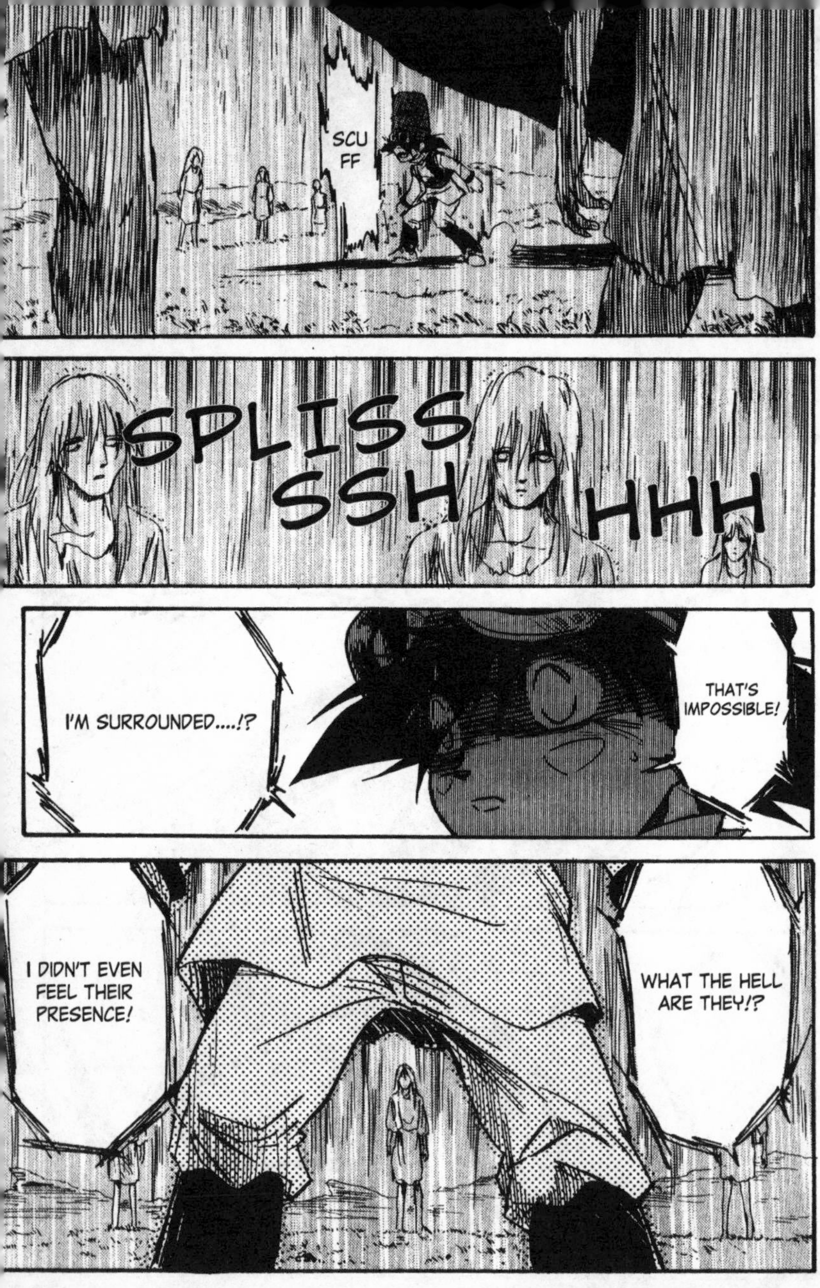
SCU
FF
SPLISS
SSH
HHH
I'M SURROUNDED....!?
THAT'S IMPOSSIBLE!
WHAT THE HELL ARE THEY!?
I DIDN'T EVEN FEEL THEIR PRESENCE!

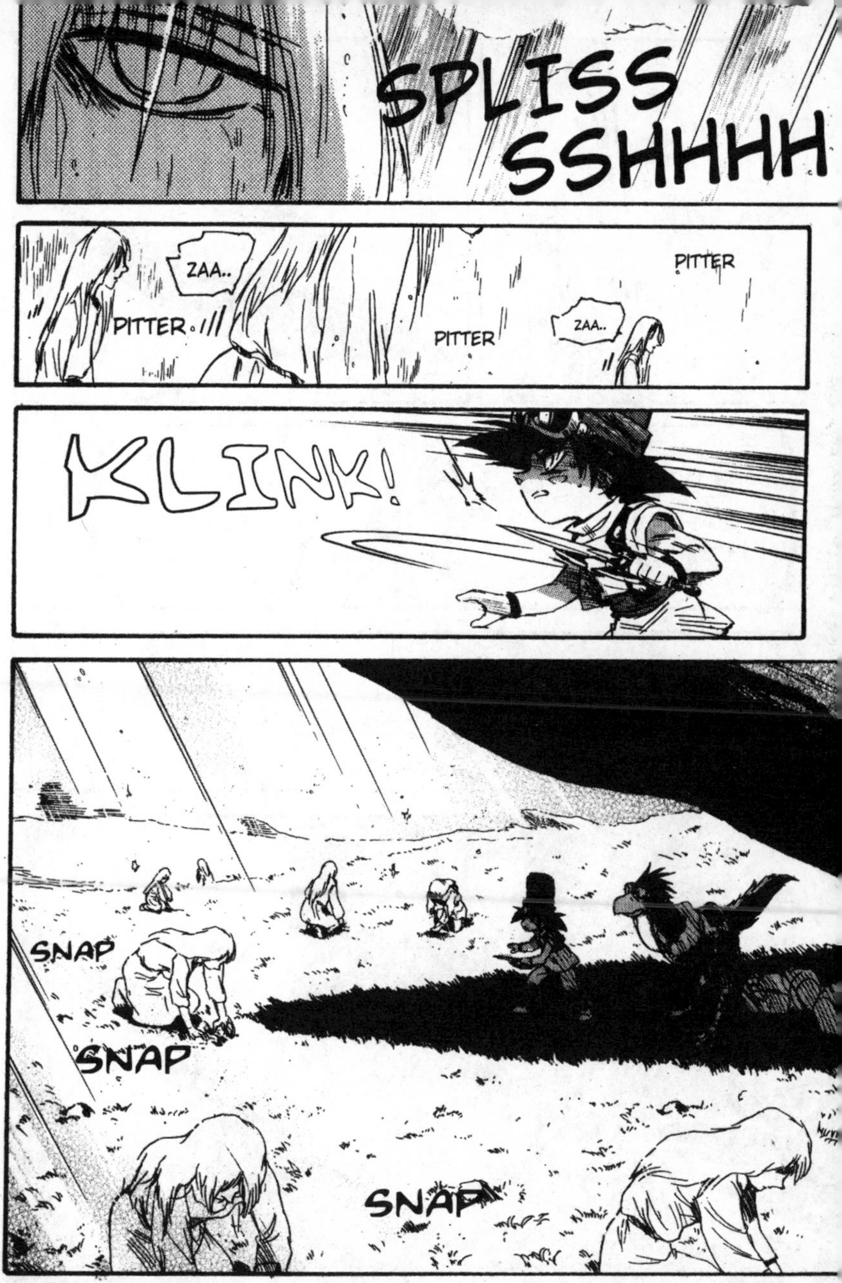
SPLISS
SSHHHH
ZAA..
PITTER
PITTER
PITTER
ZAA..
KLINK!
SNAP
SNAP
SNAP

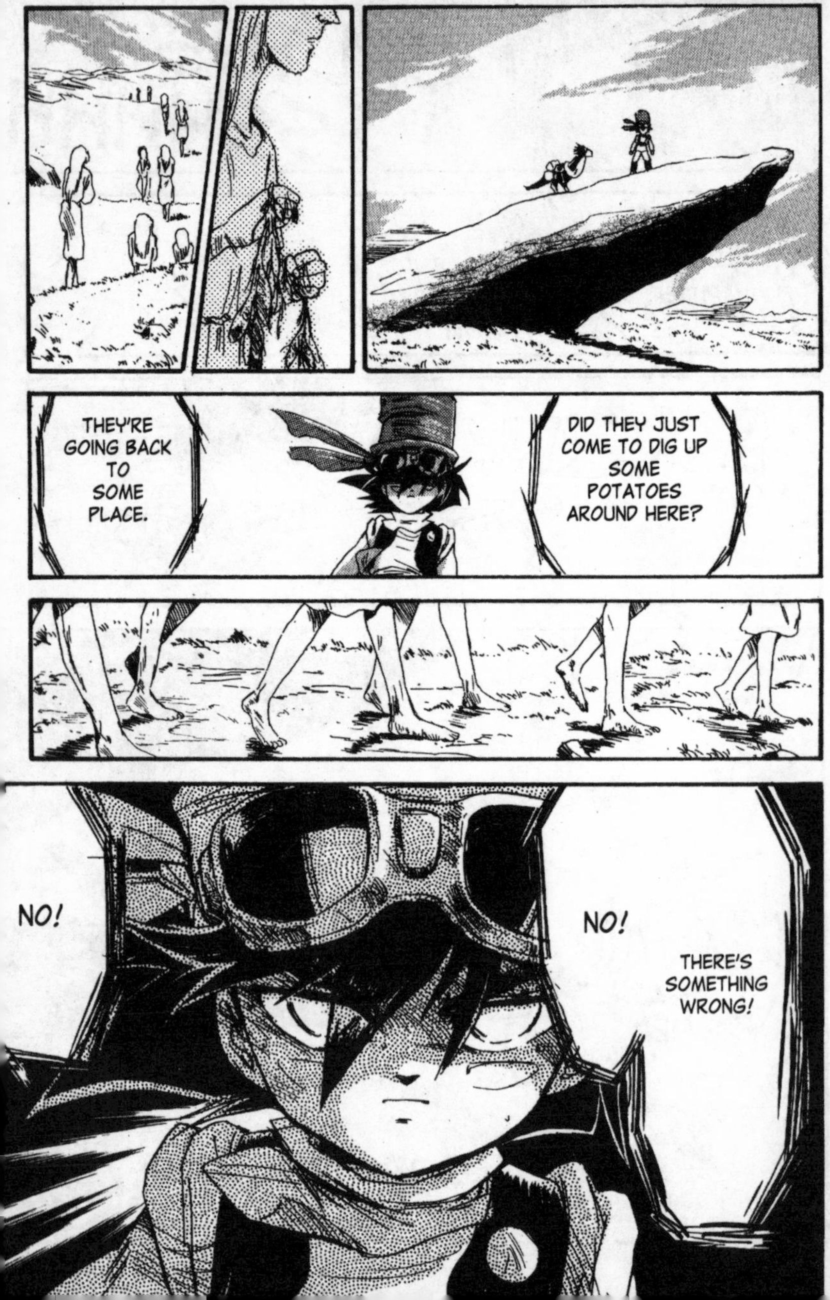
THEY'RE GOING BACK TO SOME PLACE.
DID THEY JUST COME TO DIG UP SOME POTATOES AROUND HERE?
NO!
NO!
THERE'S SOMETHING WRONG!

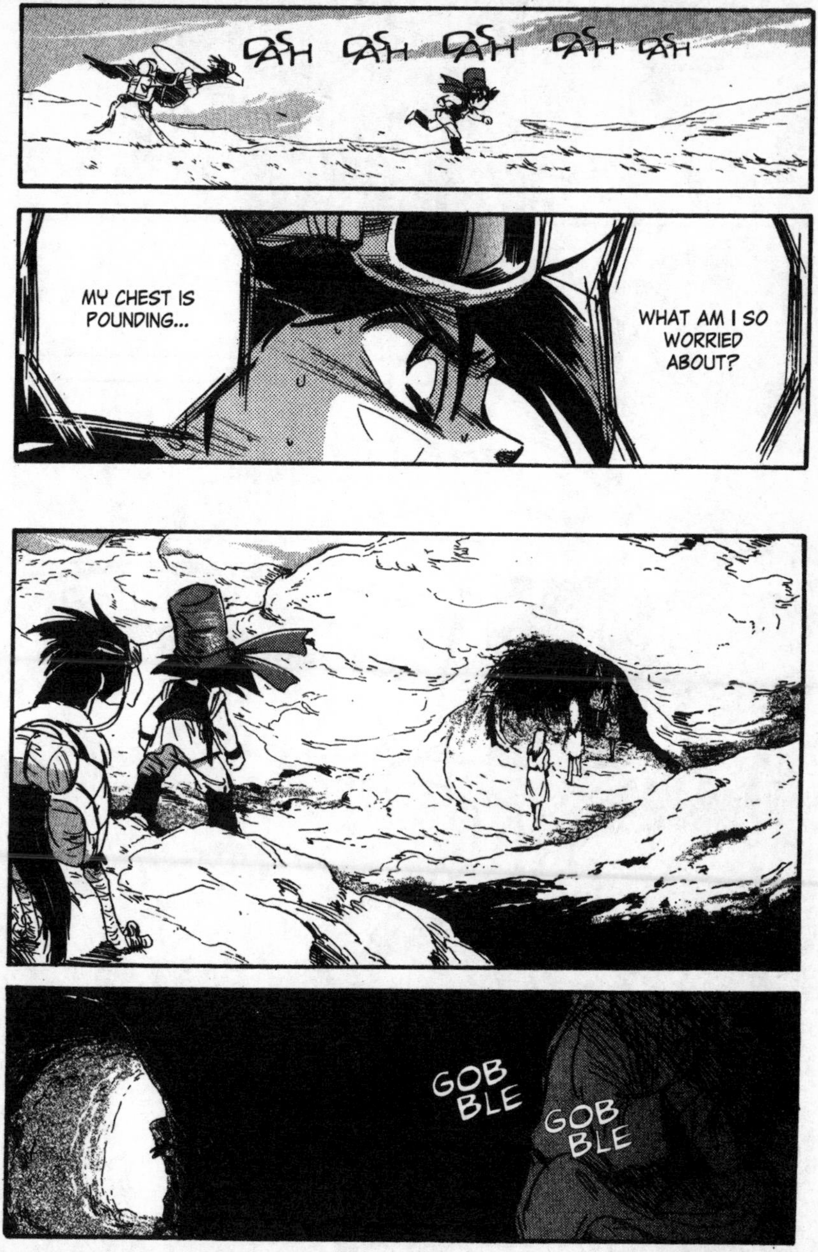
DASH DASH DASH DASH DASH
MY CHEST IS POUNDING...
WHAT AM I SO WORRIED ABOUT?
GOBBLE
GOBBLE

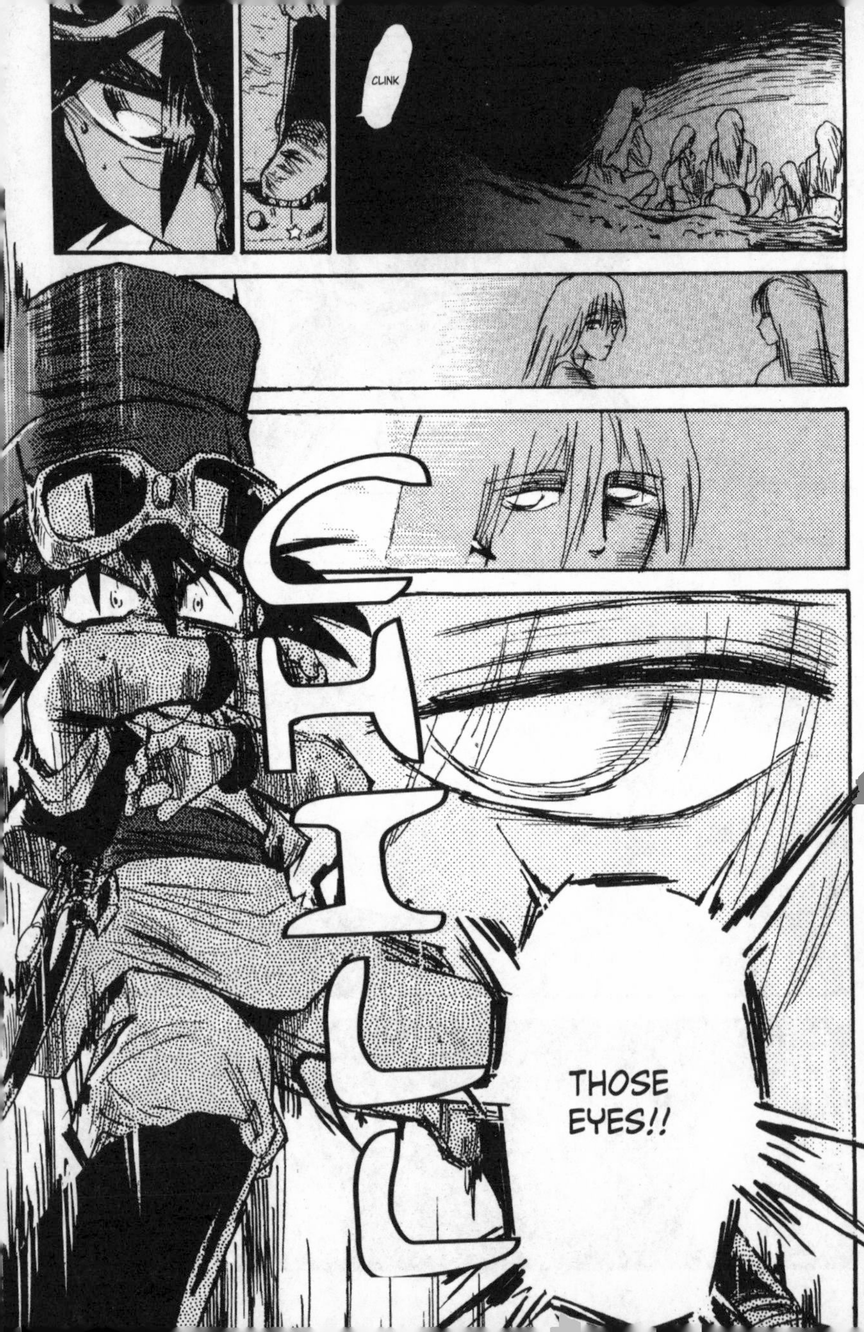
CLINK
THOSE EYES!!

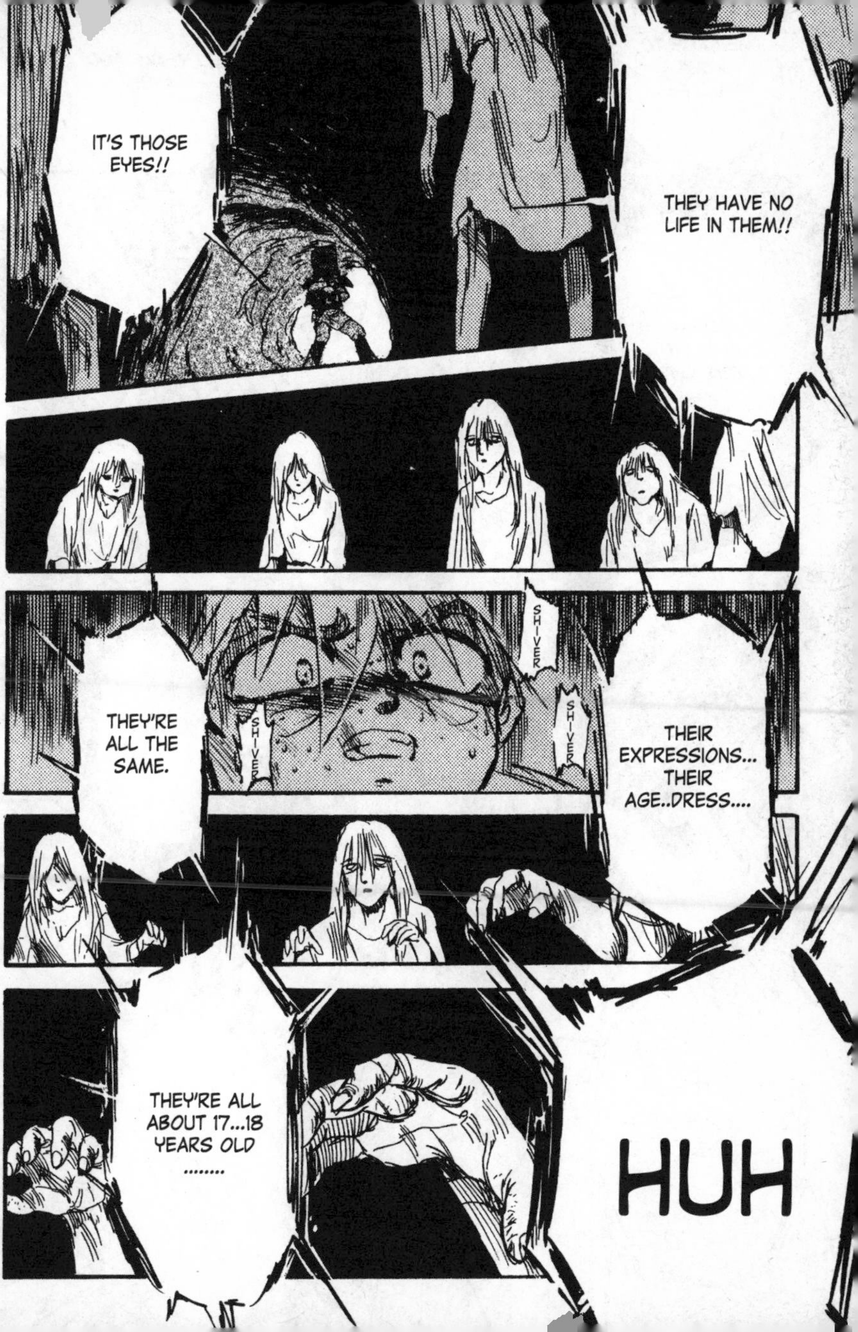
IT'S THOSE EYES!!
THEY HAVE NO LIFE IN THEM!!
THEY'RE ALL THE SAME.
SHIVER
SHIVER
SHIVER
THEIR EXPRESSIONS... THEIR AGE..DRESS....
THEY'RE ALL ABOUT 17...18 YEARS OLD ....
HUH

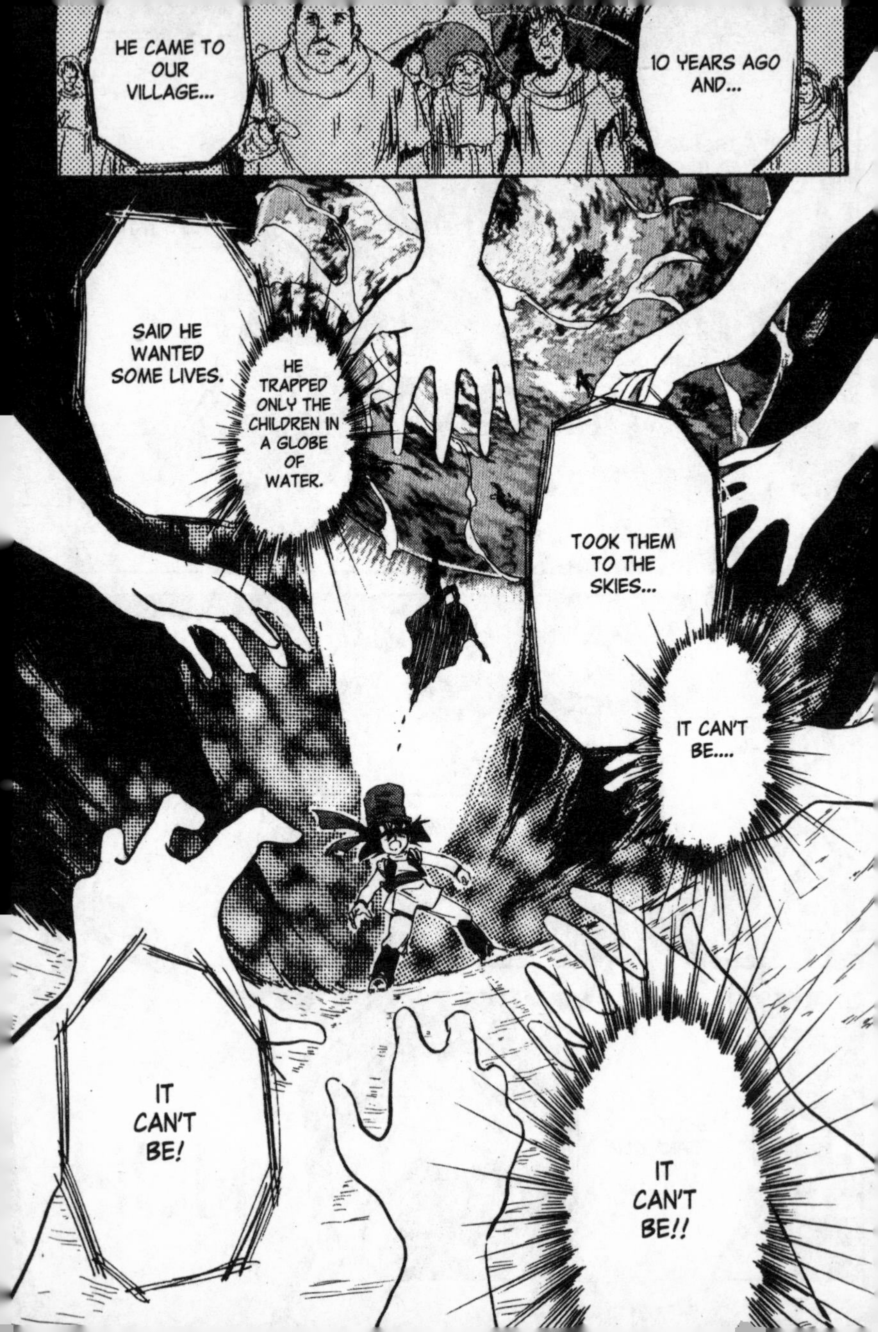
HE CAME TO OUR VILLAGE...
10 YEARS AGO AND...
SAID HE WANTED SOME LIVES.
HE TRAPPED ONLY THE CHILDREN IN A GLOBE OF WATER.
TOOK THEM TO THE SKIES...
IT CAN'T BE....
IT CAN'T BE!
IT CAN'T BE!!

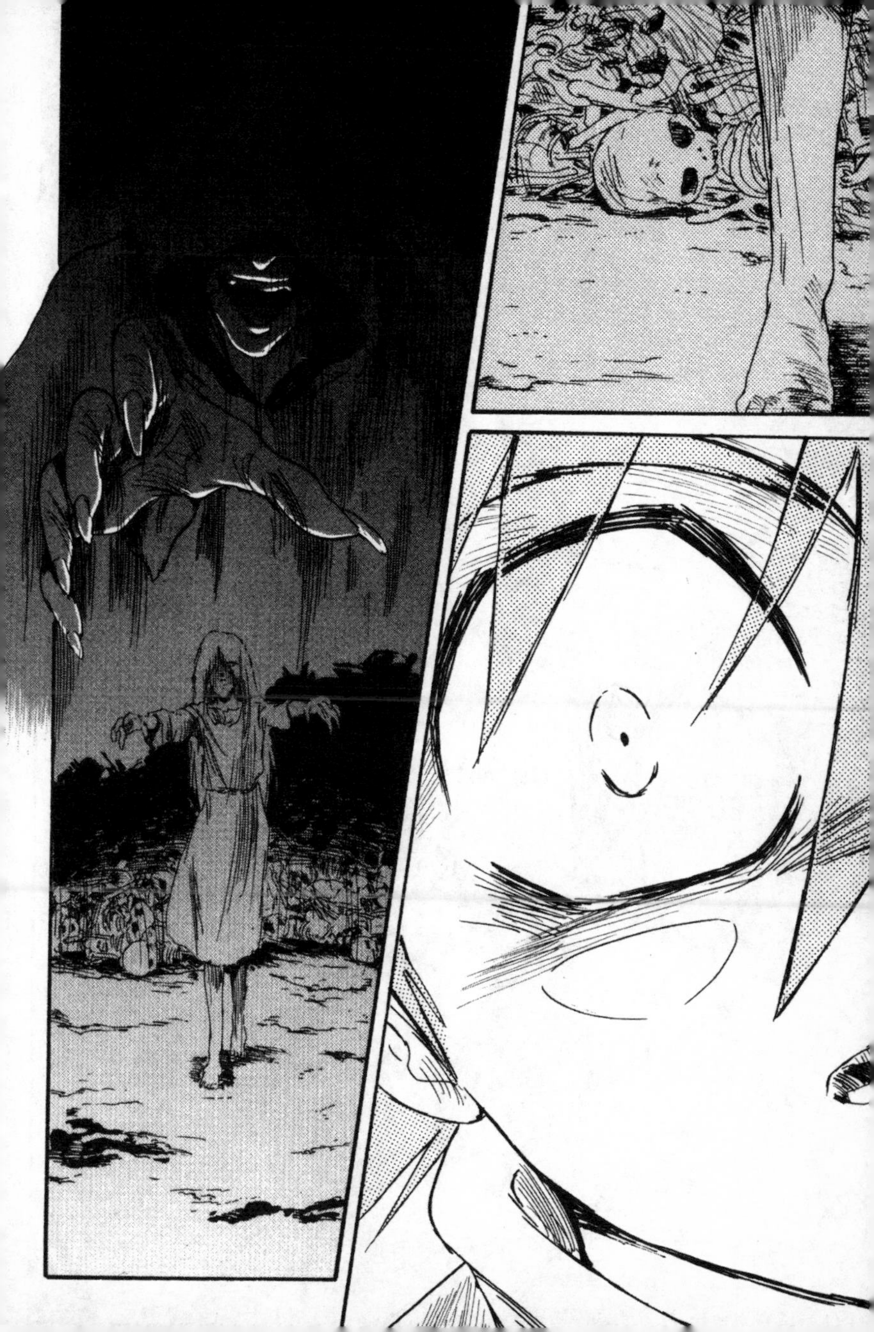

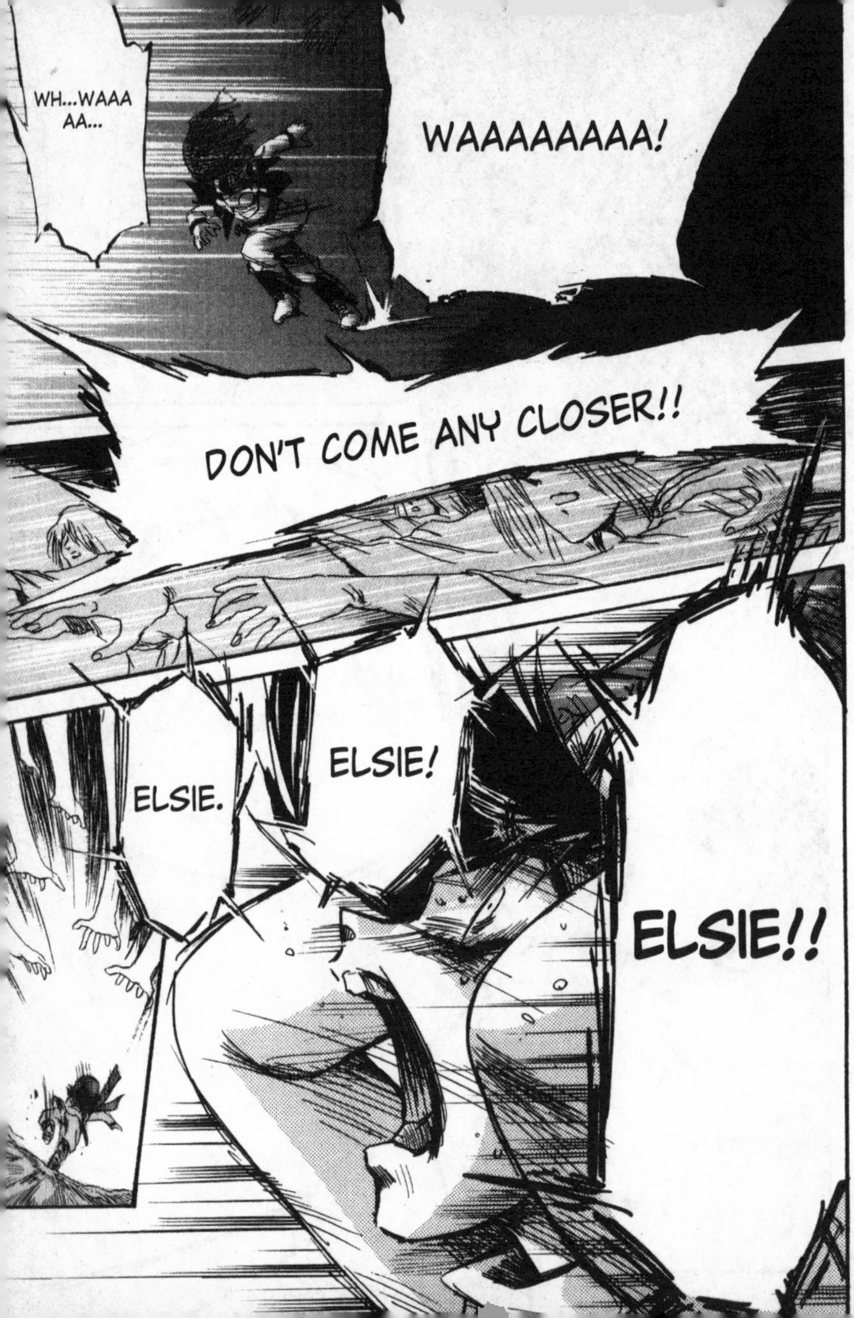
WAAAAAAAA!
WH...WAAA AA...
DON'T COME ANY CLOSER!!
ELSIE!
ELSIE.
ELSIE!!

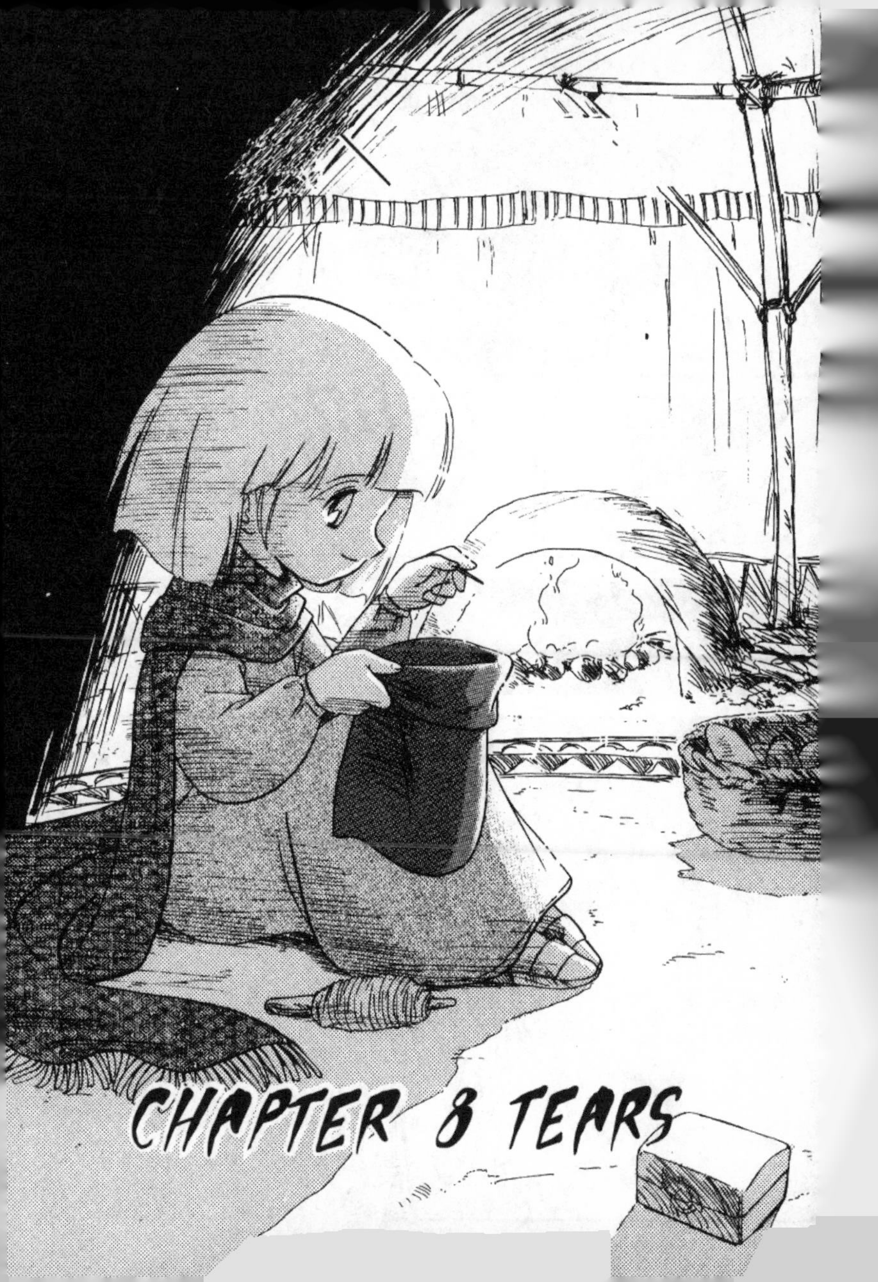
CHAPTER 8 TEARS

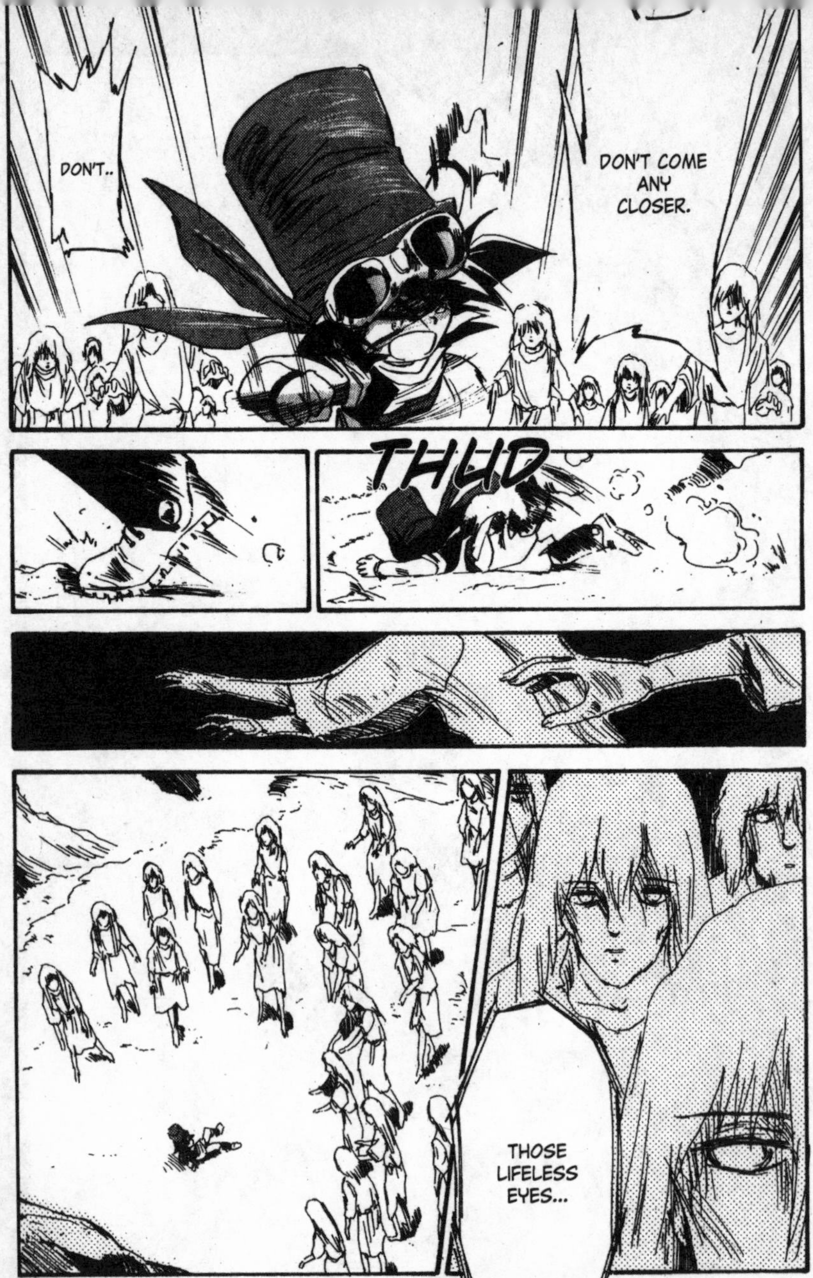

DON'T COME ANY CLOSER.
DON'T..
THUD
THOSE LIFELESS EYES...

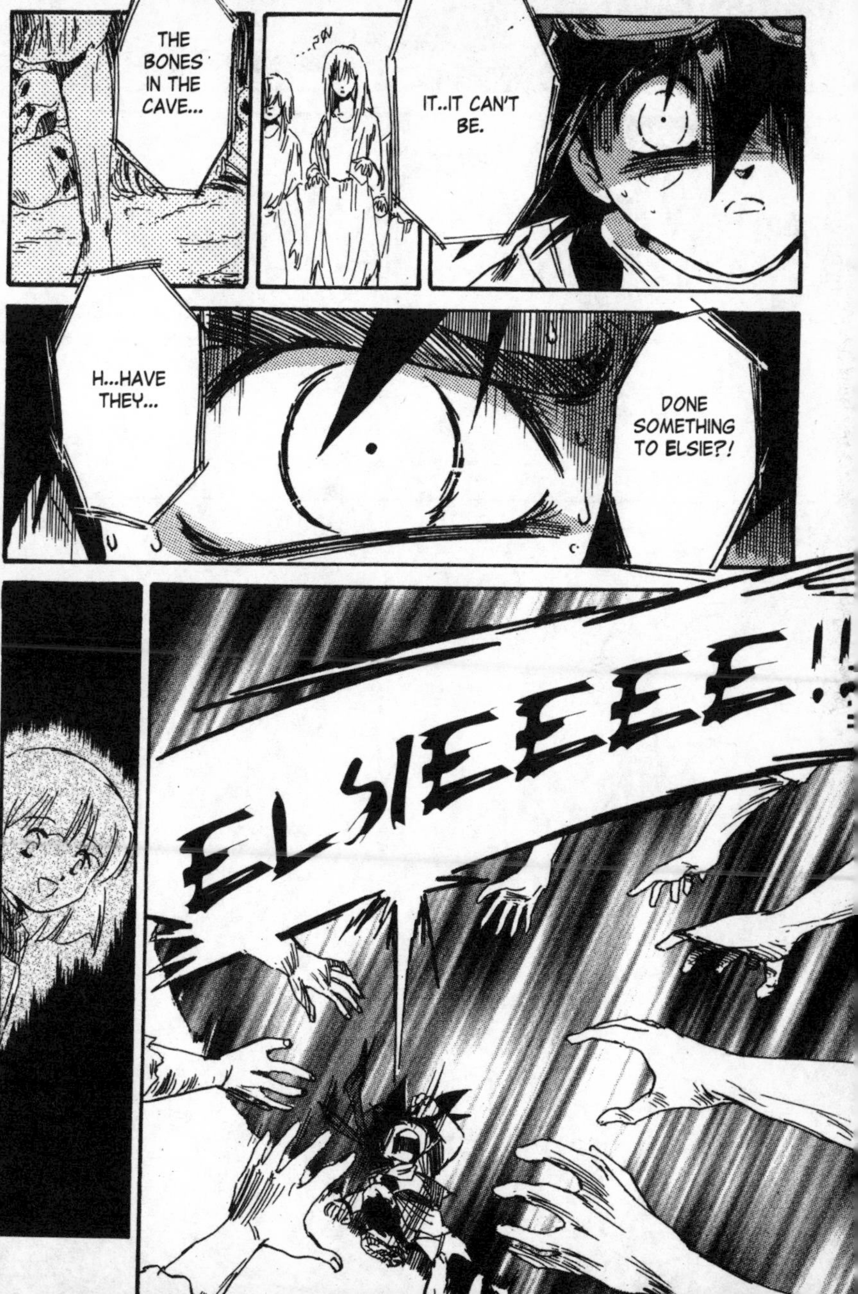
THE BONES IN THE CAVE...
IT..IT CAN'T BE.
H...HAVE THEY...
DONE SOMETHING TO ELSIE?!
ELSIEEEEE!!

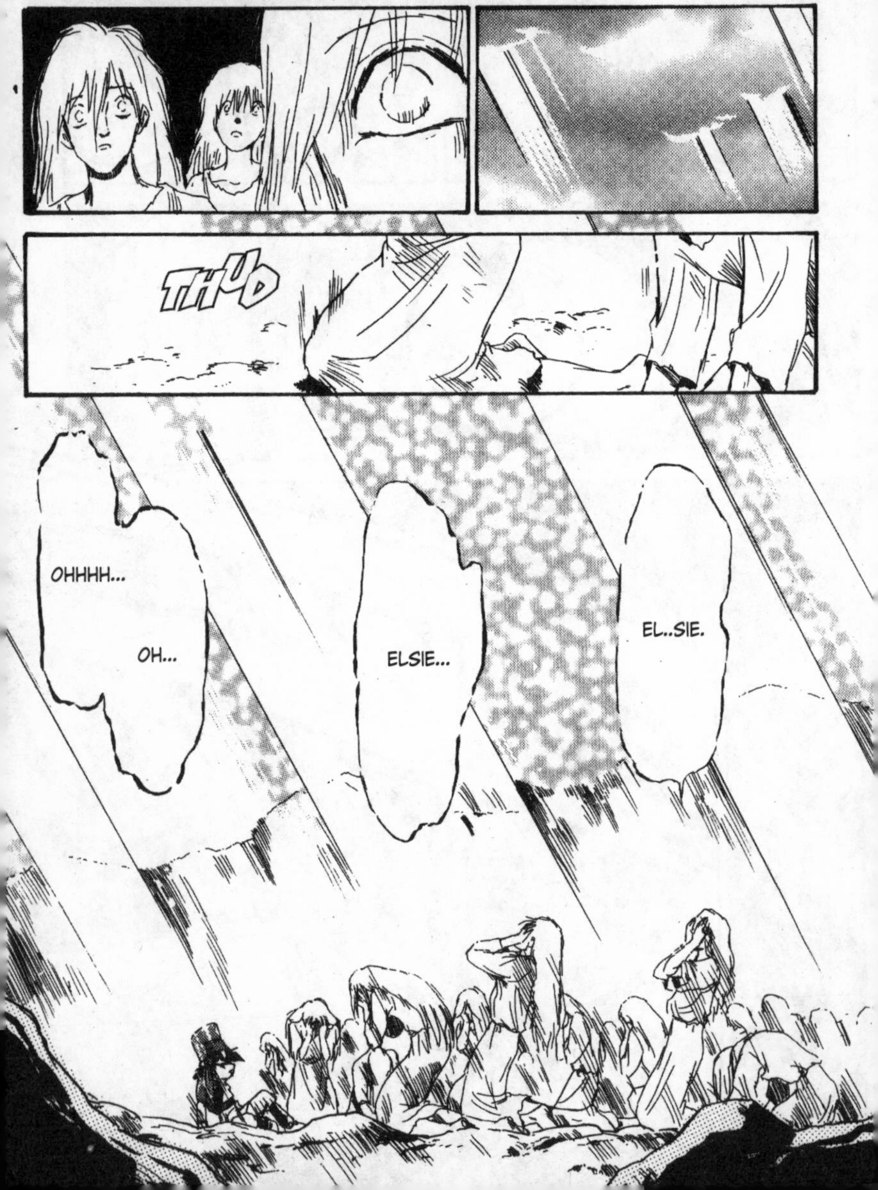
THUD
OHHHH...
OH...
ELSIE...
EL..SIE.

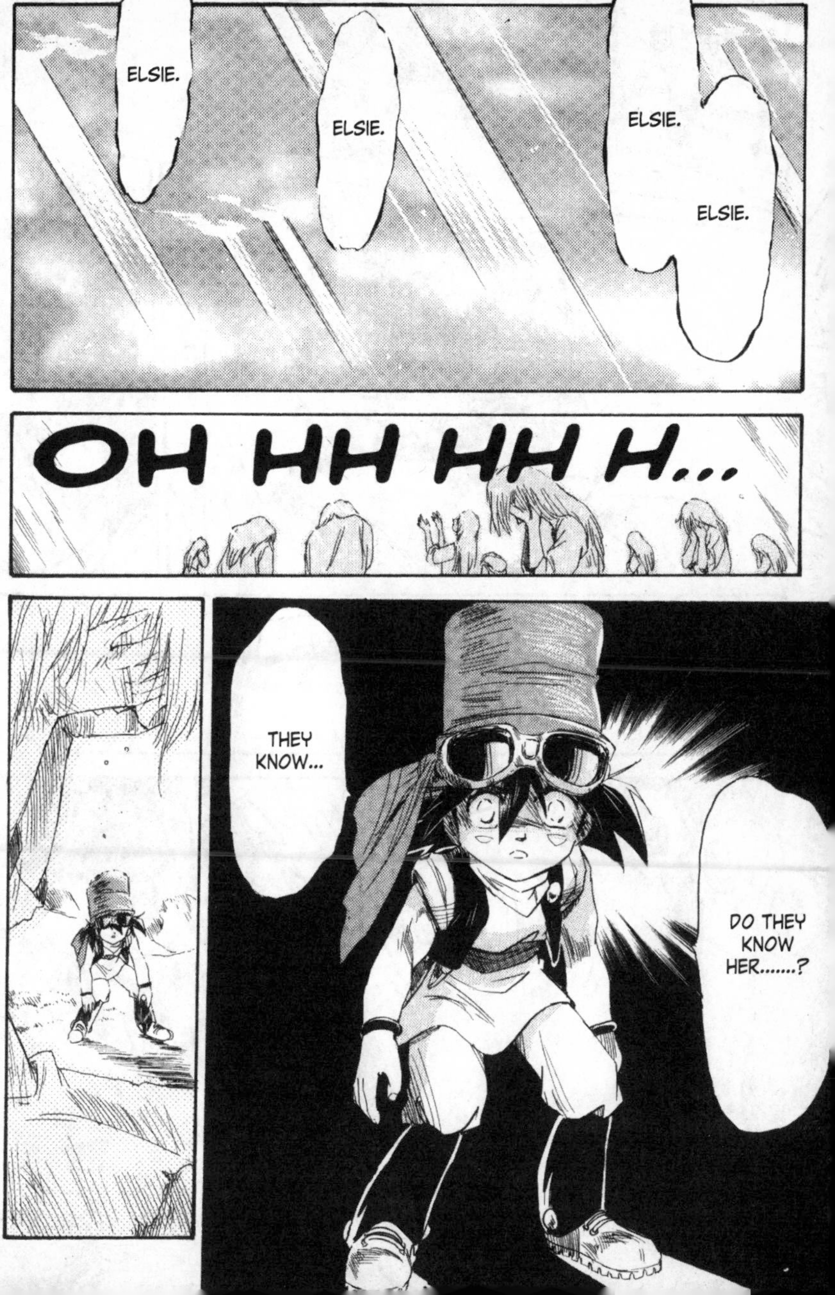
ELSIE.
ELSIE.
ELSIE.
ELSIE.
OH HH HH H...
THEY KNOW...
DO THEY KNOW HER.......?

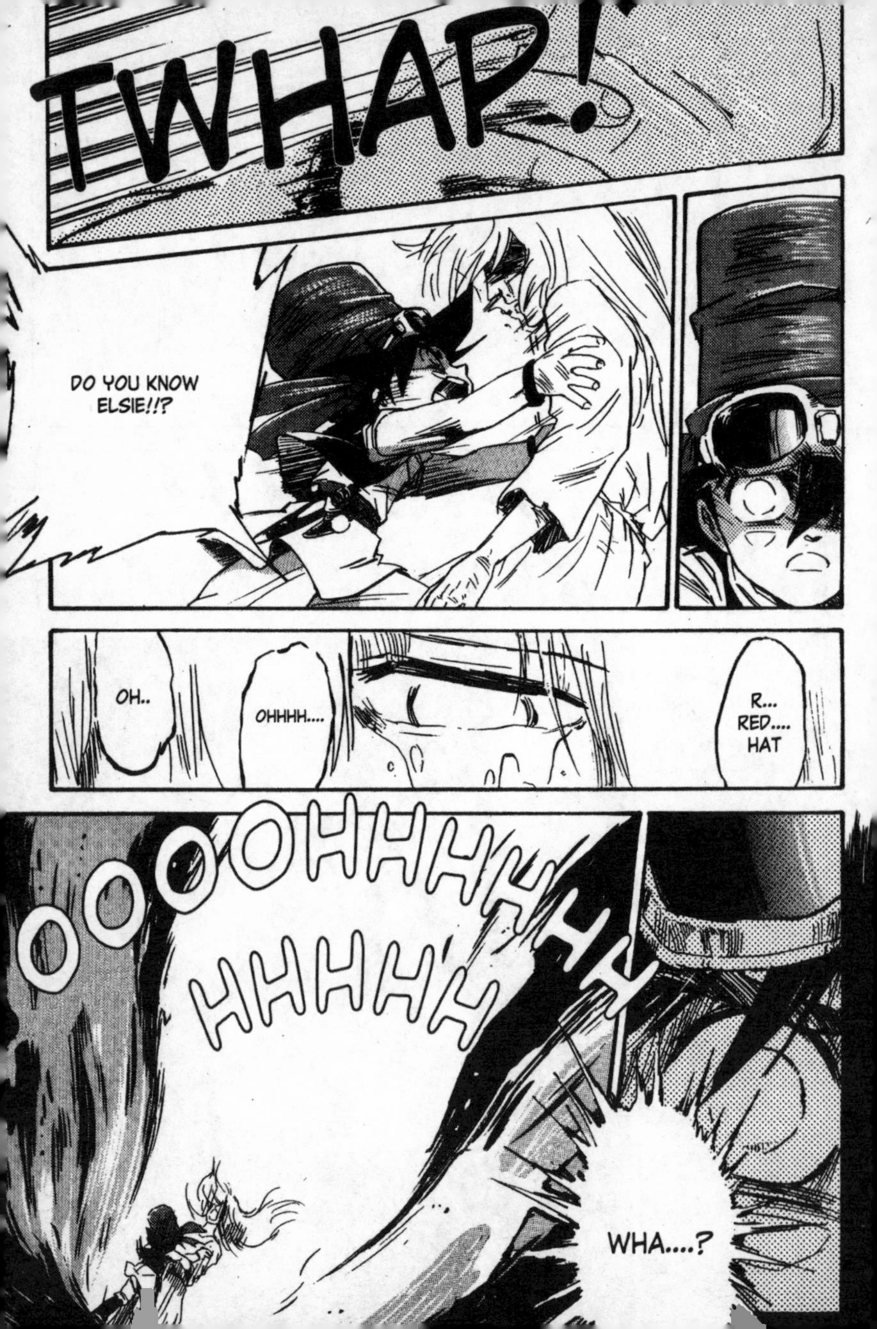
TWHAP!
DO YOU KNOW ELSIE!!?
OH..
OHHHH....
R... RED.... HAT
OOOOHHHHHHHHHHHH
WHA....?

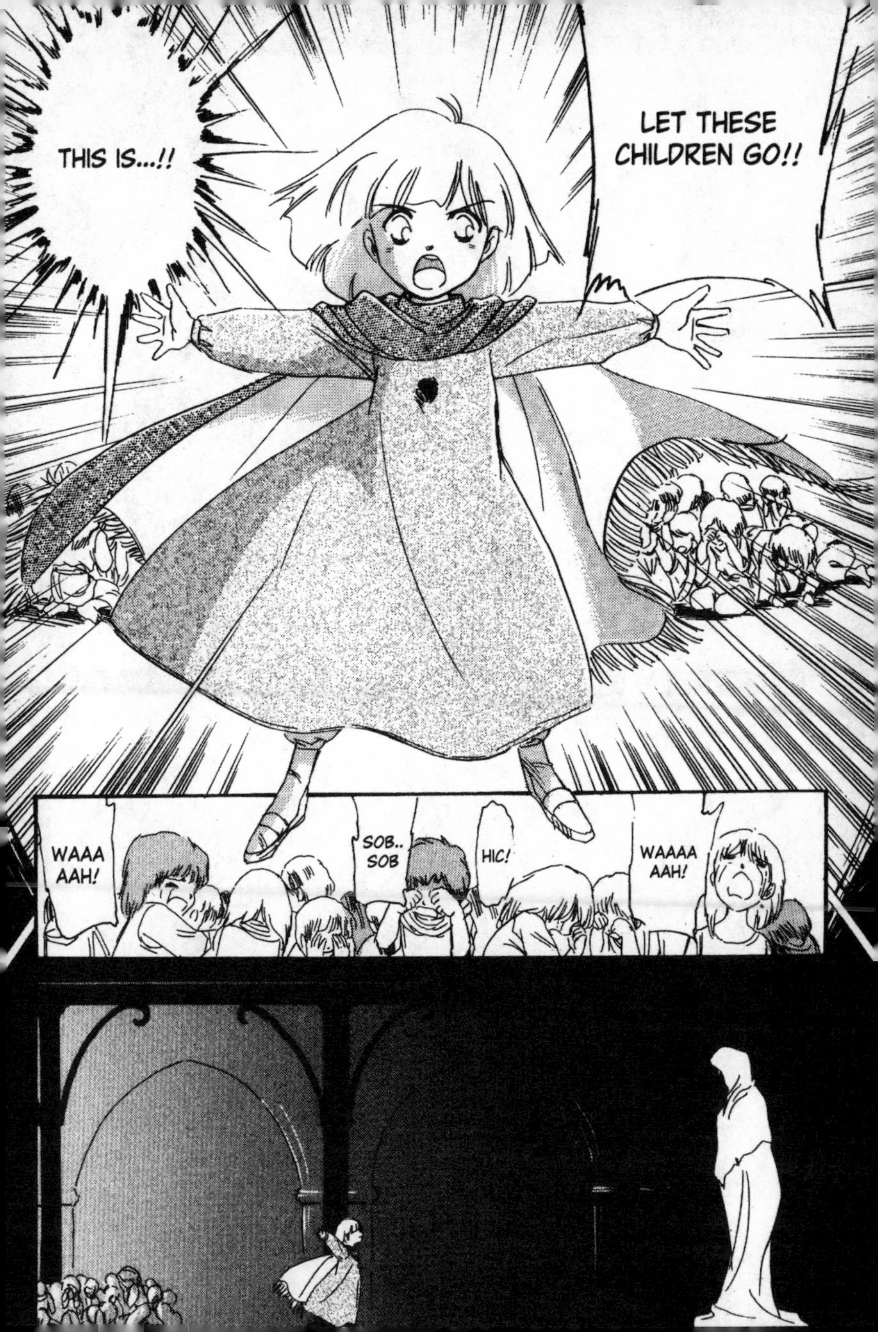
LET THESE CHILDREN GO!!
THIS IS...!!
WAAAAA AAH!
HIC!
SOB.. SOB
WAAA AAH!

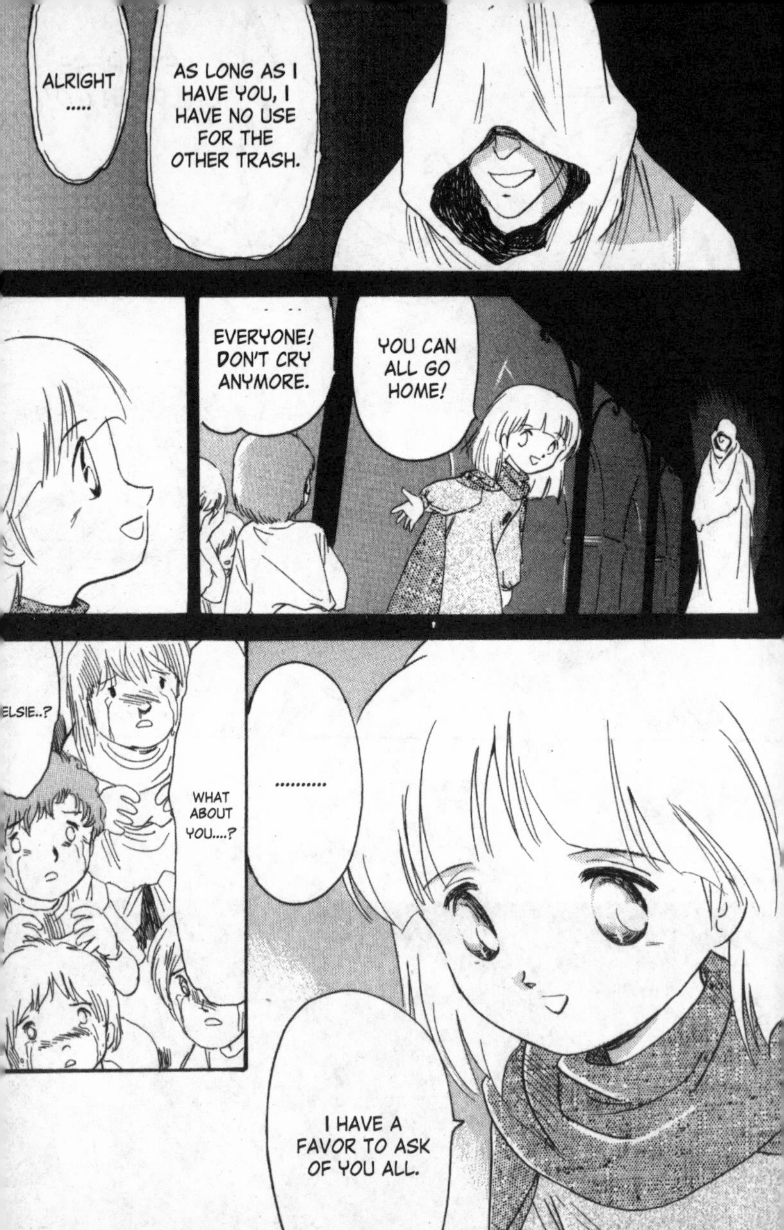
AS LONG AS I HAVE YOU, I HAVE NO USE FOR THE OTHER TRASH.
ALRIGHT .....
EVERYONE! DON'T CRY ANYMORE.
YOU CAN ALL GO HOME!
ELSIE..?
WHAT ABOUT YOU....?
....
I HAVE A FAVOR TO ASK OF YOU ALL.

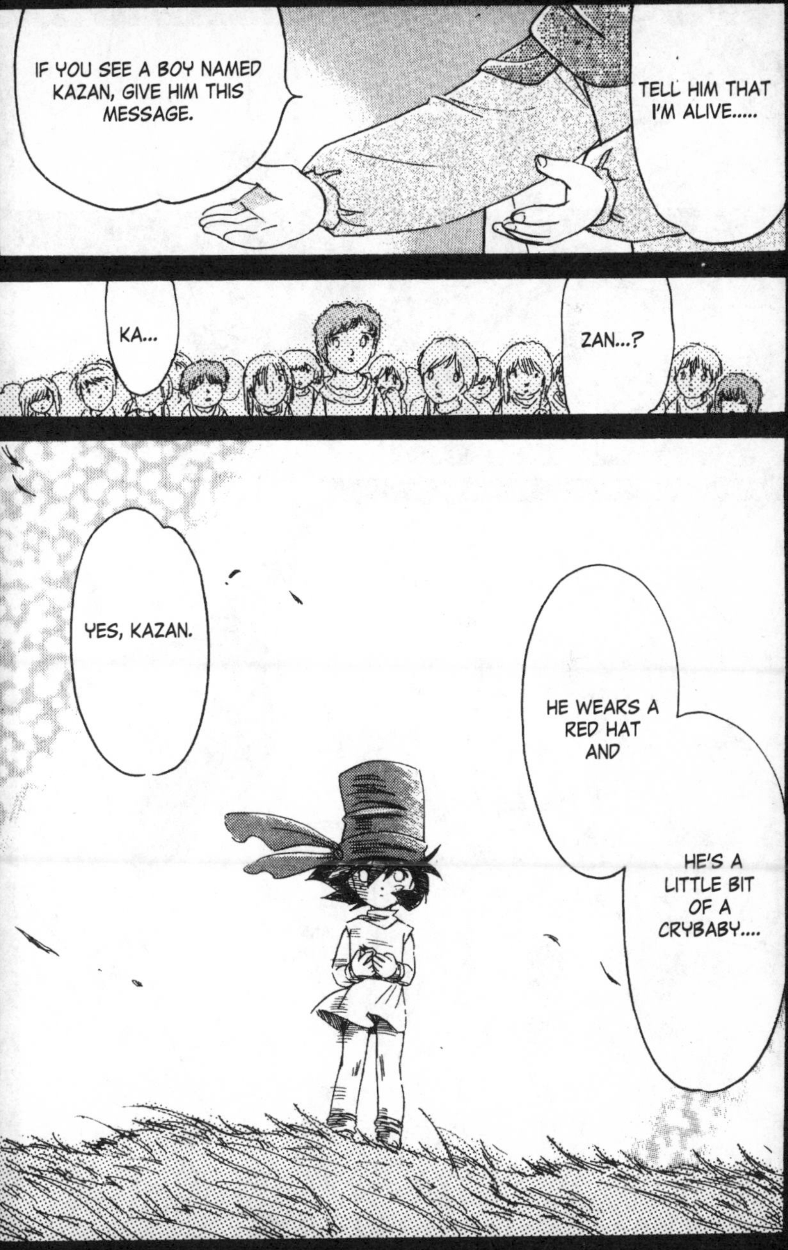
TELL HIM THAT I'M ALIVE.....
IF YOU SEE A BOY NAMED KAZAN, GIVE HIM THIS MESSAGE.
ZAN...?
KA...
HE WEARS A RED HAT AND
HE'S A LITTLE BIT OF A CRYBABY....
YES, KAZAN.

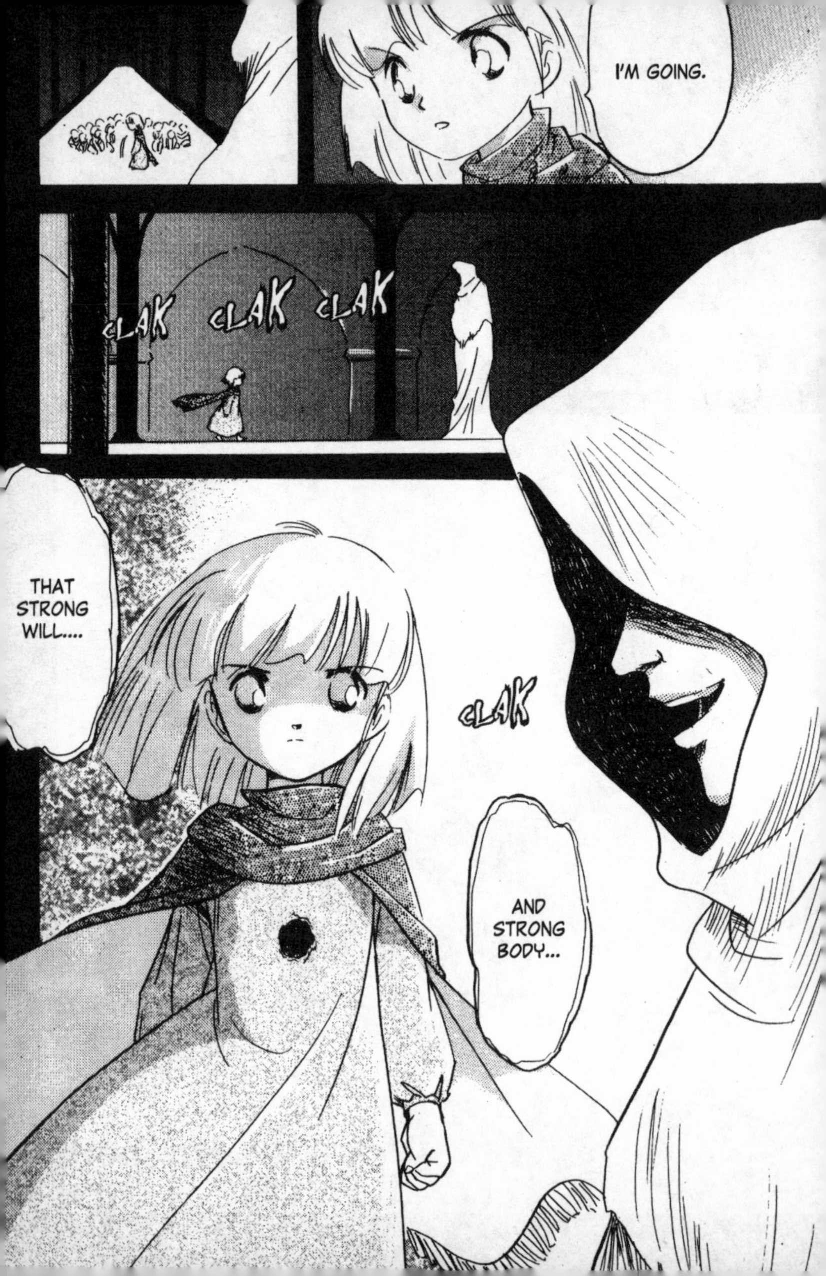
I'M GOING.
CLAK CLAK CLAK
THAT STRONG WILL....
CLAK
AND STRONG BODY...

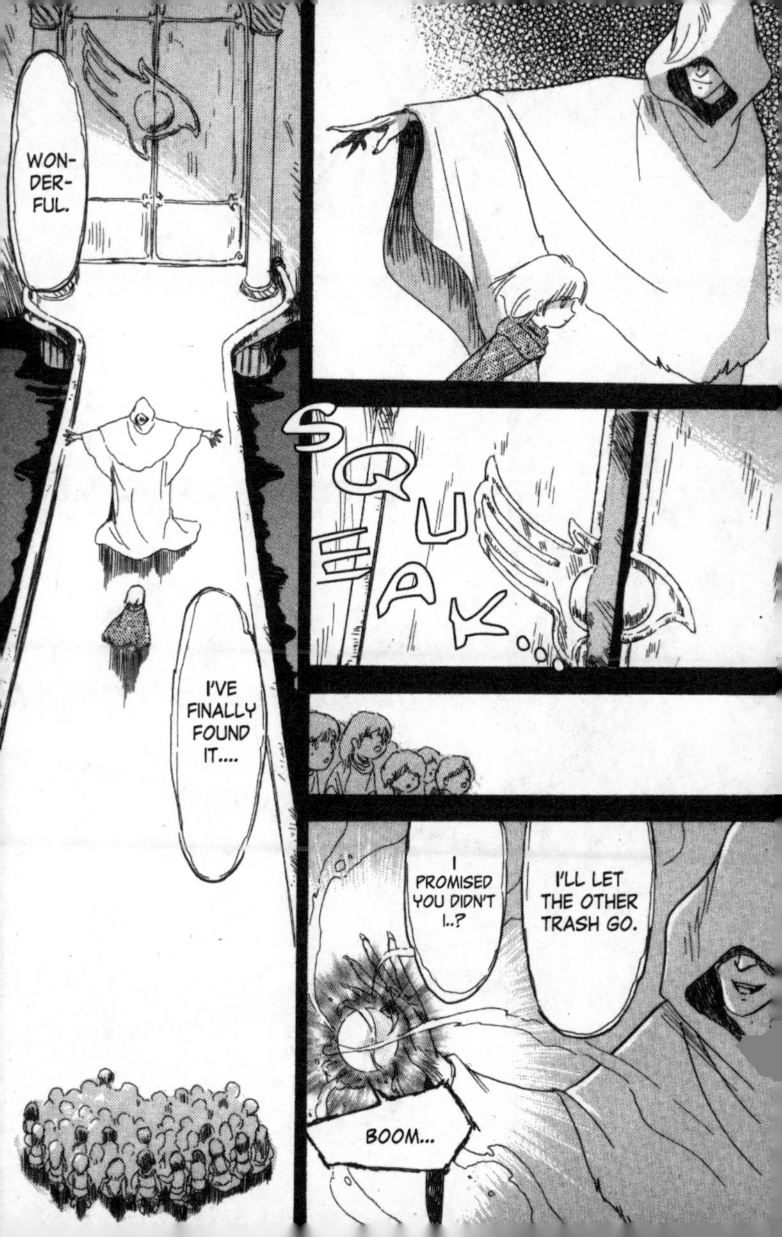
SQUEAK...
I'LL LET THE OTHER TRASH GO.
I PROMISED YOU DIDN'T I..?
BOOM...
WON-DER-FUL.
I'VE FINALLY FOUND IT....

SHOOO OOM

BWHA

BUT.....

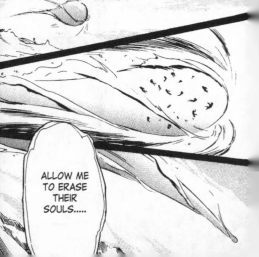

ALLOW ME
TO ERASE
THEIR
SOULS.....

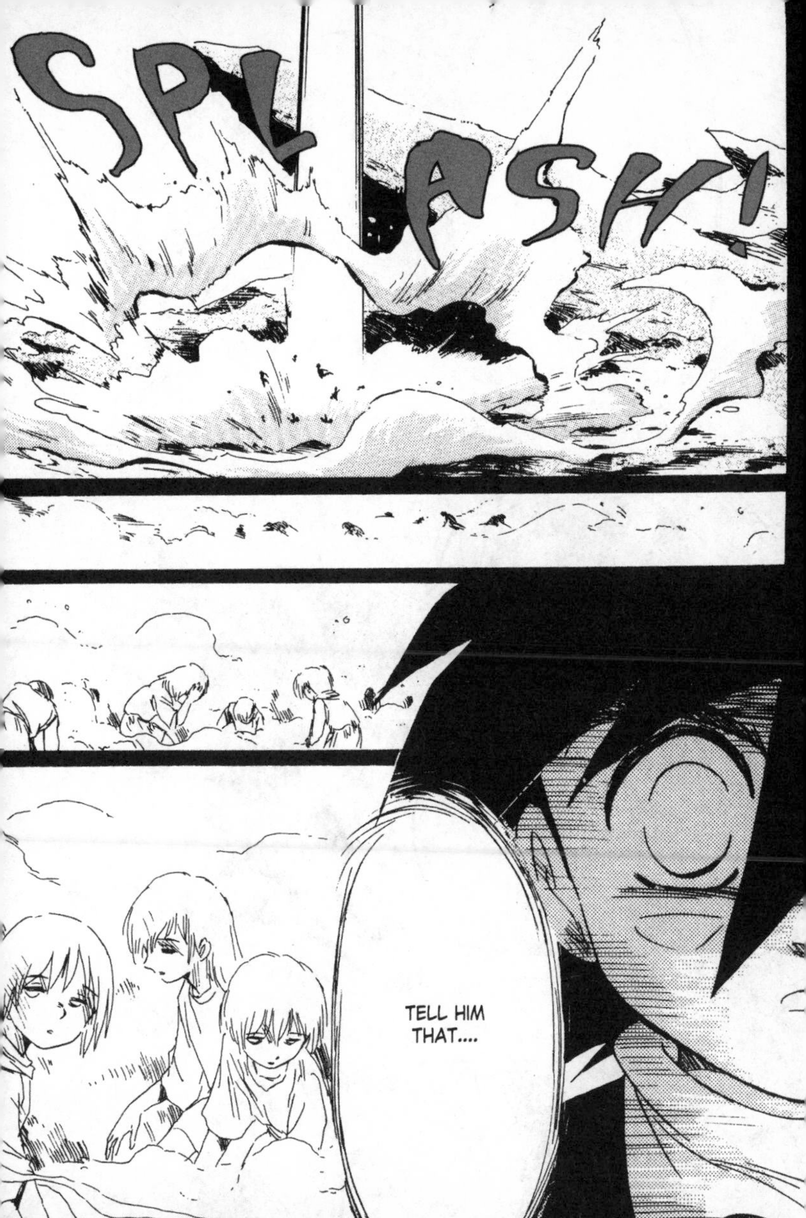
SPLASH!
TELL HIM THAT....

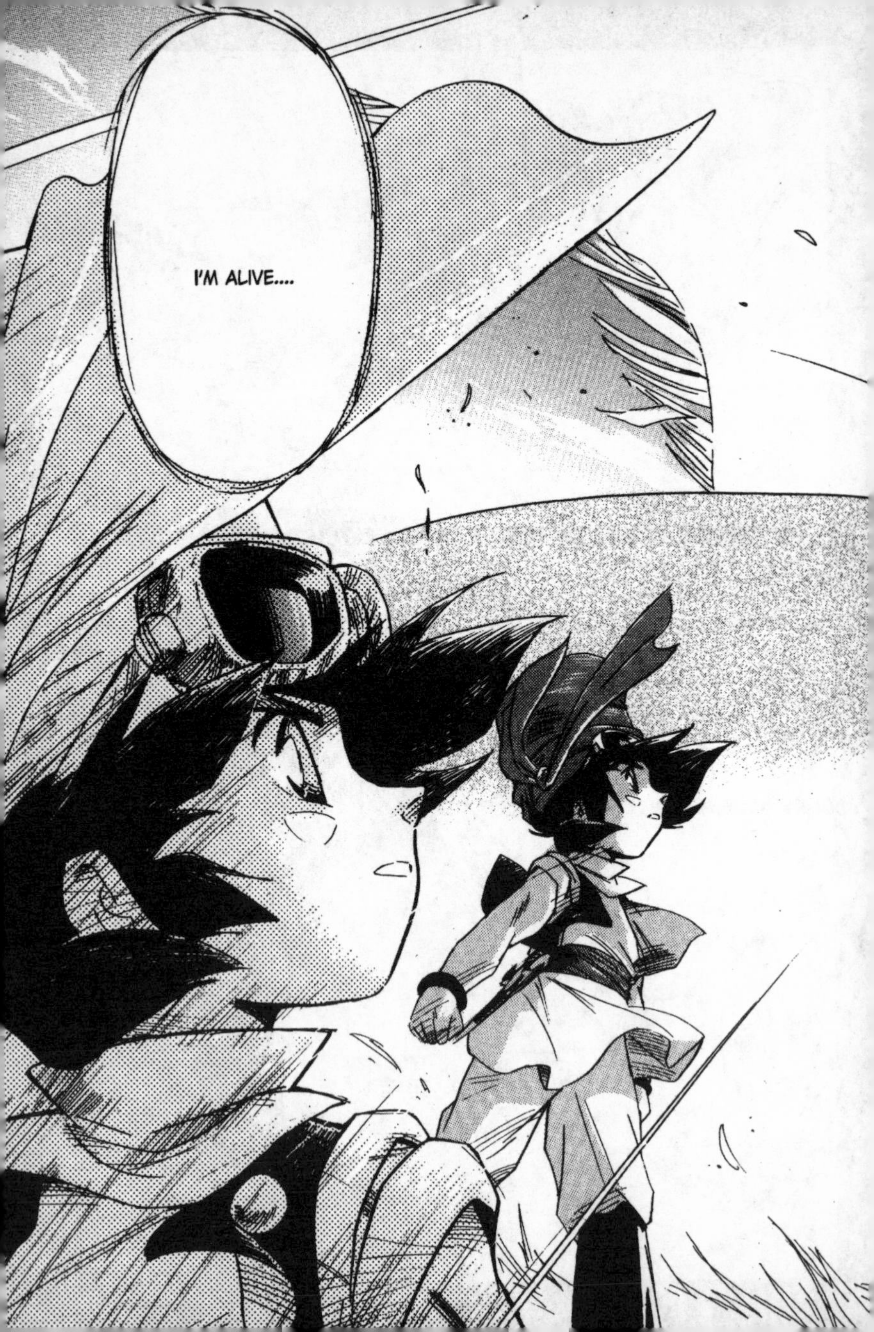
I'M ALIVE....

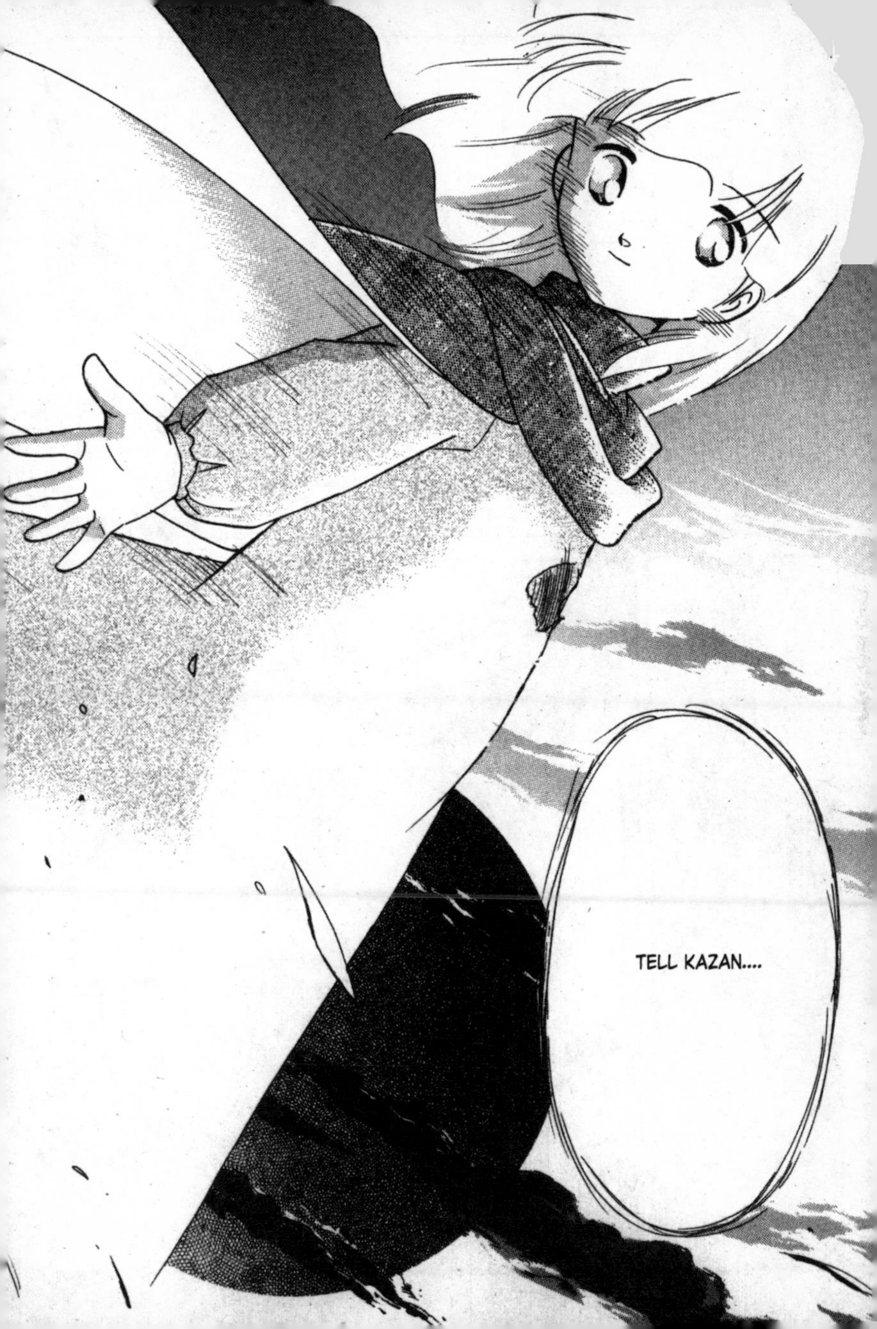
TELL KAZAN....

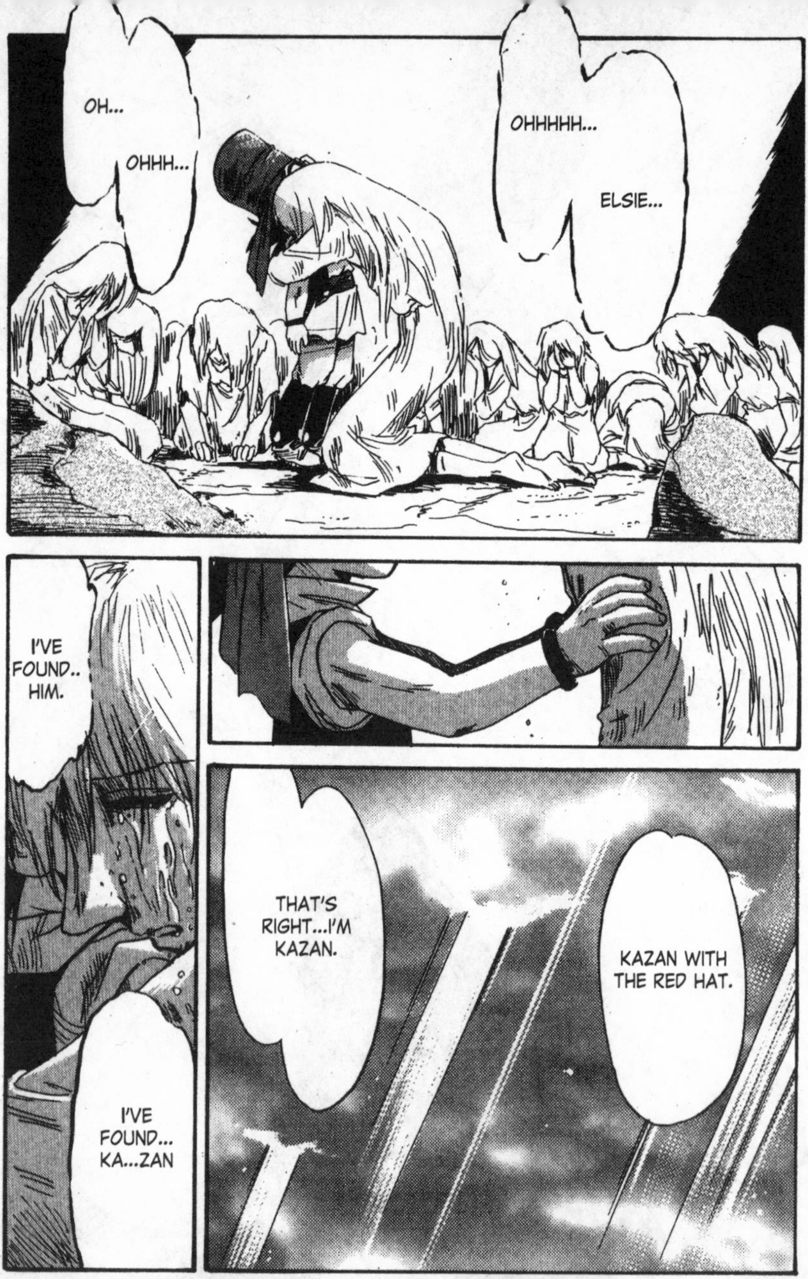
OH...
OHHH...
OHHHHH...
ELSIE...
I'VE FOUND.. HIM.
THAT'S RIGHT...I'M KAZAN.
KAZAN WITH THE RED HAT.
I'VE FOUND... KA...ZAN

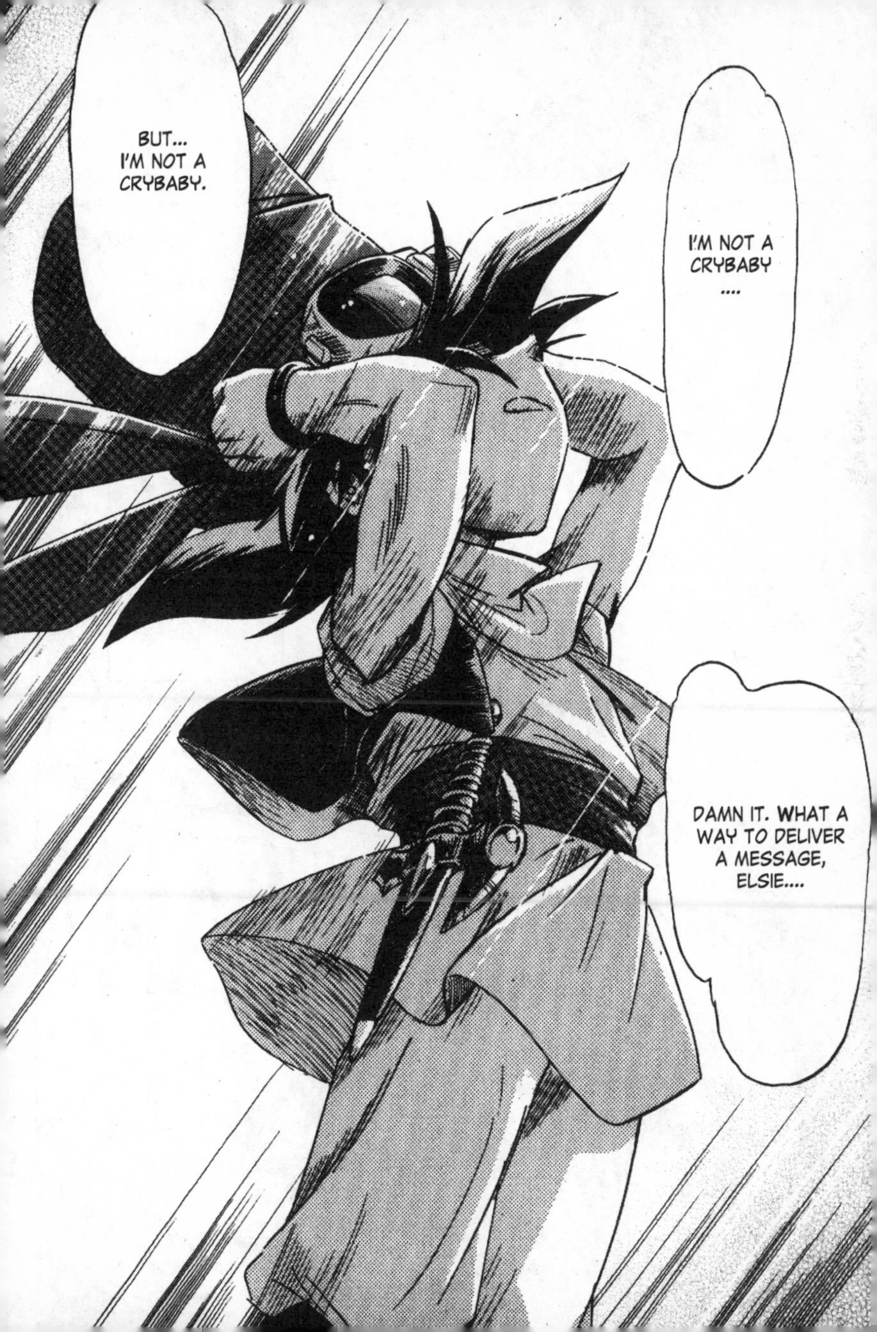
I'M NOT A CRYBABY ....
BUT... I'M NOT A CRYBABY.
DAMN IT. WHAT A WAY TO DELIVER A MESSAGE, ELSIE....

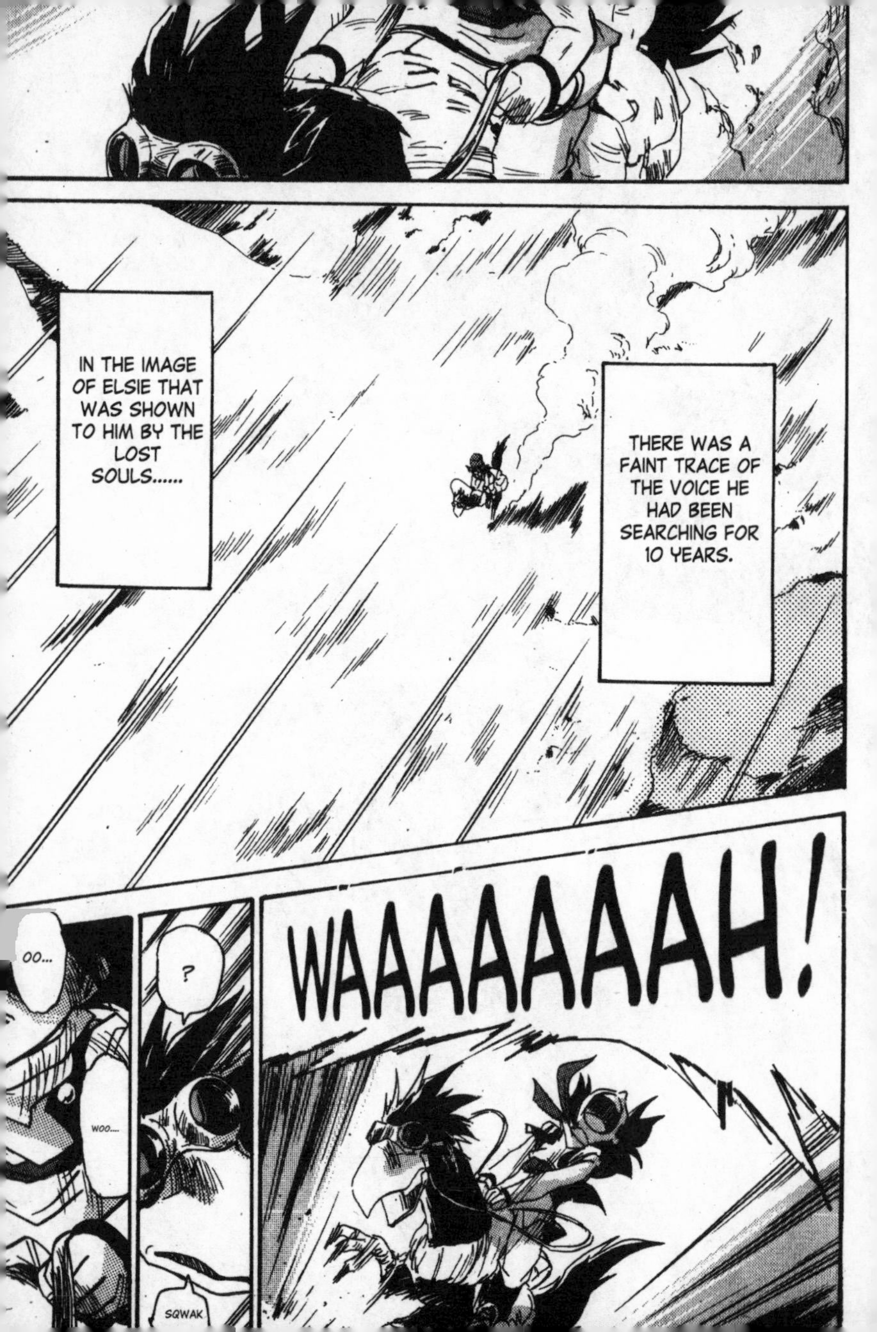

IN THE IMAGE OF ELSIE THAT WAS SHOWN TO HIM BY THE LOST SOULS......
THERE WAS A FAINT TRACE OF THE VOICE HE HAD BEEN SEARCHING FOR 10 YEARS.
WAAAAAAAH!
?
OO...
WOO....
SQWAK

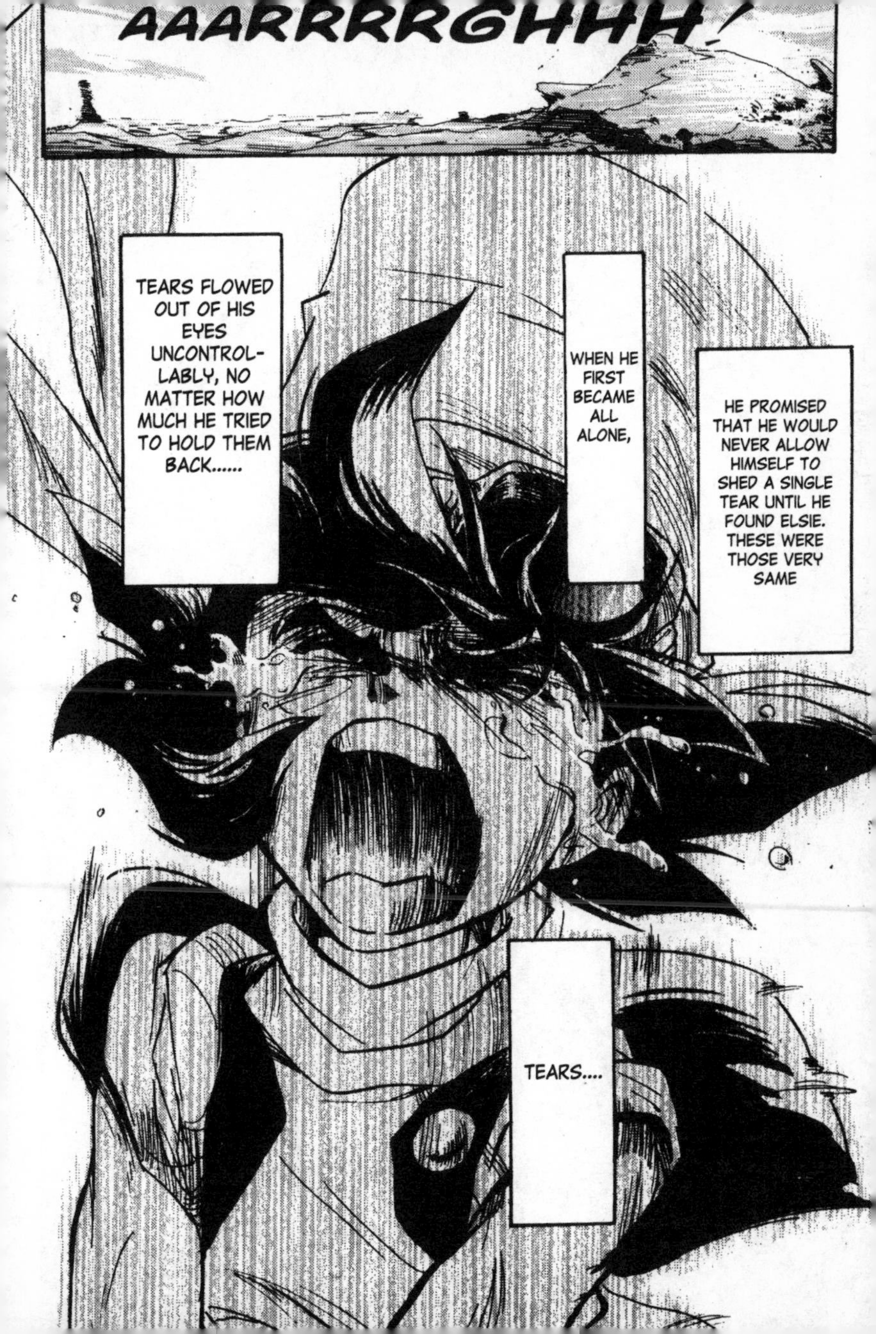
AAARRRRGHHH!
TEARS FLOWED OUT OF HIS EYES UNCONTROL-LABLY, NO MATTER HOW MUCH HE TRIED TO HOLD THEM BACK......
WHEN HE FIRST BECAME ALL ALONE,
HE PROMISED THAT HE WOULD NEVER ALLOW HIMSELF TO SHED A SINGLE TEAR UNTIL HE FOUND ELSIE. THESE WERE THOSE VERY SAME
TEARS....

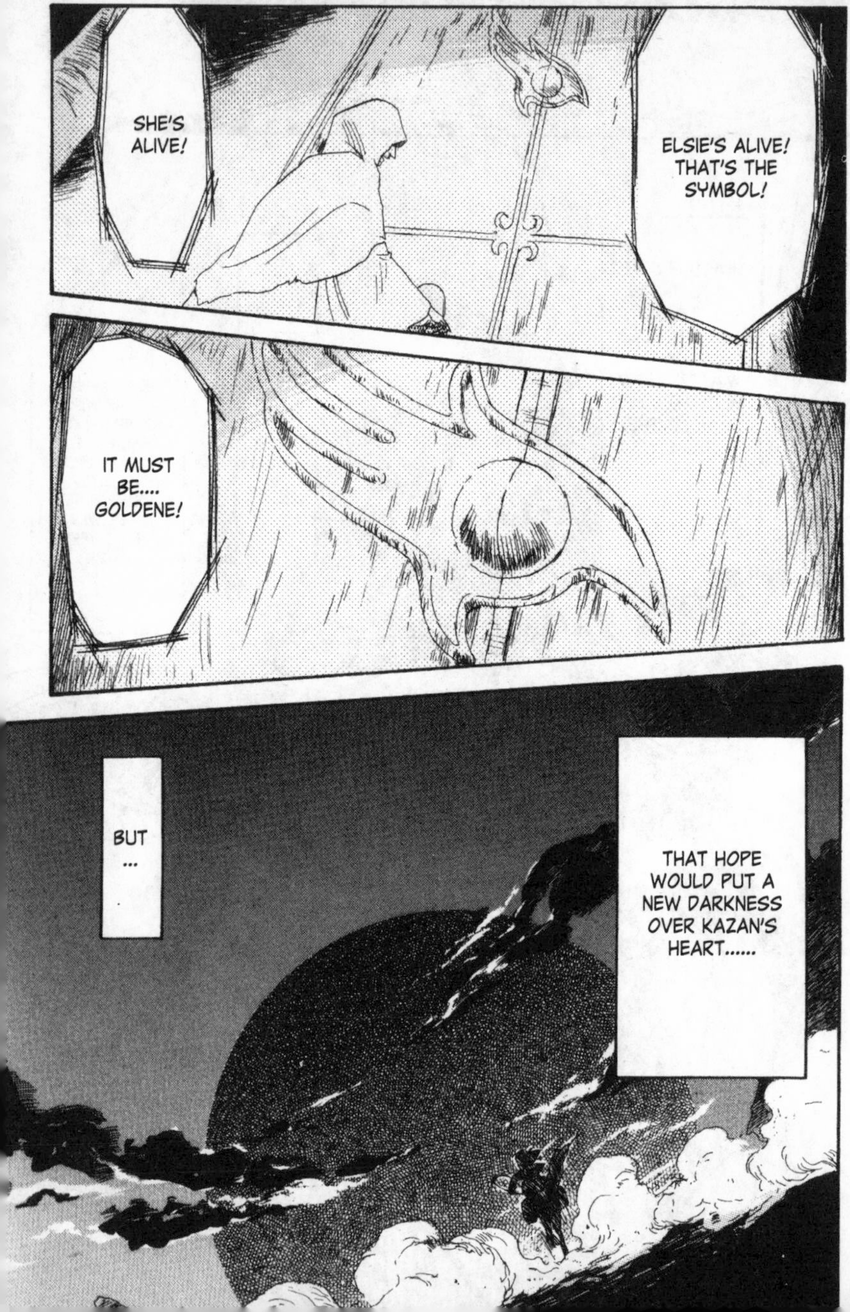
ELSIE'S ALIVE! THAT'S THE SYMBOL!
SHE'S ALIVE!
IT MUST BE.... GOLDENE!
THAT HOPE WOULD PUT A NEW DARKNESS OVER KAZAN'S HEART......
BUT ...

KAZAN

END OF VOLUME 4

CONTINUED IN VOLUME 5

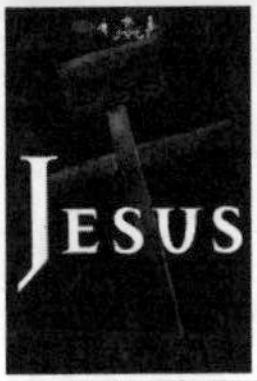
JESUS

JESUS by Yoshikazu Yasuhiko

Jesus. Teacher, healer, savior. The story of one of the most revered figures in human history is revisited in this full-length graphic novel, featuring breathtaking full-color art by Yoshikazu Yasuhiko.

*Volume 1-2 are available in ebook format.
*200-207 pages each

JOAN by Yoshikazu Yasuhiko

Emil is a young woman who may be the second coming of Joan of Arc. Following visions of Joan, Emil undergoes her own mission to unite a feudal France under the divine rule of the King.

*Volume 1-3 are available in ebook format.
*183-223 pages each

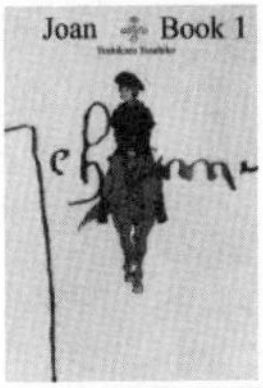
Joan Book 1

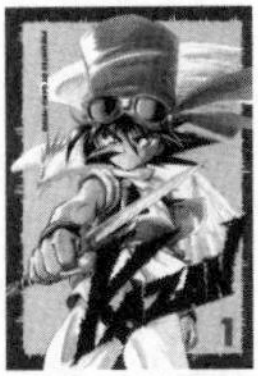

KAZAN by Gaku Miyao

Kazan is a boy warrior searching for his childhood companion on a desert planet. Magic and swordplay accompany Kazan and his friends on the road to the legendary land of Goldene.

*Volume 1-3 are available in ebook and hardcopy formats.
*187-201 pages each

MAICO 2010 by Toshimitsu Shimizu

Maico s a charming young woman who also happens to be an android--and the sexy new DJ of Japan Radio! She ends up entangled in a human love triangle, plenty of scandal and intrigue surrounding the station, and a mysterious military organization that wants her dead!

*Volume 1-3 are available in ebook and hardcopy formats.
*184-209 pages each

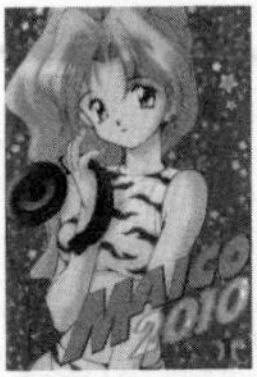
MAICO 2010

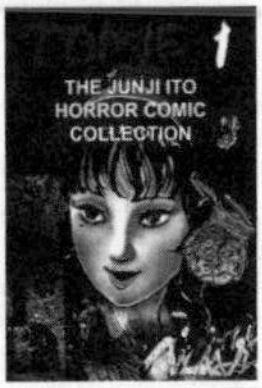
THE JUNJI ITO HORROR COMIC COLLECTION

TOMIE by Junji Ito

Tomie is the girl you wish you could forget. She is the one you shouldn t have touched, shouldn t have smiled at, shouldn t have made angry. She is quite lovely and you just might love her to death.

*Volume 1-2 are available in ebook and hardcopy formats.
*220-248 pages each

WEED by Yoshihiro Takahashi

Weed is a courageous little dog who believes he s the son of the legendary Boss Dog, Ginga. After his mother dies, Weed begins an adventurous journey to find his father in the Ohu Mountains.

*Volume 1-3 are available in ebook and hardcopy formats.
*238-240 pages each

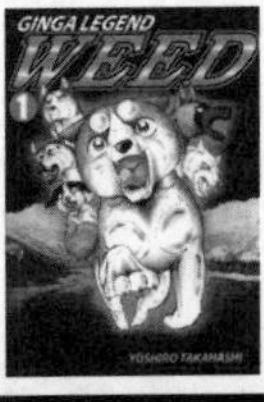
GINGA LEGEND WEED

Visit www.ComicsOne.com to see our entire selection!

comics
ONE